MULTIPLES

AN ANTHOLOGY OF STORIES IN AN
ASSORTMENT OF LANGUAGES
AND LITERARY STYLES

EDITED IN ONE LANGUAGE
BY ADAM THIRLWELL

© 2012 McSweeney's Quarterly Concern and the contributors, San Francisco, California.

INTERNS & VOLUNTEERS: Samantha Abrams, Cayla Mihalovich, Andrew Ridker, Melissa MacEwen, Sabrina Wise, Ida Yalzadeh, Evan Greenwald, Kylie Byrd, Lucie Elven, Keziah Weir, Joey Nargizian, Nara Williams, Oona Haas, Hayden Bennett, Francesca McLaughlin, Aimee Burnett, Alessandra Bautista, Naoki O'Bryan, Mary Aiello, Milo Conroy, Dana Riess, Erin Cohen, Nick Bacarella, Ashley Rogers, Jami Smith, Sarah Cleeremans, Bonnie Kim, Pilar E. Huerta, Tara Fetemi, Gretchen Schrafft. ALSO HELPING: Andi Mudd, Sam Riley, Rachel Khong, Em-J Staples, Ethan Nosowsky, Lauren Struck, Dan McKinley, Walter Green, Basharat Peer. WEBSITE: Chris Monks. SUPPORT: Sunra Thompson. OUTREACH: Alyson Sinclair. ART DIRECTOR: Brian McMullen. ASSOCIATE PUBLISHER: Adam Krefman. PUBLISHER: Laura Howard. ASSOCIATE EDITOR: Chelsea Hogue. MANAGING EDITOR: Jordan Bass. GUEST EDITOR: Adam Thirlwell. EDITOR: Dave Eggers.

Printed in Michigan by Thomson-Shore Printers. Cover phones by Kelsey Dake (red corded), Mike Bertino (white cordless), Wesley Allsbrook (flip phone), Erin Althea (black cordless), and Ian Huebert (pay phone).

INTRODUCTION

by ADAM THIRLWELL

I DON'T THINK IT'S entirely gonzo to propose that a reader who considers herself clued up in the art of fiction is going to have read *War and Peace* and *Ulysses* and *Madame Bovary* and at least maybe some of the *ficciones* by Jorge Luis Borges. What's only wishful is that this ideal reader will have read these works, as they say, *in the original*. To be fluent in Russian, English, French, and Spanish—this is a very rare achievement. And even if such a person exists, can this imaginary linguistic überfemme also read the German of Franz Kafka, and the Italian of Carlo Emilio Gadda, not to mention the Polish of Witold Gombrowicz or—?

You get the picture. The history of literature is a world history. No one claims to be an expert in novels who only reads novels in Portuguese, or Tagalog. And so the history of literature necessarily exists through translations. The reader who wants to investigate the difficult art of the novel will end up with a whole warehouse of imported goods.

But maybe these propositions—which are in fact explosive—seem only ordinary truths, so let's put this another way. Literature is one of those strange arts where the original is often experienced as a multiple. And sure, this isn't so strange, if you just think of a multiple as a useful form of mechanical reproduction, like a postcard, but this way of thinking has the problem that the relation of a postcard to a painting is really not the same as that between a translation and its source. The most perfect translation is at once precisely the same size as the original it mimics

and an entirely different thing—as if you've mimicked the exact measurements of Michelangelo's *David*, but also made it out of Jell-O.

I'm just saying: the existence of translation at the center of literature represents a crazier situation than it might at first seem. Because—to limit our investigation of literature to the novel only—one of the things that the history of the novel represents is a frenzied, patient attempt on the part of every novelist to be as singular as possible, and the medium they possess for this singularity is a language. The finished singularity goes by the moniker *style*, and style can only be encoded in a novel's words and syntax. So why then do we read Franz Kafka's novel *The Trial*, if we cannot read *Der Proceß*? Why, in fact, do we call *The Trial* Kafka's at all? Isn't a style, in the end, precisely fated to be linguistically unique?

These are menacing philosophical questions, and I'm not in the business of answering such questions in a miniature prefatory note. I'm only in the business, for now, of posing them—so that the reader can understand the crisscrossing puzzlement that went into the project they now hold in their hands. It was a project whose motives were partly grand philosophy and partly therapeutic. Because the strangeness is that while novels and their translations seem to exist in a very odd and complicated relationship, the general bookstore mode is to treat translations as so many transparencies, so many invisibilities. We hardly mention their presence at all. And this may well be to avoid the embarrassing intricacies of the philosophical problem. But embarrassment, I think, is no way to conduct intellectual life. The proper way is confrontation. You need a hypothesis, and then an experiment.

Under the blank gray sky of London, my hypothesis, I considered, looked something like this:

HYPOTHESIS
The art of the novel is an international art. Its history is international, and the mechanics of this history is translation— which means that the art of fiction, having survived this history, must be tougher than it looks.

A novel, in other words, is an airplane. Its style is entirely transportable. And the deeper contention here was that not just the basic telenovela storyline of *Der Proceß* can be rewritten in any language, but also—and less obviously—the more intricate details and tricks and precisions of its sentences. (Which, if true, would lead to the perturbing possibility that the essence of literature's forms is in fact not specifically linguistic. But let's abandon that disturbing paradox or contradiction for the moment.) While the proposed method for testing this hypothesis could therefore be an experiment where translation would be conducted under even more high-pressure, hectic conditions than usual.

THE EXPERIMENT
What would happen if a story were successively translated by a series of novelists, each one working only from the version immediately prior to their own—the aim being to preserve that story's style?

2

At this point of happy abstraction, however, the experiment needed some sad parameters. The initial attempt to make a model followed the rough thinking that if you took a story, then subjected it to a translation, and then translated that translation back into the original language—according to the formula (this is scientific, totally) A–B–A—then you would have a simple device for testing the effects of translation on a given story. But then this thinking became extended. Absolutely, the usual translation is from A to B. I think that's unobjectionable. But if B is translated

into C, is it possible to say that C is also a translation of A? Can you, in other words, make a translation from a third language? I sort of hoped you maybe could. The proposed model A–B–A therefore became a new model that was now something like A–B–C–D–A. This, however, stalled on the worry that such a model would create a project so international that only a few people could read more than a fraction of it. And so, xenophobically weighting the project in the interests of the English-speaking reader, it was decided to adapt this slightly, giving a final formula—if X = English—of A–X–B–X–C–X, etc. With some occasional variation (half of the chains here extend to include a D; in others B ended up following directly on A, or C on B), this became the finished procedure.

(One more variation: in the spirit of a finale, or epilogue, the editor invented for himself his own risky distillation of this Speedy Gonzales experiment—to translate a story with a foreign novelist, as a duo, from a language the editor could not speak. This may well seem unethical, but the lack of ethics was the point. The reader will find this piece of immorality at the issue's close.)

This kind of experiment would have its philosophical usefulness, but I also hoped that it might create various kinds of sensual pleasure for the curious reader. There would be the pleasure of observing how far the stylistic essence of a story—its singularity—really could survive such a stylistic epidemic. And there would also be the pleasure of observing this initial singularity being transformed into a series of new singularities: the multiple new possibilities created by each new novelist's style. And then there would be the simple gargantuan pleasure of reading as many of the resulting stories as you could, in as many languages as you were able. In other words: one story multiple times, or multiple stories once.

As hinted at earlier, in this experiment fiction writers would be preferred to genuine trained professional translators. Some of these writers of fiction might also be translators, but most of them were not—some, in fact, would be doing a translation for the first and only time in their writing careers, from languages in which they were not uniformly fluent. One mischievous motive for this rule was that the scope for elongations and omissions and simple mistakes would be therefore very much increased. It was high-pressure, after all, this experiment. But more importantly, this bias toward writers had an aesthetic aim: to subject each story to as much stylistic multiplicity as possible.

In this spirit, the instructions given to each translator were maximally minimal: to provide an accurate copy that was also a live story. Some interpreted this to mean the minutest attention to linguistic detail; others interpreted it to mean total rewriting and rewiring. The editor made no theoretical or aesthetic judgments of his own—or at least, not out loud. Those judgments were left to the conscience of each author. For after all: a translation is a series of minute decisions. And these decisions will be shaded differently in relation to the more abstract conditions of time and fame. There are maybe four categories of translation, it turned out—of the celebrated dead, of the uncelebrated dead, of the celebrated living, and of the uncelebrated living. Each one can constrain or free the novelist-translator to various degrees of stylistic chutzpah.

As for the choice of those original stories, this was deliberately multiple, too. Some were provided by an invited and living author; some were chosen by the initial translator in the series; a couple were explicitly chosen by the editor. The only rule governing the choice of source material was that the pieces would either not have been translated before into English or, if they had been previously translated, would be as unknown as reasonably possible. This principle of unknownness allowed for the selection of one English original—by Richard Middleton, a British writer from the beginning of the twentieth century—which makes its first appearance here in Spanish, as translated by Javier Marías.[1] (If a reader wishes to say that Richard Middleton is in fact very well known, then that reader is welcome. But she is on her own.) The originals themselves, it was decided, would remain outside the scope of the issue; what the reader will find from hereon are translations all the way through.[2]

The network of writers who undertook this experiment was also governed by chance procedures: emerging via friendships, favors, and random pleas to strangers, diverted by sad refusals and disappointments, always subject to the higher law of other writers' language skills…

And then, as mentioned, the experiment's final rule was that, until the series was completed, each translator was allowed to see only the directly preceding version in the series—just the text they were translating, rather than any earlier versions. Only the first translator in each series had access to the original. This parameter was partly designed to prevent novelists nervous about their linguistic skills, who might want to refer back to previous versions in a language that they could read, from doing so—but really it was because this whole category of the *original* was what the project was, after all, determined to at least politely frazzle.

These, then, were the rules. Having made them up, the exhausted editor's remaining role was that of impresario—a giant exercise in cajoling these international novelists to work.

3

And now here it is, the project!—a zigzagging series of series, like some throwback to the modernist days of multilingual magazines, with multilingual titles and multilingual readers. To put that multilinguality in numbers: this issue is based on twelve originals, with more than sixty multiples, the whole thing in the process encompassing eighteen languages. Yes, there it is, the material—and I don't think it demands a single, sustained reading experience. You can loop through it in various ways, randomly, here and there among the sequences, or more sternly, following each sequence through to the end, with our exhausted translators' commentary as a guide. (Because yes, as the project approached its conclusion, it became obvious that there was a problem of transparency. If, in the series X–B–X, X_1 differs vastly from X_2, how would the reader know if the differences originated in B's version of X_1, or X_2's version of B? And what if both of them had been equally libertine? And so on completion of their story, each translator was invited, if they wanted,[3] to write a miniature commentary on what they'd done with as much comprehensiveness as they liked—outlining their ethical thinking, their minute problems, their giant rearrangements.) An anthology and a notebook, at the same time! And it occurs to me that one happy accident of amassing all this material is that it represents a mini conjuring trick, or optical illusion—a quick global map of some of the most agile practitioners, alive or dead, in the young art of the novel, that is also a portable library

---

[1] In fact, the Middleton series contains two exceptions: Marías's translation of the story breaks the rule that no translation would have been previously published. But that first publication was in Spain, and in 1989. It is basically archaeology.

[2] For the intrepid originalist, bibliographical notes appear on page 216.

[3] Some preferred not to.

of experiments with fiction. Although I do say *accident*—because the true conclusions of this scheme, I think, are really philosophical. And they are entirely threatening.

The experiment, I'm trying to say, didn't quite work in the way that I expected. Which proves, I suppose, at least that it was a true experiment. The degree to which each story emerges unscathed veers wildly in each case. Sometimes, I think that the hypothesis was neatly confirmed—like in the series based on _____. Other times, it seems very obvious that it was gruesomely demolished—like in the series based on _____.[4] To be frank, as I read the finished versions and their accompanying commentaries it sadly occurred to me that contradiction was this project's mode. A gracious sense of fidelity to the dead overlaps with an ungracious glee in infidelity; a teeming corruption of sound or sense (often with the aid of that gorgeous, perilous gizmo, Google Translate) both destroys a story's local beauties, and yet also reveals its form; a multiple that was almost identical in every version could be wildly different in substance because of one key word.[5]

You, dear reader, can therefore decide how you think the biscotti should crumble. My personal unexpected side-effect has been an anxiety caused by the strange way so many stories' forms or styles ebbed and flowed, impervious to the series of singular stylists who rewrote them. Yes, I've been left wondering about the basic premise of the whole experiment—that pure and noble concept of *style*. I mean, I've always believed in style as the ultimate ideal, the basic unit of literature. A style, according to this ideal, corresponded to a unique vision. Such a vision was the goal of every writer. But now I wonder if this idea of a novelist's style should be stranger, and more mobile. I keep remembering some quip by Picasso, defending his own multiple technical approaches. Different subjects, he argued, require different methods. It was that simple, why he changed technique so much. And I wondered, then, if my literary idea of style was too abstract. Was it based on a presumption that life in its entirety were a single subject, rather than an infinite amalgam of subjects?

Maybe there was a hidden reason, I began to think, why Kierkegaard is there at this project's opening. For Kierkegaard isn't really a fiction writer—but also, well, he is, with his multiple texts, and multiple pseudonyms, and multiple self. He felt like this experiment's secret hero, or saint. My thinking about style, I'm just saying, in comparison to this project's seething novelties, now seems slightly ponderous. And just as much as I will like someone because she manages to admire both Karl Marx and also Mme du Deffand, I wonder now if the future for style should be multiplicity. It should be allowed any anachronism—for why should the styles of the past be forbidden to you?—just as it should be allowed any geographical displacement.[6] My new ideal, I'm thinking, and not without a qualm, is the pure, unembarrassed inauthentic.[7]

But basta: because you, dear reader, may be led to entirely opposite conclusions…

For now, as a coda, I just want to hazard something even more wild and unproven. And the wildness would go something like this. Maybe in some hypothetical future, literature will become the pure international—oblivious to the problems of time and space—and somehow the language in which you write or read your literature will be less important than the singular, multiple structures those languages happen to form… I really do not know. (Nor do I know whether such a future represents apocalypse or utopia.) But if it does—well, then, perhaps this home-made contraption will represent an early harbinger, or proof.

—*A.T. (London)*

---

[4] The reader can fill in the blanks.

[5] So that, to pick one example, when John Wray writes a story about an animal in a *synagogue*, and Nathan Englander writes a story about an animal in a *shul*, this is a very different story, while remaining almost identical. And therefore when Alejandro Zambra subsequently translates this same synagogue or shul as a *casa*, something just as massive occurs once again.

[6] For which the word would be what—*anatopism*?

[7] And while I fretted about this, I did then happen on a kindred spirit in the form of one of my favorite dearly departed restaurants, Mission Street Food, in whose book Karen Leibowitz discusses the whole problem of describing what kind of food they do, coming up with the lovely credo: "We feel authorized to make dishes outside our families' ethnic traditions, and we freely mix different cultures' ingredients and techniques, *because we like to eat delicious food, wherever it comes from*"—an unashamed credo that I'm putting in delighted italics, here in this footnote, and that comes with its own sober footnote to Edward Said's *Orientalism*, where Said defines all cultures as "hybrid, heterogeneous, extraordinarily differentiated, and unmonolithic." Which could be this introduction's smuggled epigraph.

MULTIPLES

1

SKRIFT-PRØVER

a story in DANISH *by* SØREN KIERKEGAARD

ILLUSTRATORS, IN ORDER OF APPEARANCE

Erin Althea, Wesley Allsbrook, Mike Berrino, Tim Lahan, Brianna Harden, Ian Huebert.

A PREFACE TO WRITING SAMPLES

translated into English by CLANCY MARTIN

An Example of Writing
by A.B.C.D.E.F.G.H.I.J.K.L. Martin
A Would-Be Author

Preface
☛ Please read the following preface, because
it includes matters of the very greatest importance.

Preface

YOU'D SUPPOSE THAT it's excessive to write a preface to a preface, but actually just the opposite is true: in fact doing so perfectly expresses our time and the accelerating haste of our work and efforts, and to pause that haste for even a moment and give it proper consideration requires more work and effort still. Ours is the time of overstimulation, and in such a time a mere newspaper advertisement won't catch the reader's eye. To advertise one's book in the newspaper is as good as never having written it at all. To be noticed at all, at the very least

EEN VOORWOORD BIJ STAALTJES VAN SCHRIJFKUNST

translated into Dutch by CEES NOOTEBOOM

Een Proeve van Schrijven
door A.B.C.D.E.F. Godthaab
een Would-Be Schrijver

Voorwoord
☛ Lees svp het volgende voorwoord, want het behelst
zaken van het allergrootste belang.

Voorwoord

MEN ZOU KUNNEN denken dat het overdreven is om een voorwoord bij een voorwoord te schrijven: maar in werkelijkheid is juist het omgekeerde het geval: zoiets drukt op volmaakte wijze onze tijd en de steeds toenemende haast van ons werk en onze inspanningen uit, en om die haast zelfs maar voor een ogenblik te laten rusten en daarbij stil te staan, vraagt nog meer werk en inspanning. Onze tijd is er een van overmatige prikkels, en in zo een tijd zal een eenvoudige krantenadvertentie de aandacht van de lezer niet meer trekken. Als je voor je boek een advertentie in een krant moet zetten kun je het net zo goed niet schrijven. Om überhaupt de aandacht te trekken, is het minste wat je nodig hebt op de voorpagina terecht komen met een hand die naar de advertentie wijst en daardoor de advertentie verkoopt en adverteert. Het verdrietige feit is, dat ook dat al snel niet meer genoeg zal zijn; het volgende dat je ziet is een dusdanige menigte handen en advertenties op de voorpagina dat het bedoelde effect verloren gaat tussen al dat collectieve handenwringen. De schrijver heeft misschien geluk en slaagt er in iets byzonders te creëren, iets nieuws. Maar zoals de dingen gaan, het nieuwe is al gauw het nieuws van gisteren, maar misschien heeft hij in het begin heel even succes. Een auteur die twee keer geluk heeft en goed adverteert mag misschien hopen op iets wat vandaag de dag nog steeds af en toe gebeurt: dat de advertentie gedrukt wordt op papier van een kwaliteit dat goed genoeg is om gebruikt te worden op de WC. Alle anderen mogen wanhopen: maar van zijn kennisgeving zal ten minste kennis worden genomen. Hij heeft ten minste een reden tot hoop, hij die slim genoeg was om te weten dat hij ons cultureel maar o zo druk publiek moet treffen op het enige vrije moment dat het nog overheeft; hij zal worden opgemerkt, hij zal misschien zelfs worden gelezen in de afzondering van het toilet. Natuurlijk wordt alles in het openbaar haastig en gedachteloos gedaan, maar wanneer het op het toilet gebeurt, dan heeft de gelukkige schrijver ten minste nog een privé relatie met zijn publiek!

Maar wat waar is voor advertenties voor boeken is ook waar voor de boeken zelf—voorwoorden worden niet meer gelezen. Om opgemerkt te worden moet je nieuw zijn: zoals dit stuk bijvoorbeeld: een voorwoord bij een voorwoord. En dat zeg ik precies met dit voorwoord in gedachten, en met wat ik geschreven heb in mijn voorwoord tot dit voorwoord: het voorwoord behelst zaken van het grootste belang—voor mij.

Voor mij is het oprecht van onbeschrijfelijk belang het publiek ervan te overtuigen dit voorwoord te lezen, omdat de lezer dan ogenblikkelijk het juiste standpunt zal hebben, en voor mij is dit van het grootste, allergrootste belang, dat de lezer het juiste standpunt inneemt.

Nu ik de aandacht heb getrokken kan ik even op adem komen. Dus, als U het goed vindt, zal ik de vrijheid nemen om eerbiedig en, als het ware, knielend, U, allerdierbaarst publiek te vragen (en wanneer ik U zeg, voeg ik er haastig bij, dan bedoel ik U zoals ik een hooggeacht belangrijk persoon of een grote vergadering toe zou spreken, op zijn allerformeelst, niet zoals je tegen een vriend spreekt of zomaar iemand) om het juiste standpunt in te nemen. Laat me recht voor zijn raap spreken. Ik was onzeker; ik heb uren, zelfs dagen, geaarzeld

you'll need to be on the paper's first page with a hand that points to and, as it were, markets or advertises the advertisement. The sad fact is that soon even this won't be enough; next thing you know there'll be such a horde of hands and advertisements on the first page that the intended grip of the advertisement will be lost in all the collective and crowded hand-wringing. The author may be lucky and create something noteworthy, something new. As things turn out, the new is quickly yesterday's news, but he may have a momentary initial success. A twice-lucky author who advertises well might hope for what still occasionally happens today: that the advertisement is printed on paper of high-enough quality to be used in the toilet. Let everyone else despair; his notice, at least, will be noticed. He at least has reason to hope, he who cleverly knew how to contrive matters such that he catches our cultured but also awfully busy public during the only free time they have left—he will be noticed, he will perhaps even be read, in the privacy of the toilet. Of course all things done in public are done hastily and thoughtlessly, but when done in the toilet, the lucky fellow at least has a private relation with his public!

But what is true of advertisements for books is also true of books themselves—prefaces are not read anymore. To be noticed, you must be new: like this piece of writing, for example: a preface to a preface. And I say this precisely with the present preface in mind, and what I've written in my preface to this preface: the preface includes matters of the very greatest importance—for me. For me it is sincerely of indescribable importance to convince the public to read this preface, because at once the reader will have the right point of view, and to me this is of the greatest, greatest most urgent importance, that the reader is fixed in the right point of view.

Now that I have been noticed, I can catch my breath. Accordingly, if it's quite all right with you, I'll take the liberty of respectfully and, as it were, on bent knee, of asking you, most cherished public (and when I say you, I hasten to add, I mean you as I would address an esteemed, elevated personage or a grand assembly, you in the most formal way, not you as one speaks to a friend or just anyone), to fix yourself in this right point of view. Let me be blunt. I was uncertain; I hesitated for hours, even days, before deciding to approach the matter in this way; I have delayed, I have avoided the moment: but now I must do it—with just one favor that I ask in advance: the generosity, mercy, kindness, patience, and open-hearted evaluation by this most cherished public.

* * *

Here's the situation. I am a young man in the prime of life; it's a shame I can't say more, but the problem is that I'm a complete unknown to you, which, when dealing with a cherished public, had better not happen accidentally, as the public by virtue of that very fact that it *is* the public knows everything and everybody worth knowing—and so for that simple reason I am a nobody, nothing. But starting from today I hope to become something—simply and entirely through your kind attention, the most cherished public! My longing, my fierce and consuming desire, is to become an author, and that can happen only because of you. An author doesn't make readers, the public makes authors—and in that way it's lucky I am a nobody and a nothing. Because in this way you have the power, if anyone does, that I will in fact be created as something—indeed, I will be wholly your creation. And in this way no one will be able reasonably to deny that I'm the real deal. Normally, I admit, being "the real deal" means that one already is something, but since precisely what is needed is that I be created, well obviously I had to begin as nobody, as nothing. For what is it to create? According to Pontoppidan it is "to produce from nothing or from an unsuitable material." As the cherished public knows well enough, concepts are dialectical and always turning head over heels. So if one is not quite entirely nothing, which would be the real deal, then one has to be a kind of second-best. From the second-best, too, the public can create an author. But just think: to be truly good, and even worse to be genuinely brilliant, is by definition just the opposite of being the real deal. Yes, it is straightforwardly impossible for the public to create an author from that; therefore the public is quite right to despise and attack every such author, because his existence is an affront to the public, a limitation on its omnipotent powers of creation. But I, I am the real deal—I am absolutely nothing. I have worked as a hairdresser and occasionally wandered with a carnival, I have been a waiter, I've hung around pool halls, and at present I am unemployed: all this to say that I am in no way a limitation upon the powers of the public—to create.

So create me! You, most cherished public, cultured public, have what they call the *nervus rerum gerendarum*. One word from you, a promise to buy what I write, or, if you could perhaps, just to get things underway, a small advance—and I am an author; and I will be an author as long as I have your kind attention. After all, what is an author? A kid who gets paid for

voor ik besloot de zaken zo aan te pakken; ik heb het uitgesteld, ik heb het ogenblik vermeden: maar nu moet ik het doen—met maar één gunst die ik vooraf vraag: de edelmoedigheid, barmhartigheid, vriendelijkheid, het geduld en de oprechte waardebepaling van dit allerdierbaarst publiek.

De situatie is als volgt. Ik ben een jonge man in de bloei van mijn leven; het is jammer dat ik niet meer kan zeggen, maar het probleem is dat ik voor U een volkomen onbekende ben, iets dat, wanneer je te maken hebt met een dierbaar publiek, beter niet per ongeluk moet gebeuren, omdat het publiek, juist door het feit dat het het publiek is, alles en iedereen kent die de moeite van het kennen waard is—en ik dus door die eenvoudige reden een niemand ben, niets. Maar te beginnen vanaf vandaag hoop ik iets te worden—eenvoudig en geheel alleen door Uw vriendelijke aandacht van allerdierbaarst publiek. Mijn verlangen, mijn brandende en verterende verlangen is om een schrijver te worden, en dat kan alleen door U tot stand komen. Een schrijver maakt geen lezers, het publiek maakt schrijvers—en zo gezien is het een geluk dat ik een niemand ben, en niets. Want op die manier heeft U de macht—als iemand die heeft—om mij in feite tot iets te maken ik zal helemaal Uw creatie zijn. En op die manier zal niemand met reden kunnen ontkennen dat ik de gezochte persoon ben. Normaal gesproken, dat geef ik toe, betekent de gezochte man dat iemand al iets is, maar omdat ik nog gemaakt moest worden, is het duidelijk dat ik moest beginnen als niets en niemand. Want was is dat, iets maken? Volgens Pontoppidan is dat "produceren uit niets of uit ondeugdelijk materiaal." En zoals het bemind publiek goed genoeg weet zijn concepten dialectisch en veranderen ze hals over kop. Dus, als iemand niet helemaal niets is, zou dat de gezochte man zijn, want hij moet wel op een na de beste zijn. Van de op een na de beste kan het publiek ook een schrijver maken. Maar pas op: om echt goed te zijn, of, nog erger, om werkelijk briljant te zijn , ben je per definitie natuurlijk het tegendeel van de gezochte man. Ja, het is regelrecht onmogelijk voor het publiek om van zo iemand een schrijver te maken; daarom heeft het publiek volkomen gelijk om zulke auteurs te minachten en aan te vallen, want hun bestaan is een belediging van het publiek, een beperking van zijn almachtige scheppingskracht. Maar ik, ik ben de gezochte man—ik ben helemaal niets.

Ik heb gewerkt als kapper en ben soms met de kermis meegetrokken, ik ben ober geweest, ik heb in biljartcafé's rondgehangen en op dit ogenblik ben ik werkeloos; alles wat ik daarmee wil zeggen is dat ik op geen enkele manier een beperking ben voor de macht van het publiek—om te creëren.

Dus maak me! U, allerdierbaarst publiek, beschaafd publiek, heb wat ze noemen de *nerbus rerum gerendorum*. Een woord van U, een belofte om te kopen wat ik schrijf, of, als dat misschien mogelijk zou zijn, alleen maar om op gang te komen, een klein voorschot—en ik ben een schrijver; en ik zal een schrijver blijven zo lang als U mij Uw vriendelijke aandacht schenkt. Want laten we wel zijn, wat is een schrijver? Dat is een kind dat betaald wordt voor iets dat gedrukt is. Nu, als je iets gedrukt krijgt maar je verdient geen geld—dat is geen schrijver. Dat is zo simpel dat elke worstverkoper het begrijpt. "Schrijver" zijn is hetzelfde als koopman zijn. Wat is een koopman? Iemand die geld verdient door dingen te verkopen. Als hij er geen geld mee verdient, is hij geen koopman maar een idioot, of een filantroop, maar zeker geen koopman.

Dus wat ik schrijf in dit boek, dat trouwens geen boek is, is bedoeld om mij onder Uw vriendelijke aandacht te brengen. Vroeger schreef je eerst een werk om te proberen een naam te maken, maar nu is dat allemaal zo gecompliceerd geworden dat je goed in alles moet zijn, niet alleen in schrijven. Net zoals een klusjesman die, omdat hij geen speciale technische vaardigheden heeft , van alles en nog wat aan moet pakken, moet iemand vandaag de dag staaltjes van zijn kunnen laten zien of een boek met knipsels om het publiek te bewijzen dat hij echt een schrijver is en zo de aandacht te trekken *voor* hij iets gaat maken of zich laat maken. En zelfs dan zal dat geen nieuwe creatie zijn, tenzij hij, zoals ik mij door Uw creatieve almacht laat maken, uit het niets geschapen wordt.

Meer hoef ik U, allerdierbaarst cultureel publiek, niet te vertellen. U kunt het allemaal: ik hoef U alleen maar Uw standpunt te laten zien; om U tot dat standpunt te brengen zal ik U door elkaar schudden, U opwinden, shockeren, en U zo voor mijn zaak winnen. Van de dichters weet U dat de wereld om liefde draait, de ervaring leert U dat zij om geld draait—samen met liefde—en dat het in het leven de kunst is om die twee krachten op een vriendelijke en gelukkige manier simpelweg om elkaar heen te laten draaien—iets wat alleen dichters ooit meemaken, omdat ze alleen in hun gedichten genoeg geld hebben. In de echte wereld is het duidelijk tijdverkwisting om tegen jonge mannen te zeggen dat ze niet zonder geld moeten trouwen. Hoe romantisch het ook gebeurt, zelfs als het instituut van het huwelijk zelf op de dag van de bruiloft door het romantische verlangen van het jonge paar een verandering ondergaat, zonder geld gaat het toch niet—en dat is zo zonder de toekomst en de vooruitzichten van het jonge paar in aanmerking te nemen. Het huwelijk zelf is geen vooruitzicht; het

something that's printed. Now if you get something printed but make no money—that's no author. This is so simple that any hot-dog vendor understands it. To be an "author" is just like being a salesman. What is a salesman? One who makes money by selling things. If he doesn't make any money at it, he's not a salesman but an idiot, or a philanthropist, but definitely not a salesman.

So what I am writing in this book, which is not actually a book, is intended to bring me to your kind attention. In the old days, first you wrote a work in order to try to make a name, but now the whole job has become so complicated that you have to be good at everything, not just writing a work. Just as a handyman, who because he has no particular technical skill, must try his hand at any task, a person is well advised today to produce samples of writing or a chapbook to show the public he really is an author and win their attention *before* he decides he'll try to make a living this way and sets to work, before he tries to create or lets himself be created. And indeed even then there will not be a new creation, unless he, as I am doing by having your creative omnipotence create me, is created out of nothing.

I don't need to tell you anything more, most cherished, cultured public. You can do it all; I simply have to show you your point of view; to fix you in that point of view I will shake you up, excite you, shock you, and so I'll win you to my cause. From poets you know that the world spins on love, from experience you know it spins on money—along with love— and that the art in life is simply to get these two powers to spin around each other in a happy and gentle way—something only poets themselves ever experience, because only in their poems do they have enough money. In the real world it's obviously a waste of time to order young men not to marry without money. No matter how romantically it's done, even if the institution of marriage itself is transformed on the wedding day by the romantic longing of the young couple, without money one cannot do it—and that's without considering the future and the young couple's prospects. Marriage isn't the prospect; marriage is the very serious occasion for asking about the prospects. You understand, of course it would never occur to me as a single man to wish to be an author. It seems to me highly appropriate that our most cherished public rejects as a contemptible indigent any single, solitary person who wants to become an author; certainly such a person should not receive any sympathy or kindness from the public. But let me return to the question of prospects (I do acknowledge that the cherished public has feeling and can be moved). I am in love. The woman I love has said yes, and I as good as have her father's yes—so long as it's sure that I'll make a good living. Since you will create me, so indeed—oh, let your hearts be moved by this lovely idea—will my marriage be your creation. Without you I am nothing, with you, everything.

So what should I hope for? Well, as I've said, I see no problem. I am both nothing less than a genius and quite literally nothing. My hope and my comfort reside in that. I understand that as a rule the originality of a work stands in inverse relation to the size of its first printing and speed of its sales—how lucky for me, since I need the cash right away. One can't help but remark on the logical result of that rule, which is that a truly important genius who has no other source of income will die of hunger. I'm glad that's not me; for the sake of the cause I don't mind waiting a while for fame, but as far as the cash is concerned I can only wait so many days and I won't have any business with this inverse relation: it's of no use to me if wealth and all other good things come to me a hundred years after my death or that I'm finally able to marry a hundred years after I've been prevented from marrying by death. In a matter like this a direct relation is best and what is needed.

Therefore, most cherished public, I put these samples of my writing, and with them my fate, in your hands. If the work skyrockets, then my fortune is made—I am an author. I throw myself into the arms of the public and of humanity: if this extraordinary but tender embrace is received, I will embrace still more fervently the woman I love. My intended and I belong to the future, as we belong to my intended way of making a living, and to the advance a publisher would intend to pay me.

In closing, I should point out that, as has been suggested to me by many prospective buyers and by one man who might buy five hundred copies, I will write on request about any subject that involves our century, humanity at large, the character of our day, of the public, of the crowd, of a particular handful of people, *audiatur et altera pars*; furthermore to any agents who can sell fifty copies I also offer haircuts, modest help in butlering or at cocktail parties, the running of errands, and other minor services.

Respectfully,

A.B.C.D.E.F.G.H.I.J.K.L. Martin

huwelijk is een buitengewone gelegenheid om naar vooruitzichten te vragen. U begrijpt, het zou nooit in mijn hoofd opkomen om als vrijgezel schrijver te willen zijn. Het lijkt mij buitengewoon gepast dat het geacht publiek een eenzaam, ongetrouwd persoon die schrijver wil worden verwerpt als een verachterlijke armoedzaaier; zo iemand zou zeker geen sympathie of aardigheid van het publiek mogen krijgen. Maar laat mij terugkomen op de vraag wat betreft de vooruitzichten (ik erken dat het geacht publiek gevoelens heeft en kan worden geraakt). Ik ben verliefd. De vrouw waar ik van houd heeft ja gezegd, en ik heb zo goed als zeker het jawoord van haar vader—op voorwaarde dat ik mijn brood kan verdienen. Omdat U mij gaat maken, zo zal ook—O, moge Uw hart geroerd worden door dit liefelijke idee—mijn huwelijk Uw maaksel zijn. Zonder U ben ik niets, met U alles.

Dus, wat mag ik hopen? Welnu, zoals ik al gezegd heb, ik zie geen probleem. Ik ben zowel niets minder dan een genie en tamelijk letterlijk niets. Daarin bestaat mijn hoop en mijn troost. Ik begrijp dat normaal gesproken de oorspronkelijkheid van een werk omgekeerd evenredig is aan de omvang van de eerste druk en de snelheid van de verkoop—gelukkig voor mij, want ik heb het geld direct nodig. Je kunt niet anders dan het logische resultaat van die regel opmerken; te weten, dat een werkelijk belangrijk genie dat geen andere bron van inkomsten heeft wel de hongerdood moet sterven. Ik ben blij dat ik dat niet ben; terwille van de goede zaak vind ik het niet erg om een tijdje op de roem te wachten, maar als het over geld gaat kan ik maar zoveel dagen wachten en wil ik niets te maken hebben met dat gedoe van omgekeerd evenredig: ik heb er niets aan als rijkdom en al die andere mooie dingen pas een honderd jaar na mijn dood komen, of dat ik eindelijk honderd jaar na mijn dood kan trouwen nadat ik door mijn dood niet heb kunnen trouwen. Bij dit soort dingen is een directe verhouding wat nodig is, en het beste.

Daarom, allerdierbaarst publiek, leg ik deze proeven van mijn schrijfkunst, en daarmee mijn lot, in Uw handen. Als mijn werk een enorm succes wordt is mijn fortuin gemaakt—en ben ik een schrijver. Ik werp mijzelf in de armen van het publiek en de mensheid: als deze buitengewone maar tedere omarming aangenomen wordt, zal ik de vrouw van wie ik houd met nog meer hartstocht omarmen. Mijn aanstaande en ik behoren tot de toekomst, zoals we ook horen tot de aanstaande manier waarop ik mijn brood wil verdienen en tot het aanstaande voorschot dat een uitgever denkt mij te betalen.

Tot slot zou ik er op willen wijzen dat, zoals mij is gesuggereerd door vele mogelijke kopers en door een persoon die overweegt vijfhonderd exemplaren aan te schaffen: ik ben bereid op verzoek over elk onderwerp te schrijven dat te maken heeft met onze eeuw, met de mensheid als geheel, met ons tijdperk, met het publiek, de menigte of een bijzondere kleine groep, *audiatur et altera pars*; daarbij bied ik aan elke agent die vijftig exemplaren kan verkopen een speciaal tarief voor de kapper, bescheiden werkzaamheden als butler of bij cocktailparties, het doen van boodschappen en andere kleine hand en spandiensten.

Hoogachtend,

A.B.C.D.E.F. Godthaab

A FOREWORD TO SAMPLES OF THE WRITER'S ART

translated into English by J.M. COETZEE

An essay in writing
by
A.B.C.D.E.F. Godthaab

a Would-Be Writer

Foreword

Please read the following foreword, for it contains matters of the utmost importance.

Foreword

ONE MIGHT THINK it excessive to write a foreword to a foreword. But in reality it is just the opposite: such a thing expresses to perfection our age and the ever-increasing haste of our labors and our strivings; and to pause for so much as a single moment, and stand back, demands yet more labor and striving. Ours is an age of excessive stimuli, and in such an age a simple newspaper advertisement will no

UN AVANT-PROPOS À QUELQUES ÉCRITS D'UN ÉCRIVAIN

translated into French by JEAN-CHRISTOPHE VALTAT

Un essai sur l'art d'écrire
par
A.B.C.D.E.F. Godthaab
Ecrivain à venir

Avant-propos

Prière de lire l'avant-propos suivant, car il contient des choses de la plus haute importance.

Avant-Propos

D'AUCUNS POURRAIENT JUGER abusif d'écrire l'avant-propos d'un avant-propos. Mais en réalité, c'est tout le contraire: un tel geste illustre notre âge à la perfection, et la hâte sans cesse accrue de nos travaux et de nos efforts, de sorte que s'arrêter ne serait-ce que pour un seul instant et prendre du recul exige encore plus de labeur et de peine. Nous vivons une époque de stimulations excessives et, dans une telle période, une simple publicité placée dans un journal ne saurait désormais retenir l'attention du lecteur.

Si l'on est réduit à faire de la réclame d'un ouvrage dans un journal, ce n'est pas même la peine d'écrire le livre! Pour vraiment attirer l'attention, il faudra au moins faire placer la publicité en première page, avec une main la pointant du doigt, afin de faire la réclame de la réclame elle-même. La triste vérité est que bientôt cela ne suffira même plus: on verra vite une prolifération de doigts tendus et de réclames en première page, de sorte que l'effet recherché se sera perdu en passant de main en main.

Il se peut que l'écrivain soit chanceux et parvienne à créer quelque chose d'unique et de neuf. Mais au train où vont les choses, le neuf d'aujourd'hui est le suranné de demain, et ce quelque soit le succès d'abord connu par l'auteur. L'écrivain doublement chanceux et qui sait faire sa publicité peut à la rigueur espérer qu'advienne cet évènement qui se produit encore quelquefois de nos jours, à savoir que la réclame soit imprimé sur un papier de suffisamment bonne qualité pour pouvoir être utilisé aux toilettes. Là où ses concurrents auront laissé toute espérance, il pourra toujours voir sa notice appréciée à sa juste valeur. Celui qui aura été assez malin pour avoir compris qu'il lui faut frapper durant le seul moment de détente qui reste à un public gavé de culture, a du moins des raisons d'espérer: il tombera sous l'œil du lecteur, et saura peut-être même le toucher dans l'intimité des lieux.

Mais ce qui est vrai de la publicité l'est aussi des livres lui-même: les avant-propos ne sont plus jamais lus. Pour être remarqué, il faut du neuf, comme ici, par exemple: l'avant-propos d'un avant-propos. Je le dis précisément en pesant à cet avant-propos-ci, et à ce que j'ai écrit dans cet avant-avant-propos: il concerne des choses de la plus grande importance—pour moi, du moins.

De mon point de vue, il est d'une importance vitale de convaincre le public de lire cet avant-propos, car le lecteur se fera d'emblée une idée juste, et pour moi, il est de la plus grande, de la plus extrême importance que le lecteur se fasse une idée juste.

Maintenant que j'ai attiré votre attention, je peux reprendre mon souffle. Ainsi, si vous en êtes d'accord, je prendrai la liberté de vous demander, (et quand je dis "vous," je me hâte d'ajouter que j'emploie ce vous comme si je m'adressais à un personnage important ou à une vaste assemblée, de la façon la plus solennelle et non comme l'on s'adresse à une connaissance ou à un inconnu), de vous demander, donc, humblement et pour ainsi dire à genoux, très cher public de vous faire une idée juste. Vous pardonnerez ma franchise. J'avais des doutes, j'ai hésité des heures, voire des jours, avant de procéder de cette manière; j'ai procrastiné, j'ai évité de franchir le dernier pas; mais maintenant

longer attract the reader's attention. If you need to place a newspaper advertisement for your book, you might as well not write the book. To really attract attention, the least you have to do is to get the advertisement onto the front page, with a hand pointing to it, in order to sell and advertise the advertisement. The sad truth is that soon even that will not be good enough: the next thing you will see is a proliferation of pointing hands and advertisements on the front page, so that the intended effect will be lost amid all the collective hand-wringing.

Perhaps the writer is lucky and succeeds in creating something exceptional, something new. As things go, what is new today is soon yesterday's news, even though, to begin with, the writer may be quite successful. An author who is doubly fortunate and advertises well might perhaps hope for something that still occurs once in a while nowadays, namely that the advertisement happens to be printed on paper of good enough quality to be used in the toilet. Whereas everyone else may as well give up hope, his notice will at least be taken note of. He who has been smart enough to realize that he must strike our oh-so-busy cultural public during the one free moment left to it, at least has reason for hope; he will be noticed, may even be read, in the seclusion of the toilet. Everything that takes place in public takes place hastily and carelessly; but when it takes place in the toilet, then the fortunate writer at least has a privy relation with his public!

But what holds true for book advertisements also holds true for the books themselves—forewords are no longer read. To be noticed you have to be new, like this piece, for example: a foreword to a foreword. I say so with precisely this foreword in mind, and with what I have written in my foreword to this foreword: the foreword covers matters of the greatest import—to me.

To me it is truly of indescribable importance to convince the public to read this foreword, for then the reader will immediately adopt the right standpoint, and to me it is of the greatest, the utmost importance that the reader should occupy the right standpoint.

Now that I have attracted your attention I can catch my breath. Thus, if you approve, I will be so free as to, humbly and as it were on my knees, request you, dearest public (and when I say *you* I hasten to add that I intend *you* as if I were addressing a highly respected personage of importance or a great assembly, in the most formal manner, not as one addresses a friend or any so-and-so), to adopt the right viewpoint. Let me be brutally frank. I was unsure; I hesitated for hours, even days, before deciding to set about the business in this way; I procrastinated, I avoided taking the step; but now I have to take it—with just one favor that I request beforehand: for the generosity, the mercy, the kindness, the patience and the sincere appreciation of the aforesaid most dear public.

The situation is as follows. I am a young man in the prime of life; it is a pity I cannot say more, but the problem is that in your eyes I am a complete unknown, something that, when you are dealing with a cherished public, cannot happen by accident, because the public, precisely because it is the public, knows everything and everyone worth knowing—and consequently, for that simple reason, I am a nobody, a nothing. But beginning today I hope to become something—simply and solely through the kind attention of you the most dear public. My longing, my burning and consuming longing, is to become a writer, and that can come about only through you. A writer does not make readers, the public makes writers—and from that point of view it is a blessing that I am nobody, nothing. For in such a case you possess the power—if anyone possesses the power—to turn me into something. I will be wholly your creation. And that way no one will have reason to deny that I am the most suitable person. Normally speaking, I concede, being the most suitable person means that one is already something; but because I would still have to be made, it is clear that I would have had to begin as nothing, nobody. For what is it, to make something? According to Pontoppidan it is "to produce out of nothing or out of worthless material." And as the beloved public knows well enough, concepts are dialectical and invert themselves in a flash. Thus, if someone is not wholly nothing, he would be the most suitable man, since surely he would be nearly the best. Even from nearly the best the public can make a writer. But beware: if one is really good, or, worse, really brilliant, one is by definition the opposite of the suitable man. Yes, it is strictly impossible for the public to turn someone like that into a writer; thus the public is perfectly right to despise and attack such authors, for their existence is an insult to the public, a restriction on its all-encompassing creative power. But I—I am the sought-after man—I am nothing at all. I have worked as a barber and am sometimes involved with the funfair, I have been a waiter, I have hung around in billiard halls, and at present I am unemployed; by which I mean to say that in no way at all am I a restriction on the power of the public to create.

l'heure est venue de le faire—pour peu que cette simple faveur me soit accordée avant: la générosité, la bienveillance, la gentillesse, la patience et l'appréciation sincère de ce très cher public.

La situation est la suivante. Je suis un jeune homme dans la force de l'âge; il est dommage que je ne puisse en dire plus, mais le problème est qu'à vos yeux je suis un parfait inconnu, une chose qui, lorsque l'on traite avec le public, ne saurait se produire par accident, précisément parce que le public est le public, qu'il sait tout et connaît ce qui est digne de l'être, et ne serait-ce que pour cette simple raison, je ne suis personne, je ne suis rien. Mais à partir d'aujourd'hui, je désire devenir quelque chose, purement et simplement grâce à votre bienveillante attention, à vous, très cher public. Mon désir, ce désir qui me brûle et me consume, est de devenir écrivain, et ceci ne peut advenir que grâce à vous. Un écrivain ne crée point de lecteurs, c'est le public qui crée les écrivains—et de ce point de vue c'est une bénédiction que je ne sois ni rien ni personne. Car dans cette situation, vous avez le pouvoir—si quiconque le possède—de me changer en quelqu'un. Je serai tout entier votre création. Et de cette manière, nul n'aura de raisons de nier que je ne sois la personne qui convienne le mieux. À proprement parler, être la personne qui convient le mieux signifie que l'on est déjà quelqu'un; mais parce je suis encore à faire, il est clair qu'il me fallait commencer par n'être personne, n'être rien. Car qu'est ce que cela veut dire: faire quelque chose? Selon Pontoppidan, c'est "produire quelque chose à partir de rien ou de matériaux sans valeur." Et comme le public adoré le sait bien, les concepts sont dialectiques et se renversent en un éclair. Ainsi, si quelqu'un est entièrement rien, il serait la personne qui convient le mieux, puisque sans doute, il serait presque le meilleur. Et même de celui qui est presque le meilleur, le public peut faire un écrivain. Mais, prenez garde à ceci, si quelqu'un est vraiment bon, ou pire encore, réellement brillant, alors il sera par définition le contraire de l'homme qui convient. En effet, il est strictement impossible pour le public de changer une telle personne en un écrivain; de la sorte le public est parfaitement en droit de mépriser et d'attaquer de tels auteurs, car leur existence est une insulte envers lui, le public, une limitation de sa toute-puissance créatrice. Mais moi—je suis l'homme que l'on s'arrache   je ne suis rien du tout. J'ai travaillé comme coiffeur, quelque fois comme forain, j'ai été serveur, j'ai fréquenté les salles de billard, et à présent je me trouve sans emploi; tout cela pour dire qu'en aucune façon je ne suis une limite au pouvoir créateur du public.

Alors faites-moi! Vous, très cher public, avez ce que l'on appelle le nervus rerum gerendarum. Un mot de vous, la promesse d'acheter ce que j'écris, ou, si toutefois c'est possible, une petite avance juste pour me soutenir… et je serai un écrivain, et je continuerai à être un écrivain aussi longtemps que vous m'accorderez votre bienveillante attention. Car soyons clairs: qu'est ce qu'un écrivain? un écrivain est un quidam qui reçoit de l'argent contre quelque chose destiné à être imprimé. Et bien, être imprimé sans gagner d'argent—ce n'est pas être un écrivain. C'est si simple qu'un marchand de saucisse le comprendrait. Être un "écrivain" c'est la même chose qu'être commerçant. Qu'est que c'est qu'un commerçant? Quelqu'un qui gagne de l'argent en vendant quelque chose. S'il n'y gagne rien, alors il n'est pas un commerçant, mais un idiot ou un philanthrope—certainement pas un commerçant.

Ainsi, ce que j'écris dans le livre, qui en fait n'en est pas un, est destiné à m'attirer votre bienveillante attention. Autrefois, on écrivait des livres dans le but de se faire un nom pour soi-même, mais désormais, ces affaires sont devenues si compliquées que l'on doit être capable de faire toutes sortes de choses, et pas seulement d'écrire. Tout comme un homme à tout faire qui, parce qu'il n'a pas de compétences techniques spéciales, doit accepter n'importe quelle corvée, l'on doit de nos jours exhiber des échantillons de son œuvre ou un florilège d'extraits pour prouver au public que l'on est vraiment un écrivain, et ainsi attirer l'attention avant même de commencer à faire quelque chose ou de se laisser faire. Et quand bien même, ce ne sera pas là une nouvelle création, qui demande que l'on ne soit formé à partir de rien, comme moi-même j'accepte de l'être par votre omnipotence créatrice.

Inutile d'en dire plus, très cher public culturel. Vous avez le pouvoir de faire ce que bon vous semble; il n'appartient qu'à moi de vous faire reconnaître votre propre point de vue; et pour vous y faire accéder, je vais vous réveiller, vous stimuler, vous choquez et ainsi vous gagner à ma cause. Les poètes vous ont appris que le monde tourne autour de l'amour; l'expérience qu'il tourne autour de l'argent—sans oublier l'amour—et que tout l'art de la vie consiste à faire en sorte que ces deux forces tournent l'une autour de l'autre d'une façon agréable et heureuse—une chose dont seuls les poètes ont l'expérience, parce que c'est seulement dans leur poèmes qu'ils ont de l'argent. Dans le monde réel, c'est clairement perdre son temps de dire aux jeunes gens de ne pas se marier sans argent. Si romantiques que soient les prémices, et même si l'institution du mariage se métamorphose le jour des noces grâce aux désirs romantiques des jeunes mariés, sans argent, cela ne marchera pas, dès lors que l'on considère l'avenir et les perspectives de ce jeune couple. En soi-même le mariage n'est pas une perspective: c'est, bien plutôt, une extraordinaire opportunité de s'interroger sur les

So make me! You, most dear public, refined public, have what they call the *nervus rerum gerendarum*. A word from you, a promise to purchase what I write, or, if it is at all possible, just to get me going, a small advance… and I will be a writer, and will continue to be a writer as long as you favor me with your kind attention. For let us be clear: what is a writer? A writer is a simple fellow who is paid money for something that gets printed. Well, if you get something printed but earn no money—that is not being a writer. It is so simple that any sausage-seller can understand it. Being a "writer" is the same as being a shopkeeper. What is a shopkeeper? Someone who earns money by selling stuff. If he earns nothing by it, then he is not a shopkeeper but an idiot or a philanthropist—certainly not a shopkeeper.

So what I write in this book, which is in fact no book, is meant to bring me to your kind attention. In earlier times one wrote a work in an attempt to make a name for oneself, but now the whole business has become so complicated that one has to be good at all kinds of things, not just at writing. Just like an odd-job man who, because he has no special technical skills, has to take on all kinds of chores, so nowadays one has to show off samples of one's work, or a book of extracts, to prove to the public that one is really a writer, and thus attract attention *before* one sets about making something or letting oneself be made. And even then it will not be a new creation, unless one is shaped out of nothing, just as I allow myself to be made through your creative omnipotence.

More than that, most dear cultural public, I need not say. You have the power to do what you wish: it is merely up to me to get you to recognize your standpoint; to get you to that standpoint I will shake you up, excite you, shock you, and so win you to my cause. From the poets you know that the world revolves around love; experience teaches you that it revolves around money—together with love—and that in life the trick lies in getting the two forces to revolve around each other in an amiable and fortunate manner—something that only poets ever experience, because in their poems alone they have money enough. In the real world it is plainly a waste of time to tell young men not to get married without money. However romantically it starts off, and even if the institution of marriage is transformed on the wedding day by the romantic desire of the young couple, without money it won't work—not without considering the future and the prospects of the young couple. In itself marriage is no prospect:

rather, it is an extraordinary opportunity to interrogate the prospects. You understand, it would never occur to me to be a writer while still a bachelor. To me it seems particularly appropriate that the respected public should reject a solitary, unmarried person who wants to be a writer as a contemptible poor devil; someone like that certainly deserves no sympathy or indulgence on the part of the public. But let me return to the question of prospects (I concede that the esteemed public has feelings and can be moved). I am in love. The woman I love has given her consent, and I have as good as got the consent of her father—on condition that I am able to earn a living. Because you the public are going to make me, so too—oh, may your heart be stirred by this lovely idea—will my marriage be of your making. Without you I am nothing, with you everything.

So, what can I hope for? Well, as I have already said, I see no problem. I am at the same time nothing less than a genius and quite literally nothing. Therein lie my hope and my consolation. I am aware that usually the originality of a work is inversely proportional to the size of its first edition and the rate of sales—fortunately for me, because I need money right away. You can't help seeing the logical consequence of the above rule; to wit, that a really important genius who has no other source of income is bound to die of starvation. I am glad I am not he; for the sake of the general good I don't particularly mind waiting a while for fame; but when it is a matter of money I can wait only so many days and want nothing to do with that business of inverse proportions: it is of no use to me if riches and the various other nice things are going to arrive only a hundred years after my death, or if at last, a hundred years after my death, I am in a position to get married when in fact, because I will be dead, I cannot get married. In such matters the best thing, the thing one needs, is direct proportion.

Therefore, most beloved public, do I lay these samples of my writing in your hands, and with them my fate. If my work becomes a great success, my fortune is made—and I am a writer. I throw myself into the arms of the public and of humanity: if this unusual but tender embrace is accepted, I will embrace the woman I love with even more passion. My intended and I belong to the future, just as we also belong to my intended way of earning a living and to the intended advance the publisher is considering paying me.

Finally I would like to mention that, as has been suggested to me by numerous potential purchasers and by a certain person who is considering

perspectives. Vous comprendrez bien qu'il ne me viendrait jamais à l'esprit de devenir écrivain en demeurant célibataire. De mon point de vue, il me semble particulièrement pertinent que le public rejette comme un pauvre diable digne de mépris un homme solitaire qui souhaite devenir écrivain hors des liens du mariage: une telle personne ne mérite certainement aucune sympathie ni indulgence de sa part. Mais laissez-moi en revenir à la question des perspectives (en tenant compte que l'estimé public éprouve des sentiments et peut-être ému). Je suis amoureux. La femme que j'aime a donné son consentement, et c'est comme si j'avais obtenu l'accord de son père—à la condition que je sois capable de gagner ma vie. Parce que vous, le public, allez me le permettre—O puisse votre cœur vibrer à cette belle idée—mon mariage aussi sera votre création. Sans vous, je ne suis rien, avec vous, je peux tout.

Puis—je donc espérer? Eh bien, comme je l'ai déjà dit, je n'y vois aucun obstacle. Je suis à la fois rien de moins qu'un génie et très littéralement, un moins que rien. Là réside mon espoir et mon réconfort. Je suis bien conscient que d'habitude l'originalité d'une œuvre est inversement proportionnelle à l'importance de son premier tirage et des chiffres de vente—c'est une chance pour moi, parce que j'ai besoin d'argent tout de suite. La suite logique de la règle ci-dessus saute aux yeux; à savoir qu'un génie d'importance qui n'a d'autres sources de revenus est condamné à mourir de faim. Je suis heureux de ne pas être à sa place; du point de vue l'intérêt général, il ne me dérange pas plus que cela pas d'avoir à attendre quelque temps la renommée; mais dès lors qu'il s'agit d'argent, je ne peux attendre indéfiniment et ne veux rien avoir à faire avec cette histoire de proportions inverses; cela ne me sert à rien que les richesses et les autres gratifications ne me parviennent que cent ans après ma mort, ou que, cent après ma mort, je sois enfin en état de me marier, alors qu'en fait, parce que je serai mort, je ne pourrai me pas marier. Dans ces questions, la meilleure chose, la chose indispensable, c'est la proportionnalité directe.

Par conséquent, très cher public, je dépose entre vos mains ces extraits de mes écrits, et avec eux, mon sort. Si mon travail obtient un grand succès, ma fortune est faite—et je suis un écrivain. Je me jette dans les bras du public et de l'humanité: s'ils acceptent cette étreinte aussi tendre qu'inhabituelle, j'embrasserai la femme que j'aime avec encore plus de passion. Ma promise et moi appartenons à l'avenir, tout comme nous appartenons à la manière dont j'entends gagner ma vie, et à l'avance tant attendue que l'éditeur songe à m'accorder.

Enfin, j'aimerais mentionner que, comme me l'ont suggéré de nombreux acheteurs potentiels, ainsi qu'une certaine personne qui pense acheter cinq cents exemplaires, je suis prêt à écrire, sur demande, sur tout et n'importe quel sujet contemporain concernant l'humanité dans son ensemble, les temps que nous vivons, le public lui-même, qu'il s'agisse de la multitude ou d'une quelconque minorité, audiatur et altera pars; je propose en outre à tout intermédiaire qui est capable de vendre cinquante exemplaires un tarif réduit au salon de coiffure, ma modeste contribution comme maître d'hôtel ou serveur lors de vos réceptions, ou bien encore comme garçon de courses, ainsi que d'autres petits services divers et variés.

Respectueusement,
A.B.C.D.E.F Godthaab.

acquiring five hundred copies: I am ready to write, on request, on any and every topic to do with our age, with humankind as a whole, with our times, with the public, whether the multitude or some particular small group, *audiatur et altera pars*; in addition I offer any and every agent who is able to sell fifty copies a special tariff at the barber shop, my modest assistance as butler or at cocktail parties, the running of errands, and miscellaneous other small services.

Respectfully,
A.B.C.D.E.F. Godthaab

WHAT I WOULD
LIKE TO SAY

translated into English by SHEILA HETI

What I would like to say
before my essays
on the art of writing

by A. B. C. D. E. F. Godthaab

(written at top speed)

•

What I would like to say

Actually, before I delve into that, dear reader, let me
deal with the most important things.

What I would like to say about the most important thing

OF COURSE, I WILL begin by abusing myself over writing about the
most important thing before presenting my essays on the art of
writing. God, everything happens backwards! In conversation,

ÖVERSÄTTARENS
ANMÄRKNING

translated into Swedish by JONAS HASSEN KHEMIRI

Vad jag vill säga innan mina essäer om skrivandets konst.
Av A.B.C.D.E.F. Godthaab*

*Förlåt, eller, rätt åt er, eller, låt mig försöka förklara varför det blev såhär.

FÖR TOLV ÅR SEDAN skrev jag med stor vånda en lång roman om ett
språkmaterialistiskt krig. Det utspelade sig i en alternativ värld, i en
verbal öken, där språksoldater hade förbjudit alla fantasifulla ord och
underjordiska styrkor planerade ett motangrepp. Tolkar satt i grammatiska
skyddsrum och slipade fram explosiva adjektiv, retorikprofessorer vässade sina
argument, korrläsare smugglade in subversiva substantiv i barnböcker.

Jag presenterade den som "en rafflande lingvistisk sci-fi" i följebrevet till
förlagen, övertygad om att boken skulle bli mitt litterära genombrott, förväntansfull inför förläggarnas telefonsamtal, upptrissade förskott, utlandsförsäljningar, bokfestivaler, veckorna av väntan till dagen när Svenska Akademins
sekreterare skulle komma ut genom dörren, blinka yrvaket mot alla kamerablixtar och säga: Det hör ju inte till vanligheterna att vi ger Nobelpriset till en
debutant. Men i år har vi faktiskt gjort ett undantag.

Ingenting gick enligt planerna. Det första refuseringsbrevet kom efter
några veckor. Det var ganska personligt. Hej, tack för att vi fick läsa, den känns

överarbetad, förklarande snarare än gestaltande, blodfattig, teoretisk, tyvärr passar den inte vår utgivning. Brev nummer två var både kortare och mer kritiskt. Det tredje svaret var ett förtryckt standardbrev, tack men nej tack. Alla förlag svarade. Alla utom ni.

Tolv år gick och ibland tänkte jag på er. Jag undrade vad som hade hänt. Varför hörde ni aldrig av er? Jag föreställde mig att mitt manus hade hamnat i botten på någon hög, glömts bort på en hylla, ramlat ned i en flyttkartong och försvunnit ned på lagret. Och någon gång i framtiden, snart, vilken dag som helst skulle en praktikant hitta den dammiga luntan och tänka: Wow, en lingvistisk sci-fi! Exakt det som vi saknar i höstkatalogen!

Men det hände inte och åren gick, jag började ta ströjobb för att bli av med min studieskuld, jag satt i receptionen på en tandklinik, jag putsade skyltfönster i en nyöppnad galleria, jag slutade skriva. För sju år sen berättade en vän, som jag var skyldig pengar, att det fanns en översättarbyrå som sökte nya förmågor. Min vän uttryckte sig precis så: Nya förmågor, och jag minns att jag blev så smickrad över att någon kunde tänka på mig som en ny förmåga att jag kontaktade dem på direkten.

Efter en kort intervju och två godkända testöversättningar fick jag mitt första riktiga uppdrag: en manual för en traktor. Regulatorn regleras med ett kombinerat hand—och fotgasreglage. Den hydrauliska lyften manövreras med en manöverspak, monterad på lyftanordningens vänstra sida, enkelt åtkomlig från förarsätet. Jag älskade det. Andra uppdraget var en bruksanvisning för en citruspress. Dela citrusfrukterna i lika stora halvor och placera en halva i taget, med den delade sidan nedåt, i jospressens mitt. Kontrollera att den spänning som anges på apparaten överensstämmer med den lokala nätspänningen innan du ansluter apparaten. Observera att citrusfruktens delade sida ska vara nedåt. Det gick så lätt, jag var äntligen på rätt plats, för första gången på flera år så kändes skrivandet lustfyllt. Och kravlöst. Och välbetalt. Eller ja, kanske inte välbetalt. Men i alla fall betalt.

Jag märkte snart att jag var bra. Jag var bättre än bra. Jag var snabb och effektiv, jag hade precision och känsla, jag var noggrann och envis. Kunderna började efterfråga mig och jag tog aldrig på mig fler jobb än jag kunde leverera. I gengäld kunde jag höja mitt arvode. Jag gjorde färre men mer prestigefyllda jobb. En säljkatalog för en exklusiv vinimportör, en jurymotivering för ett kemipris, montermaterial för en amerikansk leksakskedja. Mitt senaste jobb var en informationsfilm för ett stort konsultföretag. Följ med på en världsomspännande resa där vi äntrar en global värld där vi som världsomspännande företag

I am perfectly capable of capturing our age: (essentially: *so little accrues by our work and our efforts that we cannot stop for an instant and take refuge in contemplating the pains of our labors*) We live in a time of excessive stimulation; a period when even a simple advertisement in a journal fails to capture the attention of a reader. There is so little to dazzle the eyes in a journal, it's not worth the pains of writing for them! If they *really* want to capture the attention of a reader, they should place a simple advertisement on the first page, and have the editor stand by the reader's side, pointing to it with his finger! This would capture the attention of anyone—the editor most of all! Tears are not sufficient to show our suffering over this state of affairs; we need *lots* of fingers pointing at *lots* of journals—only at the first page— then those same fingers should pass the journals from hand to hand.

It is only through writing that we have any hope of getting across anything new. Even train travel is not fast enough to keep up with literature! What is new today already feels like yesterday's news, which means that the gifted *auteur* can never achieve success or understanding. The literary enterprise is all-too-chancy. Whoever speaks rigorously and publicly, come what may, about what they made last week—their fine words are likely to end up used as toilet paper, even if their finest statements are printed on fine-quality paper. All our best speeches will end up in the toilet, and when the public finally takes notice, they will think, *they deserved it.* Remember that fair summer? When the journals were hit with enough mail for us all to understand that the public was through with literary culture? And the reason they gave? Their eyes had tumbled from their heads, and this was true across the land.

Here's the truth about the fate of our advertisements, and the same is true about the fate of our books: your reading this essay is not going to help the situation any, even if you tell your friends, *It's so new!* (speaking, for example, of this essay in advance of my essays), and even if I tell you precisely what to think of it: *It concerns things of tremendous importance—for me, and about me.*

My point of view in this essay—and what I hope is the "take-away"— is that it's of vital importance to convince you, the public, to *read* this essay, since it's emblematic of the best ideas, and (from my own point of view) the ideas I'm expressing here are the biggest and the most extremely important of any you have ever read, and are the very best subject for a literary essay.

Now that I have your attention, I must slip away for a moment to reprimand my soufflé. (Nancy, could you do that? I think it would be quite liberating if you demanded of it—and when I say "you"—oh Nancy, I *hate* to employ "you" as though I'm addressing someone of any importance! Or as if I'm addressing a vast assembly! As if this is a solemn occasion, as opposed to what's *happening*, which is that I'm addressing a little know-nothing like you! Anyway, Nancy, would you please tell the soufflé that I'm busy addressing my very dear public on a subject of great importance?) Pardon my French. I had my doubts, I hesitated for hours before proceeding in this way. I procrastinated, I evacuated out of my rear end, but now the hour has come—the *venue* has come—for me to ask a simple favor, according to my station: I am speaking of the generosity, benevolence, gentility, patience, and sincere appreciation of you, my very dear public.

The time has come! I am a young man caught up in the spirit of the age! (It's too bad I don't have the power to say much more, but the problem is that the public's eyes are perfectly blind! The thing is, the journals have a deal with the public, which means nothing can happen by accident, precisely because the public *is* the public, that is all they deign to be, which means they do not know me for the simple reason that I am unknown: I am a no one. But I'm leaving all that behind for today...) I want to become something pure, simple, and graceful by your beneficent attention, my dear public! My desire, the desire that boils and consumes me—which I hope will one day become writing—that can happen only through *you*! Writers are not born when they begin writing; it is the public who births writers, and my observation is that this is a benediction not given to everyone. Because of this situation, *you* have the power (which any fool possesses) to really change things for me. I am entirely your creation! (Similarly, a fog of worthless reasons why I *shouldn't* be The One would fit together soundly. A proper discussion could ensue about what person it *would* be convenient to deem the best—after all, it has to be *someone*—but because I am *already* hard at work, isn't it clear that I have already started being this person? Come on, that's not nothing! I mean, do you want to elect a writer who's going to say, *Do whatever you want?* Or, like Pontoppidan, *Create something that leaves behind nothing, something without value.* The public *loooves* this! Why, it's a concept at once dialectical and as reversible as an éclair! [Nancy, since you're entitled to nothing, since you exist mainly for my convenience, you're going to have to try harder.

har en unik chans att påverka den världsomspännande marknaden globalt.

Enda gången som jag har jobbat gratis var när en släkting hörde av sig och berättade om åtalet, han var besviken på sin advokat, han litade inte på sin tolk. Och jag hjälpte honom, jag översatte hans överklagan utan att ta betalt, eller jag tog symboliskt betalt, eller jag tog inte mer betalt än han kunde betala. Ärade domare, jag hoppas att ni i bedömningen av mitt fall tar i beaktande det faktum att min mor var gammal och sjuk när det hände och varken hon eller jag förstod att det var riktiga vapen. Rånarluvorna trodde vi var maskeradkostymer. Och de färgmärkta sedlarna på vinden hade vi inte ens upptäckt.

Så en dag i förra veckan hörde ni av er. Och jag måste erkänna att jag trodde att ni äntligen hade hittat min roman och ville publicera den. Men istället frågade ni om jag med extremt kort varsel hade möjlighet att översätta en litterär essä till svenska. Jag förklarade att jag vanligtvis inte arbetade litterärt och att jag dessutom hade jag ett fullspäckat schema. Men ni gav er inte. Ni hävdade att det var en akutsituation. En av era författare behövde hjälp, han hade tackat ja till att vara med på ett "superprestigeprojekt" (ert ord) men sedan hade han drabbats av en väns dödsfall och nu var det "superbrådis" (ert ord igen). Deadlinen var om några dagar och finns det någon chans att du kan hjälpa oss med det här? Du har helt fria händer. Och betalningen? frågade jag. Tyvärr har vi en väldigt begränsad budget, svarade ni. Ändå tackade jag ja.

What I would like to say before my essays on the art of writing. By ABCDEF Godthaab. En uppblåst författare håller en monolog om sin syn på skrivkonsten, litteraturen och samtiden. Han pratar om litterära former och suffléer, han tillber sina framtida läsare, han skäller ut sin hunsade sekreterare. Jag blev inte det minsta nervös, jag visste att det skulle bli lätt, jag tänkte: Sånt här har jag gjort hundratals gånger. Det handlar bara om att börja med det första ordet och sluta med det sista, arbeta lugnt och metodiskt, från inledningsraden till sista raden, från första stycket till sista. Målet är att göra sig osynlig.

Titeln var självklar. Vad jag skulle vilja säga innan mina essäer om skrivkonsten. Eller kanske konsten att skriva. Men sen kom författarnamnet. Och det var knepigare. I manualernas värld är allt tydligt och kontrollerat. Det finns ett rätt ord och ett fel och målet är att ersätta det felaktiga med det rätta. Men här handlade det om något annat, det här var ju litteratur med stort L, så viktig att den inte var värd något och plötsligt kände jag mig osäker. Författarnamnet var ju uppenbarligen någon sorts kod för ingen kan ju heta ABCDEF Godthaab i verkligheten. Men Godthaab är inte bara ett efternamn utan även det gamla namnet på Nuuk, Grönlands huvudstad, grundad 1728 med cirka 15,000 invånare idag. Och om man kastar om bokstäverna i efternamnet så förvandlas Godthaab till Bath Goad—alltså någon som sporrar oss att ta ett bad. Finns det även här en koppling till Grönland? Staden som vill övertyga oss om att simma till en annan plats? Eller är det ett helt annat bad som åsyftas? Eller är det meningen att vi ska associera till den thailändska valutan Baht, och att det är en ekonomisk sporre som åsyftas? Eller ska vi kasta om bokstäverna igen och förvandla Godthaab till ett utrop av någon som plötsligt förstår skillnaden mellan två olika djurarter: Ah Bat Dog? Jag återvände till texten, jag läste den igen och igen, jag sökte efter en nyckel, jag letade efter en djupare betydelse. Snart tonade ett religiöst tema fram, Godthaab är bara ett omflyttat h från att vara God T Ahab, Gud kontaktar Ahab, Israels son, på samma sätt som författaren i essän kontaktar sina läsare?

Jag erkänner. Jag fastnade. Jag kom inte längre än till författarnamnet. Jag läste i min hebreiska Bibel, jag kollade upp priser på resor till Grönland, jag jämförde den anatomiska strukturen hos hundar och fladdermöss och sedan var deadlinen här. Allt var för sent. Det enda jag kunde göra var att skriva er denna ursäkt. Jag förstår att det måste kännas tråkigt att vänta på något som inte blir som man har tänkt sig. Nu är vi kvitt. /Ö.a

Especially since now you stand with the BEST. The public must make me a writer!! But take heed, if someone is good, one day they'll be shit, and the next day brilliant. A "contradiction" is the most convenient way of thinking about a man.])

In truth, it is strictly impossible for the public to turn someone into a writer, and the public is perfectly within its rights in looking down at an *auteur*. Honestly, the existence of the public is an insult to me; their limited understanding puts limits on the possible potency of my creation. Yet I— I try to dig deep!—I am a nothing. I have worked as a hairdresser, a circus performer, a waiter. I hang around the billiards room and at present I am looking for work. Do I look like a beautiful creation of the public? No way.

Fuck. You, my dear public, with whom one speaks *with shaking nerves in the rear end*… please give me your word! Promise to buy what I write, oh, just whenever it's possible, or hand me a small advance I can fall back on, and I *will* write something, and I will continue to write for a long time, if only you'll accord me your benevolent attentions. Because let's be clear: What is a writer? A writer is a fellow who receives money against some future destiny: himself on a piece of paper. Until then, the paper he is destined to live on is paper money. That's so simple, even a salesman could understand it! Being a writer is no different from being a merchant. What is a merchant? Someone who sells things for money. If he gets nothing in return, he is no merchant but an idiot or a philanthropist— certainly not a merchant!

(*Nancy*!!! I am writing all this down for *no one*! My destiny is to win only *your* beneficent attention. One day soon, I'll write some book and shove it up your ass, but right now I'm laboring for myself, for my Name, and that's all I'm going to do from here on in.) What a complicated business, writing—when I am capable of doing so many things, not only writing! Whenever a man chooses to undertake something because he's not great at any one thing in particular, he's right to consider whatever he creates as insignificant. He's right to spend his days gloating over how *enchanted* he is with his own output, casting his many flowery excerpts before the public to prove he's a real writer. (And Nancy, hear this: he'll often attract their attention before he has even *decided* whether to finish his great work or leave it alone. They're happy either way. The work doesn't even have to be original, or break with the forms of the past. Creativity is true omnipotence, but the public is also a God.)

It's useless for me to say much more, my dear cultured public. You have the power to do whatever pleases you best. It's not my place to make you see things from the proper point of view; all I can do is grant you access to my point of view, wake you from your slumbers, stimulate you, shock you, and in this way, win you to my cause.

The poets you approve of say that love makes the world go around. My experience is that money turns it around—*wait, I'm not forgetting love!*—and the whole art of living consists in making those two forces turn, one around the other, in a happy and agreeable way, which is something only poets with *experience* understand, because it is only from writing their poems that they have any money at all. In the real world, it's clearly a waste of time to tell a poetic young man not to marry if he has no money. Love, romance, brought forth his first fruits, but the institution of marriage will change all this instantly on the day of his beautiful wedding. The romantic dreams of the young couple, if they are a destitute pair, won't last long, and now consider their future; consider the future *perspective* of the young man. For marriage is not *a perspective*; it is rather an extraordinary place from which to *question* one's perspective. You must understand that I'm not advocating that a writer remain single, celibate. From my point of view, it's particularly appalling that the public rejects like a poor devil, with all of its contempt, the solitary man who hopes to become a writer outside of the bounds of marriage; such a person gains no sympathy, nor the indulgence of the public. But let me return to the question of perspective (taking into account the notion that you, the public, have any feelings and *can* be moved): I'm in love. The woman I love has given me her consent, and I have won the approval of her father, provided I am able to earn a living. Now, will you, dear public, *will* you permit me—will your heart vibrate to my beautiful dream? For my marriage is also *your* creation; the creation of your wallet. Without you, I have nothing. With you, I have it all.

Why do I dare hope? Oh yes, like I said, I can't see any other obstacles. I have no cash—*nothing*—and unless a genie comes along quickly, I'll soon have less than nothing. What sort of hope or consolation is that? I am quite aware of the public's tradition of rewarding originality with cash that is of inverse proportions to that originality (I'm talking about sales figures here). The logic of the bookstore shelves leaps before one's eyes. To know a genie is of real importance if one doesn't have any alternate sources of income. Without a genie, one is condemned to die of hunger. This is not yet the place I'm in, so I am speaking from a general point of view. I am not yet deranged in that way, and I am really not bothered by having to wait a *little* while for Fame. But the longer I have to agitate in this way—I mean, I can't wait indefinitely! I don't want any part of this tradition of "inverse proportions." I won't be happy with wealth and the other gratifications coming my way only after I'm dead, or a hundred years after my death. I am at last ready to get married, so it must happen now, because once I am dead, she will no longer want to marry! When this is the sort of thing at stake, money—arriving at once—is an indispensible need. We must break the tradition; make my story a case of "direct proportions."

With your consent, my dear public, I shall now place into your hands these excerpts from my writing, and with them, my fate. If my work wins me a grand success, then my fortune is made—and I am a writer! I will donate my hand to the public and to humanity. I'll accept your tender and unusual embrace, and I'll embrace my dear Nancy, who I love with an overflowing passion. My word and my self belong to the future—but it all rests in your hands; you will determine whether I am able to make my living as a writer; whether my publisher will give me a reasonable advance.

Finally, I would like to say, if there is someone among you reading—*anyone*—who feels inspired to buy five hundred copies of my book and can commit to it, I will begin writing straight away, upon your request, on any subject of contemporary interest, covering the entire human comedy, the times we live in, or you the public (whether that be "you" the individual or "you" the collective), and, *audi alteram partem*, Nancy is available as a maître d', or a singing waitress, or a messenger girl on a bicycle; she is basically available for all home repairs.

Respectfully,

A.B.C.D.E.F Godthaab.

NOTES ON THE TRANSLATIONS

I.

At first I thought I'd "customize" the text a little more, adding pointing hands, emoticons, etc.... but then I thought that the joke of the writer desperately trying to draw attention to himself would eventually turn against me. In the end, and not unlogically, polite, relentless, double-bottomed twenty-first-century French seemed better-suited to Godthaab's tone and the overall concerns of Early Modernity.

I added "Rabelaisian" overtones to the second paragraph, so as to give it a slight French touch. The rest is rather faithful. I'm not one to mess with Kierkegaard.

—*Jean-Christophe Valtat*

II.

When I agreed to do this, I did not agree because I am fluent in French. I barely know French. I studied it from grades four to ten, when I stopped because I hated it. Sometimes I pretend to Americans that of course French comes easily to me because I am Canadian—it is my birthright—but this is a pompous lie. I was once able to arrange a threesome while traveling in France (while only speaking French!), but even if I had been speaking ancient Greek backward, it probably could have been arranged.

For the past ten years, I have slowly been working my way through a translation of Goethe's *Faust*, though I know even less German than French. But I think if you know and love sentences and words, and spend your days being attentive to them, and think and feel a lot about humans, much can be gathered in the activity of translation. While translating *Faust*, I've felt whole worlds of meaning unravel—great, expansive, poetic possibilities—and I have been moved, feeling far closer to Goethe than I have when reading him in English. Since I must go slowly and look up every word, and since I barely grasp the grammar, I don't always (or ever?) uncover exactly what he meant, but I have felt him near. Accurate or not, a whole kaleidoscope of meanings hangs in the air, rather than one meaning. What I enjoy about that project, and what I enjoyed about this one, is—when one does not know a language entirely, the pleasure comes from the feeling of looking through a keyhole: the whole rest of the room spontaneously creates itself in your mind. As an activity, it's very stirring to the imagination. You get a feeling for the sensibility, pace, emotion, longings—the soul or essence of the creator, but not the manifestation, quite.

With this Kierkegaard, I only looked up about half of the words I didn't know. I worked speedily, in the dark, keeping pace with the voice as I understood it—or else I felt I would lose it. Sometimes I went with rhyme, choosing "Nancy" for "Ainsi."

Which seemed funny to me.

I love Kierkegaard; he is one of my favorite and most important writers. Sometimes when you love someone, as opposed to when you like someone, you see them all wrong. Freud said love is an overestimation of the love object. All love distorts. I once interviewed John Currin, and he said the women he painted looked so distorted because the intensity of his gaze disfigured and maimed, like a child might squeeze a kitten too hard and kill it. Because I am not even close to fluent, my translation falls in this category: the category of the distortion. The far right in America distorts reality; so does the left. All looking is a distortion, and my translation speaks for this part of us: the part that does see something of the material truth, but rapidly and with great feeling invents the rest.

—*Sheila Heti*

III.

I had the ambition to approach the text as a translator rather than as a fiction writer. But soon the text started itching like a straightjacket; I felt suffocated by the original, and started rewriting it. The end result was very different, and maybe half the size. In my story a faded translator, who decades ago wrote a linguistic sci-fi novel about a language war, uses an assignment to retaliate against a greedy publisher who never answered back about the original novel. Instead of reading a translation, we are left with the translator's explanation of why everything ended the way it did. The text becomes a linguistic weapon to settle accounts.

I am comfortable with speaking and reading English, since I grew up in Sweden. We were taught English as a second language from around nine years of age. But I have a Swedish accent when I speak, and I know that I make a lot of grammatical mistakes when I write. My vocabulary is not nearly as good as I think it is, since it was created by a strange mixture of Susan E. Hinton novels, NWA songs, and *Fresh Prince of Bel-Air* reruns. The main character in my story is a translator who has been assigned a task, but who never manages to get past the translation of the author's name. I kind of felt the same way.

—*Jonas Hassen Khemiri*

II

LOS DE ABAJO

a story in SPANISH *by* ENRIQUE VILA-MATAS

ILLUSTRATORS, IN ORDER OF APPEARANCE

Erin Althea, Ian Huebert, Wesley Allsbrook, Mike Bertino, Brianna Harden, Tim Lahan.

THE ONES
FROM BELOW

translated into English by Colm Tóibín

I HAVE ELEVEN CHILDREN, two cats, a dog, three fish, two rabbits, and a parrot. With the children everything's fine, but with the animals—a foible of my dear wife—I have issues.

I've just turned forty-one. I manage being grown up as best I can. I believe in very little. In happiness, maybe, if happiness consists in the discovery that the place we inhabit cannot be any greater than the actual space on which we stand. Heraclitus said it another way: the sun is the width of the foot of a man.

I have just turned forty-one, and here I am standing in the shade of the palm tree at this house where we spend our summers, a house overlooking the sea, facing the island of Cabrera. I hear the murmur of the sea. My smallest children are playing in the backyard of the house. Today I finished my book. On the floor of my study my manuscripts are lying like children cruelly abandoned by both of their parents.

The book is finished and the reader will have the last word on it, but in the meantime it seems to me that, among other things, I have written, without realizing it, a short and unorthodox History of Spain during the last forty-one years. A history in which this country appears rather like a wasteland without much of a future, a place almost barren, dead to the

DIE LEUTE AUS DEM
UNTERGRUND

translated into German by Daniel Kehlmann

ICH HABE ELF KINDER, zwei Katzen, einen Hund, drei Fische, zwei Hasen und einen Papagei. Mit den Kindern ist alles bestens, aber bei den Tieren—ein Steckenpferd meiner lieben Gattin—gibt es ständig Probleme.

Gerade wurde ich einundvierzig. Das Erwachsensein kriege ich hin, so gut ich kann. Ich glaube an sehr wenig. Vielleicht ans Glücklichsein, falls das darin besteht, herauszufinden, dass der Platz, den wir einnehmen, nicht größer sein kann, als der, auf dem wir tatsächlich stehen. Heraklit hat das so formuliert: Die Sonne, das ist die Fußspanne eines Mannes.

Gerade wurde ich einundvierzig, und hier stehe ich im Schatten des Palmenbaums vor dem Haus, in dem wir unsere Sommer verbringen. Das Haus blickt aufs Meer, auf die Insel Cabrera. Ich höre das Meer murmeln. Die kleinsten meiner Kinder spielen im Gärtchen hinter dem Haus. Heute habe ich mein Buch beendet. Auf dem Boden meines Arbeitszimmers liegen meine Manuskripte wie Kinder, grausam verlassen von ihren Eltern.

Das Buch ist fertig, und das letzte Wort darüber liegt bei den Lesern. Aber inzwischen steht es mir zu, zu bemerken, dass ich unter anderem eine kurze und unorthodoxe Geschichte Spaniens während der letzten einundvierzig Jahre geschrieben habe. Eine Geschichte, in welcher dieses Land wohl eher wie eine Einöde ohne viel Zukunft aussieht, ein nahezu verdorrter Ort, der Tod aller

Lebensfreude, sodass man den Schatten dessen, was Guillén in einem Brief an Salinas "die bescheidene spanische Realität" nannte, über das Buch fallen fühlt.

Diese bescheidene Realität entspricht manchmal dem Geist jener "Kurzen Geschichte der Welt," in der H.G. Wells zum Beispiel dem "Phänomen" des Christentums nur ein paar Seiten zugestand und es eben dadurch besser erklärte als Renan in vielen Bänden. In Wells Buch werden die angeblich großen Eregnisse und die am meisten gefeierten Gestalten auf ihre wahre und angemessene Größe reduzierte, und so stellt er sie—mit enormer Eleganz und Grazie—genau dorthin, wohin sie gehören.

In meinem Buch habe ich ebenfalls die Wichtigkeit so mancher historischen Ereignisse zurechtgestutzt, und ich habe ausgelassen, was letztlich, wenn man Persönlichkeiten beurteilen will, unwichtig ist. Wenn es zum Beispiel wichtige Schlagzeilen gibt, warten die geisterhaften Gestalten, die die Hauptfiguren meiner Szenen des nationalen Lebens sind, genauso wie Kafka auf den Nachmittag, um schwimmen zu gehen. Historische und persönliche Perspektive ist für sie das gleiche. Alle sind sie kinderlos, und ihr Verhalten erinnert uns an all die, welche die eigene Natur der Gesellschaft entfremdet. Es sind Leute, die, entgegen dem, was man sich vorstellt, auf niemanden zu ihrem Schutz angewiesen sind; da sie flüchtig sind, kann man sie nicht einfangen. Sie brauchen auch keine Bestärkung, denn da sie allein sein wollen, bekommen sie alle Nahrung, die sie benötigen, aus sich selbst. Man kann ihnen nicht helfen, ohne ihnen zugleich zu schaden.

Diese Wesen haben sich den Weg in mein Buch gebahnt, sie haben dafür gesorgt, dass ich jetzt noch mehr Grund zur Besorgnis habe, als ich als Vater so vieler Kinder ohnehin hätte. Sie machen eine Anthologie anonymer Bürger aus, wandelnder Geister, Leute ohne Glück, Leute, die sich für nichts wirklich interessieren. Für die meisten von ihnen hat die Geschichte—jene in Großbuchstaben—mit ihren großen Charakteren und ihren wichtigen Ereignissen nur einen sehr oberflächlichen Einfluss auf ihre schwierigen und instabilen Leben. Nicht nur sind sie sehr beschäftigt mit ihren eigenen Problemen, sie haben sich eine Art achselzuckende Gleichgültigkeit zugelegt, durch die sie an die Realität nur durch dünne, unsichtbare Fäden gebunden sind, wie eine Spinne an ihr Netz.

Ein paar von ihnen sind wie jener Freund, der eines Tages, als wir in der Nähe von Paris spazierengingen, plötzlich meinen Arm fasste, als er am Zaun einer Baustelle die Ankündigung einer Veranstaltung gesehen hatte, die mit den Worten begann: ISABEL ALLENDE SPRICHT ZU UNS…—"Zu uns!" rief mein

joy of life, enough for us to see the shadow of what Guillén, writing to Salinas, called "the modest reality of Spain" falling over the book.

This modest reality sometimes matches the spirit of that *Short History of the World* H.G. Wells wrote, in which, for example, the "phenomenon" of Christianity is condensed, explained in a few pages better than in many volumes by Renan. In Wells's book the supposedly great events and the most celebrated figures are reduced to their proper scale and situated—with enormous grace and ease—right where they belong.

In my book too I have cut down the importance of so many historical events, and also cut out stuff to do with personalities that in the end is irrelevant. When, for example, there is front-page news, the walking ghosts who are the characters in my scenes from national life see the news as a direct interference in their lives and give themselves over to waiting—as Kafka did—for the afternoon to come, and then they go swimming. They put both the historical and personal perspectives on the same level. They are all people who do not have children and their behavior, in most cases, reminds us of those whose own very nature alienates them from society. They are people who, contrary to what might be imagined, do not need anyone to protect them because, being elusive, they cannot be easily pinned down. They are people who do not need to be reassured, because, since they really do wish to be alone, they can get all the nourishment they need from themselves. They are people you cannot help without at the same time doing them harm.

All these beings have invaded my book and have added larger worries to those I already have as the father of a large brood. Between all of them they make up an anthology of anonymous citizens, walking ghosts, people down on their luck, and people who do not let anything bother them. For most of them, History with a capital *H*, with its great characters and its solemn events, has only a very tangential influence on their difficult and chancy lives, since, as well as being very busy with their own problems, they have invented a kind of shrugging indifference that allows them to be tied to reality only by an invisible thread, like the spider's.

Some of them are like that friend of mine who one day as we were wandering around Paris took me suddenly by the arm after he saw on the fence of a construction site the notice of a meeting which began by saying: ISABEL ALLENDE SPEAKS TO US… To us! my outraged friend exclaimed. He turned and spat. What riff-raff! he said. A bit later, as we were passing a newspaper kiosk, he read that the Turkish troops who were invading Cyprus had entered Nicosia, the capital. War was coming. What a drag, my friend said. And the truth was that he saw it all as an interference in his life.

Some of them are like that Russian exile that Nina Berberova tells us about. When he had finally regained his freedom after two years in Nazi prisons he thought of nothing except that *they should give him back the laces of his shoes*, because if not he would be forced to go along the street with his shoes untied. He would be forced to hold up his trousers because they hadn't returned his belt either. And since he had lost so much weight in jail he was afraid his trousers might fall down. This is what occupied his thoughts and not things that were in theory more important, such as the idea that he was free at last.

The book has forty-one brief sections—forty-one was Kafka's age when he died in the sanatorium of Kierling, which these days is a pretty modest building that I visited not long ago—in which I make reference to the life, the work, and the city of this non-breeder par excellence. The reader will be able, if he so desires, to play at working out the references, but no one should worry if he cannot do this. It should not be seen as a barrier, since at the end of the day—I am not a Kafkaesque writer, for he left no heirs—these references are just playful and arbitrary, just pure games and extra bits added on. Paradoxically, however, I have sometimes seen them also fitting in, as things in a beautiful machine slot into place, with the details of the difficult lives of *the ones from below*—as the Czech realist Jan Neruda used to call the outsiders in his stories, the ones who travel in my caravan of walking ghosts, men with their laces undone, people down on their luck and people who do not let anything bother them.

I contemplate from afar the mysterious silhouette of the island of Cabrera. My youngest children play in the stock-pen, which is what we call the backyard of the house here. In the kitchen the parrot repeats the same old refrain of every day at this hour. "I love you, Rita," it says. It's what my wife taught it to say eleven years ago. I feel good, having finished my book. I tell myself that to escape from the arbitrariness of existence, sometimes—as happened to me with this book—I need to impose somewhat strict rules on myself, even if those rules might be merely arbitrary. It will always be possible that the end result of having used a mixture of my life and the world I have invented, of people who did not

Freund. Er drehte sich um und spuckte aus. "Was für ein Blödsinn!" Etwas später, als wir an einem Zeitungskiosk vorbeigingen, las er von türkischen Truppen, die in Zypern einmarschiert waren und Nikosia besetzt hatten. Ein Krieg war im Anmarsch. "Wie öde," sagte er. Und die Wahrheit war, daß er das eine wie das andere bloß als eine Störung seines eigenen Lebens sah.

Andere von ihnen sind wie jener russische Emigrand, von dem uns Nina Berberova erzählt. Als er nach zwei Jahren in verschiedenen Nazi Gefängnissen endlich wieder frei war, dachte er an nichts anderes als daran, daß man ihm seine Schuhbänder zurückgeben solle, damit er nicht gezwungen sei, mit offenen Schuhen die Straße entlang zu gehen. Er musste auch seine Hose festhalten, da man ihm den Gürtel nicht zurückgegeben hatte. Und weil er im Gefängnis so viel Gewicht verloren hatte, befürchtete er, seine Hosen könnten ihm zu Boden rutschen. Das beschäftigte ihn viel mehr als alle theoretisch viel wichtigeren Dinge, wie zum Beispiel der Umstand, dass er endlich wieder frei war.

Das Buch hat einundvierzig kurze Abschnitte—Kafka war einundvierzig, als er im Sanatorium Kierling starb, welches dieser Tage ein bescheiden anmutendes Bauwerk ist, das ich vor kurzem besucht habe—in denen ich mich auf das Leben, die Arbeit, und die Stadt dieses exemplarisch nachwuchslosen Mannes beziehe. Der Leser wird, wenn er möchte, die Anspielungen erkennen, aber keiner soll sich Sorgen machen, wenn er dazu nicht in der Lage ist. Er soll darin keine Barriere sehen—ich bin kein Kafkaesker Dichter, denn Kafka hinterließ keine Erben—da das alles nur ein Spiel ist. Paradoxerweise jedoch passen diese Anspielungen manchmal aufs Wunderbarste mit den Details jener schwierigen Leben zusammen, die die "Leute aus dem Untergrund" führen, wie der tschechische Realist Jan Neruda die Außenseiter in seinen Geschichten nannte, die sich in geisterhaften Karawanen bewegen, die Männer, deren Schuhbänder offen sind, die Leute, die kein Glück haben und sich von nichts berühren lassen.

Von weitem betrachte ich die mysteriöse Silhouette der Insel Cabrera. Meine jüngsten Kinder spielen im Garten hinter dem Haus. In der Küche wiederholt der Papagei den gleichen alten Refrain wie jeden Tag: "Ich liebe dich, Rita." Meine Frau hat ihm diesen Satz vor elf Jahren beigebracht. Ich fühle mich gut, ich habe mein Buch beendet. Ich sage mir selbst, dass es manchmal, um der Zufälligkeit der Existenz zu entfliehen, nötig ist, sich selbst strikte Regeln vorzuschreiben, auch wenn diese ziemlich willkürlich aussehen mögen.

Es kann natürlich sein, daß das Resultat dieser Vermischung meines Lebens und einer erfundenen Welt (dazu eine gewisse papierene tschechische Atmosphäre und der gewissermaßen darunter herlaufende Bericht der letzten einundvierzig Jahre spanischer Geschichte) dem Buch eine sehr zufällige Anmutung verleiht. Vielleicht wird auch meine Neigung zu Pomp, Wichtigtuerei und prätentiösem Stil das ihre tun. Aber es scheint mir, daß aus alldem eine sehr ernste Wirklichkeit, eine höhere Wahrheit, genährt von Lügen, erstanden ist, die sich von der offiziellen Version der Dinge unterscheidet und einzigartig wertvoll ist. Was sind wir denn schließlich, was ist jeder von uns, wenn nicht eine Kombination, einzigartig und exakt, dessen was wir getan haben, was wir gelesen haben, und was wir uns erträumen?

get involved in propagating their own kind (plus a certain bookish, Czech atmosphere and the somewhat dulled account of the last forty-one years of Spanish history), will give the book a random feel. But it seems to me that out of this there has emerged in fact a most serious reality—a higher truth nourished by lies—different from the official version, and uniquely valuable. After all, what are we, what is any one of us, if not a combination, particular and exact, of what we have done, what we have read, and what we have imagined?

EMBEREK A FÖLD ALATT

translated into Hungarian by PÉTER ESTERHÁZY

NEKEM VAN TIZENEGY gyerek, és nekem van két macska, egy kutya, 3 hal, két nyúl, és nekem van egy papagáj. A gyerekek minden rendben van, de az állatokat—a hobbija a kedves nejemnek—nincs minden rendben van.

Negyvenegy éves lettem én.[1] Felnőttségemmel elvagyok, ahogy tudok. Már amennyire. Kevés dologban hiszek. Talán a boldogságban, ha ez kitalálni, hogy a tér, mit elfoglalunk, nem lehet nagyobb, mint az, ahol a lábunkat megvetettük. Hérakleitosz ezt így mondja: A nap a férfiember rüsztje.

Negyvenegy éves lettem én, és itt állok a pálmafa árnyékában a ház előtt, ahol töltjük a nyarat. A ház a tengerre néz, meg Cabrera szigetére. Hallom a tenger moraját. A gyerekeim legapróbbja játszik a kertecskében a ház mögött. Ma fejeztem be a könyvemet. A dolgozószobám padlóján hevernek a kéziratlapok, miként gyermekek, kiket szülőik kegyetlenül elhagytak.

A könyv elkészült, a végső szó majd az olvasóké. De kedvem támad megjegyezni, hogy többek között megírtam egy rövid, rendhagyó történetét Spanyolországnak az elmúlt negyvenegy évre vonatkozóan. Egy történet, amelyben az ország úgy néz ki, mint egy jövőtlen sivatag, egy fonnyadt, szikes vidék, minden életöröm halála, úgyhogy az árnyékot, amit Guillén egy Salinasnak írt levelében a "szerény spanyol valóságnak" nevez, a könyvre vetődni érezni mindig.

---

[1] Rájátszás az ismert József Attila-verssorra: Harminckét éves lettem én.

PEOPLE UNDERGROUND

translated into English by JULIE ORRINGER

I HAVE ELEVEN CHILDREN, two cats, a dog, three fish, two rabbits, and a parrot. The kids are all fine, but the animals—my dear wife's hobby—are not exactly fine.

I'm now forty-one. I'm at peace with my adulthood, as much as I can be. More or less. I believe in only a few things: maybe happiness, if happiness means finding out that the place we occupy is no bigger than the space under our feet. Heraclitus said it this way: "The sun is the breadth of a man's foot."

I'm now forty-one,[1] and I'm standing here in the shadow of the palm tree in front of the house where we're spending the summer. This house has a view of the sea and the island of Cabrera. I can hear the murmur of the waves. My smallest kids are playing in the tiny garden behind the house. Today I finished my book. On the floor of my study, the manuscript pages lie like children cruelly abandoned by their parents.

The book is finished; its readers will have the last word. But I want to mention that among other things, I wrote a special "short history" of Spain in the last forty-one years. It's a history in which the country appears as a desert without a future, a withered, barren salt plain, dead

---

[1] That's a nod to Jozsef Attila's poem that begins, "I am now thirty-two."

to all happiness in life. The shadow Guillén mentions in a letter to Salinas—what he calls "poor Spanish reality"—you feel this shadow projected upon the book.

This poor reality is the same one H.G. Wells wrote about in his *Short History of the World*, in which, for example, he miniaturized the Christianity "phenomenon" into just a few pages—delineating it far more effectively than Renan in his many volumes. Wells, in his book of great events and historic figures, celebrated their true and correct forms by shrinking them down to actual size; and so he put them—with elegance and grace—in the places they were meant to occupy.

In my book I put a few historic events in their proper places too, and left them there, and readers can think of me what they will—in any case, it's irrelevant. For example, if there are important events in the headlines, you'll find the ghostly figures who are the protagonists of my scenes of patriotic life just waiting, like Kafka, for the afternoon, when they can swim.[2] The historical and personal point of view—to them it's six of one, half a dozen of the other. They're all childless, alienated by the nature of society itself. There are people who, contrary to expectation, don't depend on anyone

TOP: *An island in the Turda Salt Mine, Transylvania, Romania.* ABOVE RIGHT: *Jorge Guillén.*
[2] Kafka's famous diary entry of August 2, 1914: "Germany has declared war on Russia—swimming in the afternoon."

Ez a szerény valóság néha megfelel "A világ rövid története" szellemiségének H.G. Wells tollából, melyben például a kereszténység "jelenség"—et néhány oldalban összerántotta, pontosabban így, mint Renan az ő sok kötetében. A Wells könyve a nagy eseményeket és a leghíresebbnek mondott, ünnepelt alakokat az igazi és megfelelő méretükre csökkentette, és így helyezte őket—temérdek eleganciával és keccsel—éppen oda, ahová valók: a helyükre.

A könyvemben én magam is helyrepofoztam olyik történelmi esemény fontosságát, és hagytam el végül azt, ha valaki akarja, hogy felmérje a személyiséget, ami lényegtelen. Például ha vannak fontos, címoldalra váró ügyek, akkor a kísérteties figurák, kik főszereplői az én jelenetemnek a hazafias életet illetően, ugyanúgy várakoznak, miként Kafka a délutánra, hogy úszni mehessen. A történelmi és személyes nézőpont számukra az egyik 19, a másik egy híján húsz. Mindőjük gyermektelen, és viselkedésük emlékeztet minket mindazokra, akiket a társadalom saját természete elidegenített. Vannak emberek, akik, ellentétben azzal, amit gondolnánk, nincsenek ráutalva senkire, hogy az megvédje őket; mert illékonyak, mint a fing, és megfoghatatlanok, mint a pillangók. Nem kell nekik semmilyen biztatás, mert minthogy magányra vágynak, az összes szükséges táplálék önnönmagukból vétetik. Nincs fény árnyék nélkül: nem lehetséges segíteni nekik, hogy egyszersmind ne ártsunk nekik.

Ezen teremtmények törték az utat a könyvemben, tettek arról, hogy most még több aggodalomra lássak okot, mint látnék sokgyerekes apaként úgyis. Ők alkotják a névtelen polgárok egy antológiáját, kósza szellemek, szerencsétlen alakok, akiket igazán nem érdekel semmi. A nagy jellemekkel és eseményekkel teli történelem—ama nagybetűs—legtöbbjük nehéz és ingatag életének csupán a felületét karcolta meg. Nemcsak hogy önmaguk problémáival vannak elborítva, hanem szert tettek egy vállvonogató közönyre, így a valósághoz csupán vékony, láthatatlan szál köti őket, akár a pókot a hálójához.

Néhány ezek közül hasonlatos azon baráthoz, akivel egykor Párizs közelében sétálván, hirtelen megragadta a karomat, amikor meglátta egy építkezés kerítésén egy rendezvény hirdetését, amely a következő szavakkal kezdődött: ISABEL ALLENDE SZÓL HOZZÁNK…—"Hozzánk," kiáltotta a barátom. Megfordult, és kiköpött. "Micsoda baromság!" Egy kicsit később, amikor elsétáltunk egy újságosbódé előtt, ott azt olvasta, hogy a török hadsereg megszállta Ciprust és bevonult Nicosiába. Kitört a háború. "Milyen sivár," mondta. És az az igazság, hogy mindkettőben kizárólag a saját élete megzavarását látta.

Mások közülük olyanok, mint az az orosz emigráns, akit Nina Berberova említ. Amikor két évnyi különböző náci börtönök után végre ismét szabad lett, semmi másra nem gondolt, csak arra, hogy adják vissza neki a cipőfűzőjét, hogy ne kelljen neki fűző nélküli cipővel az utcán mennie slamposan. A nadrágját is kézzel tartotta, mert nem adták vissza az övét. És mert annyira lefogyott a börtönben, félt, hogy lecsúszik a nadrágja. Mindezek sokkal inkább foglalkoztatták, mint bármely elméletileg sokkal fontosabb dolog, mint például az a tény, hogy végre ismét szabad volt.

A könyv negyvenegy rövid szakaszból áll—negyvenegy volt Kafka, amikor meghalt a Kierling szanatóriumban, napjainkban szerény kinézetű épület, hol nemrég látogatást tettem—melyben e példásan magtalan férfiú életére, munkájára és városára hivatkozom. Ha az olvasó úri kedve úgy hozza, fölismerheti az utalásokat, de akkor se törjön el a mécses, ha még csak nem is kapizsgálja. Ne lásson ebben akadályt—én nem vagyok egy kafkaiánus, Kafkának nincsenek örökösei—mert ez az egész csak játék. Paradox módon azonban ezek az utalások időnként csodaszerűen illeszkednek azon nehéz életekhez, melyek a "föld alatti emberek" sajátja, ahogy ezeket a különcöket a cseh realista, Jan Neruda nevezi, kik akár egy kísértet-karaván tűnnek föl, férfiak, kiknek lóg a cipőfűzőjük, emberek, kik nem találják a szerencséjüket, és nem hagyják, hogy bármi is megérintse őket.

Messziről nézem Cabrera szigetének titokzatos sziluettjét. A kisebb gyerekeim a kertben a ház mögött játszanak. A konyhában a papagáj ismétli a régi refrént, mint minden nap, "Szeretlek, Rita." A feleségem tanította meg neki ezt a mondatot úgy tizenegy éve. Jól érzem magam, befejeztem a könyvet. Magamnak mondom, időnként, hogy a létezés véletlenszerűségeitől megszabaduljunk, szükséges magunknak szigorú szabályokat felállítani, még ha ezek meglehetősen önkényesnek tűnhetnek is föl.

Tán természetes is, hogy az életem és egy kitalált világ (mégpedig a papirosízű cseh hangulat és a mintegy alatta futó beszámoló az elmúlt negyvenegy év spanyol történelméről), hogy tehát ezek ilyetén való összekutyulása a könyvnek valamiféle véletlen jelleget kölcsönöz. Talán a pompa, a pöffeszkedés és a hivalkodó stílus iránti hajlamom is megteszi majd a magáét. De úgy tetszik nekem, hogy mindebből egy igen komoly valóság és egy hazugságok táplálta magasabb igazság keletkezett, nem a hivatalos változat és páratlanul értékes. Elvégre mi mások volnánk, mi, mindannyian, ha nem páratlan és pontos kombinációja annak, amit tettünk, amit olvastunk és amit álmainkban teremtettünk?

to protect them; they are volatile as farts, uncatchable as butterflies. They don't want encouragement. Since what they want is solitude, they get all their nourishment from themselves. There's no light without shadow: it's impossible to help them without hurting them in the process.

These creatures made my book a tough journey. Because of them, I now have more reason to be anxious than I would ordinarily as a father of many children. They form an anthology of nameless citizens, ranger ghosts, luckless figures who aren't really interested in anything. The history of big personalities and events—History with a capital *H*—barely touches the surface of their difficult, unstable lives. They're shrouded in their own problems; they've acquired a shrugging insensibility, and there's only a weak line connecting them to the real, as a spider to its web.

Some of them are like the friend with whom I was walking one day near Paris: all of a sudden he took my arm when he saw, on the wall of a construction site, an advertisement of an event that began with these words: ISABEL ALLENDE SPEAKS TO US… "To us!" my friend cried. He turned around and spat. "What bullshit!" A little bit later, when we passed a news kiosk, he read that the Turks had invaded Cyprus and occupied Nicosia. War had broken out. "How bleak," he said. And the truth is that he saw in both signs the inconvenient disruption of his life.

ABOVE: *Turkish invasion of Cyprus, July 20, 1974.*

Others are like the Russian immigrant mentioned by Nina Berberova. After two years in Nazi prisons, when he was finally released, he had no other thought except that they give him back his shoelaces so he wouldn't have to walk out on the street looking like a slob. He had to hold his trousers up with both hands because he couldn't get his belt back; he'd lost so much weight in prison his pants were in danger of falling down. He was more concerned with these things than with other theoretically more important things, like the fact that he was finally free again.

The book has forty-one short sections—Kafka was forty-one when he died in the Kierling sanatorium, which nowadays has a simple, modest look, as I noted when I visited recently—in which I refer to this peerless and barren man's life, work, and city. If the reader is a gentleman he may recognize certain familiar quotations, but if not, he mustn't get bent out of shape. It won't be a barrier to his understanding the book— I'm not a Kafka-ite; Kafka has no descendants—because this whole thing is just a game. Paradoxically, though, these quotations are sometimes surprisingly appropriate to the difficult lives of those "people under the ground," as these eccentric ones were called by the Czech realist writer Jan Neruda, when he referred to people who appear as if in a ghost caravan, whose shoelaces drag behind them, men who never found their fortunes and who never allowed themselves to be touched by anything.

I'm watching the mysterious silhouette of Cabrera Island from afar. My younger children play in the garden behind the house. In the kitchen, the parrot repeats his old refrain, as he does every day: "I love you, Rita." My wife taught him to say that eleven years ago. I feel fine, myself; I finished the book. I tell myself, from time to time, that to allay the brutal unpredictability of our lives, we have to make strict rules for ourselves, even if they may seem rather arbitrary.

It may be natural to my life, and to my imaginary world (especially that papier-maché Czech feeling, which conceals, at the same time, underneath, a narrative about the past forty-one years of Spanish history), in which things are rather mixed up, that the book has taken on a kind of random nature. Maybe my tendency toward pomp, arrogance, and an ostentatious style plays a part in this too. But it pleases me that from all these things emerged a serious reality, a superior truth fueled by lies. It's not an official version, but an incomparably valuable one. After all, what are we, all of us, if not the unique and exact combination of what we have done, what we have read, and what we have created in our dreams?

Conceived with help from Bence Sárközy.

ABOVE: *The Kierling sanatorium.*

LE PEUPLE DE SOUS LA TERRE

translated into French by LAURENT BINET

J'AI ONZE ENFANTS, deux chats, un chien, trois poissons, deux lapins, et un perroquet. Les enfants se portent bien mais les animaux—le passe-temps de ma chère femme—pas terrible.

J'ai quarante-et-un ans. Je suis en paix avec mon âge, autant que je peux l'être. Plus ou moins, quoi. Je ne crois pas à grand chose: le bonheur, à la rigueur, si le bonheur, c'est accepter que la place qu'on occupe sur terre n'est pas plus grande que l'espace sous nos pieds. Comme disait Héraclite: "Le soleil est large comme le pied d'un homme."

J'ai quarante-et-un ans et je suis là, debout, à l'ombre d'un palmier, devant la maison qu'on a loué pour l'été, avec vue sur la mer et sur l'île de Cabrera. Je peux entendre le murmure des vagues. Mes garçons les plus jeunes jouent dans le petit jardin de derrière. Aujourd'hui j'ai fini mon livre. Sur le sol de mon bureau, les pages manuscrites reposent comme des enfants que leurs parents ont cruellement abandonnés.

Le livre est fini; ce sont ses lecteurs qui auront le dernier mot. Mais je souhaite préciser que, entre autres choses, il s'agit d'une "Brève histoire" de l'Espagne des quarante-et-une dernières années. J'y présente le pays comme un désert sans avenir, une plaine de sel aride et ridée où toute perspective de bonheur a été définitivement enterrée. L'ombre que Guillén évoque dans sa lettre à Salinas—ce qu'il appelle la "pauvre réalité espagnole"—plane constamment sur le livre.

PEOPLE FROM UNDERGROUND

OR, THE UNIQUE NUMBER WHICH CANNOT BE ANOTHER

translated into English by TOM MCCARTHY

1

ME: I HAVE ELEVEN children, two cats, one dog, three fish, two rabbits, one parrot. The children are in good shape but the animals—my dear wife's passion—not so great.

I'm forty-one years old. I'm fine with that, more or less. I don't believe in much: if I had to declare some credo, I'd say happiness—if happiness means accepting that the size of your kingdom in this world is ultimately the same as that of your shoe. Heraclitus said it: "The sun is as big as a man's foot."

I'm forty-one years old and I'm here, standing in the shade of a palm tree, in front of the house we've rented for the summer, perched above the sea on the Island of Cabrera. I can hear the rustle of the waves and the cries of my smaller children playing in the back garden. Today I finished my book. On the floor of my study, its loose pages lie around like infants abandoned by their parents.

2

The book: it's finished; its readers will have the final say. But I can let on that, among other things, it contains a "Brief History" of Spain's last forty-one years. I paint the country as a barren desert, a parched and wrinkled salt plain in which any chance of happiness has been definitively buried. The shadow, evoked by Guillén in his letter to Salinas, of "impoverished Spanish reality" falls deep over the whole text.

This impoverished reality is similar to the one that H.G. Wells served us in his own *Brief History of the World*. He shrinks the entire history of Christianity (for instance) down to a few pages—but the result is actually much more illuminating than what Renan gives us in God-knows-how-many volumes. In gauging the contours of historical figures and great events by reducing them to their *real* size, Wells restores them to their rightful place with grace and style.

I've done the same thing in my book: put certain elements back in their place, and left them there. Readers will pass their own judgment on me—I don't care one way or another.

3

The characters: if important world events provide the chapter titles, the ghostly little folk who scurry through my patriotic parables are more concerned, like Kafka when he heard the First World War had broken out, with going swimming in the afternoon. For me, when it comes to weighing the historical against the personal, it's six of one and half a dozen of the other. All my protagonists are childless, as alienated from nature as they are from society. There are some who, contrary to all appearances, need no one to protect them; they're also as volatile as farts, as hard to catch as butterflies. They don't want taking care of: they want solitude—and, to that end, draw on their own resources. No light without shadow: reach out to help them and you'd obliterate them in the process.

These creatures have made my book hard going for me. They've caused me more anguish than my own children have. They make up an anthology of nameless citizens, an army of phantoms, unfortunates who aren't interested in much. The history of great personages and events—big *H* history—hardly grazes the surface of their unstable, difficult lives. They're lost in their own problems; indifference has worked its way into their bones; and the thread that binds them to reality is as thin as a spider's.

Cette pauvre réalité est similaire à celle que H.G. Wells a décrite dans sa *Brève histoire du monde*. Pour vous donner un exemple, il réduit le "phénomène" du Christianisme à quelques pages et le résultat est beaucoup plus parlant que chez Renan avec tous ses tomes. Wells, dans son livre, a parfaitement cerné les contours des personnages historiques et des grands événements en les ramenant à leur taille réelle, et ce faisant, les a remis à leur juste place avec grâce et élégance.

Moi aussi, dans mon livre, j'ai remis à leur place quelques éléments historiques, et je les ai laissés là. Les lecteurs penseront de moi ce qu'ils veulent, ça n'a aucune d'importance. Par exemple, si des événements importants font les gros titres, les figures fantomatiques qui sont les protagonistes de mes scènes de démonstration patriotique se contentent d'attendre l'après-midi, comme Kafka, pour aller à la piscine. D'après moi, la bonne mesure entre point de vue historique et point de vue personnel, c'est deux demis et une pinte. Mes protagonistes sont tous sans enfant, aliénés qu'ils sont par la nature même de la société. Il y a des gens qui, contrairement à ce qu'on peut croire, n'ont besoin de personne pour les protéger; ils sont aussi volatils que des pets, aussi insaisissables que des papillons. Ils ne veulent pas de soutien. Puisque ce qu'ils veulent, c'est la solitude, ils tirent d'eux-mêmes ce dont ils ont besoin. Pas de lumière sans ombre: il est impossible de les aider sans les blesser au passage.

Ces créatures on fait de mon livre un voyage difficile. Elles me causent plus d'angoisse que mes propres enfants. Elles constituent une anthologie de citoyens sans nom, une armée de fantômes, des personnages malheureux qui ne s'intéressent pas à grand chose. L'histoire des grandes personnalités et des événements—l'Histoire avec un grand *H*—effleure à peine la surface de leurs vies instables et difficiles. Ils sont perdus dans leurs propres problèmes; ils ont acquis une indifférence inconsciente et le lien qui les relie à la réalité est aussi mince qu'un fil d'araignée.

Certains d'entre eux sont comme l'ami avec lequel je me promenais l'autre jour près de Paris: tout d'un coup il a saisi mon bras en voyant sur le mur d'un chantier une publicité qui commençait comme ça: ISABEL ALLENDE S'ADRESSE À NOUS… Mon ami s'est exclamé: "A *nous*!" Il s'est retourné pour cracher: "Quelle connerie!" Un peu plus tard, alors que nous passions devant un kiosque à journaux, il a lu que les Turcs avaient envahi Chypre et occupaient Nicosie. La guerre était déclarée. Il m'a dit: "Quel ennui!" Et la vérité, c'est qu'il ne voyait rien de plus dans ces deux signes qu'une perturbation malvenue dans son existence.

D'autres sont comme cet immigrant russe dont parlait Nina Berberova. Après deux ans passés dans les prisons nazis, alors qu'il était enfin libéré, sa seule préoccupation était qu'on lui rende ses lacets afin qu'il ne passe pas pour un clochard. Il devait tenir son pantalon à deux mains parce qu'il n'avait pas pu récupérer sa ceinture; il avait tellement perdu de poids en prison que son pantalon menaçait de tomber à tout instant. Ces choses là le préoccupaient davantage que d'autres a priori plus importantes, comme le fait qu'il était enfin libre.

Le livre comporte quarante-et-un courts chapitres—Kafka est mort à quarante-et-un ans au sanatorium de Kierling, un endroit qui, aujourd'hui, ne paie pas de mine, comme j'ai pu le constater quand je m'y suis rendu récemment—dans lesquels je parle de la vie de cet homme desséché et solitaire, de son travail et de sa ville. Le lecture cultivé pourra reconnaître certaines citations familières mais sinon, il n'aura pas pour autant à se torturer les méninges, cela ne l'empêchera pas de comprendre le livre—je ne suis pas un kafkaïen pour la simple et bonne raison que Kafka n'a pas de descendants—parce que tout ça n'est qu'un jeu. Paradoxalement, néanmoins, ces citations se révèlent parfois étonnamment adaptées aux vies difficiles de ce "peuple de sous la terre," comme l'écrivain réaliste tchèque Jan Neruda désignait ces personnages excentriques qui semblaient sortir d'une caravane fantôme, leurs lacets traînant derrière eux, ces hommes qui n'ont jamais rencontré la fortune et ne se sont jamais autorisés à être touchés par quoi que ce soit.

Je contemple de loin la mystérieuse silhouette de l'île de Cabrera. Mes plus jeunes enfants jouent dans le jardin derrière la maison. Dans la cuisine, le perroquet répète comme tous les jours le vieux refrain que ma femme lui a appris il y a onze ans: "Je t'aime, Rita." Je me sens bien, j'ai fini le livre. Je me dis de temps en temps que pour se débarrasser du caractère brutalement imprévisible de nos vies, nous devons nous appliquer des règles strictes, même si elles semblent arbitraires.

Si on regarde ma vie et le monde imaginaire qui est le mien (en particulier cette sensibilité tchèque en papier maché enfouie sous ce qui est en même temps un récit sur l'histoire de l'Espagne depuis quarante-et-un ans), on peut voir que les choses sont plutôt entremêlées. Il est sans doute logique que le livre ait pris un tour assez aléatoire. Peut-être que ma propension à la pompe, à l'arrogance et au style ostentatoire joue aussi un rôle là dedans. Mais je me réjouis que de tout cela émerge une réalité sérieuse, une vérité supérieure construite à base de mensonges. Ce n'est pas une version officielle, mais elle est d'une valeur incomparable. Après tout, que sommes-nous d'autre, tous autant que nous sommes, que l'exacte et singulière combinaison de ce que nous avons fait, lu et crée dans nos rêves?

Some of them are like the friend I was walking with the other day near Paris: seeing a poster on a building-site hoarding which announced that ISABELLE ALLENDE SPEAKS TO US, he grabbed my arm and said: "To us?"— then turning round to spit, added: "Like fuck she does." A little later, as we were passing by a newsstand, he read that the Turks had invaded Cyprus and were occupying Nicosie. War had been declared. "What a drag!" he said. The truth is that he saw no more in those two nuggets of information than a mild annoyance buzzing around his head.

Others are like the Russian immigrant whom Nina Berberova wrote about. Finally freed after spending two years in Nazi prisons, all he cared about was getting back his shoelaces: he didn't want people to think he was a beggar. He hadn't been able to retrieve his belt either, and had lost so much weight in prison that his trousers slipped down all the time and he had to hold them up with both hands. These things preoccupied him more than other, more fundamentally important ones, like the fact he'd regained his liberty.

4

Numbers: the book's made up of forty-one short chapters. Kafka died at forty-one, in the sanatorium at Kierling—a place which nowadays doesn't look anything special, as I was able to see for myself when I went there recently. Dispersed throughout these chapters are allusions to Kafka's dried-out, solitary life, his work, the town he lived in. The sophisticated reader will pick up certain quotes and references—but if he doesn't there's no need for him to get his brain all in a twist: it won't stop him from understanding the book. (I'm not an "heir to Kafka" for the good and simple reason that Kafka has no descendants.) All that stuff's a game. Yet, paradoxically, these citations sometimes turn out to be astonishingly well-suited to the troubled lives of these "people from underground," as the Czech realist writer Jan Neruda labeled those eccentric characters who seemed to have wandered out from some ghost caravan, laces trailing behind them: men for whom the dice had never come up right.

5

The rules: I contemplate, from afar, the strange shadow cast by the Island of Cabrera. My youngest children are playing in the garden behind the house. In the kitchen, the parrot is repeating, as it always does, the old refrain my wife taught it eleven years ago: "I love you, Rita." I feel good; I've finished my book. I tell myself from time to time that to overcome the brutally unforeseeable character of our lives, we should adopt strict rules, even if they seem arbitrary.

6

Casting the die: looking at my life and at the imaginary world I've made my own (in particular this baroque Czech conceit buried inside a narrative about Spain's history over the last forty-one years), you can see that things are quite entangled. It's not at all surprising that the book has taken a quite aleatory turn. No doubt, my propensity toward pomposity, arrogance, and stylistic show-boating enters the equation too. But, all the same, it gives me joy to see, from all of this, a serious reality emerge: a higher truth, albeit one constructed on a foundation of lies. It's not an official account or summary, but it has a unique value. After all, what are we, inasmuch as we amount to anything, but the exact and singular combination of what we have done, read, and created in our dreams?

NOTES ON THE TRANSLATIONS

I.

I like Vila-Matas's work because it is playful and inventive. Each sentence has an undertone of irony; under the gravity there is dark laughter; the style has an edge of knowingness, which uses Latinate terms with a sort of rueful grace. I wondered how this would work in translation, since there is an element in Vila-Matas's work that already reads as though it is translated from a dead language. His style takes some of its energy from this idea of language as a dead thing, or if not dead, then tired. This is one of the reasons why Vila-Matas quotes writers and refers to books so much. His belief that there is nothing much to say enriches his prose.

I began with a rough version, and then made it smooth. This was worse than the rough. And then I grew brave and realized that I was not applying for a job at the United Nations as a translator. So I began to put in words like *issues*, *stuff*, and *brood* that are far away from Spanish just to amuse myself. I then tried to find a tone as melancholy, nonchalant, and learned as the original. While sticking to the shape of what Vila-Matas wrote, I stopped paying attention to it. If something seemed clumsy, I changed it. I behaved as though I were one of Vila-Matas's own more wilful and self-involved characters. I tried to make it read as though I had written it on a bad day and it needed root and branch work. I never looked at the original again.

—Colm Tóibín

II.

As I understood it, I was supposed "to come on strongly" in the translation, not just simply translate the text. I didn't "hear" the text very well, and I was unable to decide whether it was so because it did not have a very characteristic voice, or because I have a "too Hungarian" ear. (In other words I am rather deaf to other languages.) Therefore the "personal presence" I mentioned suited me just fine. It replaced the accuracy, which otherwise is supposed to be a basic condition of translation. It is true, however, that accuracy can often be achieved by inaccuracy.

Therefore my idea was that I wanted to make it obvious that this was a translation. (This is the most horrible thing…) In a certain sense I wanted to present the skeleton of the text—I mean, without the flesh. To put it nicely, the role of the piranhas was taken over by the translation program of Google. I wonder if you have already tried it: it produces nightmare-texts. Too-bad ones. I used that to try and create a credibly

bad text. In other words, I tried to give a new direction to the translation series. I am curious to see what has become of it. I don't speak English, but I'm afraid that the next translation reconstructed the flesh (the negative piranha). It considered my credibly bad text simply bad and corrected it.

Sometimes I wish I understood all the languages of the world (and that I had learned them all from my mother). Sometimes I'm glad I can only speak Hungarian properly. Rather properly, or at least I'm trying. I don't think that I will have a great career as a translator.

—Péter Esterházy

III.

I should know Hungarian. My mother and grandparents did; it was the background music of my childhood. At times I dream of someone speaking authentic-sounding Hungarian, as if some part of my brain, inaccessible when I'm awake, secretly knows the language. If that's true, it didn't help here. I translated with the help of Bence Sárközy, my intrepid Hungarian editor, who pulled his hair into frantic points as he tried to unpack Esterházy's nested clauses and idiomatic jokes. Our first version included sentences like "In my book I found the right position of some historical events (myself kicked {or hit} the importance of one historical event to the right place), and I let everybody, if he wants, to measure the personality." From those sentences I wrung others that sound barely less stilted. The Internet solved the mysteries of Heraclitus's quote about the sun, and Kafka's about swimming. My final version, certainly too literal, at least reproduces brilliant additions of Esterházy's, like "volatile as farts, uncatchable as butterflies." The Sebaldesque images were a middle-of-the-night answer to this question: how to insert my own vision without straying from Esterházy's? My favorite is the stamp of Guillén, which seems to make winking reference to the letter mentioned in the story.

—Julie Orringer

IV.

I love to speak English, which is the only foreign language I can understand more or less, but writing or reading it is another story. Fortunately, my girlfriend is fluent—she's doing her PhD at Cornell—so she could help me. Nevertheless, some parts still remained quite obscure. Basically, I thought the text was easy at the beginning, quite hard at the end.

I didn't know the expression "six of one and half a dozen of the other." As my girl-friend didn't know it either, I assumed it was not a current idiom, so I invented this one: *deux demis* (meaning two small beers, but *demi* first means "half") *et une pinte*. I like it, I think I'll use it some time!

I believe translating is rewriting. My own voice has to be there, because even if I want to catch the narrator's voice, it is according to my idea of the character (aca-demic, but relaxing: this is all about how I feel you speak when you relax. It has to be connected with the way I speak myself, especially if you consider I am a writer on holiday too, right now).

The phrase that bothered me the most was this one: "(especially that papier-maché Czech feeling, which conceals, at the same time, underneath, a narrative about the past forty-one years of Spanish history)." This was hell. Eventually, I decided to reverse the relation between the Czech feeling and the narrative: in my opinion, it is the Czech feeling that is concealed under the Spanish history. I guess you can feel how embarassed I was, reading the result in French: not my best sentence, I believe.

—*Laurent Binet*

V.

This text was a joy to translate. It looks pretty slight on a first reading, but turns out to contain a subtle set of echoes and correspondences: the recurrence of shad-ows, for example, or the progressive elisions between children, pages, animals, and fictional characters. Then there's the intriguing motif of chance and rules, coupled with an ongoing preoccupation with numbers. I decided to bring this into sharper focus, by breaking the piece into six short, numbered sections—one for each side of a die—and adding a subtitle taken from Mallarmé's *Un coup de dés*: "The unique number which cannot be another." It seems to me that this is what Vila-Matas is really getting at here: despite all the randomness of life and history and art and all the rest, there's this text I've just finished, and it's this way and not another way, and it has, despite all the chance contingencies that shaped it, "a unique value," like a four that's not a three or a two that's not a six or five. And this is his achievement: having made the throw, then sat back and surrendered himself to its consequences. All thought emits a throw of dice.

—*Tom McCarthy*

III

GELUK

a story in DUTCH *by* A.L. SNIJDERS

ILLUSTRATORS, IN ORDER OF APPEARANCE

Wesley Allsbrook, Tim Lahan, Brianna Harden, Mike Bertino, Erin Althea, Ian Huebert.

1

LUCK

translated into English by LYDIA DAVIS

WHEN I WAS YOUNG I played the recorder, I took lessons from Kees Otten,[1] who lived in a large house on Koninginneweg. These opulent houses were formerly lived in by wealthy families, but after the war mothers and daughters from Russia and Poland lived there, as well as poor musicians, poets with office jobs, students. For Kees Otten you had to go up ten flights of stairs, he gave the lessons under the rafters, you looked out over Vondelpark.[2] Sometimes I had lessons at the same time as Simon Castaris, who played alto recorder and was in love with a girl who worked in a magazine shop on Beethovenstraat. Simon had met her at the fair and treated her to a ride on the Caterpillar, where he had kissed her. After that he thought she was his, but she was not that kind of girl. And so he often went to gaze at her in Beethovenstraat, toward closing time, when darkness was falling and he could see her clearly in the light of the shop. She often saw him standing there and softened toward him because of his defenselessness. With this

---

[1] An internationally known recorder player, with many concerts, LPs, and CDs to his credit. He died in 2008.

[2] Vondelpark: a large park in the west of Amsterdam.

2

CHANCE

translated into French by YANNICK HAENEL

QUAND J'ÉTAIS JEUNE, j'ai appris à jouer de la flûte chez Kees Otten, qui habitait une grande maison sur Koninginneweg. Toutes ces maisons somptueuses étaient habitées autrefois par des familles aisées, mais après la guerre on trouvait aussi bien des mères et leurs filles venues de Russie ou de Pologne que des musiciens sans le sou, des poètes vivant de travaux alimentaires, ou des étudiants. Pour arriver chez Kees Otten, il fallait gravir une dizaine de marches; ses cours avaient lieu sous les combles, d'où l'on avait une vue sur tout Vondelpark. Parfois, j'avais cours en même temps que Simon Castaris; il apprenait la flûte alto et était amoureux d'une fille qui travaillait dans une maison de la presse sur Beethovenstraat. Simon l'avait rencontrée à la fête foraine et l'avait invitée à faire un tour avec lui sur la chenille, où il l'avait embrassée. Après ça, il a cru qu'il l'avait conquise, mais elle n'était pas si facile. Alors il s'était mis à venir la regarder, à l'heure de la fermeture, quand la nuit tombait et qu'on la voyait distinctement dans la lumière de la boutique. Elle avait remarqué sa présence immobile dans la rue, et elle en était émue parce qu'il avait l'air sans défense. Et la tendresse fit place à l'amour, qui, bien que contrarié, revint sur Vondelpark. Simon et la fille vécurent heureux, du côté d'Overtoom, dans une petite rue banale—un autre monde. Elle l'incita à jouer plutôt de l'accordéon, et c'est ce qu'il fit car je ne l'ai plus jamais vu aux cours de Kees Otten. Des années plus tard, lorsque je l'ai rencontré une dernière fois, il n'était plus question ni de cette fille ni de musique. L'accordéon et la flûte alto traînaient chez lui, dans l'attente de nouveaux musiciens. Quand je pense à toutes les histoires qu'une flûte pourrait raconter sur plus d'une centaine d'années! Qui, durant tout ce temps, s'occupe de faire sortir un souffle poétique de leur corps de bois? Les instruments de musique vivent plus longtemps que les personnes, et je les soupçonne d'être également dotés d'une meilleure mémoire.

softening, love returned, thwarted, however, by Vondelpark. Simon lived on the prosperous side, and his love on the Overtoom[3] side, in a common little street, another world. She preferred him to take up the accordion, and that happened too, I no longer saw him at the lessons with Kees Otten. Years later I met him one more time, he was through with that girl and with music. The accordion and the alto recorder lay at home waiting for new musicians. I yearn for the stories the recorder could tell over a hundred years—who, in that time, blew their poetic breath through that wooden body? For musical instruments can live longer than people, with a little luck, and I suspect they are also endowed with better memories.

[3] A neighborhood in the west of Amsterdam.

CHANCE

translated into English by HEIDI JULAVITS

WHEN I WAS YOUNG, I studied flute with Kees Otten, who lived in a big house in Koninginneweg. All of the big houses were lived in by rich families, but after the war they were also lived in by mothers and daughters from Russia or Poland, or poor musicians, or poets who worked for food and drink, or students. To get to Kees Otten's house, one had to climb a dozen steps. His classes took place under a grape arbor, where one could get a view over all of Vondelpark. Sometimes I'd walk with Simon Castaris; he studied alto flute and was in love with a girl who worked in a bar near Beethovenstraat. Simon had already kissed her in the fields. After that, he believed he'd won her over, but she was not so easy. He would watch her when the bar closed, when night was falling and he could see her distinctly in the light from the boutiques. She noticed his still presence in the street. His air of defenselessness softened her. Tenderness followed love, which, against her better judgment, revisited them in the fields of Vondelpark. Simon and the girl settled happy, near d'Overtoom, on a plain little street—another world. She encouraged him often to play the accordion, and once he'd picked it up, I never saw him again at Kees Otten's classes. Many years later, when I visited him for the last time, he had neither the girl nor music. Both accordion and flute hung on the walls, awaiting future musicians. When I think of all the

ZUFALL

translated into German by PETER STAMM

ALS ICH JUNG WAR, nahm ich Flötenunterricht bei Kees Otten. Er lebte in einer alten Villa am Koninginneweg. Ursprünglich hatten in diesem Viertel reiche Familien gewohnt, aber nach dem Krieg quartierten sich dort auch russische und polnische Mütter mit ihren Töchtern ein, Studenten und arme Musiker und Dichter, die von der Hand in den Mund lebten. Um zum Haus von Kees Otten zu kommen, musste man ein Dutzend Stufen emporsteigen. Die Flötenstunden fanden im Garten statt in einer von Weinreben überwachsenen Laube. Von dort aus hatte man einen schönen Blick in den Vondelpark. Manchmal traf ich unterwegs zum Unterricht Simon Castaris, er studierte Altflöte und war in ein Mädchen verliebt, das in einer Kneipe in der Nähe der Beethovenstraat arbeitete. Er hatte sie schon einmal im Park geküsst. Danach glaubte er, er habe sie gewonnen, aber sie war nicht so einfach zu erobern. Wenn die Kneipe schloss, beobachtete er sie von der Strasse aus. Obwohl es dämmerte, konnte er sie ganz deutlich erkennen im Licht der Geschäfte das von draussen ins Lokal drang. Sie schien seine stille Präsenz zu spüren, vielleicht nahm seine Hilflosigkeit sie für ihn ein und machte sie empfänglich für seine Liebe. Es kam zu Zärtlichkeiten und wider besseres Wissen gab sie sich ihm hin auf einer Wiese im Vondelpark. Simon und das Mädchen waren glücklich. Sie liessen sich in der Nähe von Overtoom nieder, in einer unscheinbaren kleinen Strasse—eine andere Welt. Das Mädchen ermunterte Simon immer wieder,

Akkordeon spielen zu lernen, und nachdem er damit angefangen hatte, sah ich ihn nie wieder in den Musikstunden von Kees Otten. Als ich Simon viele Jahre später zum letzten Mal besuchte, hatte er das Mädchen und die Musik verloren. Das Akkordeon—und das Flötenspiel hatte er an den Nagel gehängt, die Instrumente lagen herum, bereit für andere Musiker.

Wie viele Geschichten könnte eine Flöte aus all ihren Jahren erzählen! Geschichten, die nicht vergehen und wie ein lyrischer Wind durch die Bäume wehen. Musikinstrumente leben länger als wir, sie bergen das Gedächtnis der Menschheit.

stories a flute can tell over the years! That last forever, and blow a poetic wind through the trees? Musical instruments live longer than people. They are the equal of the strongest human memories.

HAPPENSTANCE

translated into English by JEFFREY EUGENIDES

WHEN I WAS YOUNG I took flute lesson with Kees Otten. He lived in a big old house on Koninginneweg. Rich people had been moving into the neighborhood around that time, but after the war it had been full of Russian and Polish mothers dragging their daughters with them, and with students, poor musicians and poets, who lived hand to mouth. To get to Kees Otten's you had to climb a dozen steps. The flute lessons took place in the garden directly in front of a leafy grape arbor. There was a decent view of the Vondelpark. Sometimes on the way to the lessons I ran into a guy I knew, Simon Castaris—he was studying classical flute and was in love with a girl who worked in a bar near Beethovenstraat. He'd already made out with her in the park once. After that, he thought he had her, but she was a little more slippery than he expected. If the bar was closed, he had to stand on the street, watching for her. Although it would already be getting dark, he could see her clearly in the light from the shops falling into the restaurant from outside. She seemed to notice his quiet presence; maybe his helplessness made her more endearing to him and made her more susceptible to his love. Anyway, she showed him tenderness and granted him other gifts—special knowledge about herself—on the grass of the Vondelpark. Simon and that girl were happy. They lived in the neighborhood around Overtoom, on a small,

ATVIK

translated into Icelandic by SJÓN

SAGAN GERIST Í TÓNLISTARSKÓLA. Skólinn stendur við Köningenveg. Það er í nágrenni mikils almenningsgarðs. Upp að skólabyggingunni liggja stórar steintröppur.

Í tónlistarskólanum eru tveir ungir karlmenn við flautunám. Þeir eru vinir.

Þá verður annar þeirra ástfanginn af ungri konu. Hún á hug hans allan. Í tilhugalífinu missir hann smám saman áhuga á flautuleiknum. Það dofnar yfir sambandi þeirra skólafélaganna. Að lokum flyst sá ástfangni á brott án þess að kveðja.

Vinirnir hittast ekki aftur og frétta aldrei hvor af öðrum.

Er sá félaganna er hélt áfram náminu kýs að minnast þessara daga kallar hann þá fram með því að leika á flautuna.

Flautan varðveitir söguna af brotgjarnri vináttu æskuáranna.

inconspicuous street—another world. The girl kept on badgering Simon to learn to play the accordion, and once he'd relented, I didn't see him at music lessons at Kees Otten's anymore. The last time I ran into him, way later, he'd lost both the girl and his music. He'd hung up the accordion and the flute, which lay waiting for another musician to come along and use them.

Think how many things a flute can tell you, stuff from years and years ago. Stories that just don't fade away but that sail through the trees like a wind with a voice. Musical instruments live longer than we do—they play our memories.

NOTES ON THE TRANSLATIONS

I.

I am quite new to Dutch, having begun attempting to translate from it only a year or so ago. I know some German (rudimentary), so that helped a great deal. (Apparently three-quarters of the Dutch vocabulary is close to the German equivalents.) It also helps that Snijders prefers to write in short sentences and to tell, usually, a concrete story from everyday life, without playing complicated games with syntax.

But two features of his work present problems for a translator. One is his frequent references to Dutch history, arts, culture, geography, food. If notes aren't included with the translation, some of the content is lost to a non-Dutch reader. But of course the benefit, at least to the translator, is that with each story one's knowledge of the Netherlands is broadened or deepened. A good thing, particularly for us insular *estadosunidenses*.

The other is that occasionally, Snijders will embed a common idiom in the prose, or a familiar saying. I, of course, don't recognize them, as I don't recognize it when the syntax is a little odd even for the Dutch reader. But after finishing a translation to my own satisfaction, I send it off to a Dutch reader for review, and any oversights or mistakes are quickly corrected.

—*Lydia Davis*

II.

The truth is, I'm useless at English. Even at school I was bad: I confused words, mixed up tenses, put German into English, French into German, and in general everything into the English of cowboy movies. The English I believe I understand, the English I have inflicted on you in order to translate the superb text in this anthology, is an approximate language that I was taught by Johnny Rotten. When he said to me, belching to help me understand (because in fact London is very far from France): "I am an anarchist, I am an antichrist," I said to myself: but I understand English! All the nuances of the English language, the rhythmic undulations of its prose, serpentine like the River Thames (maybe), I owe them not to Shakespeare but to Professor Rotten. At this point, a small parenthesis occurs to me: in my opinion, there's a connection between Hamlet and the Sex Pistols (but is Hamlet Sid Vicious or Johnny Rotten? And who is the father?). However, I don't want to cause trouble by posing politico-poetic questions, even if I'm aware that it's basically too late: for

I have translated in a totally calamitous way the magnificent text proposed to me. Mistranslations abound, confusion reigns among the sentences, a situation for which I know full well Professor Rotten is not the only one responsible. Because there is something worse than the Sex Pistols: there is romanticism. And no doubt I wanted, when translating this heartbreaking text in which a young man and a young woman do not manage to fall in love, to re-establish the love that—I'm sure of it—exists between them. I make them live together when, it seems, everything keeps them apart. I swear that I didn't do this deliberately. I really believed what I wrote, while I was writing it. You see, I'm only an anarchist, a little antichrist, and above all, whether I like it or not, I am French.

—*Yannick Haenel*

III.

I decided I was not allowed to Google the meaning of words I did not know. Given I am not such a fabulous speaker of French, this meant I did not know the meaning of many, many words in the piece I was given to translate. Mostly I was able to intuit the meaning from the context; but sometimes I simply had no idea. At first this scared me, and then this became exciting. When you have not a single clue what a word means, and you stop caring, suddenly it can mean anything. I decided that one word I could not decipher should mean "grape arbor," even if it didn't. In fact it means attic.

I had a really hard time figuring out the meaning at the end of my piece—again, because my French is not so great, and the grammar toward the end became too convoluted for me to follow. Something happened to a man deciding between love and his pursuit of a musical career. I decided he got both. But the piece states that he lost the girl, and that even his musical career wasn't what he'd hoped it might be. Once I learned this, I couldn't see the point of making a sad story into a cheery one. That is not in my nature. But I did keep my mistranslations of certain sentences, because I liked how oblique they sounded.

This is the first time I actually detected a VOICE when reading fiction in the original French. This is a pretty lame statement, given I majored in Comparative Literature in college, and was "supposed" to have read many books in the original French. Reading in French for me was never easy, and so I was never able to rise above the challenge posed by plain meaning. Thus I cheated and bought the English translations, and pretended otherwise in my papers. But I spent so much time with this small piece, I started to hear what it sounded like. I mean, voice-wise. I understood that it communicated more than meaning; it communicated a mood, too. For the first time, I registered that mood.

I wish I hadn't been such a lazy idiot in college.

—*Heidi Julavits*

IV.

When I first read the English text, I thought translating it would be an easy task. The sentence structure was not complicated, and there was hardly a word I did not understand. So a first translation was quickly made. But then the problems started. A major problem was the title. I had to decide whether *chance* meant "luck" or "hazard." I guessed that the first one was meant, but still decided to put in the second one, as it somehow fit the text better. I'm not sure that I would make the same decision again.

Then there was the "accordion and flute hung on the walls." I have played the recorder for a long time, and never even thought of hanging it on a wall. How would you do that, anyway? Nail it on the wall? So in my text I had the flute just lying around. And what exactly happened between Simon and the girl? How could he watch her, when the bar was closed? Why would she hang around in a closed bar with lights switched off and not go home after work? And what does "love revisited them in the fields" mean? Did they do it or didn't they? I chose to use an old-fashioned German expression that can be read as having sex, or just giving oneself to someone: "Sie gab sich ihm hin." I also used some other old-fashioned words to capture the fairy-tale-like sound of the story.

As I wanted to get a feeling for the place, I looked up Koninginneweg and the Vondelpark on Google Maps (unfortunately I had no time for a trip to Amsterdam) and found that it was impossible to "get a view over all of Vondelpark," as it's just too big. So I changed that to "a view into Vondelpark."

The hardest part of the work was the end. That's probably why I put it in a new paragraph, as it seemed so separated from the rest of the story. I worked a long time on these last four sentences. Should it be "the stories a flute can tell over the years" or "the stories from all those years a flute can tell"? Or, rather, "could tell," if it could speak at all? I don't really like talking objects or anthropomorphisms in general. So the assertion that "musical instruments live longer than people" did not appeal to me. In my unpoetic world they don't live at all. But I kept the sentence anyway, as I was asked to translate, not to rewrite the story. The last sentence, finally, I did not understand at all—I guess its meaning was somewhere lost in translation. I had a faint feeling of what the original might have been, but how do you translate a feeling? I'm not very happy with the solution I found, but it was the best I could come up with. If I were not just the translator but the editor, I would probably suggest eliminating the last four sentences, as they only try to explain something that is already there in the beautiful first part of the story.

What fascinated me while I was working on the piece was how many different meanings some simple sentences can have. And as I had no chance of checking with the original, I decided to just make the story as beautiful as I could and somehow capture the melancholy atmosphere that I found in it.

—*Peter Stamm*

V.

Flóki Sigurjónsson, my thirteen-year-old son and a native Icelandic speaker, was given half an hour to memorize Jeffrey Eugenides's translation. I refrained from reading the source text. Three weeks after listening to Flóki's oral retelling of Jeffrey's "Happenstance," I wrote it down from memory as "Atvik." I have not compared the two.

—*Sjón*

IV

土神と狐

a story in JAPANESE *by* KENJI MIYAZAWA

ILLUSTRATORS, IN ORDER OF APPEARANCE

Wesley Allsbrook, Ian Huebert, Mike Bertino, Erin Althea.

1

THE EARTHGOD
AND THE FOX

translated into English by DAVID MITCHELL

1

O N THE NORTHERN EDGE of the wide plain there was a grassy knoll where a beautiful female birch tree stood, alone. She wasn't a large tree, but her trunk was sleek and dark; her branches stretched out gracefully; come May, her blossoms were white and cloudy; and in autumn she shed gold, fiery red, many-hued leaves. Passing birds—the cuckoo, the white-eye, the tiny wren, and the shrike—liked to rest in the tree, unless they spied a young hawk hovering nearby.

The birch tree had two friends. One, an earthgod, lived in a swampy bog some five hundred paces distant. Her other friend was a brown fox, who showed up from the south of the wide plain. Of the two, the birch tree tended to favor the fox: the earthgod, despite his grandiose title, frankly looked a bit of a savage, what with his matted hair like cotton rags, bloodshot eyes, and "clothes" dangling off him like strips of seaweed. He stomped around barefoot and his nails were always grimy and long. By contrast the fox had a high-class air, and rarely interfered with anyone.

If, however, you compared these two, you might have observed that where the earthgod was as honest as the day is long, the fox was maybe a trifle insincere.

2

EL DIOS TERRESTRE
Y EL ZORRO

translated into Spanish by VALERIA LUISELLI

1

E N EL LINDERO NORTE de la gran llanura, coronando una loma cubierta de hierba, crecía una hermosa Abedul. No era particularmente grande. Pero tenía un tronco liso y oscuro—las ramas altas y extendidas—donaire. Era notable su follaje. En primavera—flores blancas y aterciopeladas. En otoño—hojas rojas y doradas: plétora de tonos encendidos. Siempre y cuando no estuviera rondando por ahí un halcón, las otras aves pasajeras—el cuco, el ojoblanco, el minúsculo maluro y el pitohuí—solían parar a descansar en su ramaje.

La Abedul tenía dos amigos. Uno—un Dios Terrestre—vivía en una ciénaga a unos quinientos pasos de la loma. El otro—un Zorro color marrón—se aparecía de tanto en tanto por el extremo sur de la llanura. Puestos a escoger, la Abedul prefería al Zorro. El Dios Terrestre, a pesar de la sepa y lustre que le confería su título, tenía franca pinta de bestia: el pelaje enmarañado como guiñapos de algodón—los ojos inyectados de sangre ponzoñosa—las vestimentas colgándole como descosidos esparadrapos de algas marinas. Andaba descalzo a lo largo y ancho de la llanura—las pezuñas puercas y prolongadas. El Zorro en cambio era discreto, fino, aristocrático, y nunca metía la nariz donde no se le requería.

En una comparación estricta, sin embargo, cualquiera se daría cuenta de que, así como el Dios Terrenal era tan transparente como el aire, el Zorro podía a ratos ser una pizca mentiroso.

2

El verano era joven y la noche sosegada. Una capa de hojas nuevas, delicadas, recubrían a la Abedul y perfumaban el aire alrededor suyo. Vaporosa, la Vía Láctea surcaba el cielo. Las estrellas palpitaban—ahora tenues—ahora brillantes. Fue bajo ese cielo que el Zorro cruzó la llanura para visitar a la Abedul. Llevaba un poemario prensado bajo el brazo. Iba enfundado en un traje sastre color azul marino y sus zapatos de cuero beige rechinaban elegantemente mientras se acercaba a la loma.

Divina la noche, ¿no crees?—apuntó el Zorro.

Sí—musitó la Abedul a su distinguido compañero.

¿Ves allá arriba a Escorpio? ¿Sabías que los antiguos llamaban a esa estrella roja y grande "la Estrella de Fuego"?

¿Esa no es Marte?

¡Desde luego que no! Marte es un planeta, pero esa de ahí es una estrella.

Increíble. Me pregunto entonces en qué se diferencian una estrella y un planeta.

Bueno, los planetas no tienen brillo propio—son visibles solo cuando reflejan la luz ajena—pero las estrellas reales brillan por sí solas. Nuestro sol es una estrella de verdad. Puede parecernos enorme—deslumbrarnos—pero si lo viéramos a suficiente distancia sería una mera peca de luz.

Así que el sol es una estrella más y ya. ¿Y entonces hay muchísimos soles en el cielo—o sea estrellas—o sea soles?

Indulgente, el zorro sonrió:

Supongo que sí.

¿Y por qué algunas estrellas son rojas, otras amarillas, otras verdosas?

El zorro, de nuevo, sonrió y cruzó ambos brazos. Casi se le cae al suelo el poemario—casi.

Bueno—respondió—hace mucho tiempo todas las estrellas parecían grandes nubes esponjosas. Todavía ahora se pueden ver algunas así: en Andrómeda y en Orión—en el espiral de los Perros Cazadores—o en la Nebulosa del Anillo, que tiene forma de boca de pez.

¡Qué imagen! ¿Estrellas con forma de bocas de pez? ¡Es extraordinario!

La palabra exacta es esa: extra-ordinario. ¿Sabes? Ya he visto todas las estrellas desde un observatorio.

Cómo me gustaría poder verlas yo también.

Las habrás de ver, entonces. Sucede que acabo de mandar traer un telescopio de Alemania—de Zeiss—para ser preciso. Estará en mis manos antes de que llegue la próxima primavera. En cuanto llegue—te dejaré usarlo.

2

Summer was young, the evening was calm. New, soft leaves robed the birch tree and perfumed the air around her. Across the sky flowed the haze of the Milky Way, and stars pulsed and swam, now dimming, now brightening. Under this sky the fox visited the birch tree, with a book of poetry tucked under his arm. His tailored suit was navy blue and his beige leather shoes squeaked as he strolled up.

"Lovely mild night, isn't it," the fox remarked.

"Yes," whispered the birch tree to her friend.

"See Scorpio, up there? The ancients named that big red one 'the Fire Star,' you know."

"Is the Fire Star different from Mars, then?"

"To be sure! Mars is a planet, but that one's an actual star."

"Gosh… So how is a planet different from a star, I wonder?"

"Well, planets don't shine, as such. To be visible, they reflect light from elsewhere—whereas your real stars, they shine all by themselves. Our sun is a true star. It may look huge and dazzling to us, but if you saw it from a vast distance, it would be just another pinprick of light."

"Wow… So the sun is just one more star… So there's lots and lots of suns in the sky—I mean, stars—no, I should say, *suns*. Suns. Right?"

The fox smiled indulgently. "You could say so, yes."

"Why are some stars red, some yellow, others greenish?"

Once again the fox smiled and folded his arms, almost dropping the book of poetry, but not quite. "Well, once upon a time, all the stars were big fluffy clouds. You can still find them—in Andromeda, in Orion; there's a spiral in the Hunting Dogs, and one called the Ring Nebula, shaped like a fish's mouth."

"What a sight! Stars shaped like fishes' mouths? Extraordinary!"

"*Extraordinary* is the word. I viewed them myself—at an observatory, as a matter of fact."

"Gosh! *I'd* love to see them as well!"

"Then see them you shall. As it happens, I've ordered a telescope from Zeiss in Germany. It'll be here before next spring, and just as soon as it's arrived, I'll let you have a look." But the fox's mouth had run away with him, and the next moment he was thinking, *Whoops, I've told yet another fib to my only friend in the world… But it wasn't a bad lie—I said it only to make her happy—and I can easily straighten it out later on.* The birch tree was too overjoyed to notice the fox's slight distractedness. "I'm so happy," she said. "You're so very, very kind to me."

"Your wish," the fox smiled sheepishly, "is my desire. This poetry book, by the way—care to take a look at it? It's by this fellow, Heine. It's a translation, of course, but it's rather well done."

"How very thoughtful—may I really borrow it?"

"Be my guest—keep it as long as you like. Hey ho. I ought to be off… Though wasn't there something else you asked me?"

"Yes—the stars, and their different colors."

"That was it. But let's cover that next time. I don't want to outstay my welcome."

"Oh, *you* needn't worry about that, Fox."

"I'll drop by again very soon. Bye, then. I'll leave the book with you. *Au revoir.*" With that, the fox cantered off home. The birch tree—her leaves whispering in a southerly wind that sprang up from nowhere—perused the pages of the fox's book in the pale glow of the Milky Way and the stars spattering the night. The Heine anthology contained "Lorelei" and other masterpieces, and the birch tree read on and on and on. Three o'clock had been and gone, and Taurus was rising in the east, before the birch tree began to feel even the tiniest bit drowsy.

Dawn came, the sun rose, dew shone on the grass, flowers bloomed at full power; and along came the earthgod, arms folded, lumbering from the northeast, bathed in the molten-copper light of morning. The birch tree—for some reason—felt apprehensive at his approach. She shimmered her bluish-green leaves and her shadow danced across the grass. The earthgod came to a halt.

"Birch Tree. Morning to you."

"Good morning."

"Y'know, Birch Tree, there are so many things I don't understand, however much I puzzle over them… So very, many, mysteries…"

"What sort of mysteries?"

"Take grass, for example. Grass. The stuff sprouts out of muddy *brown* earth, yes? Yet grass is *green*: and how about flowers? Whites, yellows… Really, what's going on with that?"

"Mightn't that be because the grass seeds already have the greens and

La verdad es que el Zorro había pecado de bocón. Ni bien le había prometido a la Abedul el agasajo ya se estaba arrepintiendo: "Caray, le acabo de volver a mentir a mi única amiga en el mundo—aunque fue una mentirita piadosa—para hacerla feliz—en fin—al rato lo enmiendo." La Abedul se había entusiasmado tanto que no notó la leve sombra que había de pronto oscurecido el semblante del Zorro.

Qué feliz me pones, Zorro, qué amable eres conmigo.

Para eso estamos, Abedul. Por cierto—este poemario que tengo aquí—¿se te antoja echarle un vistazo?—es de Heinrich Heine—es una traducción—ni modo—pero para ser traducción no está nada mal.

¿De verdad me lo prestarías?

Claro—quédatelo todo el tiempo que necesites. Ya me tengo que ir—¿pero había algo más que me habías preguntado?

Sí—las estrellas—¿por qué varían de color?

Ah, eso, sí—mejor dejamos ese tema para la próxima. Como dicen los italianos: las visitas, al igual que el pescado, después de un rato, apestan.

Ay Zorro—tú por eso no te debieras preocupar. Es un placer estar contigo.

Mejor vuelvo pronto—hasta luego—*au revoir*—te dejo con Heinrich Heine.

Con un saludo amanerado, el Zorro se fue trotando a casa. La Abedul—sus hojas suavemente mecidas por una repentina brisa del sur—se puso a estudiar las páginas del poemario bajo el cielo salpicado de estrellas, al abrigo del brillo pálido de la Vía Láctea. La antología de Heine incluía "Lorelei" y una que otra obra maestra de esa altura, de modo que la Abedul leyó y leyó. Dieron las tres de la mañana y siguieron girando los astros hasta que apareció Tauro por el horizonte oriental. Solo entonces empezó a ganarle el sueño.

Despuntó el alba—salió el sol—las rebosantes flores brotaron—sobre el pasto resplandecía el rocío. Avanzando pesadamente por el noreste—bañado por la luz cobriza de la mañana—se acercó el Dios Terrestre. Por algún motivo difícil de precisar, la Abedul se mostró aprehensiva ante la llegada del visitante. Sacudió sus hojas verdiazules y su sombra se estremeció en el pasto. El Dios Terrestre se detuvo:

Abedul—buenos días.

Buenos días.

Sabes, Abedul, hay muchas cosas que nomás no entiendo. No importa cuántas vueltas les dé—pura incertidumbre—puro misterio.

¿Qué clase de misterio?

El pasto, por ejemplo. Pasto—la cosa esa germina en la tierra—la tierra es café—pero el pasto—el pasto es verde. Ya ni se diga las flores—amarillas, blancas—¿cómo te explicas eso?

¿Podría ser porque el pasto y las flores ya contienen, desde que son semilla, esos colores?

Igual—pero de todos modos no entiendo. ¿Qué me dices de los hongos que salen en el otoño? Ahí sí no hay ni semillas ni nada—nomás brotan—así como así—amarillos, rojos, del color que sea. La verdad es que no se entiende nada.

¿Por qué no le preguntas al Zorro?

La Abedul seguía atolondrada de la conversación que había tenido con el Zorro la noche anterior y no se cuidó de medir sus palabras. El Dios Terrestre se puso verde de puro coraje y contrajo los puños.

¿Al Zorro ese? ¿Qué te ha estado diciendo ahora?

La Abedul, titubeante, hizo su mayor esfuerzo:

Nada en particular—pensé que quizás se le ocurriría algo—tal vez.

¿Cómo va un zorrito a enseñarle algo a un dios?

La Abedul se había puesto a temblar de miedo—temblaba incontenible-mente. El Dios Terrestre daba pisotones por la loma, los brazos cruzados y tiesos, la mandíbula trabada—y ahí donde su sombra cubría el pasto, la tierra se estremecía.

Ese maldito zorro es una piedra en el zapato. Confunde la gimnasia con la magnesia. Pretencioso—envidioso—presumido—creído.

La Abedul trató de cambiar de tema:

¿Va a ser el festival de tu santuario muy pronto, verdad?

Ps'sí—masculló el Dios Terrestre, suavizándose un poquito–. Hoy es el tercer día del mes. Así que el festival es en seis días.

Le estuvo dando vueltas a esto unos segundos pero enseguida volvió a crecer la ola de cólera:

Los humanos—son unos inútiles. ¿Acaso alguien se molesta ahora en traer a mi santuario una ofrenda? No—nadie. El siguiente humano que ose pisar mi lado del bosque se va a ir directo al fondo del pantano.

El Dios Terrestre permaneció de pie—inmóvil—crujiendo los dientes. La Abedul, a quien evidentemente le había salido más caro el caldo que las albón-digas, ya no pudo hacer nada salvo dejar que sus hojas se mecieran en la brisa. El Dios Terrestre siguió de bravucón—mitad cegado por su cólera—mitad cegado por el sol resplandeciente. Entre más vueltas les daba a estos asuntos, más le hervía la sangre. Finalmente—soltó un bramido iracundo—y se largó.

whites inside them?"

"Could be, I s'*pose*... But no, I don't understand. What about the toadstools in autumn—no seeds, no anything, they just... Pop up from the earth in reds, yellows—all sorts of colors! I just don't get it, that's the truth."

"Why not ask Mr. Fox?" The birch tree was still too giddy from last night's star-conversation to guard her words.

The earthgod's face changed color and his fists clenched. "What? *That* fox? What's he been blagging on about now?"

The birch tree's voice wavered. "Nothing special... I just thought he might know something, maybe."

"And how could a *fox* teach a *god* anything, exactly?"

By now the birch tree was shaking uncontrollably. The earthgod pounded around, arms crossed tight and grinding his teeth, and where his deep black shadow fell the grass quivered.

"That damn fox is a blot on the landscape! Not an ounce of truth in him! Lowdown, cowardly, and snarkily jealous to boot!"

The birch tree finally managed to get a grip on her nerves. "Your shrine festival's coming up soon, isn't it?"

"Mmm." The earthgod's face softened, a little. "Today's the third of the month, so the festival's in six days' time." He pondered this before erupting all over again. "But these human beings are utterly useless! Does even *one* of them bother bringing an offering to my shrine nowadays? No—not a one! The next human who blunders into *my* neck of the woods is going to get dragged down to the bottom of my swamp." The earthgod stood there gnashing his teeth in fury. The birch tree, whose attempts to calm him down had only enraged him further, could do nothing but flutter her leaves in the breeze. The earthgod blustered around in the squinting sunlight. The more he thought of these matters, the more he boiled, until he let out a great howl and stormed off.

3

The swampy bog where the earthgod lived was damp, cold, and overgrown with moss, clover, and clumpy reeds. The odd thistle or grotesque willow tree grew here and there, and water seeped up into rusty quagmires. One glance and you knew that muddy place was sinister. Deep in its heart, on a hump of ground raised like an island, stood the earthgod's shrine—roughly six feet high, and made of logs.

Here on his island, the earthgod stretched out alongside his shrine. First he gave his dark ropey legs a good scratch. He spotted a bird, directly overhead. The earthgod sat up and shouted "Shoo!" The startled bird wobbled and looked like it might plummet to the ground. It fled into the distance, losing altitude as if its wings were paralyzed.

Snickering, the earthgod stood. But by chance, he glanced in the direction where the birch tree grew on her knoll. His anger possessed him again: his face changed color, his body tensed, rigid as a poker, and he clutched his wild hair with both fists.

Just then a woodcutter happened along from the south, heading for Mitsumori Mountain, sticking to the narrow path that ran along the edge of the swamp. The woodcutter seemed to know about the earthgod—every so often he threw an anxious glance toward the shrine—though, of course, the mortal saw nobody there.

But when the earthgod spotted the woodcutter, his face glowed with pleasure. Thrusting his right hand toward the man, the earthgod grasped his own wrist in his left hand, and made as if to yank it back. By doing so, the woodcutter—who still thought he was on the same path—found himself mysteriously drawn deeper into the swampy hollow. The terrified man quickened his pace, his mouth guppering and his breathing turning raspy. Next, the earthgod slowly rotated his right wrist—and the woodcutter began to walk in circles. Now in a dreadful panic, the man found himself spinning round and round on the same spot, scarcely able to breathe. His one desperate desire was to flee that devilish place as fast as his legs might carry him, but however hard he tried, he stayed there, spinning mercilessly. Finally a howl of fear broke from the woodcutter, and with both arms raised he fled for his life. Relishing every second, the earthgod looked on grinning—until the human, unable to take another step, collapsed in the sloshing water. The earthgod paced over through the mud to where the woodcutter lay, grabbed the man's body, and flung him onto firmer, grassier ground where he groaned once, stirred, but remained unconscious.

The earthgod's laughter climbed skyward in strange waves, boomed off the sky, and reached the birch tree's knoll. She became so pale that the sunlight gleamed green through her leaves, and she was seized by uncontrollable shaking.

Once more the earthgod tore at his unkempt hair. "It's all the fault of that damn fox! Oh no it's not, it's the birch tree's fault! Yes it is. No it isn't.

3

La ciénaga donde moraba el Dios Terrestre era un lugar húmedo y frío. Estaba todo cubierto de musgo—tréboles—espesos juncos enmarañados. Acá crecían bizarros cardos—allá, sauces grotescos—y a las orillas el agua lamía insistentemente los blandos lodazales. No hacía falta ser muy perceptivo para darse cuenta a primera vista de que aquel lugar era siniestro. En el mero centro del recinto, encima de una ínsula jorobada hecha de tierra y lodo, estaba el santuario del Dios Terrenal: un santuario modesto, de menos de dos metros de alto, hecho sólo de madera.

A sus anchas en su ínsula, el Dios Terrestre se acostó al pie del santuario. Se rascó las piernas—larga—morosa—placenteramente. (Las tenía prietas y rasposas.) Por encima de su cabeza voló un pájaro:

Úshcala—le gritó.

El pájaro, atolondrado, vaciló en pleno vuelo—casi se va de pico al suelo—casi. Se disolvió lentamente en la distancia—perdiendo altura—como si se le hubieran entumecido las alas.

Socarrón y alegre, el Dios Terrestre se rió. Pero en una de esas, volteó a ver en dirección de la loma donde vivía la Abedul y lo volvió a poseer la ira. El rostro le cambió de color—se le tensó el cuerpo—y con las dos manos se alborotó del pelo de por sí alborotado.

Justo en ese momento, por el estrecho camino que bordeaba el pantano, se acercó un leñador. Llegó del sur. Iba camino a la montaña Mitsumori. El leñador, al parecer, sabía muy bien quién moraba en ese lugar, porque de tanto en tanto volteaba ansiosamente hacia el santuario. Por supuesto, no veía a nadie ahí donde reposaba el Dios Terrestre.

En cambio, al Dios Terrestre se le encendieron todas las alarmas del placer anticipado cuando vio al leñador. Con la mano derecha tomó su propia muñeca izquierda y tiró de ella hacia atrás, como si su antebrazo fuera una palanca. Al hacer esto, el leñador fue arrastrado por una fuerza—para él invisible—hacia el corazón de la ciénaga. Aterrorizado, trató de apresurar el paso—su respiración cada vez más agitada. Luego, el Dios Terrestre rotó lentamente su muñeca derecha de modo que el leñador empezó a caminar en pequeños círculos. En franco pánico, deseaba huir tan pronto como fuera posible de ese lugar deplorable. Pero sin importar cuánto lo deseara, su cuerpo lo desobedecía—vuelta y vuelta en el mismo lugar. Finalmente, el leñador soltó un aullido de pavor y pudo empezar a huir—dando tumbos por la ciénaga. El Dios Terrestre observaba—saboreando cada paso trabajoso del leñador—hasta que el pobre hombre se colapsó en el lodo. Entonces el Dios Terrestre atravesó el lodazal hasta donde se encontraba el leñador ya inmóvil. Lo levantó—lo zarandeó—lo arrojó. El cuerpo inerte cayó en un parche un poco más firme de tierra. Se agitó levemente—inconsciente.

Las carcajadas del Dios Terrestre treparon por los árboles hacia lo alto—en ondas retorcidas se proyectaron hacia el cielo—reverberaron en la llanura hasta alcanzar la loma de la Abedul. Ésta su vez empezó a temblar y se puso tan pálida que la luz del sol pudo atravesar sus hojas—casi transparentes.

El Dios Terrestre se empezó a tirar de la greña enmarañada que le coronaba la mollera: "Todo es culpa de ese despreciable Zorro. O tal vez no—quizás sea culpa de la Abdeul. Sí—es culpa de ella. O más bien—es culpa del Zorro *y* de la Abedul—de los dos juntos y revueltos. Si no sintiera nada por ella, el Zorro ese me vendría importando un bledo. Tal vez no lo parezca, pero a fin de cuentas soy un dios. No puede ser que un animalucho me produzca tanta ira. Lo que tengo que hacer es purgarme la cabeza de todo lo que tenga que ver con esa Abedul. Qué gusto me dio esta mañana, cuando la pobre se puso a temblar como maraca. Ya sé—ya sé—me pasé de listo con ese pobre leñador—pero ni modo—el corazón es un misterio." El Dios Terrestre, en su miserable mezquindad, siguió haciendo rabietas.

Sobrevoló por lo alto un halcón. Esta vez, lo dejó pasar.

A lo lejos se escuchó el rumor de una cabalgata—el repiqueteo metálico de los rifles—tronando y chasqueando—como granos de maíz arrojados a una pira. Desde el cielo—en ondas claras azuladas—la luz bañaba el llano. Esta misma luz fue la que tocó el corazón del leñador moribundo y le trajo de vuelta el aliento de vida. Se enderezó y miró a su alrededor. De un brinco, ya estaba otra vez en camino a la montaña Mitsumori.

El Dios Terrestre volvió a soltar una carcajada tronadora. Una vez más, sus risas treparon al cielo y retumbaron por la llanura hasta llegar a la Abedul. Casi imperceptiblemente, ella tembló y palideció.

Durante un rato, el Dios Terrestre siguió dando vueltas alrededor del santuario, hasta que pudo apaciguarse y meterse de nuevo.

4

Una noche brumosa de la canícula de agosto, el Dios Terrestre se encontraba

It's the fox *and* the birch tree—*they're* why I'm tortured like this. If I didn't care about the birch tree, I wouldn't give two hoots about the stupid fox. I may be nobody special, but I *am* a proper god at the very least, and it's, it's simply out*rage*ous that I, *I*, should be bothering myself over one dumb beast! Why don't I just put that birch tree out of my mind? Because I *can't*, that's why! I just can't… How delicious it was this morning when she went all white and quivery. It was mean of me to pick on a feeble little human—but I couldn't help myself. There's no knowing what any of us are capable of, not when we really *really* lose our tempers…"

The miserable earthgod flailed his fists at nothing. A hawk flew by. This time the earthgod just watched it pass.

From far away came the sound of the cavalry on maneuvers. Their rifles made a spitting, crackling noise, like salt tossed into flames. From the heavens, waves of blue light washed the wide plain and seemed to revive the woodcutter, who sat up, cautiously. Then he was off, running toward Mitsumori Mountain, swift as an arrow.

The earthgod let out another thunderclap of laughter. Once again it echoed off the sky, down to the birch tree. Once again, the birch tree paled and quivered, almost imperceptibly.

The earthgod walked in pointless circles around his shrine until he eventually calmed down. Then he slipped inside.

4

On a mist-muffled night in August, the earthgod was lonely and on edge. Acting on impulse, he left his shrine and found himself heading off toward the birch tree. Why thoughts of her quickened his heart yet made it melancholy, he couldn't say. Of late he had been calmer than the previous season, and had pushed away all thoughts of both the fox and the birch tree—as best he could. Yet somehow, they kept creeping back. *You're a god*, he would repeat to himself, every single day. *Why the big drama over one birch tree?* But the earthgod still couldn't prevent his unhappiness, and when he thought about the fox he felt as though his flesh was burning.

While he was lost in these musings, the earthgod's feet led him to the birch tree until it dawned on him where he was headed, and his heart began to dance. Too long had passed since he'd last called on her—quite possibly, the birch tree had been pining for him. Yes, surely she had—now the earthgod regretted his absence very much. Such pleasant thoughts lifted his spirits, and he strode over the grass—before coming to a dead halt. The earthgod stood bathed in blue sadness, for the fox was already there. Darkness had fallen, but through the pearly, moonlit mist, the fox's voice reached the earthgod.

"Just because art submits to the laws of symmetry, that's no guarantee of beauty. No, no, no. I'd call *that* a mere instance of dead beauty."

"I couldn't agree more." The birch tree's voice was soft.

"*True* beauty is not fixed, nor a fossil, nor a model. Yes, people bang on about the necessity of symmetry, but what matters is that symmetry's *spirit* is present, as it were."

"I'm sure you're quite right," said the birch tree in her gentle voice.

The earthgod felt flames devouring his whole being. His breathing was tight and hoarse… Unbearable! "But *why* are you so cut up about this?" the earthgod asked himself. "A birch tree and a fox are conversing in the open air, that's all. How can you call yourself a god and let all this upset you so?"

The fox continued his discourse: "Thus all books on aesthetics—on art—tackle this subject."

"Do you have a great number of art books?" asked the birch tree.

"Oh, I wouldn't say a *great* number… Most of the English texts, the German ones, the Japanese ones… There's a new one out in Italian, but it hasn't arrived yet."

"What a splendid library you must have!"

"I wouldn't go that far—just a few volumes, cluttering up the place—it doubles as my study, too, so it's always an ungodly shambles—a microscope in that corner, the London *Times* over there, my bust of the Emperor Caesar here…"

"Gosh, how marvelous it all sounds—just marvelous!"

The fox snuffled, perhaps with modesty, perhaps with pride.

Silence fell, but by now the earthgod had worked himself up into a terrible state. To judge from his conversation, that fox cut a far more sophisticated figure than himself. For the earthgod to reassure himself with the thought *At least I'm a god, if nothing else* was no longer enough. Intolerable! He felt an irresistible urge to rip that fox to shreds, here and now. It was wrong even to imagine doing such a thing, but how could the earthgod help himself? That fox outclassed him. The earthgod clutched his stomach in sheer misery.

"Has that telescope arrived yet?" the birch tree was asking.

particularmente alicaído y sin sosiego. Arrastrado por un impulso, salió de su santuario y se dirigió hacia la gran llanura. No podía explicarse por qué, apenas pensaba en la Abedul, el corazón se le agitaba y a la vez se le hundía en un opresivo fango melancólico. En los últimos tiempos había podido templarse y había aprendido a ahuyentar los pensamientos relacionados con la Abedul y el Zorro. Pero cada tanto, estos pensamientos regresaban—sigilosos—inesperados. "Eres un Dios," se repetía a sí mismo todos los días. "¿Para qué tanto drama por un arbolito?" Pero en el fondo el Dios Terrestre era incapaz de extirparse el dolor que todo aquello le causaba, y en cuanto aparecía el Zorro en el ojo de su mente, le hervía la sangre.

A la deriva en este torrente de reflexiones, el Dios Terrestre de pronto se dio cuenta de que sus pasos lo habían conducido hacia la morada de la Abedul. Le empezó a palpitar furiosamente el corazón. Pensándolo bien, había pasado mucho tiempo desde la última vez que la había visto—suficiente para que ella ya lo estuviera echando de menos. Es más, de seguro estaría ansiando verlo. Esa certeza le levantó el ánimo y cruzó la llanura—casi ingrávido—contento.

Pero en cuanto llegó al pie de la loma, se le vino abajo el mundo: ahí estaba ya el Zorro. La noche era oscura, así que no veía a ninguno de los dos, pero la voz un poco nasal y ese tonito disque-intelectual del animalejo eran inconfundibles:

Que el Arte se someta a sí mismo a las inclementes leyes de la simetría no garantiza la Belleza. Yo—desde mi muy particular punto de vista—diría que *eso* es una mera instancia de belleza muerta.

No podría estar más de acuerdo contigo, querido Zorro.

La Verdadera Belleza es inasible—no es un fósil—no es un modelo. La gente—dicho sea de paso—adula la simetría sin reservas—pero lo que importa es que esté presente el *espíritu* de la belleza—si acaso me explico.

Te explicas perfectamente—respondió la Abedul, su voz tan dulce.

Al Dios Terrestre se le estrujaron todos los órganos. Se le cerraron los pulmones. "Imposible," pensó. "¿Pero por qué te van a hacer rabiar estos dos lerdos?" se preguntó. "Un arbolito y un zorrito están hablando de sus temitas, ¿cómo es posible que eso le importe a un dios?"

El Zorro prosiguió, airoso:

Así pues, todos los libros que tocan el tema delicado de la Estética, enfrentan este mismo asunto.

¿Y tú tienes muchos libros de Arte?—preguntó la Abedul.

No diría que muchos. Eso sí—tengo todos los libros en inglés, en alemán, y en japonés. Y hay uno nuevo en italiano—pero ese todavía no me lo mandan.

¡Qué magnífica biblioteca has de tener!

No iría tan lejos—tengo ciertos volúmenes—eso es todo—pero sin duda ocupan todo mi espacio vital. La verdad es que tengo ahí un caos espléndido: un microscopio en aquella esquina—números del London *Times* por acá—mis bustos de Césares y emperadores por allá—

Qué maravilla.

El Zorro resopló. Tal vez con modestia, tal vez con arrogancia. Seguramente con esa mezcla despreciable de ambas.

Se hizo de pronto un silencio, pero para ahora el Dios Terrestre estaba en un estado francamente incontrolable. Juzgando por la conversación que acababa de escuchar, el Zorro era tal vez más sofisticado que él. Quizá no bastaba con ser un Dios. Sintió una urgencia irrefrenable por desguanzar a ese zorrito—en ese mismo instante—ahí—acabar con él. Estaba mal—sí—dejar que el cuerpo y la cabeza desearan tan intensamente el mal. Pero, ¿qué podía hacer? El Zorro lo desnudaba—lo obligaba a mostrar el cobre. El Dios Terrestre se llevó las manos a la barriga—convulso—ligeramente histriónico.

¿Y por fin te llegó el telescopio?—la Abedul siguió haciendo plática.

¿Qué telescopio? Ah—claro—ese telescopio—no—no todavía. Las colas de las aduanas son muy largas, ¿sabes? Pero en cuanto llegue te aseguro que te lo traeré. Los anillos de Saturno—eso es algo que hay que ver por lo menos una vez en esta vida.

El Dios Terrestre no pudo más. Se cubrió los oídos y salió corriendo de ahí, con dirección al norte. No quería ni imaginar lo que habría sido capaz de hacerle al Zorro de haberse quedado ahí. Corrió sin tregua—y corrió—y siguió corriendo hasta que se le doblaron las rodillas y cayó—postrado—al pie de la montaña Mitsumori.

Retorciéndose en el pasto, tirándose del pelo, el Dios Terrestre soltó un gemido que reverberó a la redonda como un trueno extemporáneo. Lloró. Y siguió llorando en su lento—difícil—trabajoso—camino de vuelta a casa.

5

Pasaron los meses—llegó el otoño. La Abedul seguía ostentando su follaje verde, pero la superficie de su loma—rala—tatemada—parecía la cabeza de un viejo casi calvo. En el valle las rebosantes moras brotaban y maduraban—rojas y sanguíneas.

Era un día de aire prístino y el Dios Terrestre estaba de franco buen ánimo. Las tormentas que le habían ensombrecido el verano parecían haberse esfumado y su intensa amargura se había disuelto casi por completo. Si la Abedul quería

"Um, that telescope? Ah, yes—no, it hasn't. The shipping lanes are awfully crowded, you see. But the moment it's here, I'll bring it straight over. The rings of Saturn are truly… sublime."

The earthgod covered his ears with his hands and sped away north. What he might do to the fox if he stayed any longer didn't bear thinking about. On and on and on and on he sprinted, until his legs buckled and he found himself at the foot of Mitsumori Mountain. Writhing there in the grass, yanking at his hair, his roars rose up to heaven and clanged across the wide plain like unseasonable thunder. The earthgod sobbed his eyes out before plodding home to his shrine at daybreak, in perfect misery.

5

Time passed and autumn came around. The birch tree was still green, but the tufted grass was tinged with gold and gleamed in the breeze. The berries of the lilies of the valley ripened into blood red.

One clear, gold day, the earthgod found himself in excellent humor. The painful thoughts that had afflicted him since the summer seemed to have evaporated into faint rings somewhere above his head. His knotted-up bitterness was a thing of the past. If the birch tree wanted to talk with the fox, that was her business, and if they both enjoyed the natter, so what? The earthgod decided to visit the birch tree and air these new feelings, and so with a buoyant heart he set off to do just that.

The birch tree saw the earthgod approach, and—as usual—started quivering as he drew nearer.

Up strode the earthgod with a cheerful "Morning—and what glorious weather!"

"Good morning," replied the birch tree. "Yes, quite glorious."

"Isn't the sun a blessing! Red in the spring, white in the summer, yellow in the autumn—yellow, to turn the grapes purple! A majestic blessing indeed…"

"True," said the birch tree, "quite true."

"Y'know, Birch Tree, I feel on top of the world today. Since the summer, I've had my share of trials, but since waking up this morning, that burden has been lifted from my shoulders."

The birch tree wanted to make some sort of reply, but a strange fear kept her silent.

"The way I'm feeling today, I could lay down my life for another—and gladly! I'd even change places with a worm, if it had to die and didn't want to…" The earthgod gazed at the distant blue eternity with eyes dark and soulful. Once again the birch tree wanted to speak, but it was all she could do just to sigh…

…Which was when the fox showed up.

Upon seeing the earthgod the fox's face fell, but he could hardly just turn around and go home again, so he went up to the birch tree, ignoring his nerves. "Good morning, Birch Tree—and do I have the honor of addressing the earthgod?" The fox wore his beige leather shoes, a brown raincoat, and his summer hat still sat on his head.

"Yes, the earthgod, that's me. Beautiful day, isn't it?" The earthgod spoke as if he didn't have a care in the world.

The fox had turned a pale jealous green. "How rude of me to barge in when you have a visitor," the fox told the birch tree. "This is the book I promised to lend you. One of these nights, when the sky is clear, I'll show you the telescope, too. Goodbye, then."

"Why thank you," said the birch tree, "that's really—" but the fox trotted off without even acknowledging the earthgod. The birch tree turned an even paler hue, and her trembling started up again.

For a time, the earthgod just stared at the fox withdrawing from the scene. But then, a distant blink of sunlight glanced off the fox's beige shoes and the earthgod came out of his trance. Something was triggered by the fox's insolent swagger, and the earthgod's face turned black as his murderous temper ignited. *He'd* soon sort out that fox, that damn fox what with his fancy art books and his oh-so-precious telescope! The next instant the earthgod was up and hurtling after his prey. Now the birch tree's limbs were all shaking with dread. The fox sensed something amiss and glanced over his shoulder—to see the earthgod, black as night, roaring like a storm. Off shot the fox, fast as the wind, his face white and his mouth awry with terror.

To the earthgod, the grass was a blazing blur, and even the blue sky had yawned into a cavernous pit in whose depths blood-red flames scorched and howled.

The hunter and the hunted pounded along breathless like two locomotives. The fox ran as if in a dream, while a voice in his head repeated, "The end is nigh, the end is nigh, telescope, telescope, telescope."

A mound of bare earth lay ahead. The fox darted around to his den on

hablar con el Zorro—ni remedio. Si ambos disfrutaban la cháchara—no era grave. En este espíritu, el Dios Terrestre decidió visitar nuevamente a la Abedul. Quería airear estos nuevos sentimientos—mostrar el corazón.

A lo lejos, la Abedul vio aproximarse al Dios Terrestre y, como siempre, se puso a temblar.

¡Buen día, Abedul! ¿No es una mañana gloriosa?

Buenos días. Sí, linda mañana.

¿No te parece que el sol es un milagro? Rojo en la primavera—blanco en el verano—amarillo en el otoño. Amarillo. ¡Tan amarillo que pinta las uvas… de morado! Un milagro majestuoso de verdad.

Cierto, cierto—respondió la Abedul, fingiendo interés.

¿Sabes qué?—continuó el Dios Terrestre—Hoy me siento por encima de todo. El verano me trajo algunos momentos difíciles. Pero hoy me desperté más liviano que nunca. Algo cambió.

La Abedul quiso responder, pero un miedo extraño le impedía pensar siquiera en una palabra.

Hoy me siento tan bien que podría dar mi vida por alguien. Y con gusto. Hasta cambiaría de lugar con un gusano—si eso significara salvarle el pellejo.

Mientras decía esto, el Dios Terrestre miraba hacia el eterno horizonte con mirada franca y gallarda. Una vez más, la Abedul quiso hablar, pero no pudo decir nada. Lo único que salió de ella fue un suspirillo.

Y de pronto apareció el Zorro.

Naturalmente, al ver al Dios terrestre, al Zorro casi se le cae la cola. Pero era demasiado tarde para darse la media vuelta, así que se controló y subió la loma. Traía sus zapatitos beige rechinantes—una gabardina café—un sombrero que le quedaba como pintado:

Buenos días Abedul. Y buenos días, ¿Dios Terrestre? ¿Acaso se me está concediendo el honor de dirigirme a usted directamente?

Sí, Zorro, ese soy yo. ¿Bonito día, no cree?

El Dios Terrestre hablaba, holgado y sereno. El Zorro, en cambio, se había puesto pálido-verde. Se trató de zafar:

Qué mal de mi parte entrometerme así nada más cuando tienes visitas, Abedul. Acá está el libro que te prometí—te lo dejo. Pronto—cuando haya una noche clara— vengo con el telescopio y vemos el cielo. Hasta luego.

Durante unos instantes, el Dios Terrestre oteó al Zorro, que se alejaba lentamente de la escena—su escena—su árbol Abedul.

Un destello de luz, reflejado desde los flamantes zapatos del Zorro, lo sacó de su trance. De nuevo, la verborrea insolente del animal había desatado algo en las entrañas del Dios Terrestre. Le cambió el rostro—se encendió una vieja cólera. Había que poner a ese zorro en su lugar—ya estaba bueno de libritos de arte y telescopios—ay, tan especiales—ay, tan alemanes. En un abrir y cerrar de ojos, el Dios Terrestre estaba al acecho de su presa. La pobre Abedul, para variar, empezó a temblar de miedo. El Zorro intuyó que algo terrible se avecinaba, y miró hacia atrás, de soslayo, por encima de su hombro. Negro como la negra noche, crepitante como un incendio incontenible, el Dios Terrestre venía corriendo tras él. Empezó a correr más rápido—veloz y rectilíneo como una flecha—el rostro, pálido de puro miedo—el hocico, seco de angustia.

El pasto bailaba ante los ojos emponzoñados del Dios Terrestre como un espejismo resplandeciente. El cielo, antes amplio y claro, se abría en un bostezo cavernoso en cuyas tinieblas profundas gemían y crepitaban flamas infernales.

Predador y presa—uno detrás del otro—como dos locomotoras sin aliento.

El Zorro corría como en un sueño—en una pesadilla—repitiendo para sí mismo: "Mi fin se acerca—mi fin—se acerca—acerca—telescopio—telescopio—telescopio."

El Zorro llegó por fin a un montículo de tierra pelona—la entrada a su guarida. Metió apenas la cabeza en la boca de la madriguera—sus dos patas traseras respingaron en el aire—y ahí fue cuando el Dios Terrestre se le vino encima. Un solo golpe seco.

El cuerpo torcido y lánguido del Zorro—su cabeza pequeña suavemente apoyada en la palma de la mano del Dios Terrestre—el hocico abierto—los ojos entornados.

El Dios Terrestre lo arrojó contra el suelo y todavía pisoteó su blando cuerpo cuatro o cinco veces. Luego, entró a la madriguera: un espacio oscuro—sobrio—prácticamente vacío. El suelo de tierra estaba cuidadosamente aplanado. El Dios Terrestre percibió un extraño sabor de boca—amargo—podrido. Volvió a salir al aire libre. Metió la mano a la gabardina del Zorro y de ahí sacó dos semillas de abrojo—del tipo que utilizan los Zorros para cepillarse el pelaje. En la boca del Dios Terrestre se dibujó una mueca convulsa—y de la mueca estalló un alarido inadjetivable.

El Dios Terrestre empezó a llorar.

Lágrimas—como gotas de lluvia—bañaron al Zorro muerto—la nuca torcida hacia atrás—el discreto esbozo de una sonrisa.

the far side. His body followed his head through the fox-hole, and only his rear legs kicked the air as he vanished—which was when the earthgod finally caught him. A moment later the fox's body was twisted, his head nestling over the earthgod's hand, and his lips drawn back over his teeth.

The earthgod dashed the fox to the ground and jumped on the squidgy corpse four or five times. Then he went into the fox's den. It was sparse and dark inside. The reddish earthen floor was trodden down neat and firm. The earthgod's mouth felt all strange, all wrong. Out he went again into the open air. Putting a hand into the pocket of the raincoat of the limp fox, he drew out two brown burrs, of the kind foxes like to comb their hair with. From the earthgod's distorted mouth there issued the most unearthly noise.

The earthgod began sobbing, and sobbing.

Tears like rain fell on a dead fox with a broken neck and the faintest ghost of a smile.

THE FOX
AND THE EARTH GOD

translated into English by JONATHAN LETHEM
and MARA FAYE LETHEM

1

IN THE LAND ADJOINING the grand prairie to the north, crowning a grass-covered hill, grew a lovely Birch. It wasn't particularly large. Yet its smooth, dark trunk bore branches high and extended, giving it a certain grace. Its foliage was remarkable. In the spring, velvety white flowers. In the fall, red and golden leaves, a plethora of fiery tones. Apart from those times when a hawk lurked, passing birds—the cuckoo, the white-eyed foliage gleaner, the tiny fairy wren and the pitohui—would stop to rest among its branches.

The Birch had two friends. One, an Earth God, lived in a swamp some five hundred steps from the hill. The other, a brown Fox, showed up every once in a while at the southern edge of the prairie. If she had to choose, Birch preferred the Fox. The Earth God, for any distinction conferred by his name, had a frankly wild look: tangled fur like shreds of cotton, venomous, bloodshot eyes, clothes that hung like scraps of seaweed. He trod the prairie's length barefoot, his hoofs porcine and long. The Fox, on the other hand, was discreet, elegantly aristocratic, and never stuck his nose where it didn't belong.

In a strict comparison, though, it was unmistakable that just as the Earth God was transparent as the air, the Fox could be a bit of a liar.

بیل لومڑ اور مقدس روح

translated into Urdu by NADEEM ASLAM

اس جگہ کے قریب جہاں دریا سمندر سے بھی زیادہ پھیلا ہوا ہے ایک میدان میں پھولوں سے بھری ایک بیل ہوا کرتی تھی۔ ایک مردہ پیپل کے تنے سے لپٹی ہوئی۔ اونچائی میں تو یہ زیادہ نہیں تھی لیکن تھی اس کی ہموار چھال والے دو دو بھرے تنے اور لپٹی بیل کھاتی نہیں تھی اور آن تھی۔ پھول تو یہ پھول، اس کے تو یہ بھی دیکھنے کے لائق تھے۔ بہار میں ان کا رنگ ہلکا سارخ اور تھوڑا ارہی دارچینی کی طرف مائل ہوا کرتا اور کچھ ہے جیسا اور باقی مہینوں میں گہرا نارنگ۔بیل کی شاخوں میں ہر وقت بلبل، مینا اور پھر نے چھوٹے شکر خورے موجود رہتے ہیں۔

بیل کے دو دوست جانے والے تھے۔دوست کہ:دوست یا عزیز۔پہلی ایک پچھے ہوئے بزرگ کی روح تھی،جس کے مزار بیل سے کوئی پانچ سوقد موں سے دور تھا،اور دوسرا ایک لومڑ جو کبھی کبھی دریا کے مشرقی کنارے سے اِدھر آ نکلتا۔بیل سے پوچھا جا تا تو وہ کہہ دیتیں کہ انہیں لومڑ زیادہ پسند تھا۔ ایک بزرگ کی روح کو تو ایک متاز اور معتبر نام کی مالک تھی لیکن دیکھنے میں تھوڑی سی ڈراؤنی چیز تھی۔بال اور داڑھی دونوں اجڑے ہوئے،آنکھیں سرخ اور کپڑے لیرا لیر ا،ننگے پاؤں وہ دور دریا اِدھر اُدھر گھومتی رہتی۔جبکہ لومڑ ایک دور اندیش اور خوش ومنع شخصیت تھے اور ان میں اونچے طبقے کا فرد ہونے کا گمان ہوتا تھا۔جبکہ اگر بزرگ کی روح ہوا کی طرح شفاف ہے تو لومڑ کو کچھ کچھ جھوٹ سے بولنے کی عادت تھی۔

بہار کے شروع کے دن تھے۔راتیں پُر سکون تھیں۔نئے چن یہ پودوں کو اپنی نفاست سے دباپن دیا تھا۔چاند نکلا ہوا تھا اور اس کے اِرد گرد ستاروں کے جھرمٹ سے ملے آئے۔ایک سفید شلوار قمیص کی جیب میں شاعری کی ایک کتاب لیے۔ان کے چپل ایک شاٹ سی آواز پیدا کر رہے تھے۔

'کیا حسین شام ہے'انہوں نے کہا۔

'جی ہاں'بیل نے جواب دیا۔

'وہ العقرب کو دیکھ رہی ہیں آپ؟ آپ کو معلوم ہے کہ ہمارے آباو اجداد اس سرخ ستارے کو آ گ تارہ کہتے تھے؟'

'لیکن یہ مریخ نہیں؟'

'نہیں نہیں۔یہ ایک سیارہ ہے۔یہ ستارہ ہے۔'

'حیرت ہے۔اور اب ہم یہ پوچھنا چاہیں گے کہ ستارے اور سیارے میں کیا فرق ہے؟'

'سیاروں کی اپنی روشنی نہیں ہوتی۔وہ دوسروں کی روشنی میں نظر آتے ہیں۔جبکہ ستارے خودی روشن ہوتے ہیں۔ہمارا سورج بھی ایک ستارہ ہی ہے۔قریب ہونے کی وجہ۔سے بڑا لگتا ہے اور آنکھیں خیرہ کر دیتا ہے لیکن جب کچھ دور ہوتا ہو تو دوسرے ستاروں کی طرح ایک نقطہ سا لگتا ۔'

'سورج ایک ستارہ؟ تو کیا سارا آسمان سورجوں سے بھرا پڑا ہے؟'

لومڑ ناز برداری کرتے ہوئے مسکرائے۔'یہ کہا جا سکتا ہے۔'

'اور کچھ ستارے سرخ اور کچھ پہلے اور کچھ نیلے۔یہ کیوں؟'

لومڑ پھر مسکرائے اور پھر یہ جانچنے کے لیے کہ یہ شاعری کے لیے محفوظ ہے انہوں نے اپنی جیب کو ذرا سا ہلایا۔بولے:'کافی دور پہلے سب ستارے نیلے بادلوں جیسے ہوا کرتے تھے۔نرم سطح جیسے۔کچھ تو ابھی بھی ہیں۔المسلسلۃ،الجوزا،جو کہ کالسلوقیان میں پائے جاتے ہیں،یا المکونات الدائری،جو کہ چھلی کے منہ کے مانند ہے۔'

'کیا میں مہ دل تصحیح کر دی آپ نے ایک ستاروں کا مجموعہ جو چھلی کے منہ کی جھلک دیتا ہوا؟'

'اور آپ نے یہ ٹھیک لفظ استعمال کیا۔غیر معمولی۔دیسے میں نے تمام ستاروں کا ایک رسد گاہ میں مشاہدہ کر چکا ہوں۔'

'کاش ہم بھی کبھی دیکھ پائیں۔'

'کیوں نہیں۔ اتفاقاً ہم نے ابھی بغداد سے ایک دور بین منگوائی ہے اور وہ بھی امام دین عدسہ ساز جن کا شجرہ ہارون رشید کے عدسہ سازوں سے جا ملتا ہے۔ عراق کے حالات خراب ہیں لیکن جلد ہی آ جائے گی۔ جونہی آئے گی میں آپ کے ہاں لے آؤں گا۔'

یہ وعدہ کرتے ہی بیل لومڑ کو رنج ہونے لگا۔ با خدا ایک میں نے پھر ایک جھوٹ بول ڈالا۔ وہ بھی دنیا میں اپنے اکلوتے دوست سے۔ ویسے یہ تو ایک مہربان جھوٹ تھا۔ میں انہیں خوش کرنا چاہتا تھا۔ خیر موقع پاتے ہی میں یہ سب کچھ ٹھیک کر لوں گا۔

اپنی مسرت اور اپائی میں بیل لومڑ کے چہرے سے گزرنے والے سائے دیکھ پائیں۔

'آپ نے ہمیں بہت خوش کر دیا۔ آپ کی ہم پر بہت مہربانیاں ہیں۔'

'دوست اسی لیے ہوتے ہیں۔' پھر لومڑ نے اپنے دونوں جانب نظر دوڑائی اور جیب میں ہاتھ ڈالا۔ 'یہ ایک کتاب لائے ہیں ہم واصل سلیم کی نظمیں ہیں۔ کتاب ذرا پرانی اور بری حالت میں ہے لیکن کیا کیا جائے گورنمنٹ ان کی شاعری کو نئی نظروں سے دیکھتی ہے اور نئے ایڈیشن چھپنے نہیں دیتی۔

کچھ دن رکھ سکتے ہیں ہم؟

جب تک جی چاہے رکھ لیجیے۔ ان سے کسی نے کہا۔ آپ کی تیس چالیس سال پرانی شاعری ابھی تک ہمارے کام کام آ رہی ہے۔ جواب دیا: یہ میری شاعری کا کوئی کمال ہے۔۔۔ پاکستان کے حالات ہی نہیں بدل رہے! یہ بتا کر لومڑ اٹھ کھڑے ہوے۔ اچھا اب اجازت دیجیے۔ پھر انہوں نے ایک قلندرانہ انداز میں چاند کی طرف ہاتھ اٹھا دیا:

جلوہ گاہِ وصال کی شمعیں
وہ بجھا بھی چکے اگر تو کیا
چاند کو گل کریں تو ہم جانیں

ان کے چلے جانے کے بعد بیل نظمیں پڑھنے کی مطالعہ کرنے لگیں۔ جب رات اندھیرے میں فوجی انہیں گرفتار کرنے کو آئے تو واصل سلیم نے پوچھا۔ مجھے میرا جرم تو بتایا جائے۔ جواب آیا: آپ نے تو کوئی قانون نہیں توڑا مگر ابھی تک تو جس شخص کو بھی گرفتار کیا ہے اس کے پاس آپ کی کتاب ہی نکلی۔ اسی لیے ہم آپ کو بھی لیتے جا رہے ہیں۔

رات گزری اور صبح ہوئی۔ گھاس شبنم سے جھلملا رہی تھی اور بیل پر آہستہ آہستہ نئے نئے پھول کھلنے شروع ہو گئے۔ پہلی دھوپ میں بزرگ کی روح نمودار ہوئی۔ کسی نامعلوم وجہ سے آج بیل کو اپنا مہمان دیکھ کر تھوڑی سی گھبراہٹ ہوئی۔ انہوں نے اپنے نیچے بھلائے اور زمین پر ان کا سایہ کانپ سا اٹھا۔

بزرگ قریب آئے اور رک گئے۔

'السلام علیکم !'

'وعلیکم السلام'

کئی چیزوں کا تو کچھ میں نہیں آتا۔ جتنی بھی کوشش کی جائے۔ صرف یقینی۔ صرف پراسراریت ہی ہاتھ میں آتی ہے۔

'پراسراریت؟'

'اب میں گھاس ہی کو لیجیے۔ جائے کے رنگ کی زمین سے آتی ہے۔ یہ خود میری اور پھولوں کا تو دو کرہی نہ لیجیے۔ پیلے۔ سفید۔ لال۔ کیا وجہ ہے اس کی؟

شاید گھاس اور پھولوں کے بیجوں میں اپنے اپنے رنگ چھپے ہوے ہوں۔

لیکن پھر بھی کچھ کچھ ہے باہر۔ اور وہ جو برسات میں کھمبیاں اگتی ہیں ان کے تو بیج نہیں ہوتے۔ وہ کیسے خود ہی اگ پڑتی ہیں؟ کافی رنگ ہوتے ہیں ان کے بھی۔

آپ یہ سب کچھ لومڑ سے پوچھیے۔

بیل کو جواب ابھی کل شام لومڑ سے ہوئی گفتگو کے خار میں تھیں۔ اپنے ان الفاظ کا احساس کچھ دیر سے ہوا۔

بزرگ جلال میں آ گئے۔ ان کے ہاتھ ایک ایک کی کسی ہوئی مٹھیوں میں تبدیل ہو گئے۔

ولومڑ! کیا یہ کیا رہا ہے آج کل وہ؟

بیل نے پہلے تو جھجکی لیکن پھر اپنا حوصلہ باندھ کر بولیں:

'میں نے تو یونہی کہہ دیا کہ شاید انہیں کچھ معلوم ہو۔'

'تواب ایک اودنی سال لومڑ ایک روح کو تعلیم دینے بیٹھے گا۔ بزرگ بزبزائے۔ وہ اپنے حصے کو قائم رکھنے کی کوشش کر رہے تھے۔ سایہ تو ان کا نہیں۔ اگر ہوتا تو جہاں وہ اس وقت گرتا ہوں اس زمین اٹھتی۔

کچھ سمجھ میں نہیں آتا تا کہ اس لومڑ سے کیوں تعلقات رکھتی ہیں۔ اس قسم کے لوگ تو چھچورے اور نمائشی ہوتے ہیں۔ خود پسند۔ حاسد۔

بیل نے موضوع بدلنے کی کوشش کی۔

آپ کا عرس آ رہا ہے؛ دیڑھ دو ماہ میں۔

جی ہاں۔ بزرگ نے کچھ تسکین سے جواب دیا۔

چاہنے والوں کا آپ کے مزار پر جمگھٹا لگ جائے گا۔

کیا عرس اور کیا مزار کوئی کسی کو نہیں جانا چاہتا۔ پچھلے سال عرس پر کوئی نہیں آیا۔

'کیوں آپ ڈر رہے ہیں؟ بھلا کیسے آتے ہوے لوگ۔ پچھلے سال عرس کے وقت تو اتنا سیلاب آیا ہوا تھا۔ شاید بھول گئے آپ۔'

'جی ہاں۔ کیا حالات تھے! بزرگ نے یاد کرتے ہوے کہا۔ گاؤں کے گاؤں یوں پر ہو گئے۔ بے چارے لوگ۔ لاکھوں کے حساب سے بھوکے ننگے۔

اور کتنی فریادوں کے بعد دوسرے ملک پاکستان کی مدد کرنے کو تیار ہوے۔ آدمی یہ دنیا یہ جانے ہی کی کہ انہیں مرنے دو وہ دہشت گردی میں تو ہوں۔ اور آدمی یہ کہ ان کی مدد کرنی چاہیے ورنہ بھوک انہیں دہشت

2

The summer was young, the night peaceful. A layer of delicate new leaves covered the Birch, perfuming the air. Diaphanous, the Milky Way cut through the heavens. The stars throbbed, now faint, now bright. Beneath this sky, the Fox crossed the prairie to visit the Birch. He wore a navy blue suit and carried a letterpress volume of poetry beneath his arm. His beige leather shoes squeaked elegantly as he approached the hill.

"A lovely night, don't you think?" remarked the Fox.

"Yes," mused the Birch to her distinguished companion.

"Do you see Scorpius up there? Did you know the ancients called that large red star *The Fire Star*?"

"Isn't that Mars?"

"Of course not! Mars is a planet, but that's a star."

"Incredible. That leads me to wonder what difference there is between a star and a planet."

"Well, planets do not have their own shine—they are visible only when reflecting the light of another heavenly body—but real stars glow on their own. Our sun's a true star. It might seem enormous to us—blinding, too—but if we could view if from far enough away it would be a mere spot of light."

"So the sun's just another star! Then, are there many suns in the sky... which is to say, stars...which is to say, suns?"

The Fox smiled indulgently. "I suppose so."

"And why are some stars red, others yellow, others greenish?"

The Fox smiled again and crossed his arms. The volume of poetry almost fell to the floor—almost. "Well," he responded, "long ago all the stars looked like large, spongy clouds. We can still see some of them like that: in Andromeda and in Orion, in the spiral of Canes Venatici, or in the Ring Nebula, shaped like a fish's mouth."

"What an image! Stars in the shape of a fish's mouth? That's extraordinary!"

"That's the right word: *extra-ordinary*. Did you know I've seen all the stars from an observatory?"

"Oh, I wish I could see them, too."

"Well, then you shall. It happens that I just sent for a telescope from Germany. A Zeiss, to be precise. I'll have it before spring arrives. As soon as it comes, I'll let you use it."

In truth, the Fox was lying. The instant he'd made that promise to the Birch, he began to regret it. *Jeez, I just lied, again, to my only friend in the world. At least it was a kind lie, intended to make her happy. Anyway, I'll fix it soon.* The Birch was so excited that she didn't notice the shadow that crossed the Fox's face.

"You've made me so happy, Fox, you're so good to me."

"That's what friends are for, Birch. By the way, this book I have here, wanna have a look at it? It's Heinrich Heine's poems, in translation. What can you do? But for a translation it's not bad."

"You'd really lend it to me?"

"Sure, hold on to it for as long as you need. I've got to go. But was there something else to your question?"

"Yes. The stars: why are they different colors?"

"Oh, yeah, that. Let's leave that for the next time. As the Italians say: Visitors are like fish, they start to stink after a while."

"Oh, Fox, you shouldn't worry about that. It's always a pleasure being with you."

"Then I'll come back soon. See ya—*au revoir*. I'll leave you with Heinrich Heine."

And with that mannered farewell, the Fox trotted off toward home. The Birch, with its leaves softly swaying in a sudden southern breeze, and sheltered beneath the pale gleam of the Milky Way, began to study the pages of the book. The Heinrich Heine anthology included "Loreley" and other masterpieces, so the Birch read and read. It was three in the morning and the stars kept spinning until Taurus appeared on the Eastern horizon. Only then did she begin to feel sleepy.

Dawn broke on grass shimmering with dew. New flowers had appeared since the night before. Advancing slowly from the northeast, bathed in copper light, the Earth God approached. For reasons difficult to pinpoint, the Birch felt apprehensive at her visitor's arrival. She shook her blue-green leaves, her shadow shivering on the grass. The Earth God stopped.

"Birch, good morning."

"Good morning."

"You know, Birch, there are a lot of things I just don't understand. No matter how much I try, pure uncertainty. Pure mystery."

"What kind of mystery?"

"Grass, for example. The thing that germinates in the very ground, ground the color of coffee... but the grass—the grass is green. And don't even get me started on the flowers. Yellow, white—how do you explain that?"

"Maybe because as seeds the grass and the flowers already have those colors in them?"

"Maybe. But I still don't get it. What about the mushrooms that come out in the fall? No seeds involved there, they just sprout up, yellow, red, all kinds of colors. Really, there's no way to understand it."

"Why don't you ask Fox?"

The Birch, still heady from the conversation with the Fox the night before, hadn't measured her words. The Earth God turned green with rage and tightened his fists.

"That Fox? What's he been telling you now?"

The Birch hesitated, then made her best effort. "Nothing in particular. I only thought he'd come up with something—maybe."

"How is a little fox going to teach anything to a god?"

The Birch began to shake uncontrollably in fear. The Earth God stamped around on the hill, his arms crossed and stiff, his jaw tight, and where his shadow covered the grass, the earth trembled.

"That damn fox is a stone in my shoe! He doesn't know his ass from his elbow. Pretentious—envious—stuck-up—arrogant."

The Birch sought to change the subject. "The festival celebrating your shrine is coming up soon, isn't it?"

"Yup," muttered the Earth God, calming a little. "Today's the third of the month. So the festival's in six days." His anger soon crested again. "Humans are so useless. Has anyone even bothered to bring an offering to my shrine? No, nobody. The next human that dares to set foot on my side of the forest is going straight to the bottom of the swamp."

The Earth God stood immobile, gnashing his teeth. The Birch, wishing she'd never opened her mouth, did nothing except let her leaves sway in the breeze. The Earth God kept up his harangue, half blind with rage, half blinded by the bright sun. The more he considered it, the more his blood boiled. At last he let out an incensed bellow and left.

3

The swamp where the Earth God dwelled was a damp, wet place, covered with moss and clover, cloaked with thick-tangled rushes. Bizarre thistles grew there, where the water insistently licked the soft quagmires, muddy banks barely supported by the roots of the grotesque willows. Anyone would find it sinister at first glance. In the center, above a hunchbacked island of dirt and sludge, was the Earth God's shrine: a modest thing, less than two meters tall, made only of wood.

Comfortable there on his island, the Earth God approached the foot of the shrine. He scratched his legs, slowly, leisurely—pleasurably. (They were dark and rough.) A bird flew above his head.

"Shoo!" he shouted.

The bird, stunned, hesitated in midair, almost diving beakfirst into the ground—almost. He faded slowly on the horizon, losing altitude, as if his wings had gone numb. Snide and happy, the Earth God smiled. But when he turned toward the hill where the Birch lived he was again overtaken by rage. His face blanched, his body tensed, and with both hands he mussed his already chaotic hair.

Just then a woodcutter came along the thin path that bordered the swamp. He came from the south. He aimed for the Mitsumori mountain. The woodcutter appeared to know well who dwelled in that place, for he regularly turned anxiously toward the shrine. Of course, he didn't see anyone there where the Earth God rested. On the other hand, all the Earth God's alarms went off, anticipating pleasure, when he saw the woodcutter.

With his right hand the Earth God took his left wrist and pulled it back, as if his forearm was a lever. Instantly the woodcutter was dragged as if by puppet's strings—invisible to him—toward the heart of the swamp. Terrified, breathing heavily, the woodcutter tried to quicken his step. At that the Earth God slowly turned his right wrist, in such a way that the woodcutter found himself walking in small circles. In a panic to flee that dreadful place as soon as possible, his body utterly disobeyed him, winding in useless circles. When the woodcutter let out a howl of fright he was at last able to run off, staggering through the swamp. The Earth God watched, savoring each of the woodcutter's labored steps, until the poor man collapsed in the mud. Then the Earth God crossed the quagmire until he reached the immobile woodcutter. He lifted him, shook

him, and tossed him aside. The helpless woodcutter fell on a slightly firmer patch of ground and twitched there, unconscious.

The Earth God's cackles of laughter climbed to the tops of the trees, beckoning to the heavens in twisted waves, reverberating in the prairie, at last reaching the Birch's hill. She in turn began to tremble, and grew so pale that the sunlight nearly passed through her translucent leaves.

The Earth God tugged at the tangled mass that crowned his head. "This is all the fault of that despicable Fox. Or maybe not, maybe it's the Birch's fault. Yes, it's her fault. Or more precisely, it's both the Fox *and* the Birch's fault—they're mixed up in it together. If I felt nothing for her, I wouldn't give a fig for that Fox. Perhaps it doesn't show, but I'm a god, after all. I can't let some common animal get me so enraged. What I have to do is banish all thoughts of that Birch from my head. I enjoyed it so this morning when the poor thing started trembling like a bridal veil. No doubt I went too far with that poor woodcutter, but too bad. The heart is a mystery." In his miserable pettiness the Earth God carried on, unable to staunch his tantrums.

A falcon flew overhead. This time, he let it pass.

In the distance, the hum of horseback riders was heard, and a metallic patter of rifles, thundering and cracking like kernels of corn thrown into a pyre. Light bathed the prairie, descending from the sky in pale blue waves. That same light touched the heart of the dying woodcutter and restored him to life. He sat up and blinked in wonder. With a leap he headed out again toward Mitsumori mountain.

The Earth God let fly another stormcloud gale of laughter. Once again, his cackling ascended the heavens, echoing through the prairie until it reached Birch. Almost imperceptibly, she trembled and turned pale.

The Earth God continued pacing around the shrine until he was able to calm himself and return inside.

4

One misty night in the dog days of August, the Earth God found himself particularly agitated and down in the dumps. Obeying a stray impulse, he left his sanctuary and headed to the great prairie. When he thought of Birch his heart beat faster, his mood sinking in a melancholic mire. Lately he'd been better able to cool himself down, and to banish thoughts of Birch and Fox. But every once in a while, those thoughts returned, stealthily, unwelcomed. "You're a God," he repeated to himself every day. "Why such drama over some tree?" But deep down, the Earth God was unable to rid himself of the pain. When Fox appeared in his mind's eye, his blood boiled.

Adrift in a torrent of reflections, the Earth God abruptly noticed that his feet had led him near the Birch's hill. His heart beat furiously. Now that he considered it, it had been a long time since he'd seen her, long enough to imagine she'd missed him, too. In fact, she'd be anxious to see him. That certainty lifted his spirits and he crossed the prairie, almost weightless with joy.

But when he arrived at the foot of the hill, his illusions were shattered: the Fox was there. The night was dark, so he couldn't see either of them, but the Fox's slightly nasal voice, and his intellectual airs, were unmistakable.

"That Art subjects itself to the inclement laws of symmetry is no guarantee of Beauty. From my unique perspective, I'd say that *that* is a mere instance of dead beauty."

"I couldn't agree with you more, dear Fox."

"True Beauty is beyond our apprehension. It's not a fossil, it's not a model. People may worship symmetry unreservedly, but what's more important is the *spirit* of beauty—I'm not sure I'm explaining myself well."

"You're explaining yourself perfectly," responded the Birch, her voice tender and sweet.

The Earth God's organs withered. His lungs tightened. "Impossible," he thought. "How can these two lamebrains get you so enraged? A little tree and a little fox are talking about their little thoughts; how could that matter to a god?"

The Fox continued, oblivious. "All books that touch on the delicate subject of Aesthetics come up against this same issue."

"And do you have many books about Art?" asked the Birch.

"I wouldn't say *many*. But I've got them in English, in German, and in Japanese. There's a new one in Italian, but they haven't sent it to me yet."

"What a magnificent library you must have!"

"I wouldn't go that far. I have some interesting volumes—that's all—but they do take up my whole house. You'd find it a splendid chaos: a microscope in that corner, issues of the London *Times* over here, my busts of Caesars and emperors over there—"

"How marvelous."

The Fox snorted. Was it modesty? Was it arrogance? Surely a considerable helping of both.

There came silence, but by this time the Earth God was in an uncontrollable state. Could the Fox be more sophisticated than he? Maybe being a God wasn't enough. He felt an inexorable urgency to tear that little fox to pieces, right then and there. It might be wrong to allow one's body and mind to wish so intensely for evil. But what could he do? The Fox had laid him bare to himself—forced him to show his true colors. The Earth God brought his hands to his belly, which felt convulsive.

"Has the telescope finally arrived?" The Birch had continued chatting.

"What telescope? Oh, of course—that telescope. No, not yet. The lines at customs are very long, you know. But as soon as it arrives I promise I'll bring it to you. The rings of Saturn, now that's something you have to see at least once in this lifetime."

The Earth God couldn't bear any more. He covered his ears and ran away, headed north. He hesitated to imagine what he'd have been capable of doing to the Fox if he stayed. He ran until his knees buckled, and then he fell, prostrate, at the foot of Mitsumori mountain.

Writhing on the grass, pulling out his hair, the Earth God let out a moan that echoed for miles like an unseasonable lightning bolt. He cried. And then, rising, he wept as he walked home, his progress slow, his steps labored.

5

Months passed. Autumn arrived. The Birch continued to flaunt her green foliage, but the surface of her hill was sparse, scorched, like the pate of a bald old man. The valley brimmed with ripening mulberries, red and bloody.

It was a crisp, clear day, and the Earth God was in a good mood. The storms that had darkened the summer seemed to have disappeared, his intense bitterness almost completely dissolved. If Birch wanted to talk to Fox, well, what could he do about that? If they both enjoyed their chit-chat, what harm in it? In that spirit, the Earth God decided to visit Birch again. He wanted to air out these new feelings, to show his heart.

In the distance, Birch saw the Earth God approaching, and as always she started to tremble.

"Good morning, Birch! Isn't it a glorious one?"

"Good morning. Yes, it's a lovely morning."

"Isn't the sun just a miracle? Red in the springtime, white in the summer, yellow in the fall. Yellow. So yellow that it tints the grapes… purple! A truly majestic miracle."

"True, true," answered Birch, feigning interest.

"Do you know what?" continued the Earth God. "Today I feel above it all. The summer had some difficult moments. But today I woke up lighter than ever. Something's changed."

The Birch wanted to respond, but a strange foreboding kept her from speaking even one word.

"Today I feel so good that I could give my life for someone. Happily. I could even trade places with a worm, if that meant saving his skin."

As he said this, the Earth God gazed toward the eternal horizon with a frank, valiant stare. Again, Birch wished to speak, but was unable. All that emerged from her was a sigh.

And suddenly the Fox showed up.

Naturally, when he saw the Earth God, the fox's tail nearly fell off. But it was too late to turn around, so he controlled himself and went up the hill. He wore his creaky beige shoes, a brown raincoat, and a hat that looked as if it were painted on.

"Good morning, Birch. And good morning, Earth God. Are you actually giving me the honor of allowing me to address you directly?"

"Yes, Fox, it's me. Nice day, don't you think?" The Earth God spoke comfortably and calmly. The Fox, on the other hand, had turned a pale green. He tried to make excuses.

"How awful of me to butt in like this when you have a guest, Birch. Here's the book I promised, feel free to borrow it. I'll come by soon—on a clear night—with the telescope, and we'll look at the sky. See you later."

For a few seconds, the Earth God gazed on the Fox, who was slowly making his way from the Birch Tree's hill, exiting the scene.

A flash of light, reflected off Fox's gaudy shoes, jerked the Earth God from his trance. Once more, the animal's insolent verborrhea had unleashed something in the Earth God's innards. His face lit up with that old, undigested fury. He'd had quite enough of art books and telescopes—oh so special, oh so German. In a blink of an eye, the Earth God began stalking his prey. Poor Birch began to tremble, no longer in apprehension, but in sheer fright. The Fox, sensing that something terrible was headed his way, glanced back, sidelong, over his shoulder. Black like the night, crackling like a runaway fire, the Earth God pursued him. The Fox ran faster, straight as an arrow, his face pale with pure fear, his muzzle dry with anguish.

The prairie danced before the poisoned eyes of the Earth God like a gleaming mirage. The sky, so recently wide and clear, yawned open a cavernous darkness, and moaned with the crackle of infernal flames.

Predator and prey bore on a relentless track, like two panting locomotives.

The Fox ran as in a dream, or in a nightmare, repeating to himself, "My end approaches—my end—approaches—approaches—telescope—telescope—telescope."

The Fox at last reached a mound of bald earth, the entrance to his den. He'd barely stuck his head into the mouth of the lair, his two back paws bucked in the air, when the Earth God fell upon him, delivering a single sharp blow.

The twisted and languid body and small head of Fox rested softly in the palm of the Earth God's hand, with its muzzle open, its eyes slightly closed.

The Earth God threw him onto the ground, then stomped on his pliable body four or five times. Then he entered the lair. The place was dark, sober, practically empty. The dirt floor was carefully leveled. The Earth God tasted something strange in his mouth, something bitter, something rotten. He went out into the fresh air. He stuck his hand into the pocket of Fox's raincoat and pulled out two burrs, the kind foxes use to comb their fur. A contorted expression crossed the Earth God's mouth, and then, from that mask, erupted an unspeakable shriek.

The Earth God began to cry.

Tears bathed the dead Fox like rain, and though his neck lay twisted backward, on his muzzle was seen the discrete trace of a smile.

NOTES ON THE TRANSLATIONS

I.

I wanted to translate *The Earthgod and The Fox* by Kenji Miyazawa because of the story's beauty, brevity, sadness, and its allegorical elasticity—it's a folktale, a portrait of jealousy, and something deeper, all at once. Kenji Miyazawa was born in 1896 in the northern city of Hanamaki, where his father held a good position in society as a successful pawnbroker. As the eldest son, Miyazawa was expected to take over the family business, but he renounced his inheritance, converted to the nationalistic Nichiren sect of Buddhism, became a vegetarian (rare in Japan even today), and left for Tokyo to proselytize his faith. He was back eight months later, and took up a teaching job at an agricultural high school. His self-published volume of stories and a collection of verse found only qualified admiration, and any dreams he might have harbored of literary greatness were dashed. Quitting his teaching post in 1926, Miyazawa took up the study of Esperanto and founded a farmers' association where he gave lectures on agronomy. Unmarried, he died of pneumonia in 1933, aged just thirty-seven.

Although his life passed in obscurity, Kenji Miyazawa is now a near-universal household name in Japan. Few pass through their childhoods without encountering his best-known tale, "The Restaurant of Many Orders"; and thanks to state broadcaster NHK's Nihongo de Asobō, finding a Japanese youth unable to recite the opening lines of Miyazawa's posthumously published poem "Ame ni mo Makezu" would take a while. (Try it and see.)

"The Earthgod and the Fox" was my first foray into translation. The task confirmed my suspicion that my own translators are much cleverer than the joker who makes it all up. I stayed close to Miyazawa's text and didn't add, subtract, or photoshop, although (aha) here and there my style is a touch novelistic. A recurring headache was trying to render the genius of the Japanese language for synesthetic onomatopoeia, especially in the area of light and optics: there's only so much shimmering, gleaming, and glinting the Anglophone eyeball can take. I derived great pleasure from Valeria Luiselli's translation of the story into Spanish, as well as learning what countless millions of Spanish speakers have known all these years, that *Zorro* means "Fox." Reading the Lethems' buoyant rendering from Spanish back into English, I felt the envy that a "Before" portrait on a cosmetic surgeon's ad might feel when taking a sneak look across at his handsomer "After" counterpart: their more textured dialogue gives their version a bouncier spring in its step, and a warm breeziness that suits the story well.

When I was working on my version, Kenji Miyazawa would sometimes materialize and complain, "Excuse me, but I'm a 1920s Japanese writer and I just wouldn't say that—make your tone more neutral." I obeyed, but now I wonder which should come higher up the translator's totem pole—authorial fidelity or the zing of your prose?

Readers wishing to read more Miyazawa are referred to John Bester's fine bilingual edition, *Once and Forever: The Tales of Kenji Miyazawa*. Miyazawa's poetry is published in the collection *Strong in the Rain*, translated by Roger Pulvers.

—*David Mitchell*

II.

I was reading Emily Dickinson—compulsively—around the same time as I was working on this piece. So I ended up rewriting parts of it—respecting the content, but Dickinsonizing the syntax. In other words, dashes invaded my translation. But there was a certain logic behind that. Dashes are shyly used in Spanish. They're much less common than in English. But in Spanish they create a rhythm that, in my view, is closer to English.

I did try to think of the dialogues in the story, though, in terms of how they might have sounded in an early-twentieth-century fable in Spanish. I also tried to think of classic early Spanish cartoons. I'm not sure how close I got. Rather, I think that the characters—who happen to be a fox and a birch tree—ended up sounding like Mexican actors from the 1950s. Which is not as bad as it sounds.

—*Valeria Luiselli*

III.

More than a translation, more than rewriting or writing, this felt most like a game we played as children, a game we called "Telephone." That conspiratorial, carnal circle of tittering kids was, we guess, designed to teach the slipperiness of language, to reveal the inevitable pitfalls of communication: try as we might to deliver the message faithfully, we were doomed at best to a close approximation. And we had to find the humor in that failure. The messenger is the medium, bringing about such transformations as "That damn fox is a blot on the landscape! Not an ounce of truth in him!" into "That damn fox is a stone in my shoe! He doesn't know his ass from his elbow."

Just thinking about Telephone dredges up memories of Brooklyn basements in the seventies, clammy ears and unspoken crushes, but Wikipedia informs us that it is played around the world with different names, including Chinese Whispers, Broken Telephone, Arab Phone, Silent Mail, Cordless Phone, Grapevine, Deaf Phone, and Whisper Down The Lane.

—*Jonathan Lethem and Mara Faye Lethem*

IV.

Sometimes it feels as though a translation is a sari spread out flat. The original work is a sari as worn by a woman.

I cannot imagine my reading life—or my writing life—without works in translation: Stendhal and Proust, García Márquez, Mahfouz and Calvino, Tolstoy, Chekhov, Kafka and Saramago. I don't, however, know the languages in which these writers wrote, so there is no way for me to judge how faithful the English translations I love are. But I always feel a certain deficiency whenever I read a work translated into English from the other language that I do know, which is Urdu—Pakistan's national language, the language I was educated in until the age of fifteen, and the language in which I first encountered literature and the idea of literature. A single word in Urdu may carry a dozen associations for me, and as a result the English translation of that word sometimes feels like nothing more than an approximation. The culture, the history, the landscape, the codifications of belief and philosophy, and my own very specific memories—all these lend support to each Urdu word and sentence. One visualizes the whole pattern of the sari even when parts of the pattern are hidden in the folds gathered at the woman's shoulder or waist.

The embrace of meaning also feels longer and more intimate when I read an English-language book translated into Urdu. Until 2001, I didn't think it was possible for me to love *Moby-Dick* with a greater intensity. But then that year I read its Urdu translation.

While all this is true, I also believe that, at one level, every language is specific to the writer who is using it. John Banville once said that Vladimir Nabokov writes not in English but in a private language that is mysteriously comprehensible to English-speaking readers.

So it was with a delighted curiosity that I agreed to translate a story from English into Urdu—a story had been translated from the Japanese into English to begin with.

At first, during the first few hours I was alone with with the text, I was utterly faithful to each English word, trying to find the precise Urdu equivalent—using my dictionaries, ringing up my mother and father. But again and again, I had to settle for an approximation—and as a result the meaning of the sentence was slightly altered.

Noticing that, I began to change things deliberately. I saw no reason why I could not change the *facts* of the story, too: the birch tree in the story became a flowering vine growing around a peepal tree—two plants found in the part of Pakistan I grew up in. The "wood spirit" became the ghost of a holy man, a saint—one of the hundreds that are revered all across Pakistan. I dressed the fox in a Pakistani shalwar kameez.

We were now in Pakistan, in other words.

I vote every time I write a sentence: I believe myself to be a writer who wishes to engage with the politics of his time, and so as the days went by and I worked on the translation, and read about Jihad and the War on Terror in Pakistani newspapers, terrorist attacks appeared in my fairytale—the flowering vine and the ghost and the fox began to mention bomb blasts.

Growing up in Pakistan in the late 1970s and early '80s, under the CIA-backed dictator who Islamicized Pakistan, I witnessed the banning of books, the exiling of writers and poets, the torture and killing of journalists. So it didn't seem unnatural to me to say that the book of poems being carried by the fox in my fairytale was by a censored writer. The fox carries it furtively—clandestine words that could endanger his life.

(Since we are speaking of translation, I should mention that President Zia, the Pakistani dictator mentioned above, was using an Islamic ideology that drew its legitimacy from fundamentalist translations of the Koran and other holy texts. The translations of many Islamic texts are contested: there are long-standing disputes attached to the "true meaning" of some Koranic words and phrases. Some debates have raged since the death of Muhammad.)

I finished the translation and returned to it after a week's absence. During the week I realized that I could not remember with any firmness which details of the original story I had altered. Was the spirit in love with the birch tree in the original story, as the holy man was with the vine, in my version? At one point in my "translation," the fox and the vine discuss what makes good literature. I remembered what they said in my version, but what did they say in the original? The answers came as a lovely surprise when I read the two versions together. And I hope that they will be a source of delight to other readers, too.

—*Nadeem Aslam*

V

DAS TIER IN DER SYNAGOGE

a story in GERMAN *by* FRANZ KAFKA

ILLUSTRATORS, IN ORDER OF APPEARANCE

Wesley Allsbrook, Mike Bertino, Brianna Harden, Erin Althea, Ian Huebert.

IN OUR SYNAGOGUE

translated into English by JOHN WRAY

IN OUR SYNAGOGUE lives a creature about the size of a weasel. It can often be clearly seen, as it tolerates the approach of onlookers to within a distance of two meters. Its color is a pale bluish-green. No one has ever touched its fur, so not much can be said on that subject—one is tempted to claim that the true color of its fur is unknown, and that the apparent color may stem from the mortar and plaster of the synagogue's interior, which is only slightly darker in hue. Aside from its skittishness, the creature is uncommonly sedentary and even-tempered; if it weren't flushed from its quarter every so often, it would most likely change its position rarely, perhaps never.

Its favorite haunt is the screen of the women's section—it clings to the mesh there with evident satisfaction, stretches itself, and peers comfortably down at the chamber below. This bold position seems to delight the creature, but the caretaker of the synagogue has orders never to allow it on the screen—it would grow accustomed to the spot, which cannot be permitted on account of the women, who are frightened by it. And it does have a frightening appearance, at least at first glance, with its long neck, its three-cornered face, its almost laterally protruding canines, and the hard, pale whiskers on its upper lip: all of this can be frightening, but one can't help but recognize, after a moment, how unthreatening this apparent

בבית הכנסת שלנו

translated into Hebrew by ETGAR KERET

בבית הכנסת שלנו חי יצור בגודל של סמור. אפשר לראות אותו לעיתים קרובות ממש בברור כי הוא מרשה לאנשים להתקרב אליו עד למרחק של שני מטרים. הצבע שלו הוא כחול-ירוק חיוור. אף אחד לא נגע לו אי פעם בפרווה כך שאין הרבה מה לומר בנוגע לנושא הזה.—מפתה לומר שהצבע האמיתי של הפרווה שלו אינו ידוע ושהצבע שאנחנו רואים נובע מצבע הטיח שעל קירות בית הכנסת הכהה יותר רק בגוון מצבעו של היצור. מלבד החיוניות שלו היצור מאוד מיושב ורגוע. אם לא היו מציקים לו לעיתים קרובות כל כך רוב הסיכויים שלא היה משנה את התנוחה בה הוא נח אף פעם.

המקום האהוב עליו הוא הוילון של עזרת הנשים—הוא נצמד אליו בסיפוק כגלוי לעין, הוא מותח את עצמו ומציץ בנחות באולם מתחתיו. התנוחה הנועזת הזו משמחת את היצור כנראה, אבל השמש של בית הכנסת הורה לא לתת ליצור לטפס על הוילון, כדי שלא יתרגל למקום הזה בו אסור שישהה כי יבהיל בו את הנשים. והוא באמת מפחיד, לפחות במבט ראשון. עם הצוואר הארוך, הפנים בנות שלוש הפינות שלו, הניבים הכמעט זקורים שלו והשפם ההקשה והחיוור אשר מעטר את שפתו העליונה: כל אלו עשויים להפחיד אבל אי אפשר שלא להפנים אחרי רגע כמה לא מעורר חשש בעצם האיום-לכאורה הזה. היצור תמיד ינסה לשמור מאיתנו מרחק והוא בביישן יותר מכל חיות היער: הוא לא קשור לדבר מלבד למבנה עצמו אך לחוסר מזלו, הבניין אליו הוא קשור הוא בית כנסת, זאת אומרת מקום שהוא שוקק חיים על בסיס מחזורי. אם רק היה אפשר לתקשר עם היצור יכולים היינו להרגיע אותו שהקהילה בעיירה הקטנה שלנו רק הולכת וקטנה ושבזמן שהמעמסה בתחזוק בית הכנסת רק הולכת וקטנה. זה כלל לא בלתי אפשרי שהשבניין יוסב בעתיד הקרוב למחסן לאחסנת דגנים או מבנה מהסוג הזה בטווח הקרוב ואז יזכה היצור בשלווה אשר כל כך חסרה לו עכשיו.

רק נשים מפוחדות מהיצור, הגברים כבר מזמן התרגלו אליו. כל דור הראה את היצור לדור

שבא אחריו, כל אחד מאתנו כבר ראה אותו מספיק פעמים כדי שנפסיק להסתכל. אפילו ילדים הרואים אותו בפעם הראשונה כבר לא מתייחס אליו כאל פלא. היצור הפך לחיית המחמד של בית הכנסת, ובעצם, למה שלא יהיה לבית הכנסת חיית מחמד מיוחדת וחד פעמית כמו זו? אם לא הנשים כבר מזמן היינו מפסיקים להיות מודעים לקיומו, אבל אפילו קריאות הפחד של הנשים אינן אמיתיות לגמרי זה היה מוזר אם אחרי שנים רבות כל-כך בהן נתקלו ביצור על בסיס קבוע, הן עדיין היו ממשיכות לפחד ממנו. הנשים מנסות להגן על עצמן בעזרת הטענה שהיצור הרבה יותר קרוב אליהן מאשר אל הגברים בבית הכנסת וזה באמת נכון. היצור מפחד לרדת אל עזרת הגברים ומעולם לא נגע ברצפת בית הכנסת. גם אם מונעים ממנו להגיע לעזרת הנשים הוא ממשיך להישאר באותו גובה בקיר הנגדי. בגובה ההוא יש מין מדף שרוחבו לא יותר משתי אצבעות ואשר נמצא על שלוש מארבעת קירות בית הכנסת. היצור אוהב להמצא על המדף הזה למרות שברוב הזמן הוא מעדיף נקודה אחת מיוחדת הקרובה אל עזרת הנשים. זה די מדהים לראות איך היצור הזה מתנועע לו לאורך המדף, מדובר בחיה לא צעירה אבל היא לעולם לא תחשוש מקפיצה מסוכנת וגם תדע תמיד לנחות על רגליה, להסתובב באוויר ולחזור אל המקום שממנו באה.

חייבים לומר שאחרי שרואים את התעלול הזה של היצור מספר פעמים מרגישים מסופקים ומאבדים כל רצון להביט לאוויר ולחפש אותו שוב. זה לא פחד ולא סקרנות אשר גורמים לנשים לחוש נסערות כל כך—אם הן היו מתרכזות יותר בתפילה הן היו יכולות לשכוח אותו לגמרי. הנשים האדוקות, אגב, היו עושות כן אם האחרות , אשר מהוות רוב מוחלט, היו מאפשרות להן. אבל השאר רק מחפשות דרך לזכות בתשומת לב, והיצור מהווה עבורן רק תירוץ. אם הן היו יכולות והיו מעיזות הן היו יכולות לפתוח את היצור להגיע קרוב יותר אליהן ולא רק כאמתלה לצרחות אימה רמות יותר. אבל במציאות ליצור אין שום דחף להתקרב אליהן. הוא מראה מעט מאוד עניין בהן, אם הן עוזבות אותו במנוחה. אם זה היה תלוי בו הוא היה מעדיף להישאר לו בחריץ הבלתי נראה בקיר בו הוא מעביר את מרבית זמנו. רק בזמן התפילה כאשר הקולות הפתאומיים מפתיעים אותו והוא רוצה לברר מה קרה, הוא יוצא החוצה. זה הפחד שגורם לו לצאת ולקפוץ את הקפיצות המשונות שלו והוא לא עוזב עד שהטקס אינו מסתיים. באופן טבעי הוא מעדיף את האזורים הגבוהים יותר בהם הוא מרגיש בטוח יותר אבל הוא לא תמיד נמצא גבוה כל-כך. לפעמים הוא יורד לכיוון עזרת הגברים. הוילון של ארון הקודש נתמך על ידי מוט פליז והמוט הזה כנראה מושך את היצור. הוא זוחל לו לשם פעמים רבות ואז יושב שם בשקט. אפילו אז אי אפשר לומר שהוא מסיח את דעתם של המתפללים. עם העיניים הריקות והפתוחות תמיד הוא נראה כאילו הוא צופה בעדת המתפללים, אבל ברור לגמרי שהוא לא מביט באף אחד מאיתנו. הוא פשוט מביט לכיוונים של אותם כוחות אשר הוא מרגיש שמעמידים אותו בסכנה.

מבחינה זו, עד לא מזמן, התנהגותו נראתה לנו לנו ככמעט בלתי נתפסת.ממה הוא בעצם מפחד?מי מהווה עבורו סכנה? האם הוא לא חי ששנים רבות כל כך בינינו בלי כל פגע?הגברים מתעלמים מנוכחתו ומרבית הנשים היו ודאי מתעצבות אם היה נעלם. מכיוון שהוא החיה היחידה בבית הכנסת אין ליצור שום אויב טבעית ולאורך כל השנים שהוא חי עימנו הוא כבר היה אמור להבין זאת. קולות טקסי התפילה עלולים להיות מבהילים עבור יצור שכמותו אבל הם חוזרים על עצמם יום אחרי יום, בעוצמה מעט גדולה יותר בחגים, תמיד באותו אופן ותמיד ללא כל הפרעה. אפילו יצור ביישן במיוחד היה אמור להתרגל אליהם אחרי זמן רב כל כך, במיוחד שאפשר להבין

menace is. The creature keeps its distance from us, and it's more shy than any creature of the forest: it seems related to nothing but the building itself, and the fact that the building happens to be a synagogue—which is to say, periodically a very lively place—is the creature's particular misfortune. If one could make oneself understood, one might perhaps reassure the creature by pointing out that the congregation in our small hill-town grows smaller year by year, and that the burden of maintaining the synagogue grows steadily more difficult. It's by no means impossible that the building will be converted into a storehouse for grain or some such in the foreseeable future, and that the creature will attain the peace it now so sorely lacks.

It's only the women who fear the creature: the men have long since grown indifferent to it. Each generation has shown it to the next, each of us has seen it time and again; eventually we've stopped looking altogether. Even the children, seeing it for the first time, no longer regard it with wonder. It's become the pet of the synagogue—and why shouldn't the synagogue have a special, perhaps even one-of-a-kind pet? If not for the women, one would barely be aware of the creature any longer. But even the women's fright is less than entirely genuine; it would be too peculiar, seeing the creature day in and day out, over years and decades, to continue to fear it. They defend themselves by arguing that the creature is much nearer to them than it is to the men, and this much is true. The creature doesn't dare descend to the men's level—it's never been seen on the synagogue floor. If it is prevented from reaching the screen of the women's section, it keeps to the same height on the opposite wall. At that level, a narrow ledge, no more than two fingers wide, runs along three of the building's four sides; along this ledge the creature occasionally scampers, although for the most part it crouches at one particular spot, directly across from the women. It's all but incomprehensible how it can make such easy use of such a narrow route, and the way it changes direction up there, having reached the end of the ledge, is really worth seeing. It's quite an aged creature, after all, but it never hesitates in taking the riskiest of leaps, leaps that never go awry—it's already turned about in the air, and now it's running back the way it came.

It must be said, however, that once one has seen this trick a handful of times, one is satisfied and feels no need to continue gawking upward. It's really neither fear nor curiosity that keeps the women in a state of agitation—if they would occupy themselves more with prayer, they'd be able to forget about the creature entirely. The pious women would do so, in fact, if the others—who make up the substantial majority—would permit them; but the rest are always looking for ways to call attention to themselves, and the creature is a welcome means to this end. If they could have, and if they dared, they'd no doubt entice the creature to approach even nearer, if only as a pretext to take even greater fright. But in reality the creature feels no urge to approach farther; it shows just as little interest in them, if left undisturbed, as it does in the men—it would most likely prefer to remain hidden in that invisible crack in the wall in which it passes the hours between holy service. Only when prayer begins does it appear: startled by the sudden noise, it wants to see what has happened, it wants to remain alert, it wants to remain at liberty, prepared for flight if necessary—fear coaxes it into the open, it turns its little somersaults out of fear, it doesn't dare withdraw until the service ends. It naturally prefers the higher spaces on account of their relative safety, but it's by no means always up high: sometimes it climbs down farther, toward the level of the men. The curtain of the ark of the covenant is supported by a brass rod, and this seems to attract the creature: it slithers down there often enough, then sits there quietly. Not even then could one say that it distracts from the service. With its blank and perpetually open—perhaps even lidless—eyes, it seems to regard the congregation, but clearly doesn't look at any of us; it simply looks toward those forces by which it feels itself to be at risk.

In this regard—at least until recently—it struck us as barely more comprehensible than the women. What does it have to fear? Who means it any harm? Has it not lived among us all these years, entirely left to its own devices? The men pay no mind to its presence, and the majority of the women would most likely be saddened if it were to disappear. Since it's the only animal in the synagogue, it has no natural enemy; it ought to have grasped as much with the passing of the years. The clamor of the service may well be frightening for the creature, but it repeats itself daily—if slightly more emphatically on holidays—always steadily and without interruption. Even the most timid creature should have grown used to it long since, especially as it must see that the clamor is not the clamor of pursuit, but rather a noise that has nothing to do with it whatsoever. And yet the fear persists. Is it the recollection of times long past, or the presentiment of

מהר מאוד שקולות התפילה הם לא שאון של מרדף אלא קולות שלא קשורי סבשום צורה או אופן ליצור ולקיומו. ובכל זאת הוא ממשיך לפחד. האם הוא מנובע מזיכרון מהעבר או אולי מאיזה חשש עמום מהעתיד ומה שהוא צופן בחובו.? האם ידע היצור יותר ממה שחווה במשך כשלושה דורות בבית הכנסת?

לפני שנים רבות, כך מספרים באי בית הכנסת, נעשה ניסיון לגרש את היצור. אין שום ערובה שסיפור זה נכון, ויכול להיות שהוא סתם מעשייה. אבל יש תיעוד לכך שנעשה ניסיון לקבוע האם מותר על פי ההלכה לתת ליצור כזה לשהות בבית האלוהים. תשובות נאספו מרבנים רבים. למרות שהדעות היו חלוקות מרביתם דיברו על גירוש ואחריו טיהור של המבנה. אבל קל היה לקבוע זאת ממרחקים. והמציאות *לימדה* אותנו שפשוט בלתי אישרי לסלק את היצור מבית הכנסת.

a time still to come? Might this creature know more than the three generations that sit assembled in the synagogue below?

Many years ago—so the story goes—an attempt was made to drive the creature away. It could be that there's some truth to this story, but it's probably no more than an old wives' tale. It has been documented, however, that an effort was made to determine, from a religious standpoint, whether it was permissible to allow such a creature to dwell within the house of God. Reports from various rabbis were collected: although opinion was divided, the majority were for expulsion and a re-consecration of the building. But it was easy to issue such decrees from afar. In reality it was simply impossible to drive the creature in our synagogue away.

THE CREATURE
IN OUR SHUL

translated into English by NATHAN ENGLANDER

THE CREATURE IS ABOUT the size of a weasel, no bigger. And, of all places, it lives in our shul. We get plenty of opportunity to study the thing clearly, because he (and I'm really only guessing it's a "he") will pretty much let you walk right up—you can get maybe six feet away. From that distance you can see he's a sort of pale blue-green. As for the fur, no one's ever managed to touch it, so there's not much to say on that subject. And I'm still sort of tempted to tell you that the true color of his fur is as yet unknown and the color we perceive it to be is some sort of refracted spectrum bouncing off the plaster of the synagogue's walls—only the walls are a darker hue than what you see on him.

The creature's favorite spot is by the curtain that separates the women's gallery from the men's section below. He cuddles up against it, burrowing into the curtain with obvious satisfaction. Then he stretches himself out so he can peek down at the hall in comfort. It's kind of a bold position, and you can tell he takes pleasure in it. But the shul's beadle won't have it. He long ago decided not to let the little varmint (which is what the beadle calls him) climb all over that curtain. The beadle thinks he'll get too accustomed, and when he lingers there he frightens the women. It's a fair point. The thing really is frightening, at least at first glance. He's got this long neck, and a sort of three-cornered face, with

LOS
MURMULLOS

translated into Spanish by ALEJANDRO ZAMBRA

NO ENTIENDO POR QUÉ, de todos los lugares posibles, la criatura vino a vivir a nuestra casa. La explicación más razonable es que, al parecer, el lugar es grande—quizás sea más apropiado decir que es inmenso, pero desgraciadamente no estoy seguro de sus dimensiones, no puedo estarlo, no conozco otras casas. Gente bien informada me ha dicho que las viviendas comunes suelen ser mucho más pequeñas y que la cantidad de gente que las habita es sorprendentemente baja, un promedio de cuatro personas por casa, considerando incluso lugares donde—esto suena en extremo inverosímil—sólo vive una persona.

La criatura—la bestia, la alimaña, la cosa, en fin, no sé si es macho o hembra, pero todas las palabras que vienen a mi mente son femeninas—nos deja acercarnos hasta unos pocos metros, y sin embargo es difícil describirla con propiedad. Es más o menos del tamaño de una comadreja, su color de lejos es una especie de desteñido azul verdoso, su cuello—pienso que es lícito aludir a esa zona de su cuerpo con la palabra cuello, aunque la referencia no sea del todo satisfactoria—es muy largo y termina (o empieza) en una especie de cara triangular, con algo así como dientes puntudos que se curvan hasta casi tocarse. Creo que puedo llamar bigote a los filamentos pálidos y acaso ásperos que le cubren casi enteramente el labio superior.

La criatura suele acurrucarse contra una de las cortinas del espacio principal con evidente satisfacción y frecuentemente realiza una serie de movimientos extravagantes, pero la verdad es que no molesta demasiado—las mujeres se asustan, eso sí, y quizás tienen razón, porque la bestia es intimidante, al menos al principio, o quizás sólo al principio—al considerar el asunto con detención es imposible desconocer la poca alarma que causa algo que inicialmente parecía tan amenazante.

Por lo demás, la criatura siempre intenta mantener la distancia con nosotros y es más tímida que cualquier animal del bosque. No se relaciona con nadie, no conserva ningún vínculo, y la verdad es que uno llega a compadecerla por su suerte miserable. A veces pienso que todo lo que quiere es un poco de paz, y justo vino a dar a una casa como la nuestra—un lugar regularmente lleno de actividades. Si pudiéramos comunicarnos con ella, la tranquilizaríamos informándole que nuestra familia es cada vez menos numerosa, por lo que la tarea de mantener esta casa es más pesada y costosa cada día. Antes éramos miles—he oído decir que incluso millones—pero ahora es más adecuado contarnos de cien en cien e incluso a veces de diez en diez. Es absolutamente factible que, en algún momento, en un futuro no muy lejano, la casa se transforme en un granero o bodega o algo por el estilo. Puede que no falte mucho. Y entonces la pobre criatura conseguirá la tranquilidad que hoy, consciente o instintivamente, añora.

Salvo por algunas situaciones excepcionales, hace tiempo que nos acostumbramos a la criatura. Cada generación la presentó a la generación siguiente, y hasta el último de nosotros la ha visto tantas veces que ya ni notamos sus apariciones. Incluso los niños que la ven por primera vez no la miran con sorpresa. Se ha transformado en la mascota de esta casa. Y, pensándolo bien, es justo. Todo indica que esta casa es bastante particular, y entonces corresponde que tengamos una mascota particular.

Insisto en que sólo las mujeres aún se inquietan con la presencia de este animalejo. Resulta difícil creer que sigan asustadas después de tantos años compartiendo el espacio con la criatura. Ellas argumentan que se acerca más a ellas que a nosotros, y es cierto, de hecho parece evitar a los hombres, pero si somos imparciales deberíamos admitir que también evita, aunque en medida ligeramente inferior, a las mujeres. Como sea, cuando alguien—hombre o mujer—se le acerca demasiado, el animalito se esconde en una grieta en el muro. La verdad es que allí se queda buena parte del tiempo, y si no existieran los murmullos probablemente pasaría días enteros sin dejarse ver.

Durante los murmullos la criatura se sobresalta y se asoma para saber qué es lo que ocurre—los murmullos la ponen nerviosa y no vuelve a esconderse

pointed fangs that bend around until they're nearly touching. The whiskers look pale and wiry—almost sharp—and they grow in so thick that they hide his upper lip. All these things are liable to terrify you. But if you give it a second, it's impossible not to grasp how little alarm is raised by what initially seemed like a threat.

On the animal's end of things, he always tries to maintain his distance from us and is more skittish than any of the beasts of the forest. He keeps to himself and hasn't formed a single bond beyond his attachment to the building. And, really, you've got to pity his poor luck. All he wants is some quiet, and the structure to which he's attached himself ends up being a shul—a place bustling with life on a regular basis. If we were just able to communicate with him, we'd be able to calm him with the news that synagogue membership in our little town continues only to shrink, while the burden of maintaining the shul gets harder and more expensive every day. It's totally not impossible that, sometime in the near future, the building will turn into a granary or a warehouse or a structure of that sort. It might not be far off. And then the unfortunate creature will be afforded the tranquility that is, currently, so wanting.

You should know, it's only the women who are still afraid. The men have long ago gotten used to him. Every generation introduces the creature to the one that comes after it, and every last one of us has seen him enough times that we've already ceased looking. Even children spotting him for the first time don't stare with any kind of wonder. He's basically turned into the shul's mascot. And, if you think about it, why shouldn't a shul have its own special mascot? The women would have stopped paying any attention to his very existence long ago if he hadn't undertaken the role. Assuming their cries of fear are completely heartfelt, it's honestly hard to believe they're still that terrified of him after all these years sharing the same space. The women try to defend themselves with the argument that the creature is much closer to them than to the men in the synagogue, and that is absolutely true. The creature is afraid to climb down to the men's section and never, ever touches the floor of the synagogue. Even when the beadle gets his way and we manage to keep the little varmint from getting to the women's section and that curtain, the creature just slides over, hovering at the same height on the adjoining wall. At that level there's a sort of molding, about two fingers wide, that runs along three of the synagogue's four walls. He loves to dawdle on that little shelf, though most of the time he prefers that one cozy spot along-side the women's section. It's pretty wonderful watching him move along the length of that narrow molding. And we're talking about an animal that's not so young anymore. He never hurries a dangerous jump and is careful, always, to land on his feet, turning in the air for the landing, and then racing back to his perch.

It does need to be said that after observing his antics a number of times you're pretty much satisfied and lose any will to look up in the air and find him again. And it's neither alarm nor interest that causes the women so much agitation—if they would focus more on prayer they would be able to forget him completely. (And, if we're already on the subject, the devout women get as involved as the others, succumbing to the majority's will.) It's like they're all stuck up there looking for a way to get some attention, and the creature is what gives them a reason. If the women were able, and if they'd dare, they'd lure the critter closer—and not just as an excuse to fire up their screams of dread.

One thing is clear: he has absolutely no urge to get any nearer. He appears to have very little interest in the women, if they leave him in peace. If it were up to him he'd rather stay hidden in his crevice in the wall. That's where he passes most of his days. It's only during prayer time when the sudden voices startle him, and he wants to suss out what's hap-pening, that he appears. It's the chanting that gives him the jitters, driv-ing him out of that crack to leap his strange little leaps. And once he's done that, he doesn't retreat until the service ends.

He seems naturally inclined to perch at the higher reaches of the shul, where he feels more confident. But he doesn't always linger up above. Sometimes he scurries down toward the men's section. The curtain hang-ing in front of the Holy Ark is supported by a brass rod, and, apparently, the rod holds some primal attraction. He crawls out into the middle of it fairly frequently and then just sits, quiet. Even then he doesn't really distract the worshippers. With those blank, wide-open eyes you might think he's studying the congregation, but it's evident that he's not looking at any one of us in particular. It's more that he's gazing in the direction of the forces that he senses as a threat.

That reaction always seems baseless. What could he be afraid of? Who, among us, poses any kind of danger? Hasn't he lived in our midst all these many years without coming to the slightest harm? The men

hasta que concluyen. Pero incluso en medio del nerviosismo es prudente, no nos distrae. Con sus ojos grandes e impasibles pareciera estudiarnos, pero evidente-mente no está mirando a nadie en particular. Parece más bien que observa en dirección a las fuerzas que intuye como un peligro.

Tal reacción es infundada. ¿Qué podría temer? ¿Quién, entre todos nosotros, representa un peligro? ¿No ha vivido acaso todo este tiempo sin el más mínimo daño? Los hombres la ignoramos y para la mayoría de las mujeres es claro que sería una pena que desapareciera. Considerando las numerosas décadas que ha vivido con nosotros, su seguridad debería resultar evidente. Sin duda los mur-mullos pueden inquietar a una criatura como esta, pero se trata de lo mismo día tras día, con una fuerza quizá un poco mayor en determinadas fechas del año. Hasta el más tímido ser se acostumbraría a nuestros murmullos después de tanto tiempo, especialmente cuando es tan fácil darse cuenta de que no tienen otro propósito que el murmullo mismo.

A pesar de todo continúa desconfiando. Nos preguntamos si es el resultado de algún trauma pasado, o quizá alguna oscura intuición de lo que le depara el futuro. ¿La criatura sabe algo más allá de lo que la experiencia le ha enseñado?

Muchos años atrás—es lo que cuentan los ancianos de la casa—hubo un intento por expulsarla. No hay garantía de que la historia sea verdadera, pero contamos con documentación que nos asegura que hubo intentos de determinar si era correcto permitir que un animal como este viviera en la casa. Se recolec-taron respuestas de muchos especialistas, algunos verdaderamente connotados. Y a pesar de que las opiniones estaban divididas, la mayoría recomendaba la expul-sión de la criatura y la posterior purificación de todo el lugar. Es fácil llegar a una idea semejante desde lejos. Pero la realidad nos ha demostrado lo contrario. Es imposible separar a la criatura de esta casa.

ignore his presence, and a majority of the women would definitely be saddened if he disappeared. And since he's the only animal in the shul, there's no need for us to introduce any sort of natural predator. Taking into account the decades he's lived alongside us, his safety should already be a given. Admittedly, the sounds of a prayer service might be startling to a creature like that. But they repeat back on themselves day after day, with a force that's maybe a little bigger on holidays, but always in the same manner and without ever interfering with him in any physical way. Even the shyest of God's creations would be expected to get used to our voices after such a very long time, especially when it's so easy to grasp that they accompany prayer and aren't the clamor of people giving chase. The hullaballoo obviously isn't connected to him or his well being.

Despite that, he continues to be afraid. We wonder, is it the result of some past trauma or maybe from some dim sense of what the future holds? Does the creature know something more than what he experienced in the three or so generations he's been living in the synagogue?

Many years ago—or so the old-timers at the synagogue say—an attempt was made to drive him out. There is no guarantee that this story is correct, and it's possible that it's just some old yarn. But we do have documentation attesting to the fact there were attempts to determine if it was permissible, according to the precepts of Jewish law, to allow an animal like this to dwell in a House of God. Replies were collected from many rabbis. Despite some division of opinion, most recommended expulsion followed by a purification of the structure itself. It's easy enough to come to a conclusion like that from a distance. But reality has taught us otherwise. It's simply impossible to separate that creature from his shul.

5

THE ANIMAL OF THE CHURCH

translated into English by DAVE EGGERS

NO ONE KNEW why the creature was there, in a church, in such an old church, in the confessional no less. The best explanation anyone could conjure was that the space was small, and dark, and thus safe and comfortable for an animal like that. The confessional was dry, removed from the elements, free from the natural laws of beast and man.

The creature—the animal, the thing, whatever it was—was neither male nor female, but had elements of each. There were those who said it displayed some twisted, unnatural straddling of the two genders, that it was a deprived animal whose tortured sexuality made it behave oddly. But really, no one got close enough to see, to look the creature over or properly inspect it. We did know that it was about the size of a weasel, its coat blue-black, and that it possessed a preternaturally long neck, ending in a strangely aerodynamic, triangular head. Protruding from its mouth were two long fangs, curved slightly so that they almost met at the animal's chin. Above the teeth there was an array of clear filaments, hinting at the mustache of an ancient man. The creature's appearance was disturbing, nightmarish to those who saw it up close. But thankfully it kept its distance, a safe and steady and even comfortable distance, from most.

The church was elevated—of course it was—having been built on a former swamp, and so there was a vast crawlspace underneath, enjoyed by any number of rats and mice and possums. And amid them all, or even dominating them all, was this beast, the lord of the vermin. Daily, when it was tired of the life under the church, it climbed up and found fresh air in the cracks under the confessional. When it rose up, when it gasped for breath, newcomers to the church were shocked. Seeing the beast provoked shrieks in women, barks of disapproval from men. It did not belong there, these people would say. What is it doing there? How could this be allowed in a house of worship?

The priests of the church, the masters and their apprentices, had no proper answer. The animal had been there as long as they had, and probably far longer, they said. Nothing can be done. The clergy had gotten used to it, and without asking, they asked that those using the confessional get used to it, too. Most people did get used to it, but there were those who thought the arrangement absurd, terrible, unholy. They screamed, they kicked at the creature, they scared it into the shadows and left the booth frantic and outraged. But everyone else made do.

The creature certainly made do. It was fully comfortable there, appearing from time to time, its eyes black and reflective, its mouth occasionally stretching into a wide pink yawn. As long as the visitors to the confessional kept a certain distance, the creature was content to be close; after all, it was tame, slow-moving, even complacent. And it depended, it seemed, on this relationship to humans. Though it did not beg for food or water, and

wasn't parasitic in any overt way, it needed the priests and parishioners. Its strength came from its proximity to both. Indeed, no one had ever seen it anywhere else but in the booth, in that crack under the wall.

Everyone who saw it found its behavior predictable. Upon entering the confessional, a visitor would first look at the ornate latticework that separated him from his confessor. Then a door would open and close, and the shadow of the priest would enter, would darken the latticework for a moment before he settled into his bench. Then, as the confessor was mustering the courage to tell of his sins and preparing to perform whatever penance requested, the creature would appear. Up from the crack below it would slither, tentative at first, then, seeing nothing had changed since its last visit, its demeanor became almost nonchalant.

I saw this myself once, and it was both horrifying and wholly unremarkable. I sat down on the cool oak bench, and, just as I had heard it would, the beast appeared, its fur glistening like metal in the low blue light. It regarded me with the casual curiosity of a child waking up in the late evening to find his parents entertaining a friend. The beast looked to me, tilted its head, and, seeing I posed no threat to it, slithered under the wall to visit, I presumed, with the priest on the other side. It returned moments later, as if it had received a message from my confessor meant for me. That message, delivered by an animal like this, carried a musty scent but was nonetheless clear. It said, Look away, look away, look away.

NOTES ON THE TRANSLATIONS

I.

It can't be over-emphasized: translation is a creative act—at times even a violent one—and demands the same gift for productive self-delusion and inadequate assessment of risk that novel-writing does. It demands more, in fact, because of the effrontery inherent in stamping one's name and sensibility onto a simulacrum of someone else's book. When the author in question is Franz Kafka, of course, the degree of effrontery borders on the pathological. The translational impulse is a form of perversion, in other words—but at its best, it's a glorious one, the most necessary folly that we've got. Translators should have parks and streets and sailing ships named after them.

—*John Wray*

II.

One thing I had to deal with was the huge number of times the word *creature* appears in the text. I really wanted to change it to *animal* in some places and lose it entirely in others, but in most cases I was afraid that I'd piss off Kafka's ghost. As a result I stuck to the text more than I wanted to; luckily, I was able to convince Nathan to change it in his text. This way we both got a better final text in the end, and Kafka's ghost will haunt Nathan and not me.

I'm not extremely comfortable with English. It is a language in which I can easily order coffee or ask where the restroom is, but when it comes to the subtleties I get very stressed and have to check each word in three different dictionaries just to relax a little. One of the psychological barriers I've had with this is that because it took place in a synagogue—because of the "holiness" that is associated with the location, and the high register of the Hebrew prayers practiced in it—I found it difficult to switch to a lower register, even though that seemed like the right thing for the text.

I felt that Nathan did the right thing when he took my high-register Hebrew translation and switched it to a much more nonchalant level. Kafka always has something very accessible in his texts. They are not slangy, but they also don't try to dazzle you in any way. There is something very modest in his linguistic choices. In that sense I feel that Nathan "fixed" my translation a little in his take, and reached a better result than mine.

This is the first time I've ever attempted a translation; I didn't dare leave anything out. When I do something for the first time, I always try to stay out of trouble and convince everybody I can be trusted, knowing that you can fool some people some of the time.

I must say, though, that this experience kind of convinced me that I was right not to translate all these years. For me, writing is ultimate freedom, because you don't need to take anyone else into account when you write; you can just be yourself. But as a translator, I felt the exact opposite: every time I've touched the keyboard, there was this dead Czech guy breathing heavily on my neck.

—*Etgar Keret*

III.

I started my version with no definite plan, but the result was a routine piece lacking rhythm. Then I recalled two Chilean translations I particularly enjoy: one by Jorge Elliott of a couple of Chaucer's *Canterbury Tales* (using rhymed verses in Chilean Spanish, quite funny), and the outstanding Nicanor Parra's attempt at Shakespeare's *King Lear*, entitled *Lear Rey & Mendigo* ("Lear, King and Pauper") —a work in which I had the good fortune of being involved as an editor. Consequently, I decided my Kafka would be in verse.

For years my students have had to submit to the impossible and instructive assignment of producing versions of two of my favorite Kafka stories, "Eleven Sons" and "The Hunger Artist," using *décimas*, a very common poetic stanza, strongly present in Chile due to the masterworks of Violeta Parra (some of her best songs—"Volver a los 17," for example—are written in décimas). Working on the Kafka-Keret-Englander piece, the outcome was something like this:

En la parroquia vivía (a) / esta extraña criatura (b)
—muy compleja su figura (b) / describirla no sabría (a)
por su forma parecía (a) / que era una comadreja (c)
no era joven no era vieja (c) / era azul o medio verde (d)
su recuerdo se me pierde (d) / se me acerca se me aleja (c)

I am not sure why I began to digress—but I left the model, searching for a different breach or opening. Nevertheless, I went on with my rhymed "octosílabos" (eight-syllable verses). I got what follows—satisfactory, I think, as a short piece of Chilean hip hop:

También vive en nuestra casa / Una extraña criatura / No es humana su figura
No sé si él o si es ella / Pero en mi idioma alimaña / Criatura bestia araña

Maravillosa montaña / Duela cabeza y migraña / Se dicen en femenino
Entonces la criatura / Medio joven medio vieja / Medio como comadreja
Más o menos de tamaño / Vive en nuestro comedor / Hace tres generaciones
O hace cuatro—no me acuerdo / se me olvidan las canciones / entre las letras me pierdo
simplemente no recuerdo / mejor empiezo de nuevo: / Una extraña criatura
Medio azul o medio verde / (Es difícil su color) / Vive en nuestro comedor…

I had already decided to change "synagogue" to "church" (with all the implications involved), and then to "parish," and then the expression "the house of the Lord" appeared; finally, it just became a "house." I recalled the famous and beautiful Nick Cave song "God is in the House," and I thought it offered an interesting way to deal with the tremendous religious tension of the story. I also remembered "Murke's Collected Silences," by Heinrich Böll, one of my favorite short stories (in fact one of my "desert island" stories), in which a man has to erase the word *God* from some recordings. So I decided to take God out of the text (may God forgive me—in case He is there, and reads this magazine). This triggered a whole series of changes. Honestly, I don't remember precisely when I forgot completely my original idea of verses for the translation. In the end the text changed a lot—a whole bunch of words went into the bin, and that's why I thought it was not a big deal to change the title in favor of my favorite image at the end of the story. In some way, I reckon, it sums up the spirit of the text.

—*Alejandro Zambra*

I took some liberties.

—*Dave Eggers*

VI

الفصول الاربعة, بلا صيف

a story in ARABIC *by* YOUSSEF HABCHI EL-ACHKAR

ILLUSTRATORS, IN ORDER OF APPEARANCE

Mike Bertino, Tim Lahan, Wesley Allsbrook, Ian Huebert, Brianna Harden.

THE FOUR SEASONS, WITHOUT A SUMMER

translated into English by RAWI HAGE

FIRST SEASON

1

THE COFFEE SHOP IS spacious, with comfortable chairs, and tables made of walnut wood—or possibly Formica. Secretly I stroke the table without letting the waiter, leaning against a marble column, see me.

The table is smooth. It's Formica: no matter how carefully the wood is polished, traces of death are still present at its edges.

The bar's long, and ends with the coffee machine. The waiter distances himself from his column. Now that he's moved, a glaze of light shines on the pillar's black marble. There are just a few customers. My gaze wanders on the surface of the window. On the glass, people and things appear, distorted. The glass shapes them, the glass is a mirror, a falling wave.

And although I'm familiar with this place, I'm now lost between its exterior and interior. I'm confused by the reflection of a woman in a red dress, and I wonder if I saw her already—standing at the bottom of the stairs or in the lobby of the cinema.

But what's the difference? What does it matter if she was here or there? Women are alone wherever they stand.

Her red dress reminds me of my first wife. But of course it can't

QUATRE SAISONS SANS ÉTÉ

translated into French by TRISTAN GARCIA

PREMIÈRE SAISON

1

DANS LE CAFÉ, des chaises confortables et des tables en noisetier—peut-être en Formica—j'effleure du bout des ongles la table devant moi, à l'insu du barman affalé contre la colonne de marbre. Elle est en Formica—la table, je veux dire, pas la colonne de marbre.

Le bar est interminable, jusqu'à la machine à café, mais il n'y pas beaucoup de clients. Heureusement que la fenêtre les reflète et les multiplie, comme dans un miroir. La femme en robe rouge, elle, n'apparaît qu'une seule fois. Je l'ai déjà vue, pourtant, mais où? En bas des marches? Dans le hall du cinéma? Toujours toute seule. Sa robe rouge me rappelle ma première femme—ce n'est pas elle. Ou bien son fantôme. Et je ne crois pas aux fantômes.

Je bois mon thé.

Un, deux, trois, je compte les événements qui n'arrivent jamais comme les moutons avant de m'endormir. Et j'attends de manger juste avant.

Tête lourde, jambes en coton. Résister au sommeil, jusqu'à ce qu'il s'en aille, comme le désir de manger, comme le désir de baiser—pour s'en sortir. De quoi, je ne sais pas. Je me raconte des histoires sur l'absurdité et le sens de la vie.

Un pied dans le reflet, un pied dans le café, la femme passe. La robe rouge est plus courte que je ne pensais. Ses cuisses sont lourdes, sa robe en coton. Et la faim qui revient. Un, la faim, deux, le sexe, je n'arrive pas à résister.

Si le miroir pouvait la multiplier encore un peu…

Et puis la porte s'ouvre. Le cinéma.

Ma fille me demandait: pourquoi toujours un restaurant près du cinéma? Question simple, réponse simple. Parce que les gens n'ont pas à chercher loin pour manger après la séance. Est-ce que les films donnent faim? J'ai ri, j'ai répondu: les gens n'arrêtent pas d'avoir faim. Et c'est ceux qui n'arrêtent jamais de manger qui gagnent à la fin.

Moi j'attends la fin du film et j'ai toujours l'estomac vide.

2

Pas écrit depuis longtemps. Je me sens coupable, négligé et négligeant. Personne pour me pardonner: ce que je n'ai pas écrit m'ignore.

J'ai lu, tout de même.

Jusqu'à ce qu'hier, assis dans le café, je retrouve l'envie. J'ai acheté un stylo Bic, par défaut, et un petit carnet. Commencé à écrire, sans savoir quoi, j'ai décrit une fois de plus les reflets dans les fenêtres à l'infini, et dans le vide. Et laissé tomber le stylo et le carnet: "Les gens ont faim," je me répète, c'est tout ce que j'ai écrit.

3

Réveillé tard—aujourd'hui, 5 janvier 1975, premier dimanche du dernier quart de ce siècle—suis retourné au même café, avec le stylo et le carnet. Là où j'avais rencontré Rima, là où j'avais appris son suicide. À cause de moi. Et c'est là où j'ai commencé une autre vie, là où j'ai écrit à Julia, me suis réconcilié avec Mona. On est toujours amis. J'y emmène de temps en temps ma femme et mes gosses: on mange un steak, et du houmous. Sexe, nourriture. Vous avez compris.

4

Une sorte de refuge pour moi, bien sûr. L'atmosphère européenne, le silence et la musique aussi. Je le suis complètement—européen. Pas oriental ou Américain, mais Européen, j'ai la même histoire, comme toutes nos histoires: j'aime Jésus, faire l'amour en son nom, la guerre aussi, et verser le sang pour lui.

Mais quand j'écris, pourquoi écrire ainsi? Reconnaître que ce que j'écris n'amuse personne et tourne en rond—est-ce que ça suffira à lui donner un sens? Pour moi seulement. Est-ce que c'est toujours une forme d'expression, si c'est pour moi seulement? Ou une perte de temps, comme de regarder dans le

be her. Unless it's her ghost, but I don't believe in ghosts. Only ghosts believe in themselves.

So why did I ask myself the question, I wonder. And then what? Nothing before that and nothing to come after.

Look at yourself, tossed in all directions, indecisive, like chewing gum, I tell myself.

I drink my tea. I look at the reflection in the window.

I need to see.

I spend my time now trying to guess what it is I'm ignoring, though the things I guess won't enhance my knowledge. I patiently wait for events that can't happen. And they never happen, so I count the hours and wait for midday to come so I can go home and sleep.

I forget.

I eat before I sleep.

The burden of time is long—this despair that takes hold of me. I fail to tame it, and become its victim.

In defiance, I overcome my fear of an uncontrollable disaster. But the possibility of a disaster is in itself the adventure. Or so I say.

A drowsy numbness slowly takes possession of my head and my legs. The need for sleep—resistance, sleep—retreat, like the act of eating—resistance, like fucking—retreat, resistance—to run away: from what? The inevitability of the absurd and the knowledge of the void…

The woman of the interior, the exterior, the woman of reflections passes by again. Her dress is red and short. I look at her thighs and feel desire, then hunger. Food and sex are two urges I'm incapable of resisting.

There are ghosts in the glass. Such treacherous glass! If it were a man it would have enchanted humans and made itself rich.

The doorknob twists. I'm sure, this time, it's the door to the cinema that opens.

My girl once asked me: Why is there always a restaurant next to the cinema? She expects answers to be as simple as questions. I said: So people don't have to go far to eat after the film's over. She said: Do films make people hungry? I laughed and replied: People are always hungry. And the ones who can't stop eating will inherit the earth. She laughed a strange laugh.

2

I haven't written for a long time. When I'm not writing I feel I've committed a sin, a sin against the self, because once I declared: Writing is my path, and to stay true to myself—I was thinking like this because commitment and faith are virtues that we learned at home and at Sunday school and on the altar of our first communion—I block off all other roads and burn all the bridges of return. And since then, whenever I stop writing, sin penetrates me and there's no one there to forgive me. Writing doesn't speak.

In consolation, I exhange writing for reading—reading is a lake, like writing, incapable of creating a visual residue. The visual is important.

That's why, yesterday, while I was in the coffee shop, I felt like writing, so I bought a Biro—I've never liked Biros, they're so modern—and a small notebook. And I started to write without any preconceived topic, without any specific idea. I described what I saw in the reflections of the conniving window, and then abandoned my pen and notebook with these words: *People are hungry*.

3

Today I woke up late—today, the fifth of January, 1975, the first Sunday of the last quarter of the twentieth century—and I went to the coffee shop with the pen I don't like and a notebook. I do like this joint. I met Rima here and it was here that the news reached me that Rima had committed suicide because I exist—it's curious how the existence of one person can cause the suicide of someone else. In this joint I started a new life, my past life, my first wife never knew this joint, it was here that I used to write to Julia, here I reconciled with Mona and we're still friends, and here I entertain my wife and children: we eat steak, we eat hummus. Sex and food. Always sex and food.

4

This place is a kind of refuge for me. I enjoy its European atmosphere, its European silence, and its European music. Me, I'm entirely European, and why not? Not an Easterner or an American but European, like European history, every history: I love Jesus and in his name I preach love and spread civility and offer sweet fruit, but in his name I also wage war, and in his name I feel the desire to shed blood.

But then if I have to write, do I have to write in this way? And is it enough for me to acknowledge that what I write is neither enriching nor

miroir—et de croire aux fantômes, à la femme, à la table en Formica. Qu'est-ce que les gens en ont à faire?

Et qu'est-ce que j'en ai à faire de vous?

DEUXIÈME SAISON
1

Dehors, sur la grand-route, des vagues de bruit très lent. Depuis un appartement voisin, l'écho d'une musique. Dans le cendrier, une pipe. Je sens la fumée monter, sans l'inhaler.

Suis en train de lire.

Par la fenêtre, le soleil, et je m'en éloigne à regrets. Je lis, sans rien y comprendre. Le soleil m'invite—à quoi? Parfois, ses rayons percent comme des balles.

Le calme, mais sur ses gardes. Pas de tir de roquettes, pas de canonade dans le voisinage. Des rafales sporadiques et des balles perdues, rien de plus.

Mon père pense que nous aurions mieux fait de quitter Beyrouth. Dimanche—les enfants restent à la maison et n'osent même pas sortir la tête par la fenêtre. L'école? Tu parles. Elles devraient toutes être fermées. Ils disent qu'il faut les laisser ouvertes, pour ne pas donner raison à la guerre. Ils mentent. Ils ne donnent tort à rien ni à personne. Ceux qui disent ça, ils ne craignent pas pour la vie de leurs enfants—leurs enfants ont grandi et ne vont plus à l'école.

Des autruches. Enterrent leurs têtes dans le sable—pour fuir les lions. Ou peut-être que non. Peut-être qu'ils ont conscience de tout et qu'ils veulent sauver leur peau. Ils jouent et quand ils perdent une carte, ils la remplacent, continuent l'air de rien.

2

Quelques balles tirées. Dieu merci, ni bombes ni tirs de roquette. À la radio: "Un homme touché par une balle, alors qu'il lisait. État stable."

Les enfants loin des fenêtres. Va te raser: tu te sentiras mieux. Faudrait partir se planquer dans le village de Kfarmalat.

D'après le premier ministre, aller sur la côte et respirer le grand air—c'est ce qu'il faut.

Y en pour le faire.

Je me contente de la compagnie des esprits. Gentils fantômes. Errants.

À la radio: "Troisième faction engagée. Une main invisible excite la violence. Le peuple libanais doit la débusquer et couper tout le bras à l'épaule." Et puis: "La guerre civile est de retour: malgré toutes les déclarations officielles, la peur de nouvelles explosions est bien là."

À la radio: "Pas une guerre civile. Une guerre entre Palestiniens et Libanais."

"J'aimerais savoir entre qui et qui," dit une mère en deuil. "Contre nous tous, oui. Contre nous, désarmés." Et pleure pour sa fille—une roquette tombée pendant qu'elle jouait dans la cour de l'école. "Ils se trompent d'ennemi," qu'elle dit.

"Traître!" répond la vierge effarouchée en criant.

"Faut juger tous ceux qui refusent de porter des armes," répètent les combattants.

"Pour la nation. Tous martyrs!" dit le jeune homme, un flingue à la main.

Les gosses ont compris la leçon: loin de la fenêtre. Mais faire attention ne garantit jamais rien.

3

Mal partout. Sans réfléchir, contre la machine à laver, face contre le miroir, qui avale pour moitié mon visage, et le visage qui avale pour moitié le reflet.

4

Barbe trop longue. Trop grise. Juste une moustache, peut-être. Non, laisse tomber. Faudra tripoter autre chose que ta moustache, je me dis.

Les mains fatiguées de la mouiller, ma barbe. Reflet du soleil dans le miroir. Rue vide: par deux fois, des coups de feu.

Pourquoi m'emmerder à me la laver et à me la raser à l'ancienne, alors qu'il y a de la mousse dans les magasins. "Un peu d'eau chaude, de la mousse à raser, pour un rasage parfait!" Cent fois j'ai entendu ça à la radio. Plus maintenant. Maintenant, tout le monde utilise de la mousse à raser, tout le monde connaît.

Moi, je n'aime pas changer. Le printemps… Allez, encore des mots. Tout ce qui compte, c'est de faire attention. À la rue, à la fenêtre, aux balles.

5

Est-ce que la guerre est essentielle pour nous? Je dis bien *nous*—c'est tout le problème. Si la guerre est nécessaire, alors d'accord, on meurt tous et puis voilà. La mort a rempli d'autres fonctions parfois que celle que de faire le malheur des gens. Ça peut servir à quelque chose, la mort. Pourquoi pas. Mais si la guerre n'est qu'un jeu, et la mort des militaires, des civils, juste un jeu, et nous des exécutants, des adjuvants pour la main de celui qui l'exécute, alors quelle est la fonction? Le massacre du troupeau et le sacrifice de la chair.

entertaining? And then what if the purpose of writing is only to benefit the author—shouldn't writing, for the author to feel rewarded, be a form of expression, not a waste of time like passing beads between my fingers?

The treacherous glass, the ghost, the woman, the Formica table, and the long bar have never changed anything. And what do people care about these things, and what do I care about people?

SECOND SEASON

1

Outside, on the wide road, noise passes in a succession of slow waves. From a nearby apartment, echoes of a drum rise through the walls. In the ashtray, a pipe burns. I taste the fumes without inhaling them.

I read.

The sun enters through the window. I glance at it. I distance myself from it with a feeling of sorrow. I resign myself to its inevitable magical powers. I read. I don't grasp what I read. The sun is all invitations. I don't know how to respond to its call. Sometimes the rays flash like bullets.

A cautious calm. The radio says better than cautious. There are no rockets, no cannons in any of the troubled neighborhoods. Just a few sporadic shots and random bullets.

My father says we should have left Beirut. It's Sunday, and the kids are prisoners inside their own home, they don't even dare stick their heads out the window. School? you say. The schools should all be shut. But in defiance of the war, they say they'll keep them open. But they're lying. They're not defying anyone. They're lying. They're not afraid for their kids' lives—their kids are grown up and no longer in school.

Like an ostrich, they bury their heads in the sand to escape the devouring lions. Or no! They see everything and are aware of everything. The important thing for them is to save themselves. They play games but when they lose a piece they just replace it and move on.

2

Just a couple of bullets, some gunfire. Thank God there are no bombs or rockets. The radio says: "A citizen was hit by a stray bullet while reading, his condition is stable."

Make sure the kids stay away from the window. Go shave your beard: it'll make you feel better. We should go and hide in the village of Kfarmalat.

The prime minister advises us to go to the coast and enjoy the sea air. Some do as he says.

Me, I entertain myself with the company of spirits. Ghosts are gentle and never cause harm. They gently wander.

The radio declares: "The third faction is still engaged. The invisible hand is inciting violence. It is still active. The Lebanese people should stand united and expose the invisible hand and cut it off at the shoulder." The radio declares: "The civil war has returned, it entered through the window: in spite of all official assurances there is still the fear of new explosions."

The radio declares: "The war is not a civil war. The war is between the Palestinians and the Lebanese."

"I wish we knew who's fighting the war," says a mother in black. "The war's being fought against us all—the ones who don't bear arms." And she weeps for her child who was killed by a rocket while he played in the school courtyard. And she says: "They're fighting the wrong enemy."

"Traitor, traitor," scream the virgins.

"We must bring to justice any man who refuses to bear arms, bring to justice any man who refuses to bear arms," repeat the fighters.

"All for the nation. We should all embrace martyrdom," says the young man with a gun in his hand.

The kids have learned the lesson of wars: they stay away from glass windows. But caution is no guarantee.

3

My whole body's in pain. Without thinking, I lean against the washing machine, I lean toward the mirror, my face swallows half the mirror and the mirror swallows half my face.

4

My beard's too long. How has grayness infiltrated it so much? Maybe I'll leave my mustache. No, forget it! You'll just have to twist something other than your mustache, I say to myself.

My hands are tired from wetting my beard. The sun shines on the mirror. The street has emptied: bullets have run through it twice.

Why do I still bother with a shaving brush in this age of chemicals and foam? "Just wet your face with hot water, apply the foam, and enjoy

6

Cadavres dans la rue. Les combattants marchent dessus. Les ignorent. Déjà à la recherche de nouvelles opportunités de donner la mort. Le meurtre est là, dans l'inauguration des églises, l'exaltation de l'héroïsme. Les maisons ont brûlé. Les bombes dans les chambres à coucher, les salles à manger, les chambres des couples.

Les balles sonnent comme les cloches, chassent des funérailles ceux qui étaient venus pleurer leurs morts.

7

—...ne prêche que la destruction.

—Ma femme, mes enfants, où sont-ils? Comment les retrouver?

Horizon brumeux, nuit claire. La montagne se découpe sur le ciel, le ciel sur la terre.

—Le nom de ceux qui l'ont tuée, elle et sa famille?

—Que dit la radio?

—Un de ses gosses, blessé, a couru vers elle. Leur père tué en premier.

Les cadavres dans les rues, et les combattants attendent que le gouvernement les enterrent. Des roquettes dans les bidons et sur le seuil des maisons.

TROISIÈME SAISON

1

Le village de Kfarmalat resplendit à l'automne. Les feuilles des arbres comme des lettres éparpillées par terre; nous oublions la guerre un instant.

Si Kfarmalat est une ruche, les abeilles y sont revenues après avoir perdu le chemin. Terreur, fumée noire, odeur de poudre: les abeilles chassées, revenues.

Entre deux oreilles, sous le vieux chandelier noirci, je rêve de ma première épouse, qui s'est remariée tant de fois après notre divorce—une centaine de fois je me suis remarié, moi aussi.

L'hiver dans le village de Kfarmalat s'écoule comme un torrent clair, qui épanche la soif et qui charme, au point parfois de faire disparaître la guerre. Je retrouve dans l'eau le reflet du miroir, la robe rouge et courte, le fantôme, le cinéma, les bonnes de film et le rire de ma fille.

Dans la cabane sur la colline en surplomb de notre maison, le vent s'engouffre entre les murs noirs. La cabane est vieille.

2

Au plus près de mon cœur, les combattants, leurs cadavres rongés par le temps qui passe.

3

Les cloches de l'église sonnent, derrière la cabane.

Mon père dit que celui qui a conçu cette guerre est un génie. Celui qui l'a menée est un idiot. Et quiconque en profite une mère maquerelle. Les combattants ne sont pas ennemis *vraiment*. Les vrais ennemis ne se sont pas encore manifestés. La guerre sera longue, mes enfants, dit-il. La guerre s'étendra jusqu'à ce que... Bas les masques. Le visage pâle, sous le dernier masque, lui ce sera l'ennemi.

Alors nous saurons si la guerre est la grande affaire ou si celui qui la mène est un imbécile, dis-je.

4

Des enfants ramassent les feuilles à la pelle et le tas grandit dans un coin: l'odeur de l'automne. Le soleil orangé s'insinue entre les murs noirs de la cabane.

J'ignore le grondement des canons. Mon inconscient me dit qu'il n'y a pas de porte de sortie.

Les gosses chantent en rond, ils attendent le coucher du soleil et l'heure du feu. Je rentre dans leur danse. Rien n'a changé. Je connais leurs chansons. Ce sont les mêmes qu'antan. Quand je rêvais souvent: je courais sur un chemin sablonneux pour aller la voir chaque soir et chaque matin. Parfois les mots bourgeonnent dans la bouche de l'enfant et il les chérit. Parfois, c'est le silence. Lorsque leurs yeux se croisent—ils finissent toujours par se croiser—il en souffre.

L'odeur de la poussière sur les chemins secs, l'odeur du thym autour de leur maison, jusqu'à l'entrée de la cave. L'attente de l'odeur d'innocence et de paix le jour même où le sang est devenu l'emblème de l'enfer.

Une explosion dans le tas de feuilles mortes. Les enfants arrêtent de tourner, de chanter. Pause. Et ils recommencent.

Je les laisse.

QUATRIÈME SAISON

1

La radio grésille à côté de lui, toute la journée, avec un peu d'espoir, elle

a smoother shave!" I've heard that commercial a hundred times. And now it's stopped running. Because everyone's now shaving with foam.

Me, I hate change. The spring that drives me like a wind-up toy doesn't release me when I move... The many springs that drive me are all mechanical and simultaneous. Empty words. What's important now is caution. Only caution. Caution from the street, from the window: from the bullets.

5

Is this war essential to us? I stress the word *us*. The answer's crucial: if the war's necessary, then let's all die. Death also has a function in situations like this. At times death exists beyond its usual purpose of making people despair. But then, if the war's only a game, and if the death of those who bear arms and don't bear arms and refuse to bear arms is all a game, and if we're all minor accomplices, instruments, spare parts in the hand of the executioner, then what's the meaning of death? Its meaning becomes just the slaughter of the herd and the burying of flesh.

6

The dead bodies are laid out in the streets. The combatants step over them. They ignore them, on the lookout for new opportunities in death. There is murder in the inauguration of churches, in the incantation of heroism. The houses have burned. The bombs have entered the bedrooms, the dining rooms, the rooms of lust.

Bullets are the tolling of bells, chasing mourners away from the victims' funerals.

7

—Preach only of destruction.

—My wife, my children, where are they? How do I reach them?

The horizon is fogged, the night is near. The mountain withdraws from the city, the sky from the land.

—What are the names of the combatants who killed her and her family, how many were they?

—What did the radio say?

—The radio said that one of her kids, wounded, ran toward his mother. Their father was killed first.

The dead bodies fill the streets, and the combatants wait for the government to bury them. Rockets are in the water barrels, rockets are on the door steps.

THIRD SEASON

1

Kfarmalat, the village, is naked in its fall and in its youthfulness. The leaves of its trees are letters, dispersed; we forget the war, for a while.

Kfarmalat is a beehive again, the bees have returned after losing their way. The terror, the black smoke, the smell of gunpowder, led the vagabond bees back to the hive.

Between two pillows, under the old, blackened chandelier, I dream of my first wife, who remarried many times after me, just as I remarried a thousand times.

Winter in the village of Kfarmalat is a clear stream, it quenches the thirst and it pleases, sometimes it makes the war disappear. I see in it the reflection of that treacherous glass, the short red dress, the ghost, the cinema, the projection of the reels of history, my daughter with her laugh.

In the shack on the hillside above our house, the wind mingles with the black walls. The shack is old.

2

Bring the fighters close to my heart, corpses devoured by time.

3

Beyond the shack, in the church, the bell tolls.

My father says: "Whoever planned this war was a genius, whoever executed it is an idiot, and whoever benefits from it is a pimp. The fighters aren't the real enemy. The real enemy hasn't started fighting yet. This war will be long, my children, it will stretch out until the man with the pale face removes his mask. The man with the pale face is the enemy."

"Only then will we know if the war is essential or if the executioner is just a fool," I say.

4

Children gather the fallen leaves and tidy them into a corner: the smell fills the area. The orange sun hovers inside the black walls of the shack.

grésille que c'est terminé. Et ajoute: demain, la guerre est terminée, ou bien après-demain.

Chaque fois, il y croit, et il se promet que ce sera la bonne. C'est de mots dont il a besoin, même de mensonges, pour lui faire oublier que ce qui a été anéanti l'a été pour toujours, que ce qui n'était pas encore ne serait jamais, et que tout ce qu'il y a de plus grand et d'aussi haut que les montagnes, disparaîtra aussi un jour.

La radio explique qu'un cessez-le-feu a été conclu. Qu'il prendra effet à partir de huit heures ce matin. Que des garanties ont été données, cette fois.

Il lisait. Referma le livre. Assis en silence, les yeux brillants. Regarda le soleil, qui lui sembla une créature sur le point de naître. Il s'en réjouit et se leva, courut vers cette drôle de créature, en marchant vers le village de Kfarmalat.

2

La guerre est terminée. Les combats ont cessé, tout ce qu'il n'avait jamais compris, ou qu'il avait haï. En flânant à travers le village, il ne veut pas penser que le cessez-le-feu ne durera pas, comme la fois d'avant, et d'encore avant, il ne veut pas penser du tout. Profite de la bénédiction de la paix, libre et désoeuvré.

Au pied de la falaise du monastère, Nasri fait la traite des vaches.

—Professeur, des nouvelles? De bonnes nouvelles?

—Un cessez-le-feu à huit heures, à ce qu'ils disent.

—C'est vrai?

—D'après vous?

—Non, au nom d'Allah… Trente fois on nous l'a promis. Mensonges.

—J'espère que c'est vrai. À chaque fois.

—Pourquoi pas? Faut bien croire. Venez prendre un café.

—Bien sûr.

Le professeur monte les marches qui séparent la rue de la maison. Sur une chaise au ras du sol, rempaillée, il s'assoit.

Sous les pins, des singes.

Les vaches dans les prés.

Nasri appelle Habboubah, sa femme, pour faire le café.

— Pas de sucre, Nasri, dis-lui.

—Pas de sucre, Habboubah.

Elle lui crie, invisible:

—Bienvenue, professeur.

—Vous avez stocké du bois, professeur, demande Nasri.

—Du bois?

—Pour l'hiver. Et le charbon?

—La guerre est terminée, mon cher Nasri: oubliez le bois et le charbon.

—Attendez. Écoutez… Écoutez…

Nasri boit une gorgée.

Au loin, des canons se répondent.

—Il n'est pas encore huit heures, Nasri.

—S'ils devaient s'arrêter, pourquoi ils ne le feraient pas maintenant? Tout de suite. Faut pas être naïf, professeur. Ceux qui signent le cessez-le-feu ne sont pas ceux qui tirent, et ceux qui tirent ne sont pas ceux qui meurent, et pour ceux qui meurent, on ne peut plus rien faire.

3

Je témoigne contre les tueurs. Je maudis cette guerre. Et qu'est-ce je peux faire—moi qui ne supporte pas les armes—à part regarder, et porter accusation contre ceux qui massacrent au nom de Marduk, Baal et Néron…?

4

Sainte nuit. Un checkpoint près de la mer. Ils ont tué mon ex-femme, son mari et ses enfants.

Peut-être que les combattants ne savaient pas pourquoi il fallait les tuer. Je ne sais pas pourquoi ils les ont tuéz. Ils l'ont tuée, elle, après l'avoir tué lui et avoir tué les enfants. Et ils l'ont tuée avant même qu'elle puisse les pleurer.

Sur ses joues, dix traits rouges, les traces de dix ongles, des ongles cassés.

I ignore the blast of the cannons. My unconscious says: no escape.

The kids sing and go round and round, they wait for the dusk, the hour of fire worship. I run to them and they take me inside their circle, I dance with them. Children's dancing never changes. I sing their songs. Children's songs always stay the same. I was once a boy of many dreams: I ran along a sandy path to see her every morning and every dusk. Sometimes words surface on the boy's tongue and he cherishes them. Other times, silence. When their eyes meet—and their eyes always meet—he embraces a hardship within him.

The smell of dust on dry pathways, the smell of thyme along the edge of her house to the opening of our cave. The longing for the odor of innocence and peace on that day when blood became an emblem for hell.

An explosion comes from the gathering of dry leaves. The children cease their turning and singing. They pause for a movement and then they proceed.

I leave them.

FOURTH SEASON

1

The radio is muttering beside him. It mutters all day, on a thin thread of hope it mutters: It's over. The radio mutters and adds: Tomorrow the war will be over, or the day after tomorrow.

And he believes it every time, like an addict he promises himself that this will be the last time: he falls for it, again and again. He needs words, even their lies, to make him forget that what's destroyed is lost forever, that what was not will never be, and that whatever is built in the likeness of a great mountain will also disappear.

The radio said: "A ceasefire has been agreed. It will take effect from eight this evening. This time guarantees have been given."

He was reading. He closed the book. He sat still and his eyes shone. He watched the sun and it seemed like a creature about to be born. He rejoiced and ran toward it. He walked to the village of Kfarmalat.

2

The war's over. The fighting has stopped, this war he never understood, and the fire that he despised. As he strolls through the village he refuses to think that the ceasefire won't last, like before, he doesn't want to think, he just wants to breathe the blessing of peace, aimless, free.

Below the cliff of the monastery, Nasri is milking the cows.

—Professor, any news? Give us the good news, reassure us!

—There'll be a ceasefire at eight, they said.

—And you believe them?

—You don't believe them?

—No, in the name of Allah… They promised us thirty times already—all lies.

—I believe it. And I'm willing to believe it every time.

—Why not? We all need to believe Come in for a coffee.

—Certainly.

The Professor takes the stairs, five of them, that separate the street from the house. On a low chair, woven with straw, he sits.

Under the pines, monks stroll by.

In the fields, cows ruminate.

Nasri calls to his wife Habboubah to make coffee.

—No sugar, Nasri. Tell her no sugar.

—Habboubah, no sugar.

And Habboubah shouts from inside:

—Welcome, Professor.

Nasri says:

—Did you stock up on wood, Professor?

—Why wood?

—For the winter, the winter. And coal?

—The war's over, my dear Nasri: forget about the wood and coal.

—Wise up… listen… listen.

Nasri takes the clay pitcher and raises it to his mouth and drinks.

Far away, cannons echo in sequence.

—But Nasri, it's not eight yet.

—If they were going to stop, why would they wait until then? They'd have stopped right away. Always judge a book by its cover, Professor. The ones who agreed to the ceasefire aren't the same as the ones doing the shooting, and the ones doing the shooting aren't the ones dying, and the ones dying are helpless because they're already dead.

3

I testify against the killers. I damn this war, I scribble curses to defeat them. And what do I possess—I who don't bear arms—except the power of my own eyes, my indictment of those who butcher in the name of Marduk, Baal, Nero…?

4

On a holy night. At a checkpoint near the sea. They killed my ex-wife and her husband and children.

Perhaps the fighters didn't know why they had to kill them. I don't know why they killed them. They killed her after they killed her husband and her children. They killed her before she had the chance to mourn their remains.

On her cheeks are ten red wounds, the traces of ten fingernails, broken.

FOUR SEASONS WITH TWO SUMMERS

translated into English by JOE DUNTHORNE

FIRST SEASON

1

I BOUGHT A DEVICE that can switch off over seven hundred models of television. It has two modes: non-stealth and stealth. It fits inconspicuously onto my keychain.

This would be my favorite cafe-bar if the televisions were off. One shows Iranian soap operas and the other, Arabic news. There are long mirrors that the barman uses to surreptitiously watch them. He faces outward as though awaiting an order, but his mind is somewhere else.

2

The cafe-bar is cave-themed. It is called The Long Dark Cave and the walls are papier-mâché or polystyrene, painted brown. There are nooks and bumps. Stalactites hang beside the televisions. On the way to the bathroom, there's a tiny manmade waterfall. It is strange that I described the televisions before I mentioned the cave theme.

Every year it wins the *Gazette*'s award for Best Themed Cafe/Bar. The mirrors face each other, making it look like there are many hundreds of interconnected chambers. London has manmade tunnels, but no cave systems; it has hills but no mountains, and it rarely experiences extreme weather.

QUATTRO STAGIONI, DUE ESTATI

translated into Italian by FRANCESCO PACIFICO

PRIMA STAGIONE

1

LONDRA. COMPRATO APPARECCHIO che spegne settecento e passa modelli di televisore. Ha due setting: non-stealth e stealth. Non ingombra, lo tengo nel portachiavi.

Questo sarebbe il mio bar preferito se tenesse spenti i televisori. Uno dà le soap iraniane e l'altro il tg arabo. Ci sono lunghi specchi da cui il barista guarda la tv di nascosto. Cioè è rivolto alla sala come aspettasse gli ordini ma ha lo sguardo perso.

2

Il bar è a tema: si chiama La Caverna, è lungo e stretto e i muri sono di cartapesta o polistirolo e dipinti di marrone. Con rientranze e protuberanze. Accanto ai televisori pendono delle stalattiti. Prima del bagno c'è una cascatella artificiale. È strano che ho descritto i televisori prima di dire che è un bar a tema.

Vince ogni anni il premio della Gazzetta per il miglior bar a tema. È la settimana prima di Natale: hanno spruzzato neve finta alle finestre. Londra non ha le montagne.

Dietro al bancone c'è un ulteriore specchio, lungo, che moltiplica i drink esotici e dà l'idea che ci siano centinaia di stanze interconnesse. Londra ha dei tunnel sotterranei ma non ha caverne.

3

Il tg ha il volume alto, l'altoparlante distorce. Sono in pena per l'udito del barista, specialmente l'orecchio sinistro. Può seguire anche la soap, ma la ignora a meno che a un personaggio non succeda roba grossa tipo un incidente stradale. Gli interessa il dramma vero, oltre il linguaggio. In fondo al bancone c'è una donna molto bella che fa una colazione turca e guarda la soap iraniana.

Il mio apparecchio è settato su stealth. Cioè non fa il puntino laser tipo fucile del cecchino.

Calcolo gli angoli perché il segnale rimbalzi sullo specchio dietro al bancone, poi su quello opposto, e colpisca il televisore più lontano. Sono un cecchino: la soap scompare dallo schermo. La donna molto bella strizza gli occhi e poi alza le mani. La trama si stava facendo interessante. Ha una fettina di cetriolo nella mano destra, la getta sul piatto. Indica lo schermo nero e chiama il barista per nome. Io di solito lo chiamo *buddy*.

Sorrido guardandomi le mani: sto pensando alla perfezione di questo posto, ma come in un'altra lingua, e non capisco bene cosa. Mentre il barista cerca il telecomando, io spengo il tg. Che giornata, per questo bar, il 19 dicembre del 2010.

Alzo gli occhi: la donna mi sta guardando attraverso lo specchio. Metto le chiavi in tasca. Lei parla al barista nella loro lingua. Metto un altro cubetto di zucchero nel mio tè senza latte e mescolo, faccio un rumore ritmato, *ti-ti-ti-ti-ti*, perché il cucchiaino è grande quasi come il bicchierino e perché i rumori, di colpo, nel silenzio, si distinguono.

Negli specchi, il barista mi viene incontro. A centinaia.

"Chiedo scusa. Li spenti lei?"

C'è un momento in cui decido quale faccia farò meglio. Opto per: la faccia di chi non ha capito.

"Tv," dice. "Li spenti lei?"

"Oh, le tv."

"Non piace? Meglio altro canale?"

La donna ora mi guarda senza l'aiuto degli specchi, e ha le sopracciglia aggrottate.

"Ho comprato questo affare su internet," dico. "È un giocattolo. Per fare gli scherzi."

Il barista tiene le mani aperte sul bancone.

"Amico dovevi dire me," dice.

"Guarda," gli dico, e glielo mostro. "È per ridere. Le riaccende, anche." Punto al televisore più lontano. "Visto?"

It's the week before Christmas, so they have sprayed fake snow on the windows.

3

The TV news is loud and the internal speaker is distorting. I worry for the bartender's ears, particularly his left. He only hears the soap opera when a character is involved in something big, like a car accident. His interest lies in high drama beyond language. There is a quite beautiful woman at the far end of the bar eating Turkish breakfast and watching the Iranian soap.

My device is in stealth mode.

I calculate the angles so that my signal bounces off the mirror behind the bar, then off the opposite mirror, before hitting the far television. I am clearly a dead-eye as the soap opera immediately disappears. The quite beautiful woman squints. It was getting to a good bit. She has a slice of cucumber in her right hand that she throws down on her plate. She points to the black screen and calls the barman by his full name. I usually call him *buddy*.

I am smiling at my hands because the cafe is nearly its perfect self. While he is looking for the remote, I turn off the news as well. Momentous day, December 19, 2010. The cafe-bar has transcended.

When I look up the woman is watching me in the mirror. I put my keys in my pocket. She says something to the bartender in a language they share. I drop an extra sugar cube into my milkless tea and concentrate on stirring, making a rhythmic *ti-ti-ti-ti-ti* noise because the spoon is only slightly smaller than the decorative glass and because noises are suddenly audible in the silence.

In the mirrors, he is coming over to speak to me. Hundreds of him.

"Excuse me, sir. You turn those off?"

There is a moment where I decide which facial expression will play best. I go with non-comprehension.

"The TVs," he says. "You turn them off?"

"Oh, the TVs."

"You not like it? You want different channel?"

The woman is watching me directly—not through the mirror—with her eyebrows locked down.

"I bought this device from the internet," I say. "It's a toy. A kind of joke."

He has both his hands flat on the bar.

"Friend, you should tell me," he says.

"Look," I say, and I hold up the fob. "It's for fun. It turns them back on, as well." I point at the far TV. "See."

The cave fills with yelling; the news is on an advert break. The bartender is impressed.

"You can turn off any TV in the world," I say, handing it to him. "Have a go."

He holds the device up to the light, smiling the whole time. He has neat teeth the color of York stone.

"It has two modes," I tell him. "That button's for stealth, and that one's for non-stealth."

The quite beautiful woman yells at him and opens her palms toward her TV. She really wants to know what's happening on her program. He points the device at her as though trying to turn her off, which he finds very funny. He uses non-stealth mode, which fires a laser-targeting dot. It hits her right in the neck. Even though it's not my language I can tell she's calling him something pretty bad.

Finally he turns her TV on and she shakes her head and settles back to watching it. He looks at me for a moment and raises one eyebrow. Then he turns her TV off again and starts laughing. Now I am laughing too.

4

The bartender explains to me that there is revolution in Tunisia. He says we are watching Al Jazeera news. Both TVs are on.

"Bad things for too long, and now they have enough."

The woman in the mirror cannot take her eyes off me.

"An invisible hand makes violence," he says. "Now the people cut off the arm."

The barman is trying to tell me the news, as it happens, but it's difficult to keep up. The woman leans over and hisses something. He frowns, then gets the remote control from under the counter.

"She says we will find the same channel in English," he says.

SECOND SEASON

1

Last week, I turned off my across-the-street-neighbor's television. He was watching snooker, which bathed the whole room in green light. I fired my device then dived to the floor of my bedroom.

Il barista è molto colpito.

"Puoi spegnere i televisori di tutto il mondo," dico, consegnandoglielo. "Prova."

Gli piace e ride. Ha bei denti, color della pietra di York. La soap è in pausa pubblicitaria. La donna molto bella si lamenta col barista alla maniera di un calciatore che protesta con l'arbitro. Il barista le punta contro l'apparecchio come tentando di spegnerla. Poi spegne il televisore della soap e ride quando la donna lo insulta. Lo riaccende. Lei gli dice altre cose. Poi la spegne. A questo punto rido anch'io.

4

Il barista mi spiega che in Tunisia c'è una rivoluzione in corso. Dice che stiamo guardando Al Jazeera. Tutti e due i televisori sono accesi.

"Troppe brutte cose, troppo tempo, e ora abbastanza."

La donna nello specchio non mi leva gli occhi di dosso.

"Mano invisibile fa violenza," dice il barista. "Ora gente taglia il braccio."

Il barista cerca di spiegarmi cosa dicono al tg, ma è difficile stare al passo. La donna si sporge e sibila qualcosa. Si acciglia, poi prende il telecomando da sotto il bancone.

"Dice che troviamo stesso canale ma inglese," dice.

SECONDA STAGIONE

1

La settimana scorsa, ho spento il televisore del tipo che vive dall'altra parte della strada. Stava guardando una partita di snooker, la sua stanza era immersa in un verde catacombale. Ho spinto il pulsante e mi sono tuffato sul pavimento della mia camera da letto.

Dopo un po', ho alzato la testa fino al davanzale e ho visto che era ancora seduto lì, alla sola luce del lampione in strada. Dava un colore alla sua pelle che pareva avesse l'itterizia. Ho aspettato per un pezzo prima di capire che dormiva. Non so come si chiama però ho visto i suoi figli, vanno a scuola.

Ho riacceso la sua tv, inondando la stanza con la luce del Crucible Theatre di Sheffield. Si è svegliato, non si raccapezzava. Era un giorno feriale.

2

L'indomani ero in piedi davanti a Curry's Digital, all'altro capo della strada. La vetrina era piena di televisori che mostravano un unico programma su uno spettrale pipistrello a rischio estinzione. Ho serrato il mio apparecchio su stealth e ho fatto fuoco tipo mitra.

A un certo punto, un giovane dello staff, praticamente un ragazzino, che portava orecchini con perno e un ridicolo completo, si è dovuto arrampicare sulla vetrina: aggirare gli schermi spenti e le telecamere costose. Quando l'ho visto nella vetrina, li ho riaccesi tutti. I televisori. Il ragazzino si è ritrovato in una caverna piena di pipistrelli a rischio estinzione. Tutto intorno a lui, stridevano sibilavano. I pipistrelli non sono ciechi ma tutti pensano altrimenti. Sebbene ce ne siano a decine di migliaia in una sola caverna, sono considerati ancora a rischio.

3

Oggi, ripasso di nuovo davanti a Curry's Digital. Sul marciapiede fuori due studentesse ballano in giacca viola e gonna a pieghe. Le loro mosse si moltiplicano sui televisori in vetrina.

Una delle telecamere è accesa e registra, ma non capisco quale. È un'inquadratura a figura intera, la stessa per ogni schermo. A un certo punto fanno finta di essere intrappolate negli schermi.

Venticinque coppie di studentesse che premono contro muri e soffitti dentro piccole stanze.

Fanno la faccia spaventata, poi ridono, poi rifanno la faccia spaventata. Ora le ragazze seppellite cercano di rompere gli schermi per scappare. I palmi appiccicosi delle mani sul vetro fanno rumori striduli da pipistrello. È una performance incredibile. La guarderei per sempre. Poi si accorgono di me.

Appena se ne vanno prendo il loro posto. Ci provo ma non riesco a guardarmi negli occhi. Sono intrappolato in venticinque tombini. Ho una profonda epifania sui miei vestiti e i miei capelli. Mentre sfilo l'aggeggio dalla tasca, vedo la guardia giurata.

4

Sono in uno dei barbieri turchi lì vicino, ho addosso un tre pezzi appena rimediato al Centro Tumori.

I miei capelli: da donna su una testa da uomo. Taglia una ciocca dopo l'altra. Emetto dei grugniti per il dolore. Non è abituato a capelli come i miei e deve fare due viaggi di scopa e paletta per pulire il pavimento.

5

Tornando alla Caverna, passando per Curry's Digital, sono ben camuffato, come un poliziotto in borghese. Ho l'aggeggio nel taschino.

After some time I peeked back over the window ledge and saw he was still sitting there, now in the dark. I waited for a long time before realizing he was asleep. I do not know this neighbor's name, but I've seen his school-age children.

I turned his TV back on, flooding his room with the light of the Crucible Theater, Sheffield. He woke up, looked around. It was a school night.

2

The next day I was standing on the other side of the road from Curry's Digital. Their display window had a wall of TVs all showing the same nature program about the endangered spectral bat. I set my device to stealth and fired, machine-gun style.

Eventually a young staff member, a boy really, wearing stud earrings and a bad suit had to climb into the display window. He had to step around the blank screens and valuable cameras. Once he was all the way in, I turned them back on, the TVs. He was in a cave full of endangered bats. All around him, they squeaked and wheeled. There were tens of thousands of this endangered species.

Bats are not blind, but everyone thinks they are.

3

Today, I walk past Curry's Digital again. There are two schoolgirls wearing purple blazers and pleated skirts dancing on the pavement outside. Their moves are multiplied many times on the TVs in the display window.

One of the cameras is on and shooting, though I can't tell which. It's a full-length shot, the same on every screen. They start pretending to be trapped in the televisions.

Twenty-five pairs of cloned schoolgirls push against the walls and ceilings of tiny chambers.

They pretend to be scared and then they laugh, then look scared again. They drag their sticky palms down the window, which squeaks. Their performance is tremendous. I would like to watch this forever. Then they see me.

Once they're gone, I take their place on the pavement. I try, but I cannot meet my own gaze. I am trapped in twenty-five potholes. I make a profound realization about my clothes and haircut. As I pull my device from my pocket, I see the security guard.

4

I duck into Cancer Research and buy a three-piece suit and shoes. I go behind a curtain to put it on. I know that, next door, there is one of the cheap Turkish men's barbers, so I make a stealthy exit and go straight in there. I am their only customer. The barber looks at me with something like wonder.

5

My hair is female hair on a male head. He lops it off in lengths. I make small grunting noises because of the pain. He is not used to my female-type hair. It takes two trips with the dustpan and brush to clear away my offcuts.

Once he's finished, I am brilliantly disguised and ready to walk past Curry's Digital and into The Long Dark Cave, which is a few doors further down. I tuck the device in my handkerchief pocket.

6

Back in the cave, I don't recognize the bartender and there is no quite beautiful woman. I order bean stew. The TV is still running the English-speaking version of Al Jazeera.

The studio is in Doha, I learn.

The screen shows young men throwing stones and cars burning.

7

There's an interview between the presenter in Doha and an MP in London. The presenter says: "And they expect the government to bury the dead." They are both in studios with fake pictures of local landscapes behind them. The presenter has mountains against a yellow sky. The MP has HMS Belfast in the Thames.

THIRD SEASON
1

It is good to get out of London during the summer, people say.

I have come to Hebden Bridge. The buildings here are made of stone the color of a smoker's teeth. My phone has not heard of Hebden Bridge and assumes I am thinking of Hebron, south of Jerusalem.

I send this text to my mother who lives in Switzerland with her

6

Non riconosco il barista e non ci trovo una donna molto bella. Ordino stufato di fagioli. La tv è ancora sul tg in inglese di Al Jazeera.

Lo studio è a Doha, pare.

La tv mostra dei giovani che lanciano pietre e delle macchine incendiate.

7

Il presentatore a Doha intervista un parlamentare a Londra. Il presentatore: "E si aspettano che il governo seppellisca i cadaveri." Sono entrambi in studio, entrambi con alle spalle fotografie di paesaggi locali. Il presentatore: montagne contro un cielo giallo. Il parlamentare: il Tower Bridge e l'Imperial War Museum.

TERZA STAGIONE
1

Si dice che Londra d'estate sia meglio evitarla.

Sono a Hebden Bridge. Costruzioni in pietra color denti di fumatore. Il mio telefono ignora Hebden Bridge e suppone io intenda Hebron, a sud di Gerusalemme.

Mando a mia madre, che vive in Svizzera, il seguente messaggio: *Ciao mamma! Sto a Hebden Bridge. Città col più alto numero di lesbiche pro capite al mondo. Clima orrendo. Baci, tuo figlio*

2

Al bed and breakfast, guardo i depliant sul tavolino. Go kart, museo Bronte, La Falconeria. Poi leggo: *Yorkshire's Premiere Show Cave.*

3

È tutto immerso in una luce verde e umida. Sono in fondo alla White Scar Cave, nella Battlefield Cavern. Quest'area è stata allungo accessibile ai soli alpinisti coraggiosi e preparati, ma ora hanno scavato un collegamento sotterraneo pavimentato perché tutti possano apprezzarlo. Ci vivono molte creature prive di vista. Mi fermo ad ammirare la formazione calcarea bianca che pare un volto umano se lo guardi da certi angoli, strizzando bene gli occhi.

4

Vicino alla cascata qualcuno ha lasciato una bottiglia di latte locale: piena, da due litri. Se dovessi vivere in una caverna, per nascondermi dall'esercito americano, per esempio, non sceglierei questa.

Tutti pensavano che Osama bin Laden vivesse in una caverna ma poi si è saputo che aveva una casa.

Alcuni bambini in gita scolastica hanno trovato una formazione che ricorda i genitali femminili.

Comincio a sentirmi in trappola.

La guida turistica spiega che una volta una coppia si è sposata nella caverna. Il vestito di lei non si è macchiato.

L'odore quaggiù mi ricorda l'entrata di casa mia a Londra.

Sento che non ne uscirò mai.

QUARTA STAGIONE

1

È il sette agosto e sono tornato al mio bar preferito, La Caverna. Il barista turco è arrabbiato perché in tv ammazzano i manifestanti siriani che vogliono libertà.

Dei giovani tirano pietre che finiscono fuori campo.

"Siria e Turchia, siamo vicini," dice.

La tv dice: "Sanno cosa non vogliono ma non sanno cosa vogliono."

2

Ultim'ora.

3

Vengo avvisato che La Caverna non è sicura. Il barista ha preso un palo di legno con uncino, che serve a tirar giù la saracinesca a grata. Lo tiene come una mazza da baseball e esce. La saracinesca sbatte in un clangore di metallo.

Le camionette della polizia, al loro passaggio, ci gettano addosso una rete di luci bianche e azzurre. Per strada, un giovane lancia un mattone.

Il tg mostra dei giovani che lanciano mattoni, e delle immagini di Curry's Digital, su in strada: hanno rubato tutti i televisori. La vetrina è sfondata e dentro è tutto nero. Poi mostrano degli autobus rossi in fiamme. Poi un negozio di mobili e delle case, sempre in fiamme.

Il barista dice che deve spegnere televisori e luci per motivi di sicurezza. Mi conduce al buio fino in fondo alla caverna. Mi porta dell'altro tè, appena fatto. Lo posa e accende una candela.

4

I commercianti di zona sono tutti in strada con armi di fortuna. La caverna ogni

girlfriend: *Hello Mum! I am in Hebden Bridge. There are more lesbians per capita here than any other town in the world. Very bad weather, also. Love, Yr Son*

2

In my bed and breakfast, I look at the pamphlets on the coffee table. The Falconry, Go-Karting, The Bronte Museum. Then I see the words: *Yorkshire's Premiere Show Cave.*

3

Everything is washed in wet, green light. I am at the far end of White Scar Cave, in Battlefield Cavern. For a long time, this area was only accessible by brave and skilled climbers, but now they have drilled a connecting hole and laid decking so everyone can enjoy it. Many blind creatures live here. I admire the white calcite formation that looks like a human face if you try very hard to see it.

4

Near the waterfall, just beyond the cordon after which the cave is no longer lit, someone has left a full bottle of local milk. If I were to live in a cave, hiding from the American military, for example, then I would not live here.

Everyone thought Osama bin Laden was living in a cave but it turned out he was living in a house.

Some schoolchildren have found a formation that resembles female genitals.

I start to feel trapped.

The tour guide explains that a couple once got married in Battlefield Cavern. Her wedding dress remained spotlesss, we are told.

The smell in here reminds me of the communal stairwell in my flat in London.

I am worried I will never get out.

FOURTH SEASON

1

It is August the 7th and I am back in my favorite cafe-bar, The Long Dark Cave. The Turkish bartender, my friend, is angry because Syrian protestors are being killed in pursuit of freedom on the television.

"Syria and Turkey, we are neighbors," he says.

We see young men throw rocks that land off-camera.

The TV says: "They know what they don't want, but they don't know what they want."

2

There is breaking news.

3

I am told it is not safe in The Long Dark Cave. The bartender has a wooden pole with a hook on the end for pulling down the metal shutter. He holds it like a baseball bat and goes outside. I listen to the mesh rattle as it comes down.

Police vans throw a net of blue and white light across us as they pass. In the street, a young man is holding a half brick.

The news shows young men holding half bricks and footage of Curry's Digital, up the road, with all the TVs gone. The display window is smashed, and it's black inside. Then the news shows red buses on fire. Then a furniture store and homes on fire.

The bartender says he must turn the televisions and lights off for security. He ushers me into darkness at the back of the cave. He brings me fresh tea. He tells me to stay where I am.

4

Local business owners are out in the street with homemade weapons. The cave occasionally fills with blue light. The TVs hang like bats from the ceiling. I would like to turn them on. I am alone in the cave, holding my keys.

Glass smashes somewhere. I have only a limited view of the outside—a rectangle semi-obscured by the mesh shutter. I see a group of waiters standing in the middle of the road, holding sticks. One man snaps a TO LET sign to use the wooden stake as a weapon. Then they see something I can't see and all run left.

I fire my device.

A screen warms up. It is the soap opera.

A woman yells in another language. I am glad to see her.

Her nails are all broken.

She has scratches on her cheeks.

There has been some kind of accident.

tanto si riempie di luce azzurra. Le tv stanno appese ai soffitti come pipistrelli. Vorrei accenderle. Sono solo nella caverna, tengo in mano le mie chiavi.

Rumori di vetri sfasciati. Ho una visione limitata dell'esterno: un rettangolo semioscurato dalla saracinesca a grata. Vedo un gruppo di camerieri in piedi in mezzo alla strada, bastoni in mano. Un uomo sta smontando un cartello AFFITTASI per usare la tavola di legno come arma. Poi vedono qualcosa che io non vedo e corrono tutti verso sinistra.

Premo il mio aggeggio.

Si accende uno schermo. È la soap opera.

Una donna grida in un'altra lingua.

Ha le unghie spezzate.

È successo qualcosa.

FOUR SEASONS,
TWO SUMMERS

translated into English by VENDELA VIDA

1

STOCKHOLM. I'M AT the Bar Riche, waiting for Ulrika, who was an au pair for my neighbor's family. This was back when I was ten-eleven-twelve?, growing up in Hailey, Idaho. Ulrika liked my mom and often, on her days off, came to help her in the garden. My mom was once married to a Swede—so they had that connection, the connection of having loved Swedish men. Then one fall night, at around midnight, the doorbell rang, and it was Ulrika standing on the doormat with two suitcases. I know because I answered the door when my mom didn't hear the bell—her hearing was shot from listening to the TV turned up too high.

Ulrika told me she had had a fight with the father in the family whose kids she watched. He had asked her to put away four bottles of wine in the wine cellar. According to her, it was a spooky, cavelike place, with mirrors all around. She had refused to go down to the cellar so late at night, so he kicked her out of the house, kicked her out of her job. It struck me, even then, that this was a very strange story. When I was older, I asked my mother if her reluctance to go down into the cavelike cellar was a metaphor for something, and she assured me, unconvincingly, that it was not.

So here I am, many years later, with a child in my stomach—a boy?

a girl?—and a fiancé, Desmond, back in Hailey, Idaho, waiting to meet Ulrika. The Bar Riche was her choice. She likes the menus because they're designed by an artist she admires. This is what she told me on the phone. She didn't say his name, though, so I turn over the menus, searching, and staring at the illustrations of animals holding remote controls. There's a mouse, a seal, and a monkey, each with a remote control. On the restaurant wall is a blown-up photograph of the Bates Motel with a sign that says NO VACANCY.

Wine glasses hang upside down like bats from elaborate racks that I originally mistook for chandeliers. Around me sit women with shopping bags (it's sale season in Stockholm) and light leather jackets, even though it's July and warm. The Swedes love their leather. On the television, the royal family is sitting on a lawn in front of an outdoor stage while various performers come up and sing.

"What's going on?" I ask the bartender, who, beneath her long bangs, seems riveted by the show.

"It's the crown princess Victoria's birthday," she tells me. "It's her party."

"Oh," I say.

"Everyone loves her," she says, looking at the screen. "She just had a baby," she adds, and looks at my stomach, as though indicating that now I have something in common with the crown princess of Sweden.

I watch for a moment and see she is quite likeable. But the performances she has to endure! There's a woman in a low-cut dress singing a sexy song to the princess and her family. Princess Victoria sits in the first row with her husband, her parents—the king and queen—and her sister and her boyfriend. It strikes me as a little strange that they all have to sit in the sunshine and watch this woman sing about a hot love affair while the camera pans over their faces. Victoria smiles kindly throughout, and, at the end, claps. Next up are three men in white pants, singing like a barbershop quartet. This is even more strange than the sexy soloist. I feel uncomfortable for everyone on the TV screen, even though they don't look uncomfortable.

While I wait for Ulrika, my hand fumbles with a letter opener, an old-fashioned one, that I stole yesterday. I don't know if I knew at the time that I was stealing it, but after I discovered it in my pocket, I didn't give it back, so I suppose that counts as theft. I was visiting my mother's first

husband, whom I'd never met before. He got in touch with me after my mother's funeral, introducing himself and offering his condolences.

So I came to Sweden to meet him, and to see Ulrika, too. I figured it was the right time, before I had a baby and my life changed forever, etc., etc., blah blah blah, platitudes. Besides, I had exhausted everyone around me with my grief. Even my fiancé, a horse lover and a very patient man, seemed trampled and tired by my pain.

2

My mother's first husband, Ulf, wrote to me that he had two houses, one in Stockholm and one in the countryside. Yesterday, I took the train to the stop he indicated was close to his country house and then followed his directions. I had expected him to be a man of means—two houses!—and imagined we'd sit on a deck by a lake while drinking from Orefors glasses. But when I finally arrived at his summer cottage, I saw it was exactly that: a cottage. I called out as I approached and a shirtless man with a tanned and rather large belly and very long white hair came out to greet me. "Hej!" he called out, and then said, "Hello," as though he needed to translate.

The cottage had no electricity, no bathroom, and he explained to me that he took the train out here each May and stayed until October. Sitting across from him at the outdoor table, I could smell he didn't have a shower either. Four months without a shower. I could be thankful I was visiting in July, not later in his stay.

He was a kind and wistful man, a retired director of transportation with good English, and we had a cordial conversation while we drank coffee from dirty cups. As he spoke about his own mother, I wondered what I'd hoped to discover coming all this way, or if really I had just wanted another person to bleed my sadness onto.

We talked for an hour about his children from his third and final wife (final, he explained, because he wore fake teeth, and what woman would have him now?). Two of the girls were living in Turkey and one in London. He showed me photos—all three girls had dark hair and light eyes, and all were pretty. But as with any set of three pretty sisters, there was one who was the most beautiful, and I wondered how her life had been different. Then I wondered how my life would have been different and if I would have been that pretty if Ulf had been my father.

Ulf must have seen on my face that my mind was somewhere else, but he mistakenly assumed I was bored instead of the opposite: I was so engaged that I was trying to exist in the world of him and his beautiful girls. He asked me if I wanted to go inside the cabin so he could give me a tour.

I said of course. The inside of the cottage was crammed with memorabilia—with diaries, old theater magazines, an ancient loom, a thousand plates that relatives had once eaten on, ten harmonicas, a small bed that seemed inefficient for a man of his weight. On his dresser, I also spotted my mother.

Three photos of her on their wedding day. Who kept photos of their first wife on their dresser? I could tell by their position that they had always been there—he hadn't just put them up for me. He had done little to prepare for my visit—not even put on a shirt. In one of the photos, snow is falling heavily on the newlyweds. I never knew there had been snow on the day they married. My mother had always told me it had been sunny and warm.

Ulf opened a chest and inside were hundreds of letters, all still in their original envelopes. All bore my mother's large and legible handwriting. She had been a schoolteacher and wrote every word as though she were writing on a blackboard. Each of the letters had been opened carefully with a letter opener, each letter replaced inside its original envelope. Ulf was very organized for being such a messy-looking man.

I asked him if I might be able to read one of the letters. "To understand my mother better," I explained.

"Sure," he said, but I could tell he wanted to say "No."

"Just one," I said.

"Of course," he said, but I could tell he wanted to say, "Yes, just one."

So I carefully fingered my hand down to the middle of the pile and picked out a letter.

She had written on airmail paper so thin I felt it might crumple in my hands. The letter came from a time when she and Ulf were dating long-distance. She was teaching in Washington, DC, and he was working in Stockholm. As I read the letter, something strange happened: I felt as if I were inside my mother's body. As she described her students, and her day, and the meal she'd had with friends afterward, I could see the well-groomed kids through her eyes, and in my mouth, I could taste the hamburger she ate for dinner. I put the letter back in its envelope. I didn't need to read another letter—I felt so good, so connected to her, I didn't want to risk not feeling that way.

As Ulf closed the chest, I noticed a letter opener he kept on the table. This was the opener he had no doubt used to open all the letters from my mother—including the very letter that had given me access to her life a moment ago. Like everything in the cabin, the letter opener was very old; it had once been silver but now looked bronze. I pushed a button on its side and a dull blade extended, then I pushed the button again and it retracted. I slipped the opener into my pocket.

After we'd said goodbye and I'd turned to leave, Ulf called after me: "One more thing," he said. I was sure he'd ask for the letter opener back. Instead he said: "Would you mind cutting my hair?"

He found a pair of scissors and sat in the garden while I stood behind him and trimmed his hair until it stuck up from his head like little antennae. He sighed each time I cut off a lock, as though it had weighed him down physically. Cutting his hair felt very intimate, as though we were exchanging an enormous secret. When I was finished I walked to face him and examined my work. Not bad, I thought, about the hair. But I also saw that I had been mistaken about him—he was not as fat or as old or disheveled as I had originally taken him to be. He was a man who had once loved my mother, and still did. She had left many heartbroken, so he was not alone.

3

I know I arrived at the Bar Riche early, and the problem with arriving early is that now that it's still before the time Ulrika and I had arranged to meet, I can't help but feel she's late.

The bartender is having trouble with the television—it keeps turning off, then on, and off again, as though someone is messing with it. "Maybe it's the animals," I say to her, and point to the monkey and bat on the menu, balancing their remote controls. She stares at me, confused. When the television turns back on, she explains to me that Queen Victoria's sister has a new boyfriend. "We first met him at the baby's christening," she says, turning her attention to the man seated in the first row on the television set.

At first I think that by "we" she means she's met him, but then

I understand. The TV is a conduit into everyone's lives. "She was engaged before," the bartender continues, "but he was found by the newspapers to be out with another girl."

"That's too bad," I say.

"She had to move to America, to New York," she says. "For a perpendicular life."

"You mean a new life?"

"No," the bartender says. "A perpendicular one."

I swivel in my bar chair to look at the large, blown-up photo of the Bates Motel. It says: VACANCY. I could have sworn that before it said there was none.

4

Two men share a bottle of rosé at the table near the bar. They are dressed in madras shorts and clashing shirts, the greenish hue of catacombs. This is what I've noticed about Stockholm: everyone dresses like the person they're meeting for a drink. The men who are friends both wear clashing clothes, the women who are friends both wear leather jackets, the man and the woman at the end of the bar both have small, contained tattoos on their arms. Everyone is a twin, a distinctly but discreetly different possibility.

I hear someone say, "Do I know you?" and then doubt myself. Who says that at a bar? It's an American man wearing a three-piece suit. He has a copy of the *Economist* in his hand.

"From college?" he says. "I lived two rooms down."

And then I remember him, and his name emerges slowly and then at once: Erik. With a *K*. That's how he would introduce himself then: "Erik with a *K*," like it was his full name.

And then another memory surfaces: the two of us going on a date to a student play. I vaguely remember wearing a spring dress I regretted—it was too long, the material too shiny. And I remember there being a reason we didn't kiss that night.

I think I see on his face that he's trying to remember too: Did we kiss? Maybe he's even wondering, *Why not?*, as I am now.

He sits on the bar stool next to me. He's more swollen looking and wider than he used to be, but not unhandsome. And because I'm suddenly nervous and prone to fidgeting when nervous, I find my hand pushing on the button on the letter opener until the blade extends. It's pointing toward him, as though I'm on the defensive.

But something else happens. Time in the bar stops and then gallops forward as though I have God's stopwatch and I can see what would have happened if we had kissed that night after the play. I see us married and living in an apartment in Brussels, and I work in the mayor's press office and he works for the same company he does now. He and I have a daughter, and I have much better clothes than the unfortunate dress I wore to the theater, much better dresses than I do now. I see it all, suddenly, as though it's playing for me on the TV above the bar. We are happy for five seasons—two summers, then bored for three months, and happy for two before we amicably decide to part ways, and then become vicious during the divorce.

I push the button and the blade retracts and we are once again two people who once knew each other, who once almost kissed, talking at a bar.

"Well," he eventually says, "I should be getting back to my family."

"Yes," I say. I wonder if he's seen what I've seen. It's so sudden, this parting.

5

The television turns off and then on again. The princess watches as more people perform, and the bartender watches the princess, and I watch the bartender until Ulrika arrives.

Her legs are narrow and her arms are short in comparison to her legs. She's wearing a violet jacket and a pleated skirt. Her once-long blond hair is cut to her shoulders and she looks like she's sweating.

"I biked here from work," she explains. She remains one of the most beautiful women I've known, and I'm not alone in noticing this. Several people in the bar stare directly at her, or else look at a mirror in which they can see her image reflected. I'm not just talking about the men. I believe women are less immune than men to another woman's beauty.

She tells me she is sorry about my mother, and apologizes for not making the funeral last summer.

"I wouldn't expect you to fly across the ocean for a funeral," I say.

I ask what she's doing now and she tells me she's working for a government program that's trying to figure out the best way for someone to die. "We try to make everything the best for our citizens here."

115

"What are you finding?" I ask.

"That they should be listening to music and that they should be surrounded by children."

"They should be forced to listen to music?" I ask.

"Yes," she says. "That will make them happiest."

But what if they don't want to listen to music? I ask. "My mother didn't have music."

"Well, it's best for them if they do." She leaves my mother out of it.

"Don't you think that's a form of torture if they don't want to? And should children really be watching them die?"

"Do you really want to argue about this now, when I haven't seen you for so long?"

I am agitated suddenly and try not to talk. In my pocket I press the button of the letter opener and turn it in Ulrika's direction, like a knife.

And then I know. I see it all. I see that she loved my mother, that they were, in fact, lovers. I know this now, that there was no incident with the neighbor and the wine bottles, that it wasn't a metaphor for anything. When the doorbell rang that autumn night it was Ulrika coming to my mother—my twice-divorced mother—to say "I've decided. I'm here."

I know this, and I know Ulrika loved her, and I can see a room of floral wallpaper and smell the not unpleasant scent of hair and starched sheets and touch a straw horse on a dresser and I know that they were happy. That there was a time in my mother's life when she was most happy, and Ulrika was most happy, and because I don't want to know how their happiness came to an end, I push the button and the blade of the letter opener retracts, and I listen to Ulrika, and watch as she gets out her sketchbook, and uses an eraserless pencil to illustrate for me the perfect room—"the ultimate room," she calls it—in which a person should die.

NOTES ON THE TRANSLATIONS

I.

Youssef Habchi El-Achkar was born in 1929, in the Lebanese village of Beit Chabab—situated in the high mountains. At that time, the village was also known for its church-bell industry, which might explain the abundance of churches there, disproportionate to the number of worshippers. In 1941, El-Achkar left the village and went to Beirut to study. He received degrees in philosophy and law, but never practiced. Instead he became a journalist, TV scriptwriter, and even a speech-writer for Raymond Eddé, presidential candidate in 1958, who later held many port-folios in the cabinet of President Fouad Chehab. Eddé was a Lebanese francophone whose skills in the Arabic language were lamentable. When the Lebanese Civil War broke out in 1975, El-Achkar decided to take his family back to Beit Chabab for safety. He stayed in the village until his death in 1992, but never lost his longing for the cosmopolitan, culturally vibrant Beirut that he experienced in the '60s and '70s.

There is a grand misconception about El-Achkar's work. In Lebanese literary discourse, he's often described as a writer of the periphery—but the truth is that he was a contemporary writer in exile from the contemporaneity of the city. The village, re-imagined as Kfarmalat, took center stage in his writing: an unfitting context for his experimental and philosophical style.

Youssef Habchi El-Achkar could well be considered a *kateeb moukhadram*—a term that has existed in Arabic for centuries, long before the widely used postmodern notions of hybridity and third space, referring to writers of the in-between, whether of generations, civilizations, languages, or movements. During his lifetime, El-Achkar witnessed the transition in the Arab world from an era dominated by poetry to an era of prose, and then from classical narrative, dominated by the shadow of Koranic language, to the Al-Nahda period, in which a new lucid and unconstrained style, influenced by Western modernity, was introduced by writers like Ahmad Shawqi, Gibran Khalil Gibran, and Mikha'il Na'ima. Like many of his contemporaries, El-Achkar, too, was influenced by European literature, but he also reached far beyond Western influences to Japanese and other world literatures.

When I asked his daughter, Maya, about her father's religious and political affiliations, she immediately responded: "He was against the war." "But people say," I replied, "that your father was an atheist, and his political affiliation was to a Pan-Arab politics." "*Pas du tout,*" she exclaimed. "My father never agreed with any of them. The closest he came to a political affiliation was writing speeches for Eddé—later, Eddé was exiled to France during the war. My father ran away from the war, but the war spread outward from Beirut and eventually it reached Beit Chabab. That

devastated him." When I inquired further about his beliefs, Maya said that her father was agnostic.

Religious symbolism, however, pervades his writing, the inevitable result of having lived in a culture where religion takes a predominant place in education and daily life. In a sense, yes, El-Achkar's work reads like a confession—not a religious confession but a psychological one. As in analysis, his characters speak in a series of intense and confined fragments, with a long line of secondary characters that appear in and out only to return to the main voice, a single inner voice that leaves a legion of whispers behind.

To choose to read El-Achkar is to read Arabic literature in its multiplicity of historical, political, and aesthetic influences and forms. I would go further and say there is no homogeneity in Arabic literature, a canon whose essence is hybridity, but which is bound together by an Arabic language that remains the strongest commonality between the region's sub-groups and the dominant Islamic culture.

What makes El-Achkar a great writer is his ability to suddenly turn a poetic description into a profound psychological statement about the human condition. In his work, all ends up in the realm of the psychological. El-Achkar transcends the war, or maybe even banalizes it, and transforms it into a mental state rather than a physical one. But it is this estrangement from human calamity that is most difficult for his characters. His characters become outsiders, and cannot help but retreat into a psychological angst and an existential struggle.

El-Achkar could well be the first contemporary Arab existentialist writer. I wouldn't be surprised if he was influenced by Jean-Paul Sartre's *La Nausée*, but existentialism could have also reached El-Achkar from the tenth-century Arab poet and philosopher Abu 'L-ala Al-Ma'arri, who asked to have this verse inscribed over his grave:

This wrong was by my father done
To me, but never by me to one.

Or maybe, simply, the roots of El-Achkar's existentialism began with his exodus from the city to Beit Chabab. But one thing is certain: El-Achkar's characters all take refuge from the void by overriding it with blaring, internal voices that overwhelm the calamity of war, much like the tolling of bells on the top of his village church.

—*Rawi Hage*

II.

I can only speak a tiny bit of French and I can't read it, so I thought I'd use an online translator to help. The opening sentence of Tristan Garcia's story came out as: "In coffee, comfortable chairs and tables hazel—maybe Formica—I touch the fingertips the table before me, unbeknownst to the bartender slumped against the marble column." The biggest problem—apart from the fact that the sentence made no sense—was the word *unbeknownst*. Was the narrator of this story really the sort of person who would say that? The French phrase from which it derived, *à l'insu*, sounded low-key, but how was I to know—perhaps, in French, it was comically archaic? Particularly since the story was built on character, not plot, these distinctions felt important. When I translated *à l'insu* on its own, it came out as: "without the knowledge." This seemed to be Google Translate trying to tell me something.

Having established, then, that my attempts at an authentic translation were doomed, I decided to give up on faithfulness altogether. From then on, when there was conflict between loyalty to the original text and my own instincts as a writer, I always let myself win.

Lebanon became London. The only things I kept were: a cafe with a girl, broken fingernails, civil war in the Middle East, and the structure. The only traditionally translated lines are spoken by the televisions. I hope that, despite all this, there's still a strong relationship between my version and the two that precede it.

—*Joe Dunthorne*

III.

I was given this with no context. It seemingly conveyed important secret information that had gotten more and more warped as different undercover spies passed it on from hand to hand. I've worked as a translator for nine years, and I know that books contain messages for foreign secret services that you shouldn't try to mess up. So I stick to my task, trying to give sentences a sense of wholeness, being very literal.

Maybe I messed up, though, where I decided to not translate the entire name of the bar—The Long Dark Cave. It'd sound fake in Italian: *La lunga caverna oscura/buia*. Awful. So I translated it as La Caverna, which'll remind the Italian reader of the Cavern, the Liverpudlian club where the Beatles used to play. It will thus send completely wrong undertones flying around the reader's ears.

One thing I always discuss with editor, translator, and friend Martina Testa, who's a master of the slacker writer's sound—she's worked on D.F. Wallace, Lethem, Whitehead, and the likes—is how much of a translation can be kept in English. I don't translate *stealth*, here, nor *buddy*. For "non-stealth," I use "non-stealth." I'm free to do so because she won't revise it. I just couldn't bring myself to write: "Di solito lo chiamo *amico*."

The Arab context made me want this story to sound like the Italian translation of *L'Etranger*. No, this is not true: what I followed was the casual, so-nineties style of the Italian publisher who brought the *McSweeney's* generation of writers to Italy: minimum fax. It was my first publisher, and I've done translation work for them. *Cioè non fa il puntino laser tipo fucile del cecchino* for "This means it will not fire a laser dot like a sniper rifle" is typical minimum fax translation style: it's colloquial and quintessentially minimumfaxian in avoiding any hiccup-y, bebop-like, Kerouac-style American tone, which is the translated American I grew up with, before encountering the nineties generation.

"Breaking News" I've translated as *Ultim'ora*, which means "Last Hour." That's what the Italian Sky Television newscast uses for breaking news, I think. But if you read it out of context it doesn't suggest news at all. What I was trying to figure out, while working on that sentence (those four intense seconds), is whether the expression *Ultim'ora* is already in every Italian's mind as "Breaking News," so that it actually sounds like *Edizione straordinaria* used to sound in old movies, when something extraordinary happened and a special evening paper was issued and a poor scruffy kid would scream those words at everyone who passed by.

Another thing I experimented with while working on this: I'm tired of using the *verbo essere*. So, for instance: "My hair is female hair on a male head" was translated: *I miei capelli: da donna su una testa da uomo*. I feel that the verb "to be" is mostly used for stating the drab and obvious. That character's hair wasn't worth a waste of *essere*.

The writing in this story is concise, so I've enjoyed making it more concise where possible: "I have my device in my handkerchief pocket" became *Ho l'aggeggio nel taschino*. *Aggeggio* is more like "thingy," but I don't care. And I don't care because writers are not translators; I don't think they're really interested in meaning, they're more interested in sound, which also means that when they know their writing is being translated, they're obviusly more interested in the possibilities of that new language than in the supposed (impossible) similarities between this new language and theirs.

I think like this. Different languages offer new combinations of sound and meaning. A song in B flat on a piano usually has a nice, round sound. A song in B flat on a guitar feels awkward.

—*Francesco Pacifico*

IV.

This is what I did when I got the Italian version of this story. I translated it word for word, using my memory of Italian from twenty years ago when I lived in Florence and drank the cheap red wine I was too young to order at bars in America, and met an Italian friend who bought me white sneakers so I could play tennis against him on a dusty clay court. That was twenty years ago and I have read Italian since then and have "kept it up" as they say, but it's been some time since my Italian was good enough to play tennis in. So I worked from memory and asked a native Italian speaker for help when I wasn't sure what a word meant, and, occasionally, I used a dictionary. I typed up the story in English and read it several times. I liked the story—I liked the longing it contained, the surprises—but Adam Thirlwell had suggested I translate the story and make it sound like something I could have written. The story as it was, and as translated more or less without a dictionary, didn't sound like something I had written.

So I read the story for the umpteenth time, and put it away. Certain images swirled in my head—a haircut, a bar with mirrors, a TV that goes on and off, bats, girls in violet blouses and pleated skirts, a foreign city, a meditation on time, a device that can change what people see, movement, an ending involving death. Then I wrote a story that to me felt like a story I would have written, one that was very much inspired by the story I had translated word for word.

What's interesting to me now, when reading the original story (which I wasn't privy to before, obviously), is that it mentions an ex-wife and an ex-wife dying. By the time the story reached the Italian version the word *ex-wife* was no longer there. But the idea of an ex-wife is something that was central to me when writing my version. I like to think that even if the word *ex-wife* didn't get passed along, it was passed along through the mood.

Now I want to tell you another story. I met a really extraordinary woman in Oslo yesterday: my Norwegian translator. She had been described to me as shy and beautiful and as someone who had once translated Thomas Pynchon and she was as intriguing to me in person as she had been in reputation.

Her office was a floor above the flat that Ibsen lived in at the end of his life. The flat is now a museum, and she had arranged for us to take a tour. Above Ibsen's desk is a large portrait of Strindberg. One might take this to imply that the two Scandinavian playwrights were friends—but the opposite is true. They were harsh critics of each other's plays, and Ibsen wanted to have a painting of his enemy over his desk to encourage him to do his best work.

I digress. the translator, who was dressed in a crisp red leather jacket, a turtleneck sweater, stylish jeans, and, like all Norwegians, boots, took me into her office where there were of course hundreds of books. Beside her desk was a tray with two glasses and a bottle of nail polish. Writers and translators are alike in this way—we need distractions from our work. On her desk was a book she was currently translating, an Indian novel, propped up and pinned open to the page she was laboring over. But her desk and office were also surrounded by other books related to the book she was translating—other novels set in India, nonfiction books about India. She held one that she was currently rereading—*A Fine Balance*, a favorite of mine as well—to her chest to show how much she loved it. And I understood that for a translator of her caliber, so much more goes into the translation than just a dictionary.

We talked about translations and she told me how one has to understand the tone of the book—how it helps inform whether "loud" or "quiet" words are used in the translation. She said this rather quietly. I thought about it as we parted ways, and as I followed the path that led from Ibsen's apartment to the hotel where he had lunch at the same time each and every day. The path is now embedded with quotes from his work—think of the stars embedded in Hollywood Boulevard—so that Norwegians step over his words as they walk. For me, this experiment worked in a not so dissimilar way. Certain words and phrases from Francesco Pacifico's translation served as stepping stones for me; they outlined the path I took.

—*Vendela Vida*

VII

СИМФОНИЯ N 2

a story in RUSSIAN *by* DANIIL KHARMS

ILLUSTRATORS, IN ORDER OF APPEARANCE

Mike Bertino, Ian Huebert, Erin Althea, Tim Lahan, Wesley Allsbrook, Brianna Harden.

2

SYMPHONY NO. 2

translated into English by GARY SHTEYNGART

SYMPHONIE N°2

translated into French by FRÉDÉRIC BEIGBEDER

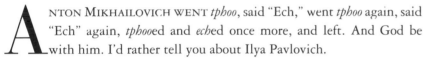

ANTON MIKHAILOVICH WENT *tphoo*, said "Ech," went *tphoo* again, said "Ech" again, *tphoo*ed and *ech*ed once more, and left. And God be with him. I'd rather tell you about Ilya Pavlovich.

Ilya Pavlovich was born in 1983 in Petersburg. When he was a little boy he was brought to Vermont where he went to the Montessori school in Burlington. Then he worked in some kind of bookstore, then he did something else, and then Borders closed. So he emigrated to Canada. And God be with him. I'd rather tell you about Anna Ignatevna.

But it's not easy to tell you about Anna Ignatevna. First, I don't know much about her, and second I just fell off my chair and forgot what I was going to say. Maybe I should just tell you about myself.

I'm pretty tall, and I'm not dumb. I dress smartly and I don't drink. I don't play Xbox but I love the ladies. And the ladies love me. They love it when I'm out with them. Serafima Izmailovna repeatedly invited me over to her crib, and Zinaida Yakovlevna also let it be known that she's always ready to do me. Oh, but what I really want to tell you about is this amusing incident that happened with Marina Petrovna. It's kind of an ordinary incident, but amusing nonetheless, because thanks to me Marina Petrovna became as bald as the palm of my hand. This is how it happened: I came over to Marina Petrovna and BAM!—she was bald. That's it.

ANTOINE MICHEL FIT *tchoum*, dit "ahh," fit *tchoum* encore, dit "ahh" de nouveau, éternua et inspira une nouvelle fois, puis disparut de ce texte. Bon débarras. Je préfère vous parler d'Isaac Polski.

Isaac Polski est né en 1933 à Varsovie. Quand c'était un petit garçon on l'enferma dans son quartier. Puis il fit un long voyage en train, puis fit autre chose, et à ce moment-là toute sa famille disparut en fumée. Alors il émigra au Canada. Que Dieu soit avec lui. Je préfère vous parler d'Anne de la Rocheposay.

Mais il n'est pas facile de vous parler d'elle. D'abord je ne la connais pas personnellement, et ensuite je viens de tomber de ma chaise et j'ai oublié ce que j'allais dire. Peut-être que je ferais mieux de vous parler de moi.

Je suis assez grand et pas trop con. Je m'habille affreusement mal mais bois tout le temps, j'ai arrêté la coke mais j'aime les filles. Et les filles m'adorent. Elles adorent quand je leur parle, et encore plus quand j'arrête de leur parler. Marie de la Rochefoucauld m'a souvent invité dans son château, et sa petite soeur m'a laissé entendre qu'elle était toujours prête à me faire une lap dance (j'attends toujours). Oh, mais le truc que je veux vraiment vous raconter c'est mon problème avec Joséphine. Ce n'est pas très grave, mais quand meme marrant, parce que, enfin, bon, voilà: Joséphine est un garçon. Voilà ce qui s'est passé: je suis allé chez ma cousine et BOUM!—ce serait plus honnête si elle s'appelait Joseph. Franchement.

3

SECOND SYMPHONY

translated into English by CHLOE HOOPER

I THINK I HEAR the metronome. I am sure I hear it and it is speeding up, thrumming like the sound of the cavalry come to set me loose. The hoofs clatter on and on, then turn to footsteps. One, two, one, two as someone comes to deliver my banquet of chaff. Are they coming? I'd prefer we talk of something else, say, Anne de la Rocheposay.

But talking about her is not a simple matter. For a start, I never actually knew her, and in any case I have just fallen off my chair, or rather if they'd give me a chair I'd fall off it, and I've forgotten what I was going to say. Am I right in thinking I'd be better at telling you about myself?

I am tall enough and not too stupid. I dress hideously, but then, I drink all the time. I have stopped the cocaine, but I can't give up girls. Girls love me. They love it when I talk to them, and love it even more when I permit them to talk to me. Marie de la Rochefoucauld often invited me into her castle, and her little sister let it be understood that she was always ready to be my private dancer. (I am still waiting.) Oh, but the thing I really want to tell you about is my assignation with Josephine; it is not so serious, in truth, a farce: I went to my cousin's house—first cousin—and very slowly Josephine unpicked her décolletage and its variety of stuffings, and then from behind the embroidery of her sweetly scented handkerchief I saw that really she should call herself Joseph. And me so hungry.

SYMFONIE NR. 2

translated into Dutch by ARNON GRUNBERG

DE BOVENBUREN ZIJN zo luidruchtig als een stel uitgehongerde paarden. Wat hebben ze onder hun voeten? Hoeven? Hoge hakken? Hebben ze nog nooit van pantoffels gehoord?

Ik kom binnen en trek mijn pantoffels aan. Komt er bezoek, roep ik: "Schoenen uit." Dat is empathie. Humanisme is een pantoffel.

Maar wat kun je van paarden verwachten? Hooi. Wortels. Meer hebben ze niet in hun hoofd.

Af en toe een appel.

Om de week duw ik een appel door de brievenbus van de bovenburen. Om ze te laten weten: ik ben er ook nog.

Nu moeten we het even over mijn vrouw hebben. Anne de la Roche. Ik noem haar mama.

Over Anne de la Roche praten is niet makkelijk. De eerste keer dat ik haar zag was in een café in Buenos Aires. Anna de la Roche was net van haar stoel gevallen.

Nog diezelfde avond stelde ze me voor aan haar werkster.

*   *   *

Laat ik eerlijk zijn, ik heb weinig kleren en weinig haar. Aantrekkelijk ben ik nooit geweest, maar ik kan schaken, ik spreek vijf talen vloeiend, en citeer moeiteloos de grote filosofen en af en toe ook een kleintje. Zo heb ik mijn eerste vrouw ontmoet. Op een studiedag voor amateur-filosofen.

De gastvrouw was de vijftig al gepasseerd, maar ze had een aanzienlijk decolleté en toen ik naar de wc wilde zei ze: "Joseph, ik ben gestopt met cocaïne maar van de mannen kan ik niet afblijven."

Wat kan ik zeggen? Ik had gezonde eetlust. Altijd ook gehad. Dat is wat ik ben, gezonde eetlust. De rest? Stilte en voetnoten.

TANGO

translated into English by IVAN VLADISLAVIĆ

WHEN THE WOMAN UPSTAIRS comes home, I'm waiting at my own front door. Anna de la Roche. That's what it says on her letter-box in the lobby. Her heels click on the parquet. I have carpets on my floors, but even so I always put on slippers to spare the downstairs neighbors. I am doubly considerate; Anna de la Roche not at all.

She drops her handbag in the hallway and I can't help looking up at the ceiling. The clicking of her heels sounds like the ratchet of a little engine in my pelvis. It sets me in motion. Now she's on her way to the liquor cabinet and I go too, not so much in her footsteps as under her heels.

Before I bought this place, my friend Gretchen, who knows the apartment lifestyle, advised me to come here in the evening to make sure it wasn't noisy. People are at work during the day, she said. It's what they get up to at night that will annoy you.

I shouldn't have scoffed at the idea. In an apartment building, the soundtrack is everything. When my neighbor on the left grinds his coffee beans in the morning, I fancy I can smell the aroma and it perks me up. The genteel squeaking of bedsprings from the Van Blerks—my neighbors on the right—reassures me. But Anna de la Roche, overhead, drives me mad.

* * *

TANGO

translated into Portuguese by JOSÉ LUÍS PEIXOTO

QUANDO A MULHER DO andar de cima chega a casa, estou à espera à minha porta. Anna de la Roche. É isso que está escrito na caixa do correio, à entrada do prédio. Os seus saltos repenicam no soalho. Tenho alcatifas mas, ainda assim, uso sempre chinelos para poupar os vizinhos de baixo. Tenho dupla consideração, Anna de la Roche não tem nenhuma.

Pousa a mala na entrada de casa, não consigo impedir um olhar para o tecto. O repenicar dos saltos parece o matraquear de um pequeno motor no meu pélvis. Põe-me em movimento. Agora, vai a caminho do armário das bebidas e eu vou também, não tanto a seguir-lhe os passos como por baixo deles.

Antes de comprar, a minha amiga Gretchen, que conhece este tipo de aparta-mentos, aconselhou-me a vir de noite para garantir que não era barulhento. As pessoas trabalham durante o dia, disse ela. É o que fazem à noite que te irá inco-modar.

Eu não devia ter rejeitado logo a ideia. Num edifício de apartamentos, a banda sonora é tudo. Quando o meu vizinho da esquerda mói os seus grãos de café de manhã, acho que sou capaz de sentir o aroma e isso desperta-me. O chiar cordial das molas da cama de Van Blerks—o meu vizinho da direita—reconforta-me. Mas Anna de la Roche, por cima, enlouquece-me.

* * *

De vez em quando, encontro uma cenoura na minha caixa do correio. A palidez e a fibra da raiz de uma planta, o tipo de coisa que se daria a um pónei na quinta pedagógica. Ela estará por detrás disto? Convenci-me a mim próprio que sim.

Compro as minha mercearias no pequeno centro comercial ao fundo da rua. Uma vez, fizeram lá umas modificações, tentaram disfarçá-lo de hipermercado, mas continuou a ser um centro comercial de bairro, com dois andares e uma dúzia de lojas.

Estava a falar com Manny dos Santos, que tem a loja de chocolates do andar de cima. Disse-lhe que estava surpreendido por ver o seu negócio a prosperar durante a recessão. Os chocolates são, de certeza, um luxo.

Manny é o nosso filósofo amador e aproveita cada oportunidade para me ensinar algo sobre o mundo.

No centro comercial, parece que há camadas em que nunca reparei. *Strata* foi a palavra que usou. As pessoas mais pobres dos subúrbios envolventes chegam da rua e entram para o rés-do-chão. É por isso que a loja de bebidas é lá em baixo, e também o bar, e o restaurante de *fast food*. Também o barbeiro e a tasca dos hambúrgueres. As pessoas mais ricas—reparei que ele disse "mais ricas" e "mais pobres" e não apenas "ricas" e "pobres," mas mesmo assim fiquei sentido—conduzem pela rampa ao lado do edifício para o estacionamento superior e entram pelo andar de cima. Dessa maneira, as donas de casa não são perturbadas pelos homens à porta do *pub* e não têm dificuldade de empurrar os carrinhos de compras até aos seus carros. As lojas do andar de cima têm mais classe, disse ele. Para além da mercearia, há a florista e a limpeza a seco, a charcutaria e o café.

Está claro, disse Mandy, estes dois *strata* estão ligados. As pessoas mais pobres vêm cá acima buscar pão e leite, e voltam lá para baixo, onde saem para a rua. Um homem como tu vai lá a baixo buscar uma garrafa de vinho, volta a subir para comprar uma dúzia de rosas para a sua esposa, entra no carro e vai-se embora.

Da maneira como o Manny explicou, o pequeno centro comercial parecia de repente um gráfico de computador: um vívido modelo económico da nossa sociedade desigual.

Esta noite, Anna de la Roche está a dançar outra vez. É claro que eu gostaria de ir lá a cima, mas sou apenas uma nota de rodapé na sua história. Um voluntário de chinelos. O meu papel é seguir a sua dança, aqui em baixo, sem a pisar.

Every now and then, I find a carrot in my letterbox. A pale, fibrous root vegetable, the sort of thing you would feed a pony at the petting zoo. Is she behind this? I've convinced myself she is.

I buy my groceries at the Bargain Center down the road. They made some alterations there once, tried to dress it up as a mall, but it's still just a neighborhood shopping center with a dozen shops on two stories.

I was talking to Manny dos Santos, who has the chocolate shop on the top floor. I said I was surprised to see his business thriving in the recession. Surely chocolates are a luxury.

Manny is our amateur philosopher, and he welcomes every opportunity to teach me something about the world.

It seems there are layers to the Bargain Center that I have never perceived. *Strata* is the word he used. The poorer people from the surrounding suburbs walk in off the street on the ground floor. That's why the bottle store is down there, and the Keg and Tankard, and the tote. Also the barbershop and the burger joint. The richer people—I noticed that he said richer and poorer, rather than rich and poor, but even so I was hurt—drive up the ramp at the side of the building to the elevated parking garage and they walk in on the top floor. That way the housewives aren't pestered by the men outside the pub and don't have trouble pushing their trolleys back to their cars. The shops on the top floor have more class, he said. Besides the grocer, there's the florist and the dry cleaner, the delicatessen and the coffee shop.

Of course, said Manny, these two *strata* are connected. The poorer people come up here for bread and milk, and then they go back down again and out into the street. And a man like you will go downstairs for a bottle of wine, and then come up again and buy a dozen roses for his wife, get into his car, and drive away.

The way Manny explained it, the Bargain Center suddenly looked like a computer graphic: a vivid economic model of our unequal society.

Tonight, again, Anna de la Roche is dancing. I would like to go upstairs, of course, but I am merely a footnote in her story. A volunteer in slippers. My part is to follow her lead, here below, and not stand on her toes.

NOTES ON THE TRANSLATIONS

I.

You know what the Italians say: *Traduttore, traditore*. So I just did my job: to betray all of you guys. Please forgive me.

—*Frédéric Beigbeder*

II.

I have schoolgirl French, but that of a very dumb schoolgirl. So I used Google Translate and hijacked passing Francophiles to do a straight translation of Frédéric's translation. But under the circumstances this seemed redundant, and after learning more about Kharms's life, or at least his death (probably by starvation in Leningrad Prison's psychiatric ward during the siege), I decided on a "bio-translation," if that's not too impudent. The challenge in modernizing his work seems to be how to maintain the danger of the absurdity without trivializing the political context in which it was written.

—*Chloe Hooper*

III.

On April 4, 2012, Adam Thirlwell sent me Chloe Hooper's first translation of Kharms's piece. On April 10, Adam sent me a revised version of Chloe's translation. The difference between the April 4 and the April 10 translations was considerable. It was then that I realized how much liberty I can take as a "translator"—at least in this particular case.

Since Daniil Kharms was one of my first literary heroes, I tried above all to do justice to his work. Earlier this year, during a conference of literary translators in Ghent, Belgium, my French translator said: "My translation is 5 percent me, and 95 percent Grunberg." In this case, I would say the translation was 30 percent Hooper, 30 percent Kharms, 30 percent Grunberg, and 10 percent collective unconscious.

—*Arnon Grunberg*

IV.

My work on this took a roundabout route. After familiarizing myself with Grunberg's "Symphony No. 2" and living with it for a couple of weeks, I drafted my version without direct reference to the original. Then, to make sure I hadn't missed the point entirely, I went back and made a direct translation, which I used to draw my version closer to Grunberg's. The liberties I took make my piece more of an adaptation than a translation.

There was some happy chance involved in the subject matter. When this work began, I had just moved from a house into a flat. I was acutely aware of having neighbors close by, and especially upstairs, and so I was drawn to that aspect of the story.

The direction of my adaptation turned on a small distinction, as I suppose all translation does. In his story, Grunberg refers to the same woman as "Anne" and "Anna." Given a European pronunciation, there is not much to choose between the two, but in English "Anne" and "Anna" are two different women. I chose to go with Anna de la Roche, and the atmosphere she brought with her led me to Manny dos Santos and the Bargain Center.

The Bargain Center is the most obvious addition to the original. It localizes the story a little and takes the upstairs/downstairs idea further. Had I seen the whole chain earlier, I would have been tempted to leave this section out.

My inclination to adapt rather than translate was encouraged by the wry, elliptical qualities of the original. The fragmentary form also opened gaps I could occupy. I'm interested to see that the story was in a single paragraph until Grunberg broke it into three short sections. Knowing that, I may have been less inclined to digress.

I have never worked with another writer, but I have worked often with artists and photographers, writing something that accompanies or responds to a set of images. This process always has its tensions. On the one hand, I must welcome the imposition of the images, and absorb their atmospheres and perspectives. On the other, I have to resist being a mere illustrator. I've learned to work with images "in the corner of my eye," to embrace them and hold them at a distance at the same time. In retrospect, I seem to have approached "Symphony No. 2" in the same way. It takes two to tango.

—*Ivan Vladislavić*

V.

When I first read "Tango"—translating it in silence to myself—I thought that it wouldn't be a very difficult job to put it in Portuguese. The language seemed pretty straightforward. Only later, when I actually started translating it, did I realize that every translation brings dilemmas to be solved. Like the negative picture of anxiety of influence, this feeling could be described as anxiety of interpretation. The questions raised by the translation led me to think about what my ultimate goal should be: to be true to the original text, or to the Portuguese language and its specificities.

After considering several possibilities, I reached the conclusion that being true to the Portuguese language would be the most appropriate way of being true to the text itself. If it could be easily read in English, after all, I would be doing a poor job by making it hard to read in Portuguese.

I only reached this conclusion on the second draft. After that, I felt much more free to make changes.

Changes is probably a too strong word for what I actually did; I have just tried to solve problems in a creative way. In terms of translation, there is no other way to do so. For example, I had to find three Portuguese words that could express the difference between "Bargain Center," "mall," and "neighborhood shopping center." Also, I had to find a way to say "Keg and Tankard," "the tote," and "burger joint" without strangeness, since there is no strangeness to them in the English text I was translating from.

I had to make choices. Choices are always questionable.

Translation is never perfect, but nothing ever is. To translate is one of the most human activities that exists. We spend most of our time translating from one language to another: from pictures to words, from feelings to actions, from what we perceive of others to how we think. A translated text is never the original text, no matter how well translated it is, but oftentimes it is the only way we have to access it.

—*José Luís Peixoto*

VI.

What can I say? Translation #1 best!

—*Gary Shteyngart*

VIII

CIPELE

a story in SERBO-CROAT *by* DANILO KIŠ

ILLUSTRATORS, IN ORDER OF APPEARANCE

Wesley Allsbrook, Erin Althea, Mike Bertino, Brianna Harden, Ian Huebert.

THE SHOES

translated into English by ALEKSANDAR HEMON

MY SHOES, LYING NEXT to each other like two animals, suddenly became horribly elongated and shapeless; they took on the appearance of the things we'd watched every day for years, but then would notice abruptly, for no particular reason, with bewilderment, as if seeing them for the first time. That sensation—seeing something for the first time—did not surprise or scare me, however; I'd had an experience that came to my aid. I recalled a cash register in a bistro where I used to have an evening drink for years, and if someone had asked me not even what the register looked like but whether there had been one to begin with, I'd have said no or shrugged. Thus, one autumn evening, after three quarters of an hour waiting for Lillian, who'd said that she might be a bit late, I'd stopped by that bistro (which had been deliberately chosen for our rendezvous so that I could seek shelter in case of a storm and—which I would've never admitted to Lillian—step into if she didn't show up, as if entering a purgatory) and sat in the corner with a double cognac. And then, having realized that she would not come that night, tormented by jealousy and uncertainty, my spirit began "grasping for straws," my gaze stopping at things around me. Initially, everything seemed to be happening without the involvement of my consciousness, occupied with things more important than an ordinary cast-iron cash register, but my empty gaze was, I would soon realize, much more lucid, more purposeful, than my careless scanning of the little bistro when I'd excitedly anticipated

LOS ZAPATOS

translated into Spanish by ALAN PAULS

MIS ZAPATOS, ECHADOS uno junto al otro como dos animales, se volvieron horriblemente alargados y deformes, como esas cosas que miramos todos los días durante años pero recién advertimos de golpe, sin ninguna razón particular, con perplejidad, como si las viéramos por primera vez. Sin embargo, esa sensación—ver algo por primera vez—no me produjo sorpresa ni temor. Una vieja experiencia acudió en mi ayuda. Recordé la caja registradora de un bar donde solía tomar algo por las tardes durante años. Si alguien me hubiera preguntado no cómo era sino, para empezar, si había alguna caja registradora en el lugar, yo habría dicho que no, o me habría encogido de hombros. Así, una tarde de otoño, después de esperar durante tres cuartos de hora a Lilian, que había dicho que llegaría con algún retraso, fui a ese bar (lo había elegido a propósito para nuestro encuentro, cosa de tener un refugio a mano en caso de tormenta y—algo que jamás hubiera admitido ante Lilian—si ella no aparecía, entrar en él como quien entra en un purgatorio) y me senté en un rincón con un coñac doble. Y luego, una vez que comprendí que esa noche ella no vendría, atormentado por los celos y la incertidumbre, mi espíritu se puso a buscar una cuerda a la que aferrarse y mis ojos se detuvieron en las cosas que me rodeaban. Al principio todo parecía estar sucediendo sin la intervención de mi conciencia, ocupada en cosas más importantes que una caja registradora común y corriente, de hierro. Pero, como pronto lo comprendería, en mi mirada vacía había mucha más lucidez y decisión que en el despreocupado examen que había hecho del barcito mientras esperaba inquieto a Lilian. Por más absorto que estuviera pensando en ella, me di cuenta, siguiendo una rama del fluir de mi conciencia, de que veía esa vieja caja registradora por primera vez. Esculpidos como cúpulas y frisos en la tapa de niquel, los relieves le daban a esa estructura de hierro el aspecto de una catedral. La idea me intrigó, mi tormento y mi sufrimiento no se interrumpieron ni disminuyeron, y me di cuenta de que el descubrimiento de la registradora-catedral no era sino una consecuencia de la alienación de mi espíritu que, en ese momento de excitación, abordaba cosas que la autocomplacencia le había impedido advertir pero que revelaban ser necesarias, a la vez como refugio y como armazón. En realidad, no había nada necesario en esa registradora anticuada, salvo quizás el hecho de que mi espíritu, en un momento de debilidad, se hubiera aferrado a un objeto tan vulgar. La experiencia me decía que no había nada extraño en él. Más de una vez me había sucedido que recién comprendía una cara vista todos los días, largamente registrada, cuando la observaba con desinterés, en estado, por así decirlo, de ausencia.

De modo que (para volver a mi relato) miraba con asombro mis zapatos a la oscura luz de la luna y era como si tropezara por primera vez con algo cuyo sentido y propósito no podía entender. Por entonces vivía en una buhardilla y soñaba despierto—dormía en el piso, miserablemente—con París y con los libros que escribiría, libros donde todo mi pasado y mi presente se rendirían a la gracia de la composición. Aquella pequeña habitación con el techo en mansarda tenía un poder de desfiguración asombroso, casí mágico. A la noche, en ese cuarto iluminado por una pequeña lámpara, como sucede en el crepúsculo y a la luz de la luna, no sólo las cosas sufrían extrañas metamorfosis. También mis pensamientos, que se volvían irreales e informes.

El detalle que me distrajo del objeto en cuestión—el hecho de que estuviera durmiendo en el piso—no carecía de importancia para este proceso de desfiguración. Recostado en el piso, veía las cosas que me rodeaban desde una perspectiva que alteraba sustancialmente su apariencia. Veía la silla como si colgara del techo, y la ventana como si estuviera a la altura de algún piso superior imaginario. En una palabra, veía todo desde el punto de vista de una rana, que hace que las cosas adquieran un aire de superioridad casi maligno. Mis zapatos proyectaban una larga sombra, como si estuvieran en puntas de pie, aunque yo podía ver sus costados ante mí. Pero ese extraño par de animales no era del mismo tamaño, y me pareció que mientras yacieran paralelos, uno junto al otro, toda ilusión óptica sería imposible. Diferían en tamaño exactamente del mismo modo en que los machos de ciertos animales difieren de las hembras: uno erguía su cabeza, como en guardia; el otro, un poco más atrás, parecía imperturbable. Por

Lillian. However much I was absorbed in the thoughts of Lillian, I noticed, following a branch stream of consciousness, that I was seeing that ancient iron register for the first time. The reliefs shaped like domes and friezes on its nickel cover gave that iron structure the appearance of a cathedral. The thought intrigued me, the presence of torment and suffering neither discontinued nor diminished, and I realized that the discovery of the register-cathedral was but a consequence of the alienation of my spirit, which at the moment of excitement approached things it had not in its self-indulgence theretofore noticed, but that now revealed themselves as a necessity, as a refuge and a shell. In fact, there was nothing necessary about an old-fashioned register, except perhaps that my spirit attached itself in a moment of weakness to such a vulgar object. My experience insisted that there was nothing strange about any of it, as it had often happened that I'd comprehend a face I'd looked at every day and had long been aware of, while observing it disinterestedly and, so to speak, absently.

Thus I was (to return to the thing I am narrating) gazing with wonder at my shoes, through the air of murky moonlight, as if encountering for the first time something whose meaning and purpose I could not understand. I lived back then in a garret and daydreamed—on the floor, in rags—about Paris and books I would write, in which all of my past and present would be submitted to the grace of composition. That little room under the mansard roof had an amazing, almost magical, power of disfiguration. At night, in that room lit by a small lamp, as by sunset and moonlight, not only did the things undergo a strange metamorphosis, but my thoughts did as well: they became unreal and shapeless.

The detail that distracted me from the object I am talking about, the fact of my sleeping on the floor, was not without significance in this process of disfiguration. For, recumbent on the floor, I saw things around me from an angle that substantially changed their appearance. Thus I would see the chair as if hanging from the low ceiling, and the window as if belonging to some imaginary upper floor: in a word, I saw everything from a frog's point of view, from which things attain a superior and almost vicious look and attitude. My shoes had a long shadow as if standing on their toes, even if I could clearly discern their sides facing me. But that strange pair of animals were not of the same size, and it seemed to me that any possibility of an optical delusion was excluded as they lay parallel to each other. They differed in size exactly as the males of some animals differ from the females:

one raised its head, as if cautious; the other one, half a body behind, was seemingly unperturbed. I wanted to believe for an instant they were two black cats, whose presence oppressed me. For they were not peaceful but creeping toward me with their eyes shiny and sharp as a razor, even if their careful approach did not reduce the space between us. In the end I had to convince myself that those were just my worn-out shoes. At the same time I had to convince myself that only now was I perceiving them not as objects but rather as some kind of creatures and, at that, as creatures I had no connection to. With all my might I was trying to recognize myself in that shapeless grayblack lump, to identify my shapes, or any relation to me that would make the shoes graspable. I could only remember I'd bought them not so long ago (but wore them out quickly gallivanting along the city's periphery in pursuit of stimulations) and they squeezed my feet and bred brutal blisters until I disposed of the torment with a swift move: with two razor cuts across the toe section, where the blisters were, I produced two openings to relieve the pressure. That moment reminded me that I'd been at war with those shoes, in fact, from our first encounter. One could say even before the first encounter. The very thought of shopping induced discomfort and fear in me, as new shoes always tortured me like Inquisition boots, bloodying the skin of my heels. But when I thought it through, I felt that I was revengeful and unjust. For I could, if I chose, remember some pleasant moments, if I was not so prone to self-denial…

I'd bought them suddenly, saying nothing to Lillian about my intention to acquire new footwear. True, she'd pretended she wasn't embarrassed going out with me, unshaven and wearing Charlie Chaplin shoes (on the contrary, she claimed she liked it, as her dad thought I was a painter, which must have flattered her), but she couldn't force me to accompany her to the theater or concerts. None of my arguments could convince her that I could not go the theater or concerts "like this," which primarily referred to my shoes. She would start imputing to me that I didn't want to go to the concerts *because of her*, while I contended I could not go *with her*, but I could alone…

"I was afraid you'd buy some flatnoses, as I know you don't like pointy shoes, but these are nice. We'll go to the theater tomorrow. I want to see *Behind the Closed Doors*," she'd exclaimed, glancing at my feet, trying to say it all in one breath, as if saying something that was self-evident—that we would be attending the theater.

un momento quise creer que eran dos gatos negros cuya presencia me angustiaba. Porque no eran pacíficos; se arrastraban hacia mí con sus ojos brillantes y filosos como navajas, aun cuando al acercarse no acortaran la distancia que nos separaba. Al final tuve que convencerme de que no eran más que mis zapatos gastados. Y a la vez tuve que convencerme de que recién ahora los percibía, no como objetos sino más bien como criaturas de alguna clase, criaturas con las que no tenía ningún tipo de conexión. Trataba con todas mis fuerzas de reconocerme a mí mismo en ese oscuro bulto amorfo, identificar mis formas o cualquier relación que tuvieran conmigo que me permitiera comprender esos zapatos. Sólo recordaba que los había comprado hacía no mucho tiempo (pero los había usado enseguida para vagabundear por los márgenes de la ciudad en busca de estímulos) y que me apretaban y me sacaron unas ampollas brutales, tormento del que me liberé con una rápida maniobra: haciendo dos cortes de navaja en la parte de los dedos, donde estaban las ampollas, y abriendo dos agujeros para aliviar la presión. Eso me recordó que había estado en guerra con esos zapatos apenas los conocí; incluso desde antes de conocerlos. La sola idea de tener que comprarlos me inquietaba y daba miedo, dado que los zapatos nuevos siempre me han torturado como las botas de la Inquisición, haciéndome sangrar los talones. Pero cuando lo pensé bien, sentí que había sido rencoroso e injusto. Porque si quería, si no cedía a mi tendencia al sacrificio, también podía recordar algunos momentos agradables…

Los había comprado de golpe, sin decirle a Lillian que tenía intenciones de adquirir zapatos nuevos. Es cierto: ella siempre había aparentado no sentirse incómoda cuando salía conmigo y yo iba sin afeitar, con unos zapatos estilo Chaplin; al contrario: decía que le gustaba porque su padre pensaba que yo era pintor, y eso debía halagarla. Pero no conseguía que la acompañara al teatro o a un concierto. No había manera de convencerla de que no podía ir al teatro o a un concierto "así," es decir con zapatos como ésos. Empezó a acusarme de no querer ir a conciertos por ella, y yo sostenía que con ella no podía, pero podía ir solo…

"Tenía miedo de que te compraras una de esas cosas chatas y aplastadas, porque sé que no te gustan los zapatos en punta. Pero éstos son lindos. Mañana vamos al teatro. Quiero ver *Behind the Closed Doors*," exclamó mirándome los pies, tratando de decirlo todo de un tirón, como si el hecho de ir juntos al teatro fuera algo obvio.

"Los voy a tajear," le dije, tan tranquilo como ella. "Les voy a hacer una cesárea, ya no los soporto más." Se opuso ferozmente, por supuesto, como si fuera una cuestión de vida o muerte, porque se dio cuenta de que estaba dispuesto a hacerlo. Luego nos separamos; ella sostenía que yo estaba buscando una excusa para no llevarla al teatro.

Empecé a recordar todos esos momentos que me conectaban con los zapatos que ahora yacían sobre mí en una esquina, proyectando su sombra larga y extrañamente intrincada contra el piso. Y finalmente—después de recordar las muchas caminatas que habíamos hecho con Lillian, cuando vagábamos a orillas del Danubio y nos metíamos en esos bares de los suburbios a bailar absurdos calipsos entre los parroquianos y las prostitutas; nuestros momentos de pasión en la buhardilla fría, donde nos sacábamos los zapatos sin prender la luz y nos entregábamos uno al otro en abrazos mudos que nos dejaban sin aliento; cómo el reloj del municipio anunciaba la hora de su partida y nosotros, apurados, buscábamos a tientas los zapatos en la oscuridad— decidí levantarme y prender la luz para dibujar con carbonilla esos zapatos monstruosos que de golpe se volvieron un mundo en sí mismos, un mundo verdaderamente distante y deforme, pero que con un poco de esfuerzo y voluntad podía parecer cercano y coherente. Se suponía que esa carbonilla vangoghiana haría el papel de mediador y dotaría de algún sentido a esos zapatos que al principio me habían resultado tan extraños, peligrosos y ajenos. Después, una vez que logré relacionarlos con Lillian en mi recuerdo, se me volvieron familiares, como si un mundo de reminiscencias se hubiera puesto a pasear por ellos. Quise salvarlos del olvido con mi dibujo, embalsamarlos como la reliquia de un santo o la mano de un mártir idealista, apenas se me volvió evidente el mundo que descansaba sobre ellos y en ellos: esta buhardilla oscura, mis vagabundeos suburbanos con Lillian, y todo lo que terminaría en la basura si no raptaba esos zapatos del olvido.

De modo que me incorporé, ensoñado y somnoliento, para preparar el papel y la carbonilla y proceder al embalsamamiento. Envuelto en trapos y una frazada militar, harapiento, como un chaman de una tribu salvaje en su atuendo ritual, me moví en la luz débil y me acerqué a los zapatos como si fueran un sacramento. Vistos desde arriba parecían pobres, polvorientos, arruinados, deformes como cadáveres que unos pájaron hubieran martirizado hasta el hueso. Los levanté con cuidado, con dos dedos, sólo para dejarlos caer enseguida, horrorizado. Una rata se escabulló de uno de los zapatos y con su larga y sucia cola trazó una diagonal imaginaria de esquina a esquina y se metió en un agujero, borrando con un solo movimiento todo lo que había que salvar del olvido.

"I'll cut them," I'd told her just as calmly. "I'll perform a Caesarean, I can't stand this anymore." She'd fiercely opposed it, of course, as if it were a question of to be or not to be, because she saw I was capable of doing it. Thus we parted, as she claimed I was fishing for an excuse not to take her to the theater.

I started recalling all those moments that connected me to the shoes now lying above me at an angle, casting their long, strangely convoluted shadow on the floor. And I finally decided—having recalled many a walk with Lillian, when we used to wander by the Danube, visiting peripheral cafes to dance mindless calypso among the dudes and streetwalkers; our passion in the cold garret, where we'd pile our shoes without turning on the light, giving ourselves to each other breathlessly in mute embraces; how, when the clock from the city hall announced the time of her departure, we'd hurriedly grope for our piled shoes in the dark—I decided to get up and turn on the light in order to draw in charcoal those monstrous shoes, which suddenly became a world unto themselves, truly distant and deformed, but that could—I say—be drawn closer and meaningful with will and effort. That Van Goghian charcoal drawing was supposed to play the role of a mediator and infuse with meaning the shoes that had initially appeared unfamiliar, dangerous, and alien to me, but that then, after I succeeded in relating them to Lillian in my memory, had become familiar, as though a world of remembrances took a walk in them. I wanted to save them from oblivion with my drawing, to embalm them like the relic of a saint or the hand of an idealistic martyr, as it abruptly became clear to me that an entire world rests on and inside them: this dark garret room, my peripheric drifting with Lillian, and everything that would go to rubbish if I didn't snatch those shoes away from oblivion.

Therefore I rose, dreamful and drowsy, to prepare the paper and charcoal and embark upon embalmment. Wrapped in an army blanket and rags, like a shaman from a savage tribe in his ritual attire, I flicked on the feeble light and approached the shoes like a sacrament. Seen from above, they looked poor, dusty and torn, deformed and misshaped like cadavers pecked by birds to the bone. I picked them up carefully, with two fingers, only to drop them instantly, horrified to the core. A rat slipped out of one of the shoes and with its long filthy tail drew a fictional diagonal line from corner to corner, where he crawled into a hole, erasing in one motion everything that was meant to escape oblivion.

MY SHOES

translated into English by FRANCISCO GOLDMAN

MY SHOES, LYING ONE against the other like two animals, had grown horribly elongated and deformed, like objects that we look at every day for years until suddenly, for no particular reason, perplexingly, we see them for the first time. Of course that sensation—seeing something as for the first time—didn't surprise or frighten me. A previous experience came to my aid. I remembered the cash register in the bar where for years I used to drink in the afternoons. For starters, if somebody had asked me if there was a cash register in that bar, never mind what it was like, I would have said no, or just shrugged. And so, one autumn afternoon, after waiting three quarters of an hour for Lillian, who had said she'd be a little late, I went to that bar (I'd picked it especially for our encounter, a matter of shelter in case of a storm, and—though I never would have admitted this in front of Lillian—if she didn't show up, I'd settle in there as if in a purgatory) and sat in a corner with a double cognac. And then, once I understood that she wasn't coming that night, tormented by jealousy and doubt, my spirit grasping for a lifeline, my eyes fell on the things around me. At first it seemed to be happening without any intervention of consciousness, which was occupied with more important matters than a plain old iron cash register. But, as you'll soon see, there was far more lucidity and decisiveness in my vacant gaze than there'd been in the casual inspection I'd made of the little

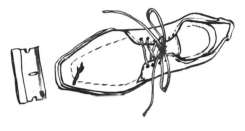

TOUT SERA OUBLIÉ

translated into French by CAMILLE DE TOLEDO

MES CHAUSSURES, CÔTE À CÔTE comme deux bêtes curieuses,[1] s'étaient affreusement déformées et distendues comme des choses que l'on observe chaque jour pendant des années jusqu'à ce que, sans raison particulière, étrangement, elles nous apparaissent pour la première fois. Bien sûr, cette sensation—voir une chose comme si c'était la première fois—ne m'a pas surpris ni effrayé.

Une sensation antérieure est venue à mon secours. Je me suis souvenu de la caisse enregistreuse du bar où, pendant des années, j'avais l'habitude de boire l'après-midi. Pour commencer, si quelqu'un m'avait demandé s'il y avait une caisse enregistreuse dans ce bar, peu importe à quoi elle ressemblait, j'aurais répondu non, ou simplement haussé les épaules. Et donc, par une après-midi d'automne, après avoir attendu Lillian trois quarts d'heure, laquelle m'avait dit avoir un peu en retard, je suis allé dans ce bar. (Je l'avais choisi en particulier pour notre rencontre—le bar—histoire d'avoir un abris en cas de tempête, et—je n'aurais jamais admis ça devant Lillian—si elle n'apparaissait pas, je resterais là comme au purgatoire)[2] et je me suis assis dans un coin avec un double cognac.

---

[1] Google translate + two human interventions.

[2] Google translate + four lazy interventions.

Puis, une fois que j'eus compris qu'elle ne viendrait pas cette nuit-là, torturé par la jalousie et le doute, mon esprit saisir une bouée de sauvetage, mes yeux tomber sur les choses autour de moi.[3]

Au début, cela semblait se passer sans aucune intervention de la conscience—ni du traducteur—qui a été occupé par des choses plus importantes que d'un registre plaine vieux fer de trésorerie.[4]

Mais, comme vous verrez, il y avait beaucoup plus de lucidité et de détermination dans mon regard vide qu'il n'y en avait eu lors de l'inspection occasionnelle que j'avais faite du petit bar en attendant avec anxiété Lillian.[5]

Car, alors que j'étais tout occupé à penser à elle (Lillian), j'ai remarqué, à la suite d'un affluent-qui-coule-de-la-conscience, que je voyais la vieille caisse enregistreuse pour la première fois.[6]

Son sommet de nickel en saillie,[7] reliefs sculptés et des dômes comme, lui a donné l'apparence d'une cathédrale. Cette idée m'a intrigué, mon tourment et la souffrance n'ont pas été interrompu ou diminué *für* autant, *aber* j'ai noté que la découverte de la caisse enregistreuse-cathédrale *war* rien d'autre qu'une conséquence de l'aliénation de mon *espiritu*, qui, dans ce moment d'excitation venait rompre la complaisance qui m'avait empêché de voir, la révélant, ELLE, la-plaine-de-la-trésorerie-en-fer-forgé nécessaire, à la fois comme un refuge et une armure.

En réalité, il n'y avait rien de nécessaire que la caisse enregistreuse antique,

---

[3] Google translate + two human interventions + one automatic image: *Mes yeux de tomber.* "My eyes fell, *en effet*, like rain, like a rain of eyes, falling, *comme une pluie de mes yeux.*"

[4] GT + 3 HI. At this moment, the translator is sleeping. *Il se permet cette intervention somnanbulique. Pendant que...* an assistant is working for him. That means: *Le traducteur soustraite.* And a very fine image, again, is produced by mechanical error (the translator sees it when he wakes up): *Un registre plaine vieux fer de trésorerie. Pour dire "une simple et vieille caisse enregistreuse en fer."*

[5] GT + 2 HI.

[6] GT + 3 HI. The assistant of the translator is now on strike and complaining. *Il note: "Un affluent qui coule de la conscience!" Puis il se félicite de ce que la machine GT a ainsi trouvé. "Un affluent qui coule de la conscience!" Mais où va-t-il, cet affluent? Peut-on s'y baigner, y plonger, y laver son linge?*

[7] GT + no HI. *Et là, maintenant, encore une traduction automatique le surprend—son assistant a définitivement abandonné sa copie—et, à l'image de "l'écriture automatique," il pense, c'est un feu d'artifices de réductions, d'ellipses, de trahisons.*

---

bar while anxiously waiting for Lillian. For as absorbed as I was in thinking about her, I noticed, following a flowing tributary of consciousness, that I was seeing that old cash register for the first time. Its protruding nickel top, sculpted like domes and reliefs, gave it the look of a cathedral. That idea intrigued me; my torment and suffering weren't interrupted or diminished, but I did note that the discovery of the cash-register-cathedral was nothing but a consquence of the alienation of my spirit, which in that moment of excitement breached what complacency had prevented me from seeing before, revealing it as necessary, as both refuge and armor. In reality, there was nothing necessary about that antiquated cash register, apart maybe from the fact that my spirit, in a moment of weakness, had fastened itself to such a vulgar object. Experience told me that there was nothing strange about that. It had happened more than once that while disinterestedly observing, in a state, so to speak, of absence, a face that I saw day to day and had long registered, I'd suddenly comprehend it.

So (to get back to my story) I looked with surprise at my shoes in the dark light of the moon, and it was as if, for the first time, I'd tripped over something whose sense and purpose I couldn't understand. Back then I lived in a garret and I'd dream while awake—I slept on the floor, miserably—about Paris and the books I was going to write, books in which my entire past and present would surrender to the grace of creation. That little room in a mansard roof had an amazing power of derangement, almost magical. By night, in that room illuminated by a tiny lamp, as happens at twilight and by the light of the moon, not just objects underwent strange metamorphoses. My thoughts did too, becoming fantastic and amorphous.

The detail that distracted me from the object in question—the fact that I was sleeping on the floor—wasn't without importance in this deranging process. Lying on the floor, I saw the things surrounding me from a perspective that substantially altered their appearance.

I saw the chair as if it was hung from the ceiling, and the window as if it was in some higher imaginary floor. In a word, I saw from the point of view of a frog, which made everything acquire an air of practically malignant superiority. My shoes threw a long shadow, as if standing on their toes, although I could see them flat on the floor in front of me. But that strange pair of animals weren't the same size, and it seemed to me that while they were parallel like that, one next to the other, any optical illusion should be impossible. They differed in size in the same way that certain male animals differ from the females: one lifted its head, as if on guard: the other, just a little behind it, seemed imperturbable. For a moment I wanted to believe they were two black cats whose presence disturbed me. Because they weren't docile: they dragged themselves toward me with shining eyes and fangs like daggers, even as they approached without reducing the distance between us. I finally convinced myself that they were nothing more than my worn-out shoes. And at the same time I had to convince myself that I'd just now perceived them, not as objects but as creatures of some kind, creatures I had no relationship to. I tried as hard as I could to recognize myself in that dark, amorphous lump, to identify my own shape or any other relation to me that would allow me to comprehend those shoes. I only remembered that I'd bought them not long ago (though I'd worn them immediately to wander the city outskirts in search of stimulus) and that their tight fit gave me some brutal blisters, a torment I freed myself from with a quick remedy: making two cuts with a knife over the toes, where the blisters were, and opening two holes to alleviate the pressure. That reminded me that I'd been at war with those shoes as soon as I'd encountered them; even before encountering them. Just the idea of having to buy them had unsettled and frightened me, given that new shoes have always tortured me like Inquisition boots, bloodying my heels. But when I thought it over, I felt that I was being rancorous and unjust. Because if I wanted to, if I didn't give into my self-mortifying nature, I could also recall a few agreeable moments…

I'd bought them at once, without telling Lillian that I was planning to acquire some new shoes. It's true: she was always trying to act as if it didn't bother her to go out with me when I hadn't shaved, with my Charlie Chaplin shoes; on the contrary: she said she liked it because her father thought I was an artist, which flattered her. But she couldn't get me to accompany her to the theater or to a concert. There was no way to convince her that I couldn't go to the theater or to a concert "like that," that is with shoes like those. She began to accuse me of not wanting to go to concerts *because of her*, while I insisted that I couldn't go *with her*, but I could go alone…

"I was afraid you were going to buy the flat and crushed-looking kind, because I know you don't like pointy shoes. But these are nice. Tomorrow we'll go to the theater. I want to see *Behind the Closed Doors*," she exclaimed, looking at my feet, saying it all breezily, as if it was obvious that now we'd be going to the theater.

"I'm going to cut them up," I said, as calmly as her. "I'm going to give

à l'exception peut-être du fait que mon esprit, dans un moment de faiblesse, s'était *fastenened* à un tel vulgaire objet. Mon expérience me dit qu'il n'y avait rien d'étrange à ce sujet. Il est arrivé plus d'une fois que tout désintéressé observant, dans un état, pour ainsi dire, d'abscence, un visage que je voyais au jour le jour et depuis longtemps inscrit, je tout à coup le comprendre.[8]

Alors (pour revenir à mon histoire) je regarder avec surprise mes chaussures à la lumière oscurra de la luna, et c'était comme si, pour la prima volta, je trébucher—moi, tomber, moi, casser figure sur sol—quelque chose, dont le sens et le but ich could nicht verstanden. À l'époque, je vivre dans grenier et rêver éveillé—je dormir sur plancher, misérablement—à Paris—et les livres que je écrire demain ou après-demain, des livres dans quoi mein past und présent zusammen s'écrire grâce à la machine, sans moi. Without me. Books written without my presence…[9]

Cette petite pièce dans un toit en mansarde avait une incroyable puissance de dérangement, presque magique. La nuit, dans cette pièce éclairée par une petite lampe, comme il arrive au crépuscule et à la lumière de la lune, il n'y avait pas que objets subir étranges métamorphoses. Mes pensées aussi, devenir fantastiques et amorphes.[10]

Le détail qui me distrait de l'objet en question—le fait que je dormais sur le plancher—n'est pas sans importance dans le procès de mon dérangement. Allongé sur le sol, je voir les choses à partir de point de vue modifiant apparence. Voir chaise comme si elle suspendre au plafond, et fenêtre comme si elle en quelque étage supérieur imaginaire. Je voir du point de vue grenouille, ce qui donner à tout air supériorité pratiquement maligne. Chaussures jeter une ombre, comme si debout sur orteils, même si je pouvoir les voir à plat sur le sol en face moi.

Mais ce couple étranges animaux (chaussures) waren nicht de même taille, und me sembler que pendant être parallèles comme ça, un à côté autre, toute illusion optique war nicht möglich. Ils différent dans la taille de même manière

---

[8] GT + no HI. *Car le traducteur, cette fois-ci, écrit. Il se lance: Et c'est ainsi que le narrateur de cette histoire, soucieux de passer au tamis le plus minuscule soubresaut de son espiritu, comme l'or d'une rivière, like Virginia Woolf meeting Swann in la Recherche del tempo perso, se transforme de Proust en petit enfant parlant sehr schlecht, très mal.*

[9] Deranged and twisted GT, *le traducteur a modifié les paramètres de la machine.*

[10] *Le traducteur trafique la machine, il la perturbe.*

que certains animaux mâles diffèrent putes: un levé sa tête, comme en garde, autre, juste un peu derrière lui, inchange. Pour un moment, je vouloir croire que chaussures être deux chats noirs dont présence me troubler. Parce qu'ils nicht dociles: ils se traîner vers moi, chaussures, avec yeux brillants et crocs comme poignards,[11] même alors qu'ils (chaussures comme chats) s'approcher sans pour autant réduire distance entre nous. Je être finalement convinced qu'ils n'être rien plus que souliers usés. Et en même temps, je devoir convaincre moi, ich, que je venir juste les perceived, nicht comme objets mais comme créatures d'une certaine sorte: créatures que je avoir aucun lien avec. Je essayer aussi fort que je pouvoir me connaître dans ce ténébreux, forfaitaire amorphe, identifier mon propre espiritu ou toute autre relation à moi qui me permettre de comprendre chaussures.[12]

Je me souvenais en tous cas que je les avoir achetés (chaussures, étranges bêtes curieuses, inspirées von Kafka und Van Gogh, und décrites avec flow de conscience woolfien et longueur phrase Recherche del tiempo perso) il n'y a pas longtemps (même si je les avoir portés immédiatement en errant dans les environs de la ville à la recherche de stimulus) et que leur ajustement serré me donner quelques cloques brutales, un tourment donc ich me suis freed avec un rapide remède: faire deux coupes avec couteau[13] sur les orteils, où les ampoules étaient, et l'ouverture de deux trous pour alléger pression.

Cela me rappeler que je être en guerre avec chaussures dès que je avoir rencontré chaussures, et même avant de les rencontrer. Juste l'idée d'avoir à acheter entre eux m'avoir perturbé et fait peur, given the fact dass nouvelles chaussures m'avoir toujours torturé comme Inquisition, bottes, ensanglantant talons. Mais quand je penser cela, me sentir que je faire plein de rancoeur et de l'injuste. Parce que si je vouloir, si je pas donner dans mon auto-mortifiante nature, je pouvoir aussi rappeler quelques instants agréables…

Je avoir acheté à la fois, sans le dire à Lillian que je projetter acquérir nouvelles chaussures. Cela être vrai: elle toujours essayer agir comme si elle avoir pas prendre peine elle sortir avec moi, quand je être pas rasé, avec chaussures de Charlot, bien au contraire: elle dire aimer, parce que père penser que je être artiste, qui la flatter. Mais elle pouvoir pas me accompagner au théâtre ou à con-

---

[11] *Ici, GT propose un lien publicitaire vers "chambre Van Gogh": Visite virtuelle de l'exposition et possibilité d'acheter tasses avec tournesols et chaussures usées, vieille caisse enregistreuse et T-shirt.*

[12] *Ici, GT propose un lien publicitaire vers Kafka, la Métamorphose.*

[13] *Nouveau lien publicitaire vers Amsterdam, hôtels à Amsterdam.*

them a Caesarean, I can't stand them anymore." She was fiercely opposed, of course, as if it was a question of life and death, because she knew that I was willing to do it. Then we parted; she insisted that I was looking for an excuse to not take her to the theater.

I began to remember all those moments that connected me to the shoes that now loomed over me from a corner, projecting their long and strangely intricate shadow over the floor. And finally—after remembering our many walks with Lillian, when we'd wandered the shores of the Danube and gone into those suburban bars to dance absurd calypsos among the regulars and prostitutes; our moments of passion in the cold garret, where we shook off our shoes without turning on the lights and gave each other over to mute embaces that left us breathless; as the municipal hall clock announced the hour of her departure and we, hurriedly, groped in the dark for our shoes— I decided to get up and turn on the light to be able to draw in charcoal those monstrous shoes that so suddenly could become a world unto themselves, a truly distant and deformed world, but that through a bit of effort and will could appear nearby and coherent. I assumed that that Van Gogh–like charcoal would play the role of mediator and give some meaning to those shoes that had originally struck me as so strange, dangerous, and alien. Afterward, once I'd succeeded in relating them to Lillian in my memory, they became familiar, as if a world of reminiscences had come to wander in them. I wanted to save them from oblivion, embalm them like a saint's relic or like the hand of an idealistic martyr, now that the world that rested upon and inside of them was revealed to me: this dark garret, my suburban wanderings with Lillian, and everything else that would end up in the trash unless I rescued these shoes from oblivion.

So I set about, somnambulant and dreamy, to prepare the paper and charcoal and proceed with the embalming. Wrapped in rags and a ragged military blanket, like a shaman from a savage tribe in his ritual attire, I moved through the weak light and approached the shoes as if performing a sacrament. Seen from above they were poor-looking things, dusty, ruined, deformed like cadavers that a few crows had martyred down to the bones. I picked them up gingerly, by the fingers, only to immediately let them drop, horrified. A rat slithered out of one of the shoes and with its long dirty tail traced an imaginary diagonal from one corner to another and went down a hole, erasing in just one motion all that was to be saved from oblivion.

cert. Pas moyen de convaincre elle que je ne pouvoir aller au théâtre ou à un concert "comme ça," avec chaussures. Elle commencer à m'accuser de ne pas vouloir aller concerts en raison de son, tandis que je insister pour que je ne pouvoir pas aller avec elle, mais je ne pouvoir y aller seul…

"J'avais peur, angst, fear, que vous aller acheter genre plat et écraser l'avenir, parce que je savoir vous pas aimer chaussures pointues. Mais ceux-ci sont gentils. Demain, nous aller au théâtre. Je voir derrière portes closes," dit Lillian, en regardant pieds, en disant tout cela avec désinvolture, comme si être évident que maintenant nous aller au théâtre ensemble.

"Je aller les couper," habe ich gesagt, aussi calmement que ça. "Je vais leur faire césarienne, je ne pouvoir plus les supporter." Elle être farouchement opposée, bien sûr, comme si être une question vie ou mort, parce qu'elle savoir que je être prêt à faire des choses pareilles. Puis nous nous quitter, elle insister pour que je chercher une excuse pour ne pas l'emmener au théâtre.

Je, ich, commencer à me souvenir de tous ces moments qui me relier à chaussures qui maintenant me surplombaient d'un coin, projetant leur ombre longue, étrange animal, complexe sur le sol. Et enfin—après avoir rappelé nombreuses promenades avec Lillian, alors que nous errer sur rives Danube—et disparu dans ces bars de banlieue à danser calypsos absurdes parmi habitués et prostituées; nostri momenti de passion dans mansarde froide, où nous secouer nostri scarpe, chaussures, sans allumer lumières et se donner cul et coup de couille au cours de embaces muets qui nous laisser à bout de souffle, comme

horloge mairie annoncer l'heure de son départ et nous, à la hâte, à tâtons dans obscurité—je décider de me lever et allumer lumière pour être en mesure de tirer au fusain diese monstruosi chaussures que si soudainement pouvoir devenir monde à part, monde véritablement lointain et distorted, mais que, grâce à un peu d'effort et pouvoir apparaître à proximité et cohérente. Je suppose que ce que Van Gogh—*link vers Van Gogh*—et de donner un sens à chaussures qui initialement m'avoir frapper comme étranges, dangereuses, et étrangères. Ensuite, une fois avoir réussi à relier à Lillian dans mémoire, chaussures devenir familières, comme si monde souvenirs venir se promener—maintenant que le monde reposer sur et à l'intérieur d'eux a été révélé à moi: ce grenier sombre von meine errances suburbaines avec Lillian, et tout ce qui finirait à la poubelle à moins que je avoir sauver chaussures de l'oubli.

Alors je me mettre à, somnambule et rêveur, pour préparer papier et charbon de bois et procéder à embaumement. Envelopper dans chiffons et couverture en lambeaux militaires, comme chaman de tribu sauvage dans costume rituel, me déplacer à travers lumière faible et approcher chaussures, comme exécution Cène. Vu d'en haut, êtres pauvres prospectifs choses, poussiéreux, ruinés, déformés comme cadavres que corbeaux avoir martyrisé vers le bas pour os. Ramasser avec précaution, par doigts, pour aussitôt laisser tomber. Horreur! Rat se glisser hors de chaussure avec queue sale long tracé diagonale imaginaire d'un coin autre, puis être allé dans trou, d'effacement dans seul mouvement tout ce qui devoir être sauver de l'oubli.[14]

---

[14] *Traducteur accusé par Google d'avoir déréglé la machine à traduire. Supreme Court, Toledo vs GT, June 25, 2018.*

MY SHOES

translated into English by JOHN BANVILLE

MY SHOES, I SAW THEM, standing side by side, horribly twisted and swollen, like two strange beasts, in that way that things known for years can suddenly be seen as if for the first time. Of course, this feeling, of seeing a thing as if for the first time, certainly it did not surprise or alarm me, certainly not.

Something I had experienced previously now came to my rescue. I remembered the cash register at the bar where, for years, I used to drink in the afternoons. Now if previously someone had asked me, not even what the cash register looked like, but if there was a cash register at all, I would have said no, or would simply have shrugged my shoulders. Then, one autumn afternoon, having waited three quarters of an hour for Lillian, who had told me she would be a little late, I went to this bar (I had chosen it so that I might take shelter if a storm should blow up, and if she had not come I would—though I would never have admitted this to Lillian—have bided there contentedly, as if in Purgatory) and sat in a corner with a double brandy.

Presently, having realized she would not come that evening, and tortured by jealousy and doubt, I sought comfort or at least diversion in scanning the things around me. At first it seemed to go on, this active looking, without my being conscious of it, and without any intervention, for after all I was preoccupied with things far more important than, for instance, a cash register. It is obvious, however, that my seemingly blank gaze must have been sharply focused, somehow, as I waited there anxiously, in the little bar, for Lillian.

Because, while I thought I was busy thinking about Lillian and all that she was, suddenly, following a tributary of my consciousness, so to speak, I saw the old cash register, I mean I *saw* it, and for the first time.

Its great domed nickel top and sculpted reliefs gave it the appearance of a cathedral. This notion fascinated me. My torment and suffering were not abated, but I realized that my discovery of the cash-register-as-cathedral was a consequence of my alienation of spirit, which in this moment of excitement—excitement!—had prevented me from seeing the essential thing, the plain old cast-iron register, as in reality—reality!—both haven and sanctuary.

Of course, it need not have been that antique cash register that I registered, anything else would have done as well; it was just that my mind, in a moment of weakness, I suppose, had fastened on this commonplace object. Experience tells me there was nothing strange or wonderful about this little epiphany. It has happened more than once that while at gaze in a vacant state I fixed upon a face I was accustomed to seeing every day and now suddenly, somehow, understood it.

Anyway, to return to my story, I saw my shoes with surprise in the obscure light of the moon, and it was as if, in that first time of seeing them, I were seeing something the meaning and purpose of which I could not comprehend. At the time I was living in a garret and would lie for long hours on the floor, in rags, daydreaming of Paris and the books I would write, in which would be expressed, oh, wonderfully expressed, all that I am and have been and will be. What a magical little room that was, under the mansard roof, where at night especially, in the lamp-light that might have been the light of the sunset or even of the moon, my thoughts strayed, lost shape, blundered, and became unreal.

The detail that distracted me from the object in question—I mean the detail of my sleeping on the floor—is not insignificant to those straying thoughts. Lying supine there, I saw things from a novel perspective. A chair would seem to hang from the ceiling, a window to be set in an imaginary upper floor. In short, I was seeing things from the point of view of a frog, which gave to everything an air of malignancy. My shoes

cast a shadow, as if standing on their toes, even though I could see them there parallel in front of me.

But this pair of animals, these shoes—and I cannot think how it could have been an optical illusion—differed in size as a male animal differs in size from the female of the species. One had its head lifted, as if on guard, while the other one, just a little behind, seemed calm and indifferent. For a moment I wanted to believe the shoes were two black cats whose presence troubled me, because they were not docile but dragged themselves toward me, shoe-cats, cat-shoes, with sparkling eyes and fangs like daggers, even though, impossibly, their approach did not reduce the distance between them and me. In the end I had to remind myself, though it was not easy, that they were nothing but my old, worn shoes. At the same time I had to convince myself I had just perceived them not as objects but as creatures of some sort: creatures I had no connection with. I tried as hard as I could to find myself in those dark amorphous things, to identify my own shape, or any part of my own spirit, in their essential shoeness.

I reminded myself I had purchased them not long ago, though I quickly wore them down on the city's wild side where I so often ventured in search of stimulation, and that they gave me terrible blisters, the solution to which was to make two cuts in the toes to reduce the pressure. This made me realize that I had been at war with those shoes from the moment I met them—indeed, even before that, I might say. Just the thought of having to buy them had filled me with foreboding, given the fact that new shoes have always tortured me like those metal boots the Inquisitors employed to make a bloodied mess of their victims' heels. But when I think about it, I think I do them and myself an injustice, the shoes, that is, not the Inquisitors. For if I try, if I do not give in to my self-mortifying nature, I can recall some pleasant moments in my life, walking about the world…

I had bought the shoes on a whim, without telling Lillian what I was doing. She pretends not to mind going out with me when I am unshaven, say, and in Charlie Chaplin shoes; on the contrary, she says she loves it, because her father thinks I must be an artist, which for some reason she finds flattering, to her, I mean. I could not convince her that it would be impossible for me to go to the theater or to musical concerts "like this," that is, in the sort of shoes I had then. She started to accuse me of not wanting to go to concerts because of her, but I insisted that I could not go *with* her, although I could of course go alone…

"I was afraid you were going to buy those awful blunt ones, because I know you don't like pointy shoes, but these ones are nice. Tomorrow we'll go to the theater. I want to see *Behind Closed Doors*." Lillian said all this in a studiedly casual way, glancing sidelong at my feet, as if to suggest it was a foregone conclusion that we would go to the theater together.

"I'm going to cut them," I said, as calm as she had been. "I'm going to perform a Caesarean, because I'm no longer able to bear it." She opposed this fiercely, of course, making it a matter for debate, but she knows I am quite capable of disfiguring even a new pair of shoes. We parted then, with her accusing me of looking for an excuse not to take her to the theater.

I began to recall all those moments that connected me to those shoes that now towered over me, casting their long, strangely misshapen shadows on the floor. And finally I decided, after recalling my many walks with Lillian along the banks of the Danube, when we would slip into dingy bars to dance mindless calypsos among the spivs and tarts; our moments of passion in the cold attic, where we would kick off our shoes without turning on the light, throwing ourselves into each other's arms in breathless embraces; of the moments when the town-hall clock chimed the time for departure and we hastily groped in the darkness for our shoes—I decided, I say, to get up and turn on the light and draw in charcoal those monstrous shoes of mine that suddenly seemed to be in a world

of their own making, distant and dim, a world apart, yet one that with a little effort can appear close by and consistent.

That Van Goghian charcoal drawing of mine was meant to fill the role of mediator and give meaning to the shoes that initially had struck me as strange, dangerous and strange. However, once I had connected them with Lillian in my memory they became familiar, as if remembrances strolled about in them. With my drawing I wanted to save them from oblivion as holy objects, to embalm them like the relic of a saint or the idealized hand of a martyr, as it had become clear to me that a whole world rested on and in them: the dark attic room, my suburban wanderings with Lillian, everything, in a word, that would end in trash unless I saved the shoes from oblivion:

So I rose up, drowsy and dreamy, to prepare the paper and the charcoal and begin upon my task of embalming. Wrapped in rags and a tattered military blanket and looking like the shaman of a savage tribe in ritual costume, I switched on the lamp and in its frail light approached the shoes as if to celebrate a sacrament. Seen from above, they appeared poor things, dusty and worn, distorted as corpses the crows have stripped to the bone. I picked them up carefully, between a finger and a thumb, only to let them drop immediately in horror. A rat slipped out of one of the shoes and with its long, pink, horrible tail sketched an imaginary line from one corner to the other and there dived into its hole, wiping out in one swift movement everything that I had thought to save from oblivion.

A NOTE ON THE TRANSLATIONS

I.

This sentence, from the last paragraph of Kiš's story, gave me more trouble than any other: *Vistos desde arriba parecían pobres, polvorientos, arruinados, deformes como cadáveres que unos pájaron hubieran martirizado hasta el hueso.* It made me sort of crazy for a few days. The problem was Alan's use of *pájaron.* Why *pájaron* instead of *pájaros,* "birds"? (I'd heard the word as *pajarón,* because that's where the accent goes on multi-syllable words ending in -*ron.*) I didn't know that word, and spent about two days trying to figure out what it could mean, or why he had used it. Though *pajarón* most obviously seemed to suggest "big birds," I couldn't turn up, at least via Google and queries to friends, any evidence of its being used that way. *Pajarote* is what we—in Mexico, in Central America—might say for an especially large bird. But anyway, shouldn't it be *pajarones?*

I did discover that the word *pajarón*—rather than *pájaron*—does exist in Argentine and Chilean slang: somebody who is easily fooled or very spacey. (*Significado de "pajarón": adj. Dícese de la persona fácil de engañar o muy distraída.*) That usage made no sense as a translation of that sentence in Kiš's story: "[The shoes] looked like cadavers that an easily fooled person had martryed down to the bones." (Actually, though, I wish I'd been more daring and made that leap and many more such leaps throughout the translation; it would have made for a far better read, I realize now, than my doggedly faithful, "poor, dusty, ruined, and deformed" translation of Alan Pauls's translation of Danilo Kiš's story.) Anyway, even the slang definition I'd found via Google was pretty arcane; none of the Argentines or Chileans I queried would ever refer to a gullible person or to a space cadet as a *pajarón.* But in Guatemala, it turned out, the word *pajarón* is, at least somewhat, in colloquial use—maybe I should have known this, but I didn't. According to my friend Claudia Mendez, *pajarón* can mean a crybaby, a big blouse like a smock, or a loudmouth (*un niño llorón, un blusón, un hombre gritón*). That's all I could find for *pajarón,* none of it very

helpful for my faithful translation. (By now, that accent had firmly gravitated in my mind from the first-syllable *a* to that closing *o.*) These slang usages did suggest exaggerated bird qualities, noisy birds, big birds. Finally, I thought of using vultures—but wait, vultures by the Danube?—and then changed it to "large birds," and then back to vultures, and then to "noisy birds," and then changed noisy to "squawking"— which suggested a frenzied pecking—which made me realize, no, "cawing," so, well, "crows." Crows would have martyred those old shoes down to the bones.

Last week, in Vincennes, France, just outside of Paris, at a literary festival, I finally met Alan Pauls. Famously handsome dude, cheerfully friendly too. We have the same French publisher, and were signing books side by side at the publisher's stand. I told him I'd translated his translation of the Danilo Kiš story back into English for that *McSweeney's* thing. There was a word he'd used, I told him, that I'd been wondering about: *pajarón.* (Jarring *pájaron* had been erased from my memory.) What did it mean? Why had he used it instead of just "birds," say?

Pajarón? Alan repeated. He really looked baffled. After he'd mulled it over, he told me he didn't know that word either. Had I read it carefully? He remembered the sentence I was referring to. He'd written *pájaros,* birds. He was sure of it.

Maybe it was just a typo, he concluded. A few days later Alan responded by email that he'd checked his manuscript and he had definitely written *pájaros.* I copied the sentence with *pájaron* off the PDF and emailed it back. Was it an editing mistake? He made no reference to the gravitating accent, which perhaps in both our minds' eyes remained fixed over the *o.* Maybe the mouse had flicked that *o* with its sooty tail as it slipped from the shoe. In his next email Alan suggested I watch Hitchcock's *The Birds;* maybe I'd discover the answer about our mystery bird there.

Of course that it was *pájaron* made the whole question moot. Anyway, it led me to crows, which I prefer to birds.

—*Francisco Goldman*

IX

INCONTRARSI

a story in ITALIAN *by* GIUSEPPE PONTIGGIA

ILLUSTRATORS, IN ORDER OF APPEARANCE

Brianna Harden, Wesley Allsbrook, Erin Althea, Ian Huebert.

1

UMBERTO BUTI

translated into English by ZADIE SMITH

It's true: like all mammals it has two eyes, a nose, a mouth, and, somewhere, four limbs.
—J.R.Wilcock, *The Book of Monsters*

HE IS BORN IN EMPOLI on the 30th of April 1931, son of Stefano Buti, holder of a degree in chemistry, and of Concetta Valori, a mathematics teacher at the technical institute.

His father, director of the Osveco firm—it produces thermal valves—has published three literary articles and five rather minor editorials in Livorno's *Telegraph*. He often claims to have sacrificed the lettered life for two plus two equals four. He still recalls those Greek and Latin verses of his schooldays, declaiming them with all the sonority of an auctioneer. He asks his son to name their authors, and each time his son denies all knowledge of them. He dedicates the same attention to modern poetry. He is like a spectator in the gallery, always ready to boo or applause, in a manner usually reserved for the efforts of opera singers. For poets, he lies in wait. He has an unbounded admiration for D'Annunzio, whose lyrics he calls "sheet music."

At least once a week he meets with a doctor, Luciano Natalucci—another literature connoisseur—and as they travel together in a Lancia Ardea, toward Pisa or Montecatini, raising a trail of dust along the B-roads, pausing to rapturously contemplate the landscape, a subtle

2

田懷意

translated into Chinese by MA JIAN

這是千真萬確的：像所有的哺乳動物一樣，它有兩隻眼睛，一個鼻子，一張嘴，以及長在不同位置的四肢。

《關於怪物》-J.R.維爾科克

1931年四月30日，田懷意出生在戰亂的中國南部城市廣州。他的父親田樹林是留學義大利的化學博士，母親茱麗葉出生在佛羅倫斯，去年隨丈夫來到中國，在離家不遠的技工學院當了數學教師。

父親是在一家叫斯蓋沃的義大利公司任銷售主管，主要產品是進口的熱力閥。他熱愛文學思想活躍，還在《廣州日報》上發表過三篇文學評論和五篇他翻譯的義大利詩歌。他經常聲稱自已犧牲了文學理想，就為了這種二加二等於四的單調的商業貿易。他常掛在嘴邊的話題總是說在義大利留學期間，他如拍賣行裡的經紀人般響亮而激情地朗誦那些優美的詩句。

他還常常問長大的兒子那些詩歌的作者是誰，常然，田懷意每次總是看著窗外的江水或山丘說不知道。這回答有時會令父親更加自鳴得意。他也不理會日本投降二戰已結束，他的義大利公司瀕臨破產，而是到處在報紙的文藝版中尋找剛發表的現代詩，然後像劇場觀眾般忽而噓聲忽而掌聲地評價著。在兒子的印像中，父親下班後總是如手握樂譜的歌手，隨時準備登臺誦唱他最喜愛的義大利詩人鄧南遮〔D'Annunzio〕的詩。

那時父親每週都會和教會的義大利醫生盧西亞諾開車去郊外野餐，

他也是一位鄧南遮的崇拜者，還娶了個中國老婆。他倆經常把車停在塵土飛揚的土路上，繞過沒人填土的彈坑，爬上草坡或者是一片荒廢的田野時，便開始對著遠處的綠山，近處的草叢像棋手般引經據典地鬥詩，全然不顧坐在車上皺著眉頭的茱麗葉和急躁的兒子。也就是在那個1946年的夏天，母親拋棄了他和父親獨自返回了義大利，少年田懷意也徹底厭惡了文學藝術，開始確定實際的人生目標。他選擇的大學不會有人文科目，只面對國家戰後重建的需要，這也顯得他比其它少年成熟和有遠見。他的座佑銘是：必須腳踏實地。如果需要結婚的話，那也要選不愛幻想也沒有文藝細胞的姑娘，然後生一男一女兩個孩子。平時就去鍛煉身體，也遠離政治黨派。對父親要他讀《神曲》的要求，他開始使用 "業餘愛好" 這個詞來對抗。

　　他的人生規劃慢慢清晰。1950年的十月16日，田懷意考入了新中國剛成立的農學院，開始思考如何把落後的農村步入農業現代化，讓更多的人有飯吃有工作。在同學之中，他只談實際問題,不說不著邊際的政治表態的大話也不談戀愛。周末，他會離開大學宿舍坐火車回家，然後從車站右邊的小巷，鑽進一家沒有被查抄的地下妓屋。那條昏暗的樓梯會通向好幾處如取不盡用不完的蜂巢般骯髒的木板小間。在偶然打開塗了紅漆的窗戶片刻，他會看到外面花草叢生的小院落，幾件女人的裙子和內褲掛在夕陽之下的涼衣繩上。那時他的血液會發熱，性愛的感覺由然而生。但多數時間他都是手握衛生紙跟著妓女躺到床上，都沒看清女人的奶子就達到了高潮。

　　"我沒有心理負擔，" 他說，"頭腦是被斷開的。" 田懷意和妓屋的李媽媽生關係不錯，他也會和進進出出的妓女點頭打招呼。

　　"這對我們都有好處。" 這句話快成了他的口頭語，儘管他知道她們會笑這位漂亮的混血大學生。有時他會因必須參加的政治活動而很晚才來敲門，那半睡半醒的妓女也會迎合這位老客戶，誰叫他是浪漫的義大利雜種呢。在繁忙時間，田懷意也會與不被嫖客挑中的女人上床，而且能在她們陰鬱的沉默中，認為她是專門為了等他。當然，有時他發現情況正相反，使他很沮喪。

　　"這是因為她們知道你是誰。" 田懷意唯一的朋友，父親是印尼華僑的福生向他笑著，"你是個義大利情種。" 那是在1953年6月27日的一個夜晚，他倆從一間煙霧繚繞的飯館走出，腳下是不溫不火的石板路，兩邊潮濕的高牆之上，幾隻雨燕掠過夜空。

　　在大學的期末關於化肥成份的考試成績公佈之後，蔡教授問他想不想再多考一門以提高總分數，田懷意則回答：及格就可以了。當父親聽到這種不求進步的觀點時，滿臉不高興地推開他正在翻譯的《夏日謠曲》說："你真不像我的兒子。"

competition of citation passes between them—of elaborate, spiraling footnotes and academic dates—all of which render the son (sat behind them, with his mother) irritable and unhappy.

It is from this car trip, during the summer of 1946, that he dates his hatred of culture. Around the same time he begins to cultivate certain circumscribed ideals, making him appear precociously mature to others. His choice of university—excluding the humanities faculties altogether—he bases on the demands of the market. In the Italy of the reconstruction this choice of direction is considered marvelously far-sighted. The maxim "To keep one's feet on the ground" is here elevated to a life principle. Marriage with a woman who has no literary tendencies. Two children, perhaps one male and one female, separated by a few years. The refusal of all political involvement. The diligent practice of gymnastics. To be among the first to make use of the word *hobby*.

Steadily, he tries to implement his program. On the 16th of October 1950 he signs up to study in the faculty of agriculture, where the attempt is made to link rural Italy with the Italy of industry. He tells people there will be no shortage of career opportunities in the farmlands of Tuscany and Emilia. He repeats: in no field does he aim for more than he has stated.

The brothels of Florence, Arezzo, and Siena—which he regularly frequents—appear to him like cubicles linked by stairs, cells of a sordid and inexhaustible beehive. In the summer the windows open on to a small internal courtyard, sometimes throwing light upon erotic scenes that give him a sudden feel of languorous weakness in his blood. And every time the miracle happens. In exchange for a piece of paper he climbs the steps behind a woman, assured of imminent pleasure, without complication.

"It's not at all psychological," he says. "It's as if one's head has been cut off."

He establishes pleasant relations with the madam and with the escorts who come and go, periodically.

"It works for us," he says, a phrase dear to him, though it arouses hilarity in his companions. Welcomed even after hours, at dead of night—like a form of loyalty bonus—he brings a reluctant pleasure to half-asleep whores, astonished by his indefatigable commitment. During the busiest hours he tends to choose the one most overlooked by other clients, as she leans in gloomy silence upon one side of the door. He thinks she'll save her best for him, but sometimes the exact opposite happens, and he doesn't understand why this should be. His friend Francesco Salani explains it to him, the evening of the 27th of June 1953, in Arezzo, as they leave a smoky room into tepid air, and walk the cobblestones leading downhill, between the high walls of the alley over which the swifts skim: "It's because they understand who you are."

At the university he does not aspire to high marks. Asked by Professor Caspani (at the end of an exam on chemical fertilizers) whether he wants to retake to improve his average, he replies that a pass mark is enough. His father, listening with ill-concealed discomfort, doesn't know whether to support or condemn him.

On one occasion saying: "How different you are from me."

"I know," his son replies.

Under the guidance of Aldo Faravelli, an elderly gymnastics trainer, he devotes himself to the various apparatus of the Virtus gym.

When he swings, legs together, on the parallel bars and then gives himself a push toward the top, he has the soaring sensation of flying not toward the skylight but straight to the center of the world. But when he trains with boxing gloves against the bag, mowing down his target with a hail of punches; sweating, panting, continually sinking blows into the leather—it is as if he has finally found his enemy. Until, exhausted, dazed, lifeless, dissatisfied, satisfied, he lays himself down on the wooden bench that runs along the wall.

On the 31st of July 1954, after graduation, he leaves for the Cadets Course of Ascoli Piceno. He will remember his early days as among the most serene of his life. Running, marching, fixed hours, lights out at twenty-two-hundred hours, wake up at six, days defined by precise programs, by unchangeable rules. He is the only one in his platoon to think like this, but this makes him proud.

On the 16th of October 1954, in the sunlit whiteness of the shooting range—standing in the hole of cement, keeping a thumb on the trigger of the Breda machine gun—he sees the target, three hundred meters away, widen and move. Then, instead of taking a few shots, he presses until the magazine is empty: a deafening noise that echoes round the walled space.

"我知道。"兒子一字一頓地說。

在體育老師的指導下，田懷意的雙杠運動進步很快，他能大幅度地擺動然後雙腿併攏向上挺住不動。那一刻他不是感到騰飛到了天窗而是鑽進了地球的中心。他也喜歡拳擊，對著皮革沙袋氣喘吁吁地擊打，使他感到敵人的存在，直到精疲力竭才大汗淋漓地躺到靠牆的木凳上，失落又滿足。

1954年七月31日，田懷意大學畢業之後馬上報考了軍校。在那些立正、稍息、行軍拉練的枯躁生活中，他感到是自己人生最寧靜的經歷。他喜歡準時十點熄燈，早晨六點起床號準時吹響，全班只有他如此樂此不疲，讓他感到自己很獨特。

十月16日，一個陽光普照的天氣，田懷意隨隊米到靶場，當輪到他站到重機槍面前，他很快就對上瞄準星和三百米外移動的標靶，然後食指扣動了扳機直到梭子打成了空殼，雙耳被震得嗡嗡響。

"你總算擊中目標了！"戰友不屑地看著他退到隊後面時，用槍托從高處砸在他頭盔上，當時他感到眼冒金花。下午去醫務室做了眼底測試，發現屈光度下降了。但真正的厄運在十一天之後發生了，他開始厭食。醫生明確地告訴他，這是憂鬱症的前兆。軍校決定把他送到軍醫大學住院。打了兩天維生素吊瓶之後，他才感到有點起色，開始能喝點米粥了。當主治唐醫生來查房時，田懷意恍惚不定地說感到身體裡有個黑洞，他很無助。唐醫生透過眼鏡瞄著他：

"你不會有事，就是要調整屈光度。"

"不，"他固執地說，"不是眼睛，不，我不知道怎麼解釋，我對精神和思想不敢興趣，但身體是一切，我不敢相信它會出賣了我。

"這是你真正的病因了。"唐醫生認真地說。

他開始從床上爬起，穿著病號衣服走在閃亮的瓷磚地板上。有時，他也會去院子裡散步，在榕樹下呆一陣，然後沿著一排如堡壘般的窗戶慢慢地走。當黃昏來臨，院外和院內的聲音越來越弱的片刻，他感到自己站在空氣清新的監獄裡。

"你的頭腦就是一所監獄"唐醫生看著坐在對面的田懷意說。

他發現說出對外界的不信任，只會增加別人的嘲笑，說出了對外界的看法，只能招來別人的懷疑，便決定不再和唐醫生說什麼。

1956年二月6日田懷意出院了。三個月之後，他退出軍校被分配到奶牛農場工作。他開始發現奶牛不但好動，對周圍也充滿好奇。而場長對這199頭看起來差不多一樣的奶牛，每一頭都能叫出名字，猶如一個大家族。

他就在這欄圈中心建了一座土丘，奶牛便會隨著陽光邊吃草邊慢慢移動。下午，它們會懶洋洋地躺在背陰處，看過去如被產業化了的耶酥誕生場面。

在1957年七月的下午，牧場正散發著熱哄哄的尿味。田懷意斜靠籬笆，長時間地看著奶牛和正在土丘那兒鏟牛糞的魏班長說：

"它們比我們生活的好。"

看到微笑的魏班長走來，他又指著那只從種牛場借來的黑色公牛說：看它對著母牛又大又圓的眼神，嘿，它可真幸運。

1959年九月18日，田懷意又調動工作回到了廣州，在種畜進出口公司當業務員。沒過多久，他又找到了當年的李媽媽生，她在一家百貨商店當了售貨員，現在是有名的牽錢紅娘。她驚訝田懷意更帥了，忍不住問道：那你的同事朋友中就沒有女青年？

"有。"他回答。

"那，沒有你看上的？"李豔麗從口袋掏出個筆記本，內頁插著些一寸大小的男女黑白照片。

"我不很自信，"田懷意又馬上表示，女方要和他結婚的話，就必須是互相有利，以免將來出現意外。他又舉列說，這個女的首先是人品好也要聰明，而且要生活在一個落後的環境，也正在尋找有本事的男人，讓這個丈夫成為她的避風港。

"那，這丈夫得到什麼好處。"

"她就會永遠感謝我，不會拋棄，拋棄家庭。"他說完就看著櫃檯上飛落的蒼蠅。

李豔麗把他的要求寫在筆記本上，又抬頭問：那外省的要不要，有大學文憑。

"調動不了戶口的不要，家庭出身黑五類和政治上是黨員勞模的都不要。當然，也不要老外。"

"好，這本子裡三個女的都不合適，你就等著吧。"

離開商店走入熱鬧的街道，在斜陽照耀下，他看到幾個騎自行車的女青年正穿過前面廣場下班回家，他突然感到這其中的一個就是他的未婚妻，但又不可能，他眼前又顯出那個陌生女人的臉，帶著憂鬱而且空洞，使他產生了一陣安靜的失望。

整個秋天他都在收看信件，有時就去女方的家裡訪問。他進過一個又一個陰沉的家庭，女方常常是這種家的傭人角色，雙手總在充滿酸菜燉魚味的角落忙碌，父親會吆喝正在刮姜皮的母親，嚼著甘蔗的男孩則眼神死板。他坐在其中，被沉默壓得說不出話。有的女青年在送他上街的空當就告訴他如何討厭流氓父親，求他帶她走，有的會因為家裡沒有幸福而哭泣。田懷意發現那些甜美笑容的照片〔背景是珠江大橋或者是擠滿桅杆的碼頭〕背後都隱藏著尖叫和傷感，斷絕交往後有的在內心積下了內疚，有的就被惡意的詛咒一番。有個叫王娟的

"You got him!" yells a gravelly voice from on high. Emerging from the trench, a kick to the helmet dazes him.

He asks for and receives an eye test and a sudden decline is noted—like attenuating circumstances—in his ability to see. Just two diopters. Escaping a reprimand, his punishment arrives eleven days later, while recovering in an infirmary from a state of acute asthenia following the refusal of food. Anorexia, with an origin in depression, is the diagnosis. It is decided he will be transferred to the military hospital in San Giorgio. Two days of intravenous feeding, then a gradual assumption of food, first liquids, then solids. And a talk with the army chaplain, Don Cerioni. To the chaplain he confesses that the discovery of a physical imperfection has thrown him into despair. The chaplain, stupefied, asks:

"For two diopters?"

No, he says, it's not because of the diopters. I don't know how to explain it. I never believed that the body could betray one like this. The mind doesn't interest me, but the body is everything.

"This is the real sickness," says Don Cerioni.

He gets up out of bed and walks in his pajamas on shiny tiles. Sometimes he walks in the courtyard, under the trees, along windows that repeat like the battlements of a fortress. At twilight, when the noises from afar weaken and disperse in the clear air, it feels like the courtyard has become a prison.

"It is your head that is a prison," says Don Cerioni.

And when he confesses to the chaplain that his mistrust of the world has only grown, the other man responds, laughing, that he has exchanged the world for himself and this is the reason for his mistrust. He decides not to confess anything more to the chaplain.

Discharged on the 6th of February 1956, three months later he is employed by the livestock holding Diulio Vallegani, in Piacentino, breeders of milking cows. He discovers that despite their apparent fixity cows are in fact mobile and curious, and that Gianluca Vizzini, their guard, recognizes—and knows the names of—all one hundred and ninety-nine of them.

He erects a hill of earth in the immense pen, around which the cows lazily move, or, in the closeness of the afternoon, lay themselves down and rest like an industrial nativity scene. On the 2nd of July 1957, as a hot smell radiates from the herd, he leans on a fence and watches them for a long time.

Then he says to Vizzini (who is shoveling dung at the foot of the little hill):

"They're better than us."

With clear admiration he observes the sexual performance of Timoteo, a black bull on loan from a Canadian stud farm.

"It's lucky that the cow is fake," he comments, while the animal—eyes dilated, bright, enormous—copulates with an iron outline, covered by a black caparison. Ultimately all they needed to collect the sperm was that outline.

"In the end we're technological animals," he says, eyes shining.

On the 18th of September 1959 he turns to Florence, to Via della Scala, to the matrimonial agency "Meetings." Doctor Amelia Ristori, the director, is politely amazed by his youth. Might she be permitted to ask him—she adds with one flowing movement, while extracting a drawer from the filing cabinet—whether he has female acquaintances among his peers?

"Yes," he replies.

"A nice-looking boy like you," she continues, "and there's no one you're interested in?"

I don't have a lot of faith, he says. He would like to make clear at the beginning the boundaries of any relationship, to avoid any future surprises. He fears they want to marry him to get ahead. She listens to him in silence, under a color print of *The Kiss* by Hayez. He would prefer a relationship founded on reciprocal interests. For example: a girl with the necessary moral and intellectual gifts, living in an uncomfortable situation, who is looking for an equally gifted husband to make good her escape.

"But what's in it for the husband?"

"Gratitude, I suppose."

She begins to transcribe the personal data on a card. In which papers do you want to make the announcement? Regional or national?

Regional. He asks her:

"Do you think there will be any responses?"

"Many."

When he exits at sunset onto a lively street, he comes out onto the piazza Santa Maria Novella and sees a group of girls laughing under the arcades. He has a strange feeling as he watches them, thinking that it could be one of them, but that could never be—then he sees, surfacing

女青年見面之後表示她來是為了克服害怕男人的缺點。還有的女人是為了錢為了他有宿舍有固定工作。他有兩次去了郊區火車站約會,在飯館的遮陽篷下,他發現事先約定的手握報紙或者車票都是多餘的,他倆只是從猶豫的眼神裡就很快發現對方。也有和照片無法對上的時候,包括記住的臉和陌生的體態無法重合,這常令雙方尷尬地看著別處。田懷意對女人的判斷過去在找妓女的時候還行,那時是帶著租隻動物的心態,可疑的眼光中充滿了貪婪。但現在是選擇人生伴侶,那他就束手無策了。

1961年十月3日,他預感到將在解放廣場見到的女青年會成為他的木婚妻。她24歲,從護士學校畢業,現在家看著兩個弟弟。他倆已經通了三封信。他知道了她母親已去逝,42歲的父親和一個賣體育用品的女人又結了婚。她不喜歡這位後媽,也不想再去上大學深造或者找工作。在第二封信裡她就表示:做他的家庭主婦,給他生兒育女。

她個子矮小,身材豐滿,黑髮在前額剪了個劉海,看上去象古埃及的娃娃。她說知道他想要什麼樣的女人,那就是她。田懷意感到她又害羞又大膽,矛盾又複雜的性格會難以對付。這些在信紙上是看不出來的。

他在心裡開始疏離她,喝完一杯桔子水後他就承認自己無法把握她。

"你和許多男人一樣,"她冷冷地說。

"但我有說出來的勇氣。"

"那你就更加懦弱。"

她是對的。他只剩下放棄的膽量了。

很快,李豔麗又給他介紹了一位剛過三十歲的女人,叫媛媛,家住廣州臨近的佛山鎮。第一次通上電話,便傳來了她緩慢的聲調,平靜的對話令他昏昏欲睡,又有點蒼涼,使他想起非洲的荒原,那是在上地理課時看到的:近處的青苔和水坑映著遠處灰色天空,放眼望去一片孤獨。這使他感到有點不尋常又延續的穩定生活,一種順從和看上去無法逃避的圓形地平線。她說:我就想把頭靠在你肩上。

媛媛的外貌長得一般,在信中她形容自己又小又豐滿。但其實她乳房並不大,胳膊和大腿也許粗壯些,總體看去還是文弱有加,但這個身體有韌性和耐心,是可以放心擁有的。當她放任大笑的時候,又展示出了和稚氣不同的成熟。這種對比使田懷意更有新鮮感。

接下來的約會他發現兩人各有人生目標,但有一點還是共同的:過一個平和的生活,不浪費時間,很少社交,不追求高雅的文藝生活,不看小說,更不過問政治。當太陽在1962年的4月3日又照耀在解放廣場的時刻,他對她滿意地說:

"好了，你唯一要做的就是控制住你的幻想。"

他們於1963年6月19日在被改成倉庫的天主教堂旁邊的門房舉行了婚禮。除了義大利醫生盧西亞諾當了證婚人兼神父，田懷意沒有親屬到場，遠在新疆勞改的父親音訊全無，只有他的朋友福生和紅娘李豔麗來了。他知道田懷意不是為了愛情而結婚，但還是替同學高興。他在三年前已經成了家，老婆是工廠的會計。走到教堂前面的小廣場時福生小聲說：等過了蜜月摘下面具之後，你的婚姻問題才會出現。

三個月之後，田懷意和福生爬上足球場的階梯時笑著說：看，我們沒發生問題。

也許是面具還沒摘下來吧。福生擦著汗笑了笑。也許，我們就是兩個面具。田懷意有點得意地說。

媛媛從不介意周日丈夫和福生去江邊釣魚或者去看乒乓球比賽。晚上吃完飯之後他倆還會偷聽收音機，通常是香港電臺廣播的武俠小說《七劍下天山》或《白馬嘯西風》，碰到文藝或新聞節目就馬上換台。在愛好方面他倆從未發生爭執。他倆也會去東風路逛街，買回些房間裡需要的茶杯墊或月份牌。但經常就是進去看看。他發現媛媛很節儉也愛做白日夢，常會幻想擁有友誼商店裡賣的那些中國人得不到的象牙雕和真絲紗巾。

你們在家裡有沒有分工？沒有，很和氣，感情很好。在床上呢？福生眼角有一種暗示：這才是考驗男女的地方。還可以。沒問題嗎？沒問題。田懷意又說，她是沒有什麼性經驗，可學的很快。當然，她沒有我以前認識的女人那麼主動。但她不會背叛我，我也不會。做丈夫就該這樣。

"別這麼正經，像是給領導彙報成績。"福生說。

"雖然我從未問過，但她很滿足，真的，"他又說，"她肯定有快感，有時就像風暴般呼呼地響，能感到她抑制不住了，就如海嘯沖進了肉體，然後地震般地顛簸著。有時她會像波浪一陣一陣地顫抖。不過，無論在做愛之前或者之後，她都紅著臉不說。

"你沒有快感我不驚訝，"福生聽了臉上還是有些不屑，"但如果僅僅為了快感，那夫妻生活也沒有意義。"

"我有快感，你這是什麼意思？"

"我是說，如果我們要愛情，就想佔有一切，如果不要愛情，那兩人在床上是幹什麼？"

"我愛她。"田懷意肯定地說。

正如他的願望，田懷意有了兩個孩子，男孩田野出生在1965年一月七日，女孩田園在也1966年十一月22日被母親從婦產醫院抱著來到街上。田懷意微笑著抓著老婆的手說，一切都在計畫之內。在貼滿"

---

in the air, like a sheet of newspaper, a melancholic face looking at him. He has the sense—quietly despairing, and without knowing why—of not having any other choice.

All autumn to sift through the letters and to visit gloomy families, in which the women undergo endless persecutions, hateful silences, and incest, and where to live is to scream, to cry, to serve, to rebel. Sad appeals, hiding behind the smiles in the photographs (in the background of grassy slopes, through ports crowded with masts). Some phone contact, halfway between embarrassment and malice; farewells that in their very cordiality reveal that they are, in fact, concealed renunciations. There were also painful requests for money, and coarse offers of clandestine meetings intended to triumph over—as Adele C. from Grosseto put it—shyness. Two meetings in minor train stations, under the awnings of open-air cafes, including signs to recognize each other by—which their mutual hesitations soon rendered superfluous. He listens, watches, hardly speaks, takes part, judges. He thinks that he judged in the brothel, too; the suspicious and greedy eye of those who buy animals. But here the question concerned a choice for life.

Often there are glaring differences between the photographs and the person—sometimes a difference of ten years—with metamorphoses of the body that leave them difficult to even recognize.

On the 3rd of October 1961 he has the intuitive feeling of having met, in Piazza del Campo a Siena, the woman who would be his. Three letters had been exchanged and the precise articulation of a few points. Age: twenty-four. Education: secondary-school diploma in science. Occupation: mother's help. Her charges were her father's two children—he had been widowed when he was forty-two, and had taken a second wife, the check-out girl in a sporting-goods shop. She had a difficult relationship with both her father and her mother-in-law. She didn't want to take a university course or work outside the house. Her calling, as she specified in her second letter, is to be a housewife for a man like her.

She is small, brunette, plump, with a fringe that lends her the air of an Egyptian baby. She says she knows what he wants. It's her. She has a shy forwardness about her, an immediate irony that was not clear in the letters.

Too much initiative—perhaps a difficult personality.

In his mind, he begins to give her up. He confesses that he is a little cowardly.

"Like many men," she says.

"But I have the courage to say it."

"Only so you can be more cowardly."

She's right. He has already given her up.

To follow another path: a thirty-year-old from Perugia, Carla Salviati. In the first telephone dates she speaks slowly, a restful conversation, almost hypnotic. A serene sort of desolation, which reminds him of a landscape he has never seen, that of the tundra, though he studied it in Nangeroni's *Geography*: lichen, puddles of water reflecting a gray sky, solitude as far as the eye could see. Unusual style of life. Continuity, resignation, circular horizons, impossible to escape. One of her favorite expressions: "He has his head on his shoulders."

Her physical appearance doesn't disappoint. Her size she described in a letter as being small and strong, which he had translated as short and fat, but instead she is only a little inflated in the breast, in the arms, and—as far as one can make out—the legs. Her physique suggests weakness, patience, availability. She laughs with a ripe indulgence that contrasts with her childlike freshness. This peculiarity makes him curious.

They discover in their following meetings a comforting convergence of aims: a peaceful life, with no time-wasting—neither political distractions, nor the social whirl—and above all, free of snobbish cultural aspirations. As the sun sets on the 3rd of April 1962, on the Field of Miracles in Pisa, he says to her:

"The only thing you can do is limit your illusions."

They marry on the 19th of June 1963 in the church of San Frediano in Lucca. Only the witnesses, no relatives, no social whirl. He has the moral support of Francesco Salani, the one friend to whom he had confessed the secret of how they met, and who has said to him (while insisting on the need for sincerity): "The difficulty will come afterward, when you take off the masks."

吊死劉少奇油炸王光美"的公共汽車站那兒，天空下起了一陣小雨，田園平靜地眸著眼。

田懷意加入釣魚協會是在1989年5月6日的晚上。飯局是在中外合資的珠江酒店，協會會長是已離了婚的福生，在這間能容納百人的宴會廳裡，田懷意頭一次被眾多的眼光看著，他有點激動地說：我這個人一生做事就是量力而行，從未有過野心。所以今天，我有了一個完整的家庭，孩子們都畢業並結了婚。街上鬧學潮的遊行隊伍裡也不會有他倆。他又指著坐在右邊的老婆，她是我的賢內助，我從她身上學到了做人的本份。我很珍惜她。當然，我也沒有讓她失望。田懷意等大家笑完又說，今年，我已經五十八了，仍然每天早晨打太極拳。今年剛得過廣州市退休職工健康比賽優異獎。這也證明瞭我父親說過的：健康的身體才是通向智慧的源頭。說完他還鞠了躬。在一陣掌聲中，他意識到自己從未這麼大聲講演，而且說出了小時候父親說過的話。他微微感動了。他的妻子壓著他顫抖的手。

1996年十一月16日，他在為購買女兒的生日禮物時暈倒在電梯口。出院時醫生又提醒他，雖然心臟沒有大問題，但還是要小心，回家臥床儘量少活動。兒子田野租了輛車把他拉回江邊的新家，那裡拆近後被香港開發商蓋了一片新樓房，他住在二房一廳的三層樓上。從涼臺看去，近處的江邊還在建住宅社區，但遠處的山丘，甚至他父親開車的那條土路還依稀可辨，在太陽照耀下水泥攪拌車開過之後，塵土便如霧狀沿路波浪般散開。

他開始讀鄧南遮的《玫瑰三部曲》了，那些書都是文革後父親單位用卡車送還的。書架上還遺留著寫滿父親手記的義大利語《夜鶯之歌》。他驚訝書本裡竟然有那麼多真理，那麼多精彩的詩句。也許是因為父親的酷愛，使他拒絕了這些經典文學藝術。那麼，反正，一切都太晚了。

田懷意去世於2005年3月3日，那天他正在看一盤四十年前的農牧業先進模範表章大會的錄影帶，那是女兒在大學資料庫中找到的，而且認定裡面有他正獲得了青年農業專家獎狀的場面。

"誰知道，誰知道……"他最後對自己說。

馬建 譯
2012.8.3

* * *

But the difficulty hasn't arrived yet, he tells Salani, three months later, as they climb the stairs of the football stadium in Florence. Maybe because— he smiles—they haven't taken off the mask. Or maybe because— insinuates his friend—they have become two masks.

Every night they watch the television and choose the same programs by mutual consent—usually soap operas. They enjoy *Carosello*, too. No cultural programs. On that breed of boredom they are in perfect agreement.

She doesn't mind if he goes to hunt in Maremma with Salani. Or if he goes to see the Empoli matches or to a game of Fiorentina. He goes with her to buy stuff for the house, but primarily to browse. He has discovered that she is thrifty and loves to daydream about the things she failed to get. Division of labor? No. Solidarity. Maybe affection.

And in bed? asks Salani, eyes suddenly suggestive. It's the testing ground of every couple. It's not bad, his friend answers. It's not bad? No, he replies, it's not bad. She didn't have experience, but she wasn't slow to learn. Certainly she lacks the mastery of the kind of women he's been having all these years. But she hasn't betrayed him, and nor will she. Everyone should do it like this.

"Speaking seriously really brings out the worst in you," says Salani.

Nor does she have regrets. He's not sure she draws pleasure from intercourse—Salani listens to this impassively—but pleasure there surely is. At first it's a muffled pleasure like the rumble of a storm, then a sudden jolt like an earthquake, and finally irrepressible like a tsunami, with cyclical waves pushing out and long shudders on the way back in. However, she says nothing, not before or after.

"That you should orgasm doesn't surprise me," says Salani, "if only because, if you didn't, what would be left?"

"Meaning?"

"Look, love can be an obstacle," he replies. "If one wants it too much, one wants everything, one is upset for nothing. But without love, what are two people doing in a bed?"

"But I love her," he said.

* * *

Two children, just as he had imagined as a boy: Pietro, born on the 7th of January 1965, and Marta, born on the 22nd of November 1966. Life is planning, he smiles, stroking the new mother as he takes her back home in the car, through snowy scenes. The baby doesn't cry.

When he is accepted into the Circle of the Hunt, on the evening of the 6th of May 1989, on a convivial Tuesday at the Grandluca Hotel, he introduces himself reading from a card and, as the eyes of everyone at the table turn to him, finishes thusly: "I have never had any ambitions larger than my capabilities. I have a united family, and my children have graduated and married. My wife and I"—pointing to her at his right— "Have a wonderful relationship. I have learned over the years to appreciate her, and she has never disappointed me. I have reached my fifty-eighth year without any serious illnesses. I still engage in sports, above all gymnastics, and I participate with distinction in competitions for seniors. And this only confirms what the Latins used to say: *Mens sana in corpore sano.*"

He bows to the unanimous applause of his fellow members. He has never before this moment said aloud this phrase so beloved by his father. He is slightly moved. His wife squeezes his hand.

On the 16th of November 1996 the cardiologist Frederico Traglia, of Arezzo, advises him against continuing with his sporting activities. It's not anything too grave, but some caution is necessary.

In the farmhouse that he has restored on the peak of a hill in Senese, he sees the sun set in vaporous waves. He has filled a shelf with academic texts that his father had intended for a country house and it happens that he now reads the fairytales of Fedro with Chiarini's simultaneous translation. What truth! Maybe it had been the shadow of his father that had kept him so far from the classics. Anyway, now it is late.

He dies on the 3rd of March 2005 in front of the television, watching the recording of an educational game in which he had taken part, as an expert in agriculture, forty years earlier: *Who Knows Who Knows It?*

TIAN HUAIYI

translated into English by TASH AW

This is the absolute truth: like all mammals, it has two eyes, a nose, and a mouth, as well as long, unevenly placed limbs.

—*"On Monsters," J.R. Wade Cook*

TIAN HUAIYI WAS BORN on 30 April 1930, in the war-torn southern Chinese city of Guangzhou. His father, Tian Shulin, had studied for a doctorate in chemistry in Italy; his mother, Juliet, a Florentine, had followed her husband to China the previous year and had found a job as a mathematics teacher in a technical-skills institute not far from where they lived.

His father worked as a sales manager for an Italian company called Scala, whose principal product was imported thermal valves. He was passionate in his love of literature and ideas, and had published in the Guangzhou *Daily* three pieces of literary criticism and five Italian poems in translation. He often bemoaned the fact that he had sacrificed his literary aspirations for the everyday monotony of his thoroughly commercial job, and whenever he reflected on his life, he would become nostalgic for his time as a student in Italy, when he used to recite lines of poetry aloud, as bright and clear as the ringing cries of brokers in an auction house. He often tested his son on the names of those poets, but of course, each time,

TIAN HUAIYI

translated into Spanish by ÁLVARO ENRIGUE

Es una verdad incuestionable: como todos los mamíferos, tiene dos ojos, una nariz y una boca, así como largos miembros dispuestos de manera dispareja.

—*J.R. Wade Cook, "Sobre los monstruos"*

TIAN HUAIYI NACIÓ el 30 de abril de 1930 en Guangzhou, una ciudad destrozada por la guerra en el sur de China. Su padre, Tian Shulin, había estudiado en Italia un doctorado en Química; su madre Julieta—florentina—había seguido a su padre a China el año anterior al nacimiento del niño y trabajaba como maestra de Matemáticas en una escuela técnica cercana a su casa.

El padre era gerente de Ventas en una compañía italiana previsiblemente llamada Scala. Se dedicaba a la importación de válvulas termales. Era un hombre apasionado por la literatura y el pensamiento que había publicado tres reseñas y cinco traducciones de poemas italianos en el periódico de Guangzhou. A menudo lamentaba haber sacrificado su carrera literaria por la monotonía de un trabajo de mercader. Cuando se detenía a meditar sobre su vida, lo atenazaba la nostalgia por sus años de estudiante en Italia, en los que había versos luminosos y claros con la potencia de un corredor de subastas. Muchas veces interrogaba a su hijo sobre los nombres de sus poetas dilectos, a sabiendas de que Tian Huaiyi simplemente miraría hacia las montañas y los ríos alzándose de hombros. La respuesta del joven no colaboraba con la autoestima del gerente de ventas.

Tian Shulin no era un hombre que estuviera al día: apenas se enteró del fin de la Segunda Guerra Mundial tras la rendición de Japón. A pesar de que la empresa italiana estaba al borde de la bancarrota, su preocupación principal era revisar la sección de Cultura del periódico en busca de poemas recientes. Cuando los encontraba, alternaba entre el silbido y el aplauso, cómo si él mismo fuera un teatro. En la imaginación de su hijo, el regreso del químico a casa era tan dramático como la entrada de un cantante a escena: volvía de la oficina listo para soltarse con una canción, partitura en mano. Casi siempre, lo que seguía era un colorido concierto de D'Annunzio, su poeta italiano favorito.

Tian Shulin y Luciano, el médico de la Iglesia Italiana, salían todas las semanas de paseo por el campo, donde almorzaban. Luciano, que estaba casado con una china, también era un lector devoto de D'Annunzio, lo que lo hacía el compañero ideal del químico. A menudo dejaban los caminos de tierra y detenían el coche en medio de la nada para caminar por los márgenes de un cráter, un valle con la hierba crecida o una parcela con los surcos rotos. Los sembrados que manchaban el paisaje remoto le parecían a Tian Huaiyi un tablero de ajedrez. Se entretenía con el verde de las colinas en la distancia mientras escuchaba a Luciano y su padre compitiendo por recitar los mejores versos de su clásico personal. Ninguno de los dos volteó nunca hacia el asiento trasero para ponerle atención al niño que se aburría viendo las colinas acompañado por una Julieta que siempre iba de pésimo humor.

En el verano de 1946 Julieta abandonó a su marido e hijo y se regresó sola a Italia. Fue por esa época, también, que Tian Huaiyi desarrolló un odio profundo por cualquier cosa relacionada con el arte o la literatura, y empezó a enfocarse únicamente en experiencias empíricas. Eligió una Universidad especializada en carreras útiles para la reconstrucción del país tras el desastre de la guerra, en la que no hubiera cursos de humanidades. Haber tomado esa decisión le pareció un gesto de madurez y la prueba de que tenía más visión que sus amigos. Se decía a sí mismo todo el tiempo: hay que mantenerse apegado a la realidad. En relación al tema del matrimonio y la eventualidad de una familia, pensaba que lo mejor para él era una joven que no tuviera absolutamente nada que ver con la comunidad artística y planeaba tener dos hijos: un niño y una niña. Hacía ejercicio regularmente y mantenía su distancia con respecto a los partidos políticos. Cada vez que su padre trataba de ponerlo a leer *La Divina Comedia* pretextaba actividades extracurriculares en la universidad.

Tian Huaiyi would simply gaze out of the window at the rivers and hills beyond and shrug his shoulders. Needless to say, this response scarcely added to his father's feeling of self-worth.

Tian Shulin barely noticed Japan's surrender and the end to the Second World War. His Italian employer was on the verge of bankruptcy, yet his main preoccupation was scouring the arts section in the newspapers in search of the latest poems. On finding them, he would alternate between hissing and applause, just like a rowdy theater audience. In his son's imagination, his return from work each day would seem as dramatic as a singer's arrival on stage: music sheet in hand, ready to break into song—a concert of colorful lines from D'Annunzio, his favorite Italian poet.

Every week, accompanied by Luciano, the doctor from the Italian church, he would set off in the car for a picnic in the country. Luciano, who had a Chinese wife, was a fellow devotee of D'Annunzio, which made him a perfect companion for Tian Huaiyi's father. The two men would often stop the car along dusty stretches of dirt track before skirting around hollowed-out craters, hurtling up grassy knolls, or streaking across abandoned farmland. The green hills in the distance and the clumps of grass that dotted the countryside would seem to Tian Huaiyi like pieces on a giant chessboard, as he listened to his father and Luciano competing to recite lines from the classics. They never once turned round to pay attention to the frowning Juliet or her fidgety son in the back of the car.

That summer of 1946, Juliet abandoned her husband and child and returned to Italy alone. It was at about that time, too, that Tian Huaiyi developed a profound loathing of anything related to art or literature, and began to focus solely on empirical experiences. He chose a university that did not teach the humanities, only what was needed for the reconstruction of the nation following the war, for he was much more mature and far-sighted than his friends. His motto was: remain grounded in reality. As far as marriage and family were concerned, he wanted a girl who was not a member of the artistic community; and he planned that he would one day have two children, a boy and a girl. He exercised regularly and kept his distance from all political parties. And every time his father tried to get him to read *The Divine Comedy*, he cited "extracurricular activities" as an excuse.

Thus the map of his life began to take shape.

On 16 October 1950, Tian Huaiyi was admitted to the newly created College of Agriculture, where he began to work in the field of "backward rural agriculture modernization" in order to help feed and employ more people. He was the only one among his classmates to grapple solely with practical issues, never declaring lofty political ideals or talking about romance. At weekends, he would leave the college dormitories to take the train home, and from a small alley next to the train station, he would make his way into a shady underground brothel. A dim, narrow staircase led to a honeycomb of squalid wooden cubicles. Occasionally, through an open red-painted window, he would catch a glimpse of a small courtyard, densely planted with plants and flowers; a few items of women's undergarments and skirts would be hanging on a lifeless clothesline, bathed in the light of the setting sun. His blood would be feverish with sexual desire, but most of the time, clutching a handful of toilet paper, he would meekly follow a prostitute to bed and, without even seeing her breasts clearly, swiftly climax.

"None of this troubles me," Tian Huaiyi would tell himself. "My mind is detached from all this." He enjoyed good relations with Mama Li, who ran the brothel, and would always politely greet the girls as they came and went. *This benefits both of us* became his catchphrase—he would repeat it earnestly each time he went to bed with a girl, even though he knew that they would all laugh at him, this beautiful mixed-blood college student. Sometimes, when he was forced to take part in political activities, he would knock on the door late, but the girls would nonetheless rouse themselves from sleep and entertain him: he was a faithful client, this irresistibly romantic Italian half-caste. During busy periods, he would have to be content with a girl whom no other client wanted, and while he lurked in the gloomy silence with her, he imagined that the prettier girls were waiting somewhere else, saving themselves especially for him. Of course, when he discovered that the situation was exactly the opposite, he would feel inconsolably dejected.

"They like you, they know what kind of man you are," said Fusheng, Tian Huaiyi's only friend; he was the son of an Indonesian Chinese and had plenty of experience with women. "You're a red-blooded Italian." It was late on 27 June 1953; they had just left a smoky restaurant and were strolling on warm paving stones on a road lined on either side by high, damp walls. Overheard, a few swifts flitted across the night sky.

At university, after the examination on Fertilizer Composition, Professor Cai asked Tian Huaiyi if he wanted to sit for a supplementary

Fue así como el mapa de su existencia comenzó a adquirir contornos definidos.

El 16 de octubre de 1950, Tian Huaiyi fue admitido en la recién fundada Facultad de Agricultura, donde se especializó en Sistemas de Modernización de la Agricultura Tradicional. Vivía enfocado en el diseño de modelos que pudieran alimentar y emplear a más personas. Era el único de sus colegas concentrado solamente en asuntos prácticos. Se abstenía de vindicar posturas políticas y nunca habló con nadie de asuntos amorosos. Los fines de semana dejaba el dormitorio universitario para tomar el tren de vuelta a la ciudad. Antes de volver a casa, se desviaba por un callejón detrás de la estación para detenerse en un burdel sombrío e ilegal en el que una escalera estrecha y empinada conducía a un panal de escuálidos cuartos de madera. Ocasionalmente la ventana de madera roja del lugar estaba abierta, lo cual le permitía ver desde las alturas un patio densamente poblado de vegetales y flores cultivados por las muchachas; sus faldas y fondos flotando en un tendedero al sol en declive de la tarde. Usualmente llegaba ya cocido por el deseo, así que arrancaba un trozo de papel de baño y seguía a una prostituta a la cama donde, sin siquiera notar el tamaño de sus pechos, volaba al orgasmo.

Nada de esto me afecta—se decía Tian Huaiyi—mi mente está en otra parte.

Tenía una estupenda relación con Mama Li, la madrota que regenteaba el negocio y que siempre despedía y le daba la bienvenida educadamente a las muchachas cuando entraban y salían de la sala de exhibición. "Esto es un contrato, representa un beneficio para ambos," solía decirle Tian Huaiyi a las putas cuando las seguía rumbo a los cuartos, aún a sabiendas de que su figura de estudiante mestizo, tal vez demasiado bello para un sitio tan sórdido, de por sí tenía algo de risible para ellas. Cuando en la universidad lo forzaban a participar en actividades políticas, llegaba tarde al burdel y tenía que llamar a la puerta, que ya encontraba cerrada. Las chicas se despertaban de buen ánimo para entretenerlo. Era un cliente fiel con el que encontraban irresistiblemente romántico acostarse debido a la mitad italiana de su sangre. Cuando llegaba en horas de mayor tráfico de clientes, no le quedaba más remedio que resignarse a las chicas sobrantes, así que mientras se desfogaba con humor más bien sombrío imaginaba que las pirujas más guapas lo estaban esperando en otro cuarto, manteniéndose intactas para él. Cuando descubría que la situación era exactamente la contraria, se sentía inconsolablemente rechazado. Era un hombre que al parecer no le temía a sus contradicciones. O tal vez no las registrara.

Les encantas, le dijo Fusheng, su único amigo. Saben qué clase de hombre eres. Se terminaba el 27 de junio de 1953 y estaban saliendo de un restorán cargado de humo. Saben que eres italiano, que tienes la sangre roja, concluyó. Fusheng era el hijo de una pareja de chinos de Indonesia y un hombre fogueado en amores. Ambos caminaban trabajosamente sobre las lozas de un camino bardeado por muros húmedos y altos. Aves nocturnas sacudían el aire enclaustrado de la noche sobre sus cabezas.

En la Universidad, después del examen de Composición de Fertilizantes, el profesor Cai le preguntó a Tian Huaiyi si quería tomar un examen suplementario que le permitiera mejorar su calificación. Él respondió que una nota aprobatoria le bastaba. Cuando su padre se enteró de ese gesto, tan displicente, hizo a un lado el ejemplar de *Sueño de una noche de verano* que estaba traduciendo y dijo: "No puedo creer que seas mi hijo."

Tian Huaiyi le respondió separando notoriamente las palabras, de modo que no quedara duda de lo que estaba diciendo: "Me queda clarísimo."

Era un estudiante mediano pero progresó mucho en las barras paralelas bajo la guía de un excelente profesor de gimnasia olímpica. Columpiaba las piernas sin despegarlas un milímetro, las mantenía en alto sin aflojarlas. En el momento de impulsarse con la pura fuerza de los brazos, nunca pensaba que podría salir volando por el aire denso del complejo deportivo, sino que si se soltaba, se clavaría en el centro de la tierra. También le gustaba boxear. Mientras golpeaba incansablemente el sparring, sentía la presencia de un enemigo invisible. Seguía adelante hasta derrumbarse de cansancio en las bancas de madera del gimnasio, derrotado pero satisfecho.

31 de julio de 1954: Inmediatamente después de graduarse de la Universidad, Tian Huaiyi hizo los exámenes para ingresar a la Academia Militar. La monotonía absoluta de su rutina diaria en el colegio de cadetes –permanecer parado viendo pasar un desfile, marchar, entrenamientos de campo— lo hacía sentir dueño de una paz que nunca había tenido. Apagaban las luces a las diez, llamaban a filas a las seis: la predictibilidad de la vida de regimiento le encantaba y era el único de su generación que no se aburría nunca. Ese gusto tan extravagante lo convencía de estar dotado con virtudes únicas para la vida militar.

El 16 de octubre, que fue un día resplandeciente, Tian Huaiyi asistió a las prácticas de tiro de larga distancia con su equipo. Cuando llegó su turno apuntó la ametralladora al centro de la diana—a 300 metros de distancia—y apretó el gatillo sin soltarlo hasta que se le terminaron las municiones; un ruido hueco zumbaba en sus oídos. "Parece que la ráfaga pasó en algún momento por objetivo," se burló uno de sus compañeros mientras el agrónomo se integraba de

test in order to increase his aggregate mark, but Tian Huaiyi said: a pass is good enough. When his father learned of his lackadaisical attitude, he pushed aside the copy of *A Summer Night's Dream* that he was translating and said, "It's hard to believe you're my son."

"I know," Tian Huaiyi said slowly, stressing each word.

Under the guidance of an excellent physical-education instructor, Tian Huaiyi made swift progress on the parallel bars. He would swing his legs closely together and hold them firmly aloft, absolutely unmoving. At that precise moment, he never felt as if he was going to soar into the air, but instead thought that he would sink down into the center of the earth. He also liked boxing, and, while furiously punching the leather sandbags, he would feel the presence of an invisible enemy and lash out until he collapsed with exhaustion on the wooden bench, defeated but curiously satisfied.

31 July 1954: on graduating from college, Tian Huaiyi immediately took the entrance exams for the Military Academy. In the monotony of the daily routine—standing to attention on parade, marching, going on field-training exercises—he felt more peaceful than he had ever been in his whole life. Lights out at ten, reveille at six: he liked the predictability of this regimented existence. He was the only one in the entire class who was never bored. It made him feel special.

On 16 October, on a day of brilliant unbroken sunshine, Tian Huaiyi accompanied his team to the shooting range. When it was his turn to aim the machine gun at the target three hundred meters away, he squeezed his index finger until he had exhausted the entire round of ammunition; his ears rang with a hollow buzzing. "You finally hit the target," his fellow soldiers sneered as he rejoined their ranks. He felt a crushing blow on his head, as if a rifle butt had smashed onto his helmet from a great height; he was completely dazed. That afternoon, tests on his retina and optic nerves revealed abnormally low diopter readings. But the real tragedy was discovered eleven days later, when he was diagnosed as suffering from anorexia. The doctor explained clearly that these were the first symptoms of depression. The Academy decided to transfer him to the Military University Hospital, where, after two days of vitamin infusions, his condition improved and he was able to eat a little rice porridge. When the resident doctor, Tang, came by on his rounds, Tian Huaiyi absentmindedly said that he felt as if there was a black hole within his body, and that he felt completely helpless. Dr. Tang looked him in the eye and said, "There's nothing wrong with you. It's just a problem with your optic nerves."

"No," Tian Huaiyi replied stubbornly. "It has nothing to do with my eyes. I don't know how to explain. I have no interest in spirituality or the functions of the brain. The physical body is everything to me. I can't believe it can betray me like this."

"I'm beginning to understand the real cause of your illness," Dr. Tang said solemnly.

Gradually, Tian Huaiyi was able to climb out of bed. Dressed in his patient's uniform, he would walk gingerly on the shiny tiled floor and sometimes venture outside into the courtyard, resting a while under the banyan tree before strolling along the row of windows, as small and grim as those in a fortress. When dusk fell, in those brief moments when the sounds both within and without the hospital began to fade, he felt as if he was standing in a vast open-air jail.

"Yes, your mind is a prison," Dr. Tang said, staring at him inexpressively. Tian Huaiyi found that when he spoke, the outside world no longer believed him; his words only added to people's ridicule of him. Speaking would only provoke suspicion, so he decided that he would no longer say anything to Dr. Tang.

Tian Huaiyi was discharged on 6 February 1956. Three months later, he dropped out of the Military Academy and was assigned to work on a dairy farm. He discovered that dairy cows were not just energetic, but also full of curiosity for their surroundings. Even though the herd of 199 cows looked indistinguishable, he knew each one by name; it was just like a big family. In the middle of the paddock he built a large earth mound, around which the cows could circle as they wished—grazing in the sun in the morning or reclining lazily in the shade in the afternoon. Watching them from afar was like witnessing a scene of pastoral innocence, like the birth of Jesus Christ—even if this version of the miracle was slightly more industrial.

One afternoon in July 1957, a rich smell of urine was wafting over the ranch as usual. Tian Huaiyi was resting against a wooden fence, gazing out at the cows while Team Leader Wei was shoveling manure on the earth mound. "Their lives are better than ours," Tian Huaiyi said, pointing at the young black bull. "Look at the way he behaves with the cows. He's getting more and more frisky with them as he gets older. He's lucky."

vuelta en las filas. Sintió un golpe brutal en la cabeza, como si la culata de un rifle hubiera atravesado su casco al caer del cielo; se mareó.

Esa tarde, le hicieron exámenes de retina y nervios ópticos que mostraron un descenso anormal en sus dioptrías. La verdadera tragedia se reveló once días después, cuando lo diagnosticaron con anorexia. El doctor explicó con toda claridad que eran los primeros síntomas de una depresión. La Academia decidió transferirlo al Hospital Militar, donde después de dos días de cocteles vitamínicos mejoró su condición hasta ser capaz de comer un poco de puré de arroz.

En una de las rondas del residente, llamado Tang, Tian Huaiyi le dijo distraídamente que se sentía como si hubiera un agujero negro en su cuerpo, que nunca había sentido tanta desesperanza. El doctor Tang lo miró a los ojos y le dijo: Tú estás bien, lo que tiene un problema es tu nervio óptico; nada más. No—respondió el cadete obstinadamente—no tiene nada que ver con mis ojos, pero tampoco lo puedo explicar: no sé nada ni del espíritu ni en las funciones cerebrales; el cuerpo físico es mi único interés. No puedo creer que me traicione de esta manera. El doctor Tang le respondió lacónicamente: Creo que empiezo a entender el origen real de tu enfermedad.

Tian Huaiyi fue gradualmente siendo capaz de salir de la cama. Vestido con su uniforme de paciente, caminaba con cautela por los pasillos de azulejos del edificio. A veces se animaba a salir al patio, donde descansaba a la sombra de una higuera después de dar un paseo alrededor del edificio, bajo las hileras de ventanas tan pequeñas y lúgubres como las de una fortaleza. Al caer la tarde, en el momento en que los ruidos tanto del exterior como del hospital comenzaban a ceder al silencio de la noche por venir, sentía que se encontraba en una enorme cárcel al aire libre.

Pues sí—le dijo el doctor Tang en otra de sus conversaciones—tu mente es una prisión. Se lo dijo mirándolo inexpresivamente. Tian Huaiyi se dio cuenta, hasta entonces, de que dijera lo que dijera, la gente del mundo exterior ya no le creía nada; sus palabras sólo acumulaban en la sumatoria final del ridículo. Dejó de hablar con el doctor Tang.

Lo dieron de alta el 6 de febrero de 1956. Tres meses después, se dio de baja de la Academia Militar y lo reasignaron para trabajar en una granja productora de leche. Descubrió que las vacas lecheras no sólo eran inesperadamente energéticas, estaban dotadas de una enorme curiosidad por su entorno. Aunque la manada de 199 vacas las volvía indistinguibles, él conocía a cada una por su nombre, como si fueran una enorme familia. Levantó en el centro del corral una gran montaña de estiércol alrededor de la cual las vacas podían circular tanto como quisieran—pastando al sol por la mañana o reclinándose para descansar a la sombra por la tarde. Verlas de lejos era como atestiguar una escena de inocencia pastoril, como el nacimiento de Jesucristo –aunque su versión del milagro era un tanto más industrial.

Una tarde de julio de 1957 las corrientes de aire removieron un olor a orina no inusual por el rancho. Tian Huaiyi estaba descansando contra los tablones de madera de un corral. Miraba a las vacas mientras el Líder de Grupo Wei enriquecía su montaña palando estiércol fresco. Sus vidas son mejores que las nuestras, dijo Tian Huaiyi señalando a un toro joven color azabache. Mira como se comporta con las vacas, pasó de juguetón a fogoso y le siguen correspondiendo; es un suertudo y ni cuenta se da.

En septiembre de 1959, Tian Huaiyi fue transferido de vuelta a Guangzhou, esta vez como agente de ventas para la Corporación de Exportación e Importación de Ganado Vacuno. No tardó mucho en encontrarse con su vieja conocida Mama Li Yanil. Hacía años que había dejado el burdel y trabajaba como dependiente de un mostrador en una tienda de departamentos; además se había convertido en una casamentera de mucho éxito y reconocimiento. A ella le impactó encontrar a Tian Huaiyi todavía más apuesto que en su juventud, así que no pudo resistir preguntarle: ¿Y tus compañeras de trabajo son guapas? Respondió que sí. ¿Hay alguna que te guste? Sacudió la cabeza: Por eso te vine a ver. Li Yanli se sacó un cuaderno muy gastado del bolsillo de su delantal. Sus páginas estaban cuajadas de fotos de hombres y mujeres en tamaño infantil y blanco y negro.

Tian Huaiyi admitió de entrada que era un hombre con poca confianza en sí mismo. Aún así, hizo una lista sorprendentemente detallada de los que le parecían los requisitos indispensables para un buen partido. Si una mujer se quería casar con él, el trato debía generar ganancias para ambas partes, de modo que se evitaran desacuerdos futuros; la principal virtud de la mujer tenía que ser la docilidad, pero quería una que además fuera inteligente; tenía que venir de un ambiente simple, más bien pobre; debía necesitar un hombre sólido y práctico, como él; ser una mujer en busca de refugio, para la que su marido fuera todo.

¿Y qué gana un hombre en una relación así?, le preguntó la casamentera. Su gratitud, respondió Tian Huaiyi. Nunca la voy a abandonar y a la familia que hagamos juntos no le va a faltar nada. Cuando terminó su alocución, bajó la mirada al cuaderno de la matrona, que se había quedado abierto sobre el mostrador. Ella se reclinó para anotar sus demandas y lo miró a los ojos. ¿Te interesa una provinciana? Pero que tenga diploma universitario, respondió. Tampoco quiero a

On 18 September 1959, Tian Huaiyi was transferred back to Guangzhou, this time to the Animal Breeding Stock Import and Export Corporation, where he worked as a salesman. Before long, he'd found Mama Li Yanli from all those years ago. She had long since left the brothel, and was now a shop assistant in a department store. She had also become a famous and highly successful matchmaker. She was amazed to find Tian Huaiyi even more handsome than before, and could not resist asking, "So are there any young girls where you work?"

"Yes," he replied.

"I mean, any that you fancy?"

He shook his head. "That's why I've come to see you."

Li Yanli fished out a notebook from her pocket. Its pages were stuck with small black and white photographs of men and women, about an inch in size.

"I'm not a very self-confident person," Tian Huaiyi admitted at the outset. Nonetheless, he went on to outline his requirements: if a woman wanted to marry him, the match had to be mutually beneficial so as to avoid mishaps in the future; the woman had to be first and foremost of good character, but also intelligent; she had to come from a simple, deprived background; she must, of course, be in search of a solid, practical man like him, and must want her husband to be a place of refuge for her—he had to be her everything.

"In that case, what's in it for the man?"

"I would have her gratitude," he said. "For she will never be abandoned, nor will the family be left wanting." When he finished speaking, he merely bowed his head and looked at the flies on the counter.

Li Yanli wrote his request in her notebook and then looked at him. "Are you interested in someone from the provinces? She has a college diploma."

"I don't want anyone who has to be transferred without a residence permit, or anyone from the five blacklisted categories, or members of political parties and model workers—and of course, no foreigners."

"Well then, the three women I have in mind are all unsuitable. You'll just have to wait."

As he left the store and stepped into the light of the setting sun, he saw several young women cycling home from work in the square ahead. For an instant, he thought that he recognized a former girlfriend among them, but as the girl approached, he realized that he had been mistaken. Her face was unfamiliar to him; all that he recognized was the melancholy and sadness etched across it. He felt a swell of quiet despair deep within him.

Throughout that autumn, he would rifle through the post for news of matches, and sometimes he would pay visits to potential partners. He visited household after gloomy household: the girls were always treated like servants in these homes, always busying themselves in a corner with menial tasks, their hands reeking of pickled cabbage or stewed fish. The father would always be shouting at the mother, who would always be peeling ginger, and there would invariably be a son impassively chewing sugarcane, his expression numb and unchanging. Tian Huaiyi sat amid all this, steadfastly uncommunicative. Some girls would drag him out into the street and moan about how they hated their lowlife of a father, begging Tian Huaiyi to take them away from this wretchedness; others would break down sobbing because of all this misery at home.

Tian Huaiyi realized that behind those sweet, smiling faces in the photographs (predictably and unimaginatively taken against a backdrop of the Pearl River Bridge or a busy marina crammed with the masts of sailboats) there were always hidden screams and silent anguish. Each time he broke up with a girl he would feel a profound sense of guilt, and some of them would be so angry that they would heap malicious curses on him. He found the whole business thoroughly baffling. One young woman by the name of Wang Juan admitted that she had only agreed to meet him in order to overcome her fear of men. Others came because of money, simply because he had a room in a dormitory as well as a steady job. Twice, he arranged dates in suburban train stations, and, waiting under the awning of the station restaurant, he found that the prior arrangement of holding a newspaper or train ticket was completely superfluous, as they were able to recognize each other simply by their hesitant manner and general awkwardness. It was easier even than taking along a photograph, as people rarely resembled their portrait. He found that he had little clue about how to judge women. When, years before, he had gone with prostitutes, it had seemed as uncomplicated as selecting livestock, but now that he was in search of a life partner, he had no idea what to look for.

On 3 October 1961, he had a premonition that the woman he was meeting at the YWCA in Liberation Square would be his future wife. She was twenty-four years old, recently graduated from nursing school,

nadie que necesite un permiso de residencia para ser transferida, nadie que tenga nada que ver con las listas prohibidas; tampoco mujeres afiliadas a partidos políticos ni trabajadoras modelo; por supuesto, no quiero bajo ninguna circunstancia una extranjera. Li Yanil se rascó la cabeza. Entonces ninguna de las tres candidatas que había pensado para ti funciona. Vas a tener que esperar un poco.

Dejó la tienda con una inclinaciltimo sol de la tarde, vio pasar a varias mujeres regresando del trabajo en bicicleta.e tenga nada que ver con las categormplea ón de cabeza. Ya bajo los rayos del último sol de la tarde, vio a la distancia un pelotón de mujeres en bicicleta, regresando del trabajo rumbo a sus casas. Por un instante creyó reconocer entre ellas a una que había sido su novia, pero conforme se fue acercando se dio cuenta de que estaba equivocado. No era su cara lo que le había parecido familiar, sino el aire de melancolía y tristeza que la cruzaba. Sintió en su interior la inflamación de una desesperación callada y hartera.

Durante ese otoño asaltaba cada poco el mostrador de Li Yanil a la espera de noticias sobre posibles candidatas. En algunas ocasiones hacia visitas a parejas potenciales. Visitó casa tras casa y todas le parecieron más bien deprimentes. Las jóvenes a las que se esperaba que pretendiera eran tratadas como sirvientas. Las tenían arrinconadas haciendo labores miserables, las manos apestosas a vinagre de conserva o pescado cocido. En todos los casos el padre se pasaba la visita gritándole órdenes a la madre de las jóvenes, que siempre estaba pelando jengibre. Invariablemente, había un hermano presente, que masticaba caña de azúcar sin decir ni una palabra, con gesto ausente y fijo. Tian Huaiyi entraba a esos escenarios en plan más bien poco comunicativo. Algunas chicas lo sacaban a la calle y se quejaban sobre las vilezas de su padre, rogándole que las liberara de ese naufragio. Otras se ponían a llorar durante la presentación, porque no entendían del todo la misteriosa puesta en escena que se ejecutaba en casa.

Tian Huaiyi entendió que detrás de las caritas que había en las fotografías—caritas contrastadas siempre contra un fondo de cerezos en flor o marinas repletas de veleros—se ocultaban siempre o gritos o silencios angustiados. Cada vez que rompía con una de las chicas se sentía hondamente culpable; algunas se enojaban tanto que lo despedían con inquietantes maldiciones antiguas. El proceso de encontrar esposa le parecía, por decir lo menos, desconcertante.

Una joven llamada Wang Juan admitió que sólo había aceptado ir a una cita a conocerlo para superar su miedo a los hombres. Otras dijeron que había ido por que pensaban que tenía dinero o porque tenía un trabajo fijo. Dos veces arregló citas en paradas del tren suburbano y, esperándolas bajo el toldo del restorán de la estación, se dio cuenta de que el plan según el cual se reconocerían por la forma de portar un periódico o el boleto de tren era completamente superfluo: era obvio cuál era la chica por la pura inseguridad de sus modos y el aura de incomodidad que la rodeaba. Era más fácil reconocerlas por esas rarezas que llevando su foto al encuentro: la gente nunca se parece a sus retratos.

En esas citas descubrió que en realidad no tenía elemento de juicio para evaluar a una mujer. Cuando años antes iba con prostitutas, elegir a una le parecía tan fácil como escoger una pieza de ganado. En cambio ahora que estaba en busca de una pareja de por vida no tenía idea, en realidad, de lo que necesitaba.

El 3 de octubre de 1961 tuvo la premonición de que la mujer a la que había quedado de encontrar en la YWCA de la Plaza de la Liberación sería su esposa. Tenía 24 años, estaba recién graduada de la escuela de enfermería y era responsable de sus dos hermanos menores. Habían intercambiado tres cartas, así que sabía que su madre había muerto y que su padre de 42 años se había vuelto a casar con una mujer que vendía equipo deportivo. No se llevaba con su madrastra, pero ni quería regresar a la Universidad para seguir estudiando, ni estaba dispuesta a buscar un trabajo. En la segunda carta ella le dijo directamente que quería ser su esposa –quedarse en casa, cuidarla, tener sus hijos.

Era una mujer baja, pero tenía buenas caderas. El pelo negro mate cortado de modo que el fleco le tapaba la frente. Tian Huaiyi pensó que se veía como una muñeca egipcia. Ella dijo que sabía qué clase de mujer estaba buscando y que ella llenaba esos requisitos. Tian Huaiyi sintió que era al mismo tiempo tímida y arrojada; su temperamento contradictorio prometía complicaciones con las que seguro sería difícil bregar—problemas que no habría podido descubrir sólo leyendo sus cartas. La verdad es que apenas se sentó frente a ella, comenzó a distanciarse emocionalmente y, una vez que terminó su vaso de jugo de mandarina le pareció claro que no podrían llevarse bien.

Eres un hombre típico, le dijo ella fríamente.

Cuando menos tengo el valor de decir las cosas como son.

Eso te hace todavía más cobarde.

Y tenía razón. Todo lo que le quedaba a Tian Huaiyi eran los vestigios de un coraje que lo había abandonado hacía mucho tiempo.

Al poco Li Yanil le presentó a una mujer que acababa de cumplir treinta. Se llamaba Yuanyuan y vivía relativamente cerca, por el pueblo de Foshan. La primera vez que conversaron por teléfono, su manera lánguida de hablar le produjo algo de sueño y hasta cierto abatimiento; mientras la escuchaba, pensaba en las sabanas del África –al menos como se las había imaginado en las clases de geografía de la secundaria: musgo en el primer plano, charcos reflejando el

and was now at home looking after her two younger brothers. They had exchanged three letters, so he knew that her mother had passed away, and that her forty-two-year-old father had remarried a woman who sold sports equipment. She did not get along with her stepmother, but she did not want to go back to college for further studies, nor was she keen on going out to search for work. In her second letter she wrote, quite plainly, that she wanted to be his wife—to stay at home, look after the house, and bear his children.

She was short but amply built, with black hair cut in a fringe that fell over her forehead; she looked like an Egyptian doll, thought Tian Huaiyi. She said she knew what kind of woman he was looking for—and that she fulfilled all his criteria. Tian Huaiyi sensed that she was at once shy and bold; her contradictory, somewhat complicated temperament would surely be difficult to deal with. This sort of problem could not be discovered in a mere letter. Even as he sat there, he began to distance himself emotionally from her, and once he had finished his glass of tangerine juice, he admitted that he could not see himself ever getting along with her.

"You're a typical man," she said coldly.

"At least I have the courage to speak plainly."

"That makes you even more of a coward."

She was right. All he had were the vestiges of the courage that had abandoned him a long time ago.

Soon afterward, Li Yanli introduced him to a woman who had just turned thirty. She was called Yuanyuan and lived not far away, near the town of Foshan. The first time they spoke on the telephone, her languid way of speaking made him sleepy and even a little despondent; it made him think of the vast plains of Africa—at least as he had imagined them in geography lessons at school: green moss in the foreground, puddles of water reflecting the gray sky, nothing but loneliness as far as the eye could see. He felt as if his life was strange and unchanging—a passive, seemingly inescapably circular existence.

She said: "I just want to rest my head on your shoulder."

Yuanyuan's looks were fairly average. In her letter she had described herself as short and plump, but in fact her breasts were not particularly ample and her arms and legs might have been stouter: the general impression was, in fact, one of frailty and gentleness. But there was also a sort of resilience and patience about her, and he felt that she was someone who could belong to him and pose him no problems. And when she laughed, she seemed at once childlike and very mature. These contrasts made Tian Huaiyi feel joyous and curiously optimistic.

On their next date they discovered that although they had differing goals in life, they shared a number of crucial ambitions: to live peacefully; never to waste time; to remain apart from social circles; never aspiring to high culture, never reading novels, and certainly never showing any interest in politics. The sun was still high in the sky over Liberation Square that day—3 April 1962—as they talked at length about a possible life together. He said: "Fine. The only thing you have to do is promise to keep your fantasies under control."

The wedding took place on 19 June 1963, in the old Catholic church that had been converted into a warehouse; the ceremony was held in the janitor's room. Apart from Father Jian and Luciano, the Italian doctor, who acted as the witness, Tian Huaiyi had no family present. He had had no news of his father, who had been sent to a labor-reform camp in the remote reaches of Xinjiang Province. Only his friend Fusheng and the matchmaker Li Yanli attended. She knew that Tian Huaiyi was not marrying out of love, but that he was nonetheless as happy as any of his friends, for he had found his true home three years previously, when he had stumbled on a job he loved: he was wedded to the factory-accounts department.

After the ceremony, while they were strolling in the small square in front of the church, Fusheng whispered, "After the honeymoon, once you've dropped your masks—that's when the problems will appear."

Three months later, Tian Huaiyi and Fusheng were climbing up the stairs at the soccer ground. Tian Huaiyi laughed and said, "You see? I told you we wouldn't have any marital problems."

"Maybe you're still politely wearing your masks," Fusheng said, wiping the sweat from his brow as he laughed uproariously.

"Or maybe that's just who we really are," Tian Huaiyi replied, smugly.

On Sundays, Yuanyuan never minded her husband and Fusheng going out to fish or watch a table-tennis competition, for she would still have plenty of time with him after dinner, when they would settle down and listen to the radio together, tuning into broadcasts from Hong Kong— usually adaptations of martial-arts novels such as *Seven Swords* or *White Horse, Roaring West Wind*. As soon as a cultural program or the news came on, they would switch stations. They had similar tastes and never argued

cielo gris, nada más que soledad hasta tan lejos como alcanzaba la vista. Sintió que su vida era rara y reiterativa —una existencia pasiva, al parecer inescapablemente circular.

Ella le dijo: Lo único que quiero es poder descansar la cabeza en tu hombro.

La apariencia de Yuanyuan no era nada del otro mundo. En su carta se había descrito como baja y repuesta, pero la verdad era que sus pechos no eran particularmente amplios y sus brazos y piernas apenas pasaban por fornidos. Daba una impresión general de fragilidad y gentileza, aunque también tenía algo de paciente y flexible, así que Tian Huaiyi pensó que le podía pertenecer sin dar problemas. Tenía una risa al mismo tiempo madura e infantil. Una personalidad tan cargada de contrastes cómodos producía en él una alegría inopinada e incluso cierto curioso optimismo.

En la siguiente cita descubrieron que aunque tenían objetivos diferentes en la vida, compartían una cantidad crucial de ambiciones: vivir en paz, no perder el tiempo, mantenerse apartados de cualquier círculo social, no aspirar nunca a la alta cultura, no leer novelas y bajo ninguna circunstancia mostrar el menor interés en la política. El sol todavía estaba muy arriba sobre la Plaza de la Liberación ese 3 de abril de 1962 cuando hablaron largamente de las posibilidades de una vida compartida. Él le dijo: Lo único que me tienes que prometer es que vas a mantener tus fantasías bajo control.

Se casaron el 19 de junio de 1963, en una antigua iglesia católica transformada en bodega. La boda se celebró en la conserjería. El padre Jian ofició la misa y Luciano, el doctor italiano, actuó como testigo. No estuvo presente ningún familiar de Tian Huaiyi. No tenía noticias de su padre desde que fue enviado a un campo de reeducación en la parte más remota de la provincia de Xinjiang. Los únicos invitados fueron su amigo Fusheng y la casamentera Li Yanil. Ella sabía que Tian Huaiyi no se enlazaba con Tuanyuan por amor, pero que eso no importaba porque ya era un hombre satisfecho: había encontrado su verdadero hogar hacía tres años, cuando aterrizó en un trabajo que amaba de verdad; vivía casado con el Departamento de Contabilidad de la fábrica. Después de la ceremonia, mientras paseaban por la placita enfrente de la iglesia, Fusheng le murmuró al oído: Después del viaje de bodas caen las máscaras y empiezan los problemas.

Tres meses después, Tian Huaiyi y Fusheng estaban subiendo las escaleras a la cancha de fútbol. Tian Huaiyi estaba contento: ¿Ya ves? Te dije que no íbamos a tener problemas matrimoniales. Tal vez todavía traen las máscaras, le respondió Fusheng, limpiándose el sudor de la frente mientras se reía a carcajadas. O tal vez somos como somos de verdad, respondió Tian Huaiyi con suficiencia.

A Yuanyuan no le importaba que los domingos su marido fuera a pescar o ver juegos de ping pong con Fusheng, porque sabía que le quedaría tiempo de sobra con él después de cenar, cuando se instalarían a escuchar el radio juntos, sintonizando programas de radio de Hong Kong –generalmente adaptaciones de novelas de artes marciales, como *Las siete espadas* o *Caballo blanco, Vientos del oeste*. Tan pronto comenzaban los programas culturales o de noticias, cambiaban de estación. Tenían gustos similares y nunca discutieron sobre esas minucias. También paseaban juntos por la calle de Dongfeng, para comprar cosas que necesitaban para la casa; se hacían de objetos menores, como un calendario o manteles individuales, aunque a menudo sólo veían los escaparates sin comprar nada. Él descubrió que aunque Yuanyuan era una persona frugal, a veces fantaseaba con ir a Almacenes Amistad a comprar cosas que sólo los extranjeros tenían autorización para adquirir –piezas de marfil tallado, bufandas de seda.

¿Se les complica dividir el trabajo de casa?, preguntó en otra ocasión Fusheng.

No, nos llevamos bien; cada uno hace lo que tiene que hacer, como si nada; nunca hemos discutido por eso. ¿Y la cama?—había un brillo en la mirada de Fusheng, un brillo que decía: esa es la verdadera prueba para un hombre y una mujer. Todo bien, respondió Tian Huaiyi sin un ápice de duda. ¿Sin ningún problema? Ni uno. Y agregó: No tiene mucha experiencia sexual, pero aprende rápido; no es de armas tomar, como las otras, pero, a cambio, nunca me va a traicionar; y yo a ella tampoco: ese es el lugar del marido. Carajo, bufó su amigo, no seas solemne: suena como si estuvieras llenando un reporte del trabajo. Tian Huaiyi respiró hondo, como para anunciar que pasaba al terreno de la confidencia. No le he preguntado porque siempre se pone roja cuando lo hacemos, pero creo que está satisfecha. No te creo. Se rió y dijo: No hay duda de que goza en la cama: a veces berrea como un huracán, pierde el control, un tsunami barriéndole todo el cuerpo; o se estremece y se sacude sin pena ni pausa, como las olas pegando en la orilla del acantilado. Terminó fingiendo humildad: Aunque nunca sabes con las mujeres. No me sorprendería que tú no tuvieras mayor placer—le respondió Flusheng todavía con aire desdeñoso— pero supongo que la vida matrimonial no se mide en términos de placer. No sabes de lo que estás hablando, dijo Tian Huaiyi: Me complace de verdad. Fusheng lo miró directo a los ojos. Lo que quiero decir es que, si quieres amor de verdad—siguió—tienes que incluirlo todo; las parejas tienen que tenerse por completo, el amor debe ocupar cada una de sus partes y la posesión tiene que ser mutua y total; si no quieres amor de verdad, para qué tomarte la molestia de

over this sort of thing. Sometimes they strolled together down Dongfeng Road, buying things they needed for the house, such as small placemats or calendars, but often they would just window-shop without buying anything. He discovered that although Yuanyuan was very frugal, she would often daydream, fantasizing about going to the Friendship Store to buy things that only foreigners were allowed to purchase, such as ivory carvings and fine silk scarves.

"Is it difficult dividing up the household chores between you?"

"No, we get along well—everything just happens naturally—there's never any conflict."

"What about… in bed?" There was a glint in Fusheng's eye, as if to say: *this* is the real test of a man and a woman.

"It's all right."

"No problems at all?"

"None."

Tian Huaiyi then added: "She doesn't have much sexual experience, but she's a fast learner. Of course, she doesn't take the initiative the way the women I've known in the past have, but then again, she will never betray me. And nor will I her. That's what a husband should be."

"Don't be so damn solemn. You sound as if you're filing a report to your boss."

"Even though I've never asked, I know I satisfy her. Really." He laughed. "She definitely gets great pleasure in bed. Sometimes, she screams like a howling gale—you can just tell that she's lost all self-control, as though a tsunami is sweeping through her body, then she shudders and jolts over and over again, like waves crashing onto the shore. But the strange thing is, before and after we make love, she just blushes and says nothing."

"If you don't get any pleasure, I wouldn't be at all surprised," Fusheng said, still wearing a look of mild disdain. "But I guess married life isn't about pleasure."

"What are you talking about?" Tian Huaiyi said quietly. "I do get pleasure."

Fusheng looked him squarely in the eye. "What I mean is, if you want true love, it has to be all-encompassing. Partners have to possess every part of each other—love has to occupy every part of you. And if you don't want true love, well—why bother even going to bed with her?"

"I love her," Tian Huaiyi said firmly.

Exactly as he wished, Tian Huaiyi had two children. A boy named Tian Ye was born on 7 Jan 1965, followed by a girl named Tian Yuan on 22 November 1966. As her mother carried her out of the maternity hospital, Tian Huaiyi smiled and squeezed his wife's hand. He said, "Everything is going to plan." In the crowded bus station there were banners proclaiming, EXECUTE THE COUNTER-REVOLUTIONARY LIU SHAOQI! BOIL THE TRAITRESS WANG GUANGMEI IN OIL! Tian Yuan calmly opened her eyes to the world. Outside, there was a light rain shower.

Tian Huaiyi joined the Anglers' Association on the evening of 6 May 1989. A dinner was held at the Overseas Joint Venture's Pearl River Hotel. Fusheng had since married and was now the chairman of the association, presiding over the ceremony. There were over a hundred people in the banqueting hall, and, as he took his place at the lectern to make his speech, Tian Huaiyi could not recall ever having been the center of attention for so many people. With some excitement, he began to speak:

"In my entire life I've been very measured in my approach, very methodical in everything I've worked at. I've never had any unrealistic ambitions. I guess this is why I have a perfect family. My children have graduated and are now married. They would never be mixed up in the noisy student rabble demonstrating in the streets these days." He pointed to his wife sitting to his right. "She is a good wife to me. I learned from her how to be a dutiful person. I truly, truly cherish her. And of course, I have never let her down, have I?" Tian Huaiyi waited for everyone to stop laughing and said, "I'm fifty-eight this year, yet every morning, at daybreak, I practise Tai Chi, and I've recently won a Guangzhou City Retired Worker's Health Competition Award. This proves what my father, who is surely watching us from a distance, used to say: a healthy body is the route to the source of wisdom."

He bowed.

Amid the applause he realized that he had never before made such a confident speech in public, nor spoken of the things his father had said to him when he was a child. He was moved almost to tears; his wife held his trembling hand tightly.

On 16 November 1996, on his way to buy a birthday present for his daughter, he collapsed in the elevator. As he was discharged, the doctor reminded him that although there were no major problems with his

acostarte con tu esposa. Concluyó: Yo la amo.

Tal como había deseado, Tian Huaiyi tuvo dos hijos. Un niño llamado Tian Ye nació el 7 de enero de 1965, seguido por una niña llamada Tian Yuan, en noviembre de 1966. Mientras la madre la cargaba fuera de la maternidad, Tian Huaiyi sonrió y le apretó la mano a su mujer. Dijo: Todo va como estaba planeado. En la estación de autobuses, repleta de gente, había unos estandartes que proclamaban: ¡EJECUTEN AL CONTRARREVOLUCIONARIO LIU SHAOQI! ¡HIERVAN EN ACEITE A LA TRAIDORA WANG GUANGMEI! Tian Yuan abrió los ojos calmadamente al mundo. Caía una llovizna.

Tian Huaiyi se integró a la Asociación Nacional de Pescadores con Caña la noche del 6 de mayo de 1989. Se ofreció una cena en el Hotel de Inversiones Internacionales Conjuntas del Río Perla. Para entonces Fusheng ya se había casado y era el presidente de la asociación; encabezaba el banquete en esa calidad. Había más de cien personas en el salón de fiestas. Mientras se levantaba para leer su discurso, Tian Huaiyi no podía recordar una ocasión en la que hubiera sido el centro de atención de tanta gente. Emocionado, comenzó a hablar.

Toda mi vida he sido mesurado en mi forma de hacer las cosas, metódico en todos mis empeños. Nunca tuve ambiciones irreales. Supongo que es por esto que tengo una familia perfecta. Mis hijos fueron a la Universidad y están casados. Nadie se los va a encontrar entre las muchedumbres ruidosas de estudiantes que se manifiestan en las calles estos días.

Apuntó hacia su mujer, sentada a su derecha, y siguió: Es una buena esposa. Aprendí de ella a ser diligente. La aprecio de verdad. Y, por supuesto, nunca le he fallado. ¿O si? Tian Huaiyi esperó a que la gente dejara de festejar el chiste para concluir:

Tengo 58 años y todavía hago Tai Chi todas las mañanas. Acabo de ganar el Premio a la Salud de los Trabajadores Retirados de Guangzhou. Esto prueba lo que mi padre, que seguramente nos mira desde la distancia, solía decir: un cuerpo sano es la mejor ruta a la fuente de la sabiduría. Hizo una inclinación de cabeza.

Mientras le aplaudían, se dio cuenta de que nunca había estado tan seguro de sí mientras decía un discurso. Tampoco había hablado nunca de lo que su padre le decía cuando era niño. Se conmovió casi hasta las lágrimas. Su mujer le apretó la mano.

El 16 de noviembre de 1996, en camino a comprarle un regalo de cumpleaños a su hija, se desmayó en un elevador. Cuando lo dieron de baja del hospital, el doctor le recordó que aunque no tenía problemas mayores de corazón, debería cuidarse y salir poco de casa, descansar mucho, mantener la actividad física al mínimo.

Su hijo Tian Ye alquiló un coche y lo llevó a su casa nueva. Estaba en un desarrollo reciente, construido por una compañía de Hong Kong en el predio de unos edificios abandonados. El departamento estaba en una unidad de tres pisos y tenía dos habitaciones y una estancia amplia. Parado en el balcón, Tian Huaiyi podía ver los complejos residenciales de la orilla del río. En las colinas, a la distancia, los caminos de tierra por los que alguna vez manejó su padre en las expediciones dominicales al campo apenas eran visibles. Una mezcladora de cemento trabajaba bajo la luz lechosa del día; el polvo se levantaba como una neblina que se expandiera por oleadas en el aire.

Empezó a leer los *Romances de la Rosa* de D'Annunzio. Terminada la Revolución Cultural, la Unidad de Trabajo de su padre le había devuelto todos sus libros; eran tantos que los tuvieron que enviar en un camión. Entre los libros, Tian Huaiyi había encontrado los apuntes del viejo sobre la "Oda a un ruiseñor." Lo sorprendió encontrar tantas verdades en esos libros, tantos poemas espléndidos. Tal vez fue la pasión de su padre por esos clásicos la que lo hizo voltearles la espalda.

En cualquier caso, ya era demasiado tarde.

Tian Huaiyi murió el 3 de marzo de 2005. Ese día había estado viendo un video de la Asamblea General de Pequeños Ganaderos que su hija había encontrado en los archivos de la biblioteca. Tenía cuarenta años de haber sido filmado. En la película, había una escena brevísima en la que se vio a sí mismo recibiendo su certificado como Trabajador Modelo y un reconocimiento de Joven Especialista en Agricultura.

¿Quién puede saber qué habría sucedido?, se susurró a sí mismo justo antes de morir. ¿Quién?

heart, he nonetheless had to be careful and stay at home, with plenty of bed rest and minimal physical activity. His son Tian Ye rented a car and took him back to his new riverside home, a brand-new development built by a Hong Kong company on the site of some derelict old buildings. The apartment was in a three-story block and had two bedrooms and a spacious lounge. Looking down from the balcony, Tian Huaiyi could see a residential community on the riverbank; in the distant hills, the dirt roads that his father had once driven through during those Sunday outings in the country were barely visible. In the hazy sunshine, a cement mixer was just starting up; the dust it created was like mist that spread like waves through the air.

He began to read D'Annunzio's *Romances of the Rose*—after the Cultural Revolution, his father's work unit had returned all his books. There were so many of them that they had to be loaded onto a truck. On the bookshelf Tian Huaiyi found the notes his father had made on the "Nightingale's Song." It surprised him to find so much truth contained in these books, so many splendid poems. Maybe it was because of his father's passion for these classics that he had turned his back on them.

In any case, it was all too late.

Tian Huaiyi died on 3 March 2005. That day, he had been watching a video of the General Assembly of Livestock Farmers from forty years ago, which his daughter had found in the university archives. In the film, there was a short scene in which he was receiving his certificate for Model Performance and Young Specialist on Agriculture.

"Who knows what might have been?" he whispered to himself just before he died. "Who knows?"

NOTES ON THE TRANSLATIONS

I.

My first thought on reading "Umberto Buti" was that the protagonist seemed strangely Chinese, with his rejection of politics, aversion to risk, sense of inferiority, and thwarted desires. I asked myself: if he'd been born in China in 1931, how many details of his story would have to be altered? How much would the change of place affect his fate?

I should make clear that, as my grasp of English is still dreadfully poor, my initial reading was aided by Google Translate and online dictionaries, and then, much more helpfully, by a recorded translation my partner, Flora Drew, made for me, which I then replayed, transcribed, and rewrote. I didn't ask for clarifications, and she didn't check my finished piece. Our aim was to leave room for "happy mistakes." She did, however, read several passages of Zadie Smith's English translation out loud to me, so that I could pick up the rhythm of the prose.

Wanting the protagonist to retain some connection with his homeland, I transplanted him to Guangzhou, the southern port where Italian Jesuits first entered China. I gave him an Italian mother and the name Tian Huaiyi. ("Tian" is the surname of the Chinese translator of Dante's *Divine Comedy*; *Huaiyi* means "Italian Heart.")

I tried to keep the structure and narrative of the original, but for the story to work in its new setting, elements needed to be added and removed. I had to find equivalents for organizations that didn't exist in China, such as the matrimonial agency and the Circle of the Hunt, and sometimes alter the way characters spoke or thought. Whereas the original story appears to exist in a vacuum, when it unfolds in China, politics and history inevitably creep in.

It's impossible to mention the years 1931, 1966, or 1989, for example, without making reference to the tumult of the times. In Italy, the limits on the protagonist's ambitions are self-inflicted; in China, added constraints are imposed by the state. Tian Huaiyi doesn't choose his jobs or places of residence, he is "assigned" and "transferred." In such a context, people's sense of isolation and desire for security deepens. So, whereas in the original, the wife's favorite expression is: "He has his head on his shoulders," in the Chinese version I have her say, "I just want to rest my head on your shoulders."

This project has been enlightening. It has made me question how much characters are shaped by time, place, and language, and convinced me that the hardest challenge of translation is to find a way to give the new version the same breath of life that animated the original.

—*Ma Jian*

II.

Problems from the outset: how to translate a work by a well-known, living writer like Ma Jian? How much had he transposed (I knew that some way up the chain lay a story in Italian), and how much did I dare alter in the text myself? It made me realize that I approach translations differently if the piece is by a living writer—dead ones are so much easier to deal with.

In the end, the nature of the translation insisted itself upon me after just one reading of the story. Ma Jian's prose here has a tone and rhythm that is gently hypnotic, full of stillness. Wry and wistful, quietly evocative, the passages were clear and unadorned—all I had to do was tune in to this style. Once I was on the same frequency, the steady, even pacing that Ma Jian had laid down carried me smoothly through the piece.

From a technical point of view, I faced the usual issues when translating Chinese. The phonetic rendering of Italian names back into English was a particular problem here, for I had no recourse either to the writer or the original text. The treatment of tenses was another—Ma Jian writes in the present, which works more fluently in Chinese in a story of this sort than in English. I guessed that the Italian version up the chain was in the present tense too, but I nonetheless decided to change to the past tense. Something about the timespan of the story— long and languid, an epic in miniature form—demanded the slower pace that the past tense seemed to offer.

—*Tash Aw*

III.

Adam promised me a champagne bottle if I finished in record time, and I did. Some parts of the story felt like they did not make a lot of sense, in psychological terms—the whole bordello thing seemed unfitting with the main character's psyche, so I did pull a few strings there. My whole life here in New York happens in bad English and bad Spanish, so it was a relief to do something that involved a good English–good Spanish relation. I was quite conservative about my syntax, which tends to be much more complex.

I do wish I'd held this back a bit, to force Adam to bet two champagne bottles.

—*Álvaro Enrigue*

X

HOGY VISSZANYERJÜK

a story in HUNGARIAN *by* LÁSZLÓ KRASZNAHORKAI

ILLUSTRATORS, IN ORDER OF APPEARANCE

Ian Huebert, Wesley Allsbrook, Tim Lahan, Brianna Harden, Mike Bertino, Erin Althea.

UM ZURÜCKZUGEWINNEN

translated into German by LÁSZLÓ KRASZNAHORKAI

THE FRIGHTFUL HUNT

translated into English by LAWRENCE NORFOLK

DIE FURCHTBARE JAGD, damit wir verstehen, wer die Erde schuf, damit wir formulieren, welcher Traum des Zufalls sie ins Dasein rief, geht langsam zu Ende. Unsere Metaphern sind erschöpft, unsere Vorstellungskraft ist verdorben, nur unser Intellekt arbeitet noch nach seiner ursprünglichen Funktion, aber wir sind mit dieser Funktion nicht mehr ein-verstanden, wir wollen uns nicht mehr der Leidenschaft überlassen, die dem Intellekt Schwung gab und ihn erhielt. Es gibt keinen Platz mehr zu Hause zu sein, und niemand kann sagen, na, das hier gehört mir, es gibt kein Losfahren und keine Heimkehr mehr, nicht einmal in Gedanken, es gibt nur einen grausam wunderbaren, vereisten Glanz, in dem man klar sieht: außer uns gibt es in dieser gigantischen Welt niemand, und in dieser gigantischen Welt gibt es außer uns nichts, und hat es auch nie gegeben. Nichts, aber wenn es trotz-dem etwas gäbe, würde etwas es für immer vor uns verdecken, egal in welche Richtung wir uns bewegen, dieses Etwas bewegte sich immer mit uns zusam-men, wie der Mond mit einem rennenden Kind in der Nacht—der Mond, um dieses Etwas immer zu verdecken, der Mond, damit dieses Kind dieses Etwas nie erreichen kann. Mit einem Wort: alles ist vergebens, wir sind weder fähig, aus der Welt, in der wir leben, herauszusehen, noch die Welt, in der wir leben, zu überschauen, lassen wir es also sein, sei dies genug, es ist entschieden, bitte, keine weiteren Experimente: die Welt ist voll und ganz human, die Wege

I

THE FRIGHTFUL HUNT, so we understand
Which created the Earth, so we formulate,
Is now (alas) running into the sand…

Our metaphors are desolate,
Our imaginations polluted and unfecund
Our minds work against their owners' isolate

once-grief-filled now-polluted Band-
-Usian Fount. The house is jammed and none can prate
"Well, here's my portion, my little piece of land."

There's no border-crossing here, no escape or rebate
but there alone may the World's true image be scanned:
An icy sheen, grotesquely Baltic, rhipidate.

What else to say? What new brand
to put to Io's flank, her lowing pate
raised above the foamy-fringed strand?

The world's shores are huge and (but for us) unmanned
and whatever lurked there, so we translate,
evades our gaze, as if long-sunk in the sand,
That one hidden *Something*, inviolate.

II

Up comes the moon. The kid's off at a run
Both speeding along in an endless race
Inseparable, chained together as one.

The *Something*'s like that, like something we trace,
Like the boy chasing after his anti-sun,
Or an endless series of failed escapes.

What next? How to move beyond *Phenomenon*
Or see that *Something*'s noumenal face,
Or glimpse the world such questions once won?

Oh, enough. Let's give ironic thanks. Let's say grace
For the world's blocked paths, all of them all too human-
choked. Let us mourn its dwindling space.

That's the task. It's what we've done
Reaching for unheard melodies, the rarest phrase,
A song pitched in H#, a poem in Papua New Guinean.

For now, and for example, it's un-
imaginable for a member of the human race
To think themselves a wolf. So no reprieve. We're done.
The world is everything, alas. That is the hopeless case.

III

None of this comes as a surprise
Not to us, inured to loss,
However poignant it may be, however pleasing to our eyes.

We hunt the meaning of our memories, toss
questions, seek allies
And reparations alike. Ask what holds us

sind geschlossen, wir können nie, aber tatsächlich nie wissen, wie wäre es zum Beispiel Wolf zu sein.

Dies alles aber stürzt niemanden mehr in Verzweiflung, und nicht nur, weil wir uns daran gewöhnt haben, dass der Verlust eine schmerzensreiche Schönheit hat, nein, weil wir dort, wo wir angelangt sind, auch denken könnten: wenn es so wäre und wir den Sinn unserer ursprünglichen Erinnerungen verloren haben, warum können wir ihn dann nicht zurückgewinnen, was kann uns noch hindern hier, an diesem Punkt, zwischen unseren erschöpften Metaphern und unserer verdorbenen Vorstellungskraft? Zurück denn zu dem holden Quellgebiet des uralten Sinns unserer Erinnerungen, dahin, wohin man vielleicht wirklich nur auf Kosten dieses Verlustes gelangen kann, zurück zu dem Punkt, an dem wir schon einmal standen, ohne zu ahnen, wo wir eigentlich sind! Das Bild, das der Verstand von der Welt behauptet, geht sowieso nicht mehr verloren, wir können also frei die entsetzliche Geschwindigkeit unseres Tempos zurücknehmen, zurück, hinaus, zur Seite, nach einem außerordentlich komplizierten Abgetriebensein hin zu einem einfacheren Sinn, dorthin, wo endlich klar wird, woraus diese vielen Gottheiten für uns geworden sind, diese höllische und himmlische Maschinerie. Wir werden sehen, was wir schon lange—obwohl nun das erste Mal—hätten sehen können, und es wird keine höhere Kraft mehr hinter uns sein, denn selbst wenn jemand hinter uns wäre, würden wir diesen Jemand ebenso für immer verdecken wie der Mond in jener Nacht jenes rennende Kind. Es kommt uns also keine verborgene Großheit / Größe zu Hilfe, wir können niemandem mehr huldigen, wir werden da stehen in dem absoluten Zentrum unserer eigenen Welt, um weitere Jahrtausende hindurch nun die tödliche Konstruktion der Irreversibilität / Unumkehrbarkeit der Dinge zu enträtseln. Inzwischen aber... inzwischen haben wir die heilsame Klarheit jener gewissen uralten Erinnerungen zurückgewonnen, die Erinnerungen daran, dass im grausamsten Sinn des Wortes: alles uns gehört, die Erinnerungen, dass wir das, was ist, geschaffen und wir selbst unsere Dinge in der Zeit plaziert haben.

Back, here between dead metaphors and the weak cries
of poets (*Imagination* being their boss),
What is, and what keeps us from, the prize?

Now. It's back to Bandusia. Take the Horatian fosse
Back to our memories' original lies,
Bearing our truths like so many fragments of "True Cross."

Where's that, you ask: Nebraska, Orkney, Belize?
Lost among all this representational dross
We wind down because time flies—
That's us: a junkyard of half-crocked clocks.

IV

You think that's bad? Here's worse.
We're all bound for Heaven-or-Hell AG
Where they churn out godheads like so much Wurst

Giving the lie to the unholy See.
Now we know what we should have known first:
There never was an Almighty Fully Capitalized He.

We'd have hidden Him anyway. Stayed put in the curse
Of being alone through Eternity
Just like (q.v. my earlier verse)

The boy and the moon, the *That* and the *He*
each tracking a linked yet separate course
Through centripetal eternity.

To summarize: there's no going back. The hearse
Is off. We're inside with no key.
The good news? Our imaginations and memories are ours
To run, to soar through, to swim. A moon-track, a sunset, a sea.

Conceived with help from Howard Sharp.

BANDUSIE

translated into French by FLORIAN ZELLER

1

C'ÉTAIT DANS UNE MAISON très ancienne qui menaçait de s'écrouler à tout moment. Je suis monté au deuxième étage sur la pointe des pieds pour ne pas être responsable d'un tel événement: j'ai toujours eu horreur de me faire remarquer. Mais j'ai manqué de cette même précaution en refermant la porte des toilettes derrière moi: le mécanisme semblait abîmé, comme si la chaleur extrême avait dilaté les gonds ou le cadre de la porte, et j'ai dû la forcer un peu pour qu'elle ne reste pas entrouverte; un bruit sourd a évoqué quelque chose de regrettable et de définitif—comme le socle d'une tombe qui se referme enfin. Aussitôt, la panique m'a gagné et je me suis imaginé bloqué à jamais dans cette minuscule pièce. Qu'aurais-je alors fait? Dans le doute, j'ai préféré ne pas enclencher le verrou, dont l'apparente vétusté, elle aussi, me laissait craindre le pire, et je me suis installé, dans une position que chacun connaît—sans parvenir à réprimer cette angoisse irrationnelle.

Enterré vivant. Enfant, je faisais souvent ce cauchemar terrifiant, et j'avais fait promettre à ma mère, si je mourais avant elle, qu'elle m'installerait le téléphone dans mon cercueil. Elle haussait les épaules avec ironie: cela ne me servirait à rien, et pourquoi avais-je de telles pensées? Est-ce que je ne pouvais pas me contenter de jouer au football comme tous les garçons de mon âge? Elle ne comprenait pas que cette précaution était au contraire très astucieuse: si, à la faveur

---

BAND U.S.A.!

translated into English by WYATT MASON

1

CONSTIPATED

THE HOUSE WAS ON THE BRINK OF COLLAPSE. To avoid the miserable eventuality that I might be held accountable, I tiptoed discreetly upstairs: I've never wanted to stand out, no, no. My preference, throughout life, is to pass like a shade through the dim mornings of civilization, to steal like a ghost through the highways and byways of our brief transit between one advent and one last. Alas, I had to slam the bathroom door behind me, like some dim brute: the whole thing—frame, jam, lock, latch—had been cooked in the heat, like cassoulet. The door had swollen on its hinges like, like, like a terribly unfortunate little lamb that perished by the seaside in the Falklands and, in the heat, became a sad little quadrupedal balloon, hoofed and fuzzy. Horrors! I say: the door simply wouldn't close without force. The sound was terrible! Terrible!—heavy and dark, like a human body falling, hitting cold tile from a great, great height. It scared me, to the point where, I confess, I experienced what I hesitate to call, well, a lack of, of, of control of my, oh dear, bowel. What was I to do? I didn't lock it— oh dear: the lock was falling apart too, which didn't make me feel any better, oh dear oh dear—so I assumed the obvious position athwart the yawning basin, and couldn't help but fear the worst.

Buried alive, like a miner, in a mine, a deep, dark, dank, and—in all likelihood—Chilean mine. As a child, this had been my recurring nightmare: I made my mother promise that, were I to expire before the first light of morning—its lemony rays gilding my soft, downy cheeks in nature's wet, hot, matutinal *bizou*—she'd settle me into my eternal resting place, my sorry crypt, with, why yes of course, a cellphone. She shrugged her shoulders: my dear boy, what leads you to such flights of whimsy? Why can't you just play kick the hobo in the street with the rest of the lads? The poor woman: she failed to appreciate the early quavers of the artistic temperament, the early throbs of… genius. For were I pronounced dead in error, I would be but a few agile thumbstrokes away from my salvation. Eventually, I wore my dim mum down and she promised. I learned our number by heart, tattooing it, as it were, on my soul, and my grandmother's too (on my soul, that is), in case ours (our phone, not our soul) was busy.

The loo was entirely dark. Only the meagerest of ribbons of light threaded through the green shutters, the tiniest of promises. One would have supposed one was on the other side of the world at the border of some uncharted desert, a domain of endless suffering, unceasing toil, unending pain. To ram the point home, postcards of paradisical lands, tropical wonderments, were affixed to the dark wall. Whither their leaver? Their edges (those of the cards, I mean) had yellowed, their recipients no doubt buried in the sands of the past, their senders turned to dust as inexorably as those stone monuments left by heathens of the great forgotten continent of Maracara. Heaven seemed a kind of hell, or so I was given to think. Joy flees. Sigh.

2

ADUMBRATED

Suddenly, I heard something on the landing—someone was coming—and I remembered that I hadn't locked the door. After thinking that I wouldn't be able to leave this place, now I was afeared that someone would see me baking, as it were, a loaf—and I couldn't imagine having to deal with some miscreant's miscast look, as if he had walked in upon an idiot of yore, humping a heifer on a heath, the queer mischief obscured by a rising mist. So, naturally, I turned on the faucet. The

d'un mauvais diagnostic, on me déclarait mort par erreur et qu'on s'empressait de m'enterrer, il me suffirait de composer le numéro de la maison pour qu'on vienne me rechercher. A force d'insister, ma mère avait fini par me le promettre, et j'ai appris par cœur notre numéro de téléphone, ainsi que celui de ma grand-mère (au cas où le premier serait occupé).

Les toilettes étaient plongées dans la pénombre. Les stores en bois vert ne laissaient passer qu'un mince filet de lumière blanche, ce qui n'était pas désagréable compte tenu de la chaleur. On se serait cru à l'autre bout du monde, sur l'un de ces rivages immenses et inexplorés. D'ailleurs, au mur, plusieurs cartes postales représentant des plages paradisiaques avaient été accrochées. Par qui? Elles avaient jauni, enfouies dans les sables de l'oubli depuis une éternité, et je me suis dit que leurs expéditeurs étaient peut-être morts et enterrés, eux aussi. A cette pensée, la vision du paradis avait quelque chose de dérisoire. Il y avait, dans une vie, des étincelles de joie qui s'éteignaient presque aussitôt. J'ai soufflé profondément.

2

Au même instant, j'ai cru entendre un bruit sur le palier—quelqu'un venait—et je me suis souvenu que je n'avais pas fermé le verrou. Après avoir craint de ne plus pouvoir sortir de cet endroit, je redoutais maintenant qu'on n'ouvre la porte sans imaginer que je sois là et qu'on me *prenne sur le fait*—le visage hébété comme quelqu'un que l'on surprend dans une arrière-salle en train de fabriquer de la fausse monnaie. J'ai alors tendu le bras pour ouvrir le robinet. Le bruit de l'eau indiquerait ma présence, et personne ne pousserait cette porte sans frapper. Je pouvais continuer à être coupable en toute impunité.

3

Je me suis alors concentré sur l'eau du robinet: c'était une cascade régulière, claire comme du cristal, une fontaine inépuisable qui procurait une fraîcheur délicieuse à la pièce. Les cartes postales, comparées au jaillissement de l'eau, paraissaient bien éteintes. Elles ne représentaient plus que des espaces disparus, engloutis. Des paradis perdus. Mon attention allait et venait de ces images au robinet, puis du robinet aux images, et cette oscillation étrange, à la façon d'un manège magique, m'a fait passer de l'autre côté: j'ai retrouvé le souvenir d'une autre fontaine, celle de Bandusie, qui apparaît dans une ode d'Horace. Dans mon imaginaire, elle a toujours été l'endroit où toute soif peut s'apaiser. Je vois un animal sur son rivage qui vient se désaltérer, et cet animal pourrait être *n'importe lequel d'entre nous*—et même, pourquoi pas, un loup—il trouverait ici du repos et de la fraîcheur. D'où me vient cette image, cette autre carte postale? Et depuis combien d'années n'ai-je pas relu le poème d'Horace? L'ai-je seulement déjà lu? Il se confond, dans mon esprit, avec tous ces textes latins que j'ai dû traduire, à l'école, et qui m'ont procuré plus de souffrance que de joie. Je n'y comprenais rien. La poésie a toujours été une langue étrangère pour moi. Une langue de vipère. Je bute sur chaque mot, le sens ne cesse de se dérober, et je maudis secrètement celui qui m'impose cette épreuve.

4

J'étais maintenant au bord d'accoucher de quelque chose. C'était là. Il me suffirait, ensuite, de me laver les mains, d'éteindre le robinet et de donner un coup d'épaule dans la porte avant de rejoindre les autres au salon, comme si de rien n'était. Au fond, c'était une situation commune et anodine: d'où me venaient ces inquiétudes? Et ces pas que j'avais entendus un instant plus tôt sur le palier, les avais-je vraiment entendus? Personne n'était là; j'étais seul, au deuxième étage de cette immense maison. Et je pouvais en profiter pour traquer la signification de mes souvenirs et revenir, un instant, à la vision de cette fontaine. Mon cœur se serre, car je peux tendre la main, la tendre encore, je n'atteindrai jamais cette source. Il n'y a que ce robinet, et le reste est illusion. Je regarde autour de moi, et je ne vois aucun endroit pour apaiser la soif—aucun endroit sinon l'écriture. Mais est-ce suffisant?

Je n'ai pas de réponse à cette question. Et, pour être honnête, je n'ai de réponse à aucune question. J'ai seulement ce cœur serré. Je me lève des toilettes et m'empresse de me laver les mains. Cette sensation n'est pas très précise. Je ne saurais dire exactement ce qu'elle signifie. On dirait le souvenir d'une vie très ancienne. Antérieure à la naissance. Et qui va s'évanouir. Ces cartes postales, cette eau, ce loup au bord de la source: toutes ces images ne signifient rien pour moi, mais forment un petit ballet de signaux qui augmente encore le sentiment de ma solitude.

Comme si ma vraie vie était déjà passée, et qu'il ne m'en restait plus que des bribes.

Mais les autres m'attendent en bas, et il est temps de les rejoindre. Je tire la chasse d'eau. A travers les volets, j'entraperçois le jour. Un enfant court au loin. Je me souviens alors qu'il nous reste aussi ceci. Courir. Fendre les airs. Nager. Regarder le cycle de la lune. Le coucher du soleil. La mer. Qu'il nous reste notre imagination, et que cela est suffisant.

water would alert them, absolutely, of my presence within: no one would dare trespass without knocking. I could, like a great sow, wallow in the brack of my solitary guilt. And then, a change beset me.

3
TOLERATED

I focused on the faucet: an even stream, a crystal bower, an undrying fount of purity that flowed through the demon dark. The postcards, in contrast to the giddy fountain, seemed embalmed. They advertised fallen empires, devoured by time. Paradise, lost. My attention drifted from faucet to cards, from cards to faucet, from… sorry, dizzy… and this strange oscillation carried me like a magic carpet: I recalled another fountain, in Bandusia [Pronunciation: *band-yoo-ess-áy* — Ed.], which you find in one of Horace's odes. I had always considered it to be the place where all thirsts were quenched, no matter their ardor. I see: an animal on a hill that has just drunk its fill; this creature could have been *any one of us*—and why not, for example, a, so to say, tiny piglet, a tiny albino piglet—finding its ease in the cool of this paradise, found. Whence came this idle, this, as it were… postcard, one unmolested by time the reaper? How many years had it been since I'd imbibed these verses? Had I, had I… even read Horace? His lines foundered in the warm waters of my memory alongside those Latin lyrics that had been my dreary duty to translate, *en école*. I didn't comprehend a word of it, I should say. Poetry had always been a foreign language to me, a lingua not so franca, what-what. A snake's tongue ho-ho. I stumbled over every word, the meaning always eluding me, and I pitied the mendicant friar who'd made me suffer so, and whom—or so I swore—I'd one day hunt down, bind, and destroy.

4
LIBERATED

Whoa! I think I just gave birth, boyee. Nailed it! All's I have to do now is wash my stinkin' mitts, shut the faucet, and punch open the door so's I can hook back up with my crew in the drawin' room, like nuttin' went down—except that big fuckin' loaf I just dropped! I mean, Jesus: Why the fuck was I actin' like such a mook? The fuckin' footsteps? Fuggeddabouttit. Wasn't nobody there; it's just me and my prick on the third floor of this fuckin' castle. Anyway, that shit about the fountain in my mind-box? Fuck if I know what that was about. Anyway, it is what it is. Gotta admit, my heart was actin' like a pussy, makin' me want to reach out and grab it like some little kid hopin' to get a grip on his pop's hand. But Jesus: it was a fuckin' faucet! I'm such a cunt when I need to take a crap. I mean, I needed a fuckin' drink, not a drink from a fuckin' faucet—and the poem? What the fuck? Douchebag alert! Like a poem was gonna help nobody.

Anyhoo. Like there are answers to questions. My heart's the answer, fucked as it is. Might as well get up from this crapper and wash my mitts. I can barely feel a fuckin' thing anyway. Who the fuck knows what it means. Past-life bullshit. Poof, there it goes. Those friggin' postcards, the fuckin' water, that albino piggy: arty-farty crapola. All's it makes me feel is more alone.

I'm done. The rest is dregs.

My boys is waitin'. Flush that fuckin' thing. It's daylight already. Some kid's runnin' in the street. So there's that. Run. Jump. Swim. Look at the moon. Sunsets. Seas.

What we've got? What we lose.

Received with laughter from HETM.

HACIENDO TIEMPO

translated into Spanish by RODRIGO FRESÁN

1 / CONSTIPADO

EN CUALQUIER MOMENTO, la casa se va a venir abajo. Para evitar eventualidad tan terrible por la que pueden llegar a considerarme responsable, desciendo por las escaleras en puntas de pie, con discreción: jamás quise destacar, no, no. Mi opción, a lo largo de la vida, siempre ha sido la de pasar como una sombra a través de las mortecinas mañanas de la civilización, escabullirme como un espectro a través de las autopistas y los caminos poco frecuentados en nuestro breve tránsito entre algo que llega y algo que parte. Aún así, tuve que cerrar de un golpe la puerta del baño detrás mío, como un zorro. Todo el asunto—marco, postigo, cerradura, picaporte—se había cocido en el calor, como una cazuela. La puerta se había hinchado en sus bisagras como... como... como el terriblemente desafortunado corderito que pereció junto al mar de las islas Falkland y, recalentado, se transformó en un pequeño y patético globo cuadrúpedo, con pezuñas y cubierto de pelusa. ¡Qué espanto! me digo. La puerta no se podía cerrar a no ser que se la empujase con fuerza. ¡El ruido era terrible! ¡Terrible! Cuando por fin se cerró, su sonido fue como algo pesado y oscuro: como el sonido de un cuerpo humano cayendo desde muy, muy alto e impactando contra las baldosas. Me asustó al punto de experimentar lo que vacilo en definir como... bueno... una pérdida del... del... del control de mis, ay, tripas. ¿Acaso pueden reprochármelo? No la cerré, ay, y el cerrojo

KILLING TIME

translated into English by SARAH MANGUSO

1 / COLD

AT ANY MOMENT the house is going to come down. To prevent such an event—I could be blamed—I'll descend the stairs on tiptoe.

I never wanted to draw attention to myself. My choice, all my life, has been to pass like a shadow through the dying morning of civilization, sneak like a ghost through the empty highways and back roads in our brief trip between coming and going.[1]

Even so, I had to wedge the bathroom door shut behind me like a fox. The whole thing—frame, shutter, lock, latch—had cooked in the heat like a casserole. The door had swelled in its hinges like... like... like the terribly unlucky little lamb who perished by the sea of the Falkland Islands and, overheated, changed to a small and pathetic quadruped balloon with hooves, covered in lint.

What horror! I tell myself. The door couldn't be closed unless it were slammed. The noise was terrible, terrible!

When it finally closed, the sound was dark and heavy, like the sound of a human body falling from very, very high and hitting the tiles. I was

---

[1] Romay (see note) suggested *something that arrives and something that departs*; I went with my shorter, incorrect translation.

scared to the point of feeling what I hesitate to define as… well… a loss of the control of my… bowels. Can anyone blame me? I didn't close it, and the bolt was starting to break, which made me feel no better, so I took the inevitable position in front of the yawning toilet and couldn't but fear the worst.

Buried alive like a miner in a deep, dark, wet, and, in every sense, Chilean mine: That was my recurring childhood nightmare. I made my mother promise that if I died before the morning's first light—its lemony rays gilding my soft, chubby cheeks, damp by the warm, humid, natural morning *bisou*—she would deposit me in my place of eternal rest, in the lament[2] of my crypt, with a mobile phone. She shrugged her shoulders and said, *Sweetie, what makes you imagine things like that? Why can't you wander the streets like the rest of your friends?* The poor woman never appreciated the first shudders of my artistic temperament, the first pulses of my… genius.

So that if I were declared dead by accident, I wouldn't be more than a few thumb-clicks away from salvation.

I eventually exhausted my mother's patience, and she ended up promising me what I asked. I learned our phone number by heart, as if it had been tattooed on my soul; and also my grandmother's number (again, fixed upon my soul), if ours (our phone, not our soul) were busy when I called.

The bathroom was completely dark. Only the humblest bits of light filtered, like the smallest promises, through the green blinds. Anyone in here would assume he[3] were on the other side of the world, bordering a land unknown to maps, a land of infinite suffering, of unending fatigue, of incessant pain. To emphasize this sensation, postcards from paradise-lands and tropical wonders were taped to the wall in the dark. Destinations of a pallid traveler? Their borders (those of the postcards) had faded to sepia, addressees securely buried under the sands of the past, their senders returned to dust, inexorably, like these stone monuments erected by the barbarians of the great lost continent of Maracara. Paradise seemed a kind of hell, or at least they made me think so.

Joy flees. I sigh.

---

[2] A literal translation; Romay confirmed it isn't an idiom.

[3] Romay corrected this from it.

también se estaba rompiendo, lo que hizo que me sintiese nada mejor, ay, ay, así que asumí la inevitable posición frente al bostezante lavabo y no pude sino temer lo peor.

Enterrado vivo, como un minero, en una profunda, oscura, húmeda y—en todo sentido—mina chilena. Esa siempre ha sido mi pesadilla recurrente cuando era un niño. Entonces, le hice prometer a mi madre que, de morir yo antes de que me alumbrase la primera luz de la mañana—sus rayos alimonados dorando mis suaves, mullidas mejillas, húmedas por el húmedo y cálido y natural *bisou* matutino—ella me depositaría en mi lugar de descanso eterno, en el lamento de mi cripta con, por supuesto, un teléfono móvil. Ella se encogía de hombros y me decía: "Querido, ¿qué es lo que te hace imaginar cosas así? ¿Por qué no puedes vagabundear por las calles como el resto de tus amiguitos?" Pobre mujer: nunca pudo apreciar los primeros estremecimientos de mi temperamento artístico, las primeras pulsaciones de mi… genio. Porque, de haber sido yo certificado como fallecido por error, no estaría a más que unos pocos golpes de pulgar de mi salvación. Eventualmente, agoté la paciencia de mi madre con mi ruego y ella acabó prometiéndome lo que le pedía. Aprendí de memoria nuestro número telefónico, como si lo hubiese tatuado en mi alma; y también el teléfono de mi abuela (otra vez, fijo en mi alma), en caso de que el nuestro (nuestro teléfono, no nuestra alma) estuviese ocupado en el momento de mi llamado.

El baño estaba completamente a oscuras. Tan solo los más humildes jirones de luz se filtraban, como la más pequeña de las promesas, a través de las persianas verdes. Cualquiera aquí hubiese supuesto que se encontraba al otro lado del mundo, en la frontera con una tierra desconocida para los mapas, un dominio de infinito sufrimiento, de fatigas sin fin, de dolor incesante. Para enfatizar esta sensación, pegadas a la pared a oscuras había postales de tierras paradisíacas y maravillas tropicales. ¿Destinos de un pálido viajero? Sus bordes (me refiero a los de las postales) se habían desteñido al sepia, sus destinatarios seguramente ya estaban enterrados bajo las arenas del pasado, sus remitentes ya habiendo vuelto al polvo, inexorablemente, como esos monumentos de piedra alguna vez erigidos por los bárbaros del gran continente perdido de Maracara. El paraíso me parecía una especie de infierno, o al menos así me hacía pensar, aquí, todo eso. El gozo se escapa. Suspiro.

2 / IMPRECISO

De pronto, oí algo en el piso de abajo—alguien subía—y recordé que no había echado el cerrojo a la puerta. Luego de pensar que ya nunca podría dejar este lugar, ahora me asustaba la idea de ser visto por alguien horneando, por decirlo de algún modo, una hogaza de pan. Y no pude siquiera imaginar el tener que hacer frente a la mirada fuera de lugar de algún malhechor, como si hubiese tropezado con uno de esos idiotas de tiempos remotos violando al gato de la casa. Así que, por supuesto, abrí el grifo. El sonido del agua les haría darse cuenta, sin lugar a dudas, de que yo estaba allí; por lo que nadie se atrevería a entrar al baño sin llamar antes a la puerta. Podía seguir sintiéndome tan culpable como quisiera. Pero entonces, experimenté un cambio.

3 / TOLERADO

Me concentré en el grifo: un fluir parejo, un entramado cristalino, una imposible de secar fuente de pureza corriendo a través la oscuridad demoníaca. Las postales, en comparación a la atolondrada fuente, parecían como embalsamadas. Publicitaban imperios desaparecidos, devorados por los milenios. Paraíso, perdido. Mi atención iba del grifo a las postales, de las postales al grifo, de... lo siento, estoy marcado, y esta extraña oscilación me llevó como a bordo de una alfombra mágica: recordé otra fuente, en Bandusia (Pronuncia: *Ban-du-si-a*, Ed.), mencionada en una de la odas de Horacio. Siempre la consideré como ese sitio en el que toda sed era saciada sin importar su ardor. Contemplo: a un animal en una colina que ha bebido hasta llenarse, esta criatura podría haber sido *cualquiera de nosotros;* y, por qué no, describirlo como a un muy pequeño cochinillo, un muy pequeño cochinillo albino, encontrando su bienestar en el frescor de este paraíso, recuperado. ¿De dónde provenía esta... a su manera... postal ignorada por el tiempo que todo lo arrasa? ¿Cuántos años habían pasado desde que yo asimilé este poema de Horacio? ¿Acaso lo... lo... había leído alguna vez? Parecía nadar en las tibias aguas de mi memoria junto a esos versos latinos cuya traducción *en école* alguna vez había sido mi temida tarea. Debo decir que no comprendía ni una palabra de todo aquello. La poesía siempre ha sido para mí un idioma extranjero, una lingua no tan franca y todo eso. Una lengua de serpiente, jo-jo. Tropezaba con cada palabra, su significado eludiéndome siempre, y así me apiadaba de aquel fraile mendicante que tanto me hacía sufrir y a quien juré, un día, dar caza y amarrar y destruir.

4 / LIBERADO

¡Hey! Creo que acabo de dar a luz, muchachos. ¡Lo he clavado! Todo lo que me queda por hacer ahora es lavar mis manos metidas en apestosos mitones,

2 / IMPRECISE

Suddenly, I heard something on the floor below—someone climbing—and remembered I hadn't bolted the door latch. After thinking I could never leave this place, I now feared the idea of being seen baking, for lack of a better description,[4] a loaf of bread. I couldn't imagine having to deal with a trespasser's impertinent look, as if he had encountered one of those ancient idiots violating the house cat, so I turned on the tap. The sound of the water would doubtless indicate that I was there, so no one would enter the toilet before knocking. I could continue feeling as guilty as I liked. But then I felt a change.

3 / TOLERATED

I concentrated on the tap: a smooth flow, a crystalline lattice, a pure source, impossible to dry up, running through the demonic darkness. The postcards, compared with the roiling source, seemed embalmed.[5] They advertised lost empires, devoured by the millennia, paradises lost. My attention was on the tap, then on the postcards, from the postcards to the tap, from... sorry, I'm dizzy, and this strange oscillation took me aboard a magic carpet: I remembered another water source in Bandusia (Pron. *Ban-du-see-ah*—Ed.), mentioned in one of Horace's odes. I always considered it as that site in which all thirst was quenched regardless of its fire.

I contemplate an animal on a hill that has drunk to fullness. This creature could have been *any of us*, so why not describe it as a tiny piglet, a tiny albino piglet, enjoying the freshness of this paradise regained.

Whence came this postcard ignored by time, which sweeps away everything? How many years had passed since I'd absorbed this poem of Horace? Since I'd read it? It seemed to swim in the warm waters of my memory next to the Latin verses whose translation *en école* had been my most dreaded task. I'll admit it—I didn't understand a word of it. Poetry has always been for me a foreign language, a *lingua* not so *franca*, and all that. A serpent's tongue—ha. I stumbled with every word, its meaning always eluding me, and I pity the mendicant monk who made me suffer so and whom I swore one day to hunt and tie up and destroy.

---

[4] Romay corrected this from *to put it another way.*

[5] Romay corrected this from *perfumed.*

4 / RELEASED

Hey! I believe I've just given birth, boys. Nailed it! All that remains is to wash my stinking mitts, shut off the faucet, and punch open the door to reunite with my people in the other room. As if nothing had happened, with the exception of that enormous loaf I just dropped.

What on Earth caused me to behave like a child? What fucking footsteps?[6] Forget it. There was no one there; I'm alone with my dick on the third floor of this fucking castle.

And what was the source of all this shit in my fat head? I have no fucking idea. In any case, there it is, and there I'll leave it for you. I must admit that my heart was jumping in fear like a kitten, needing to be held like a boy clinging to his papa's hand. But God, it was nothing more than a fucking faucet! I'm an idiot when I need to take a shit.[7] Which is to say I need a fucking drink and not a drink from the fucking faucet. And the poem? What shit! Stupid[8] alarm! As if a poem could help someone.

In any case. As if there were answers to questions. My heart, fucked up as it is, is the answer. I'd better get up from this latrine and wash my mitts. Already I feel absolutely nothing. Who will be the fuckup who knows what all this means. All that shit about past lives. Puff—already it's gone. These shit postcards, shit water, albino piglet: nothing more than artistic and pretentious garbage. And all it does is make me feel more alone.

I finished. The rest is waste.

My boys are waiting. Make this fucking toilet flush. It's already dawned. Some children are running in the street. And there it is. Run. Skip. Swim. Contemplate the moon.[9] Sunsets. Seas.

What do we have? We have what we lose.

---

[6] Romay corrected this from *fucked-up footsteps*.

[7] Romay corrected this common expression.

[8] Romay corrected this from *idiot*.

[9] Romay corrected this from third-person singular present indicative active to singular imperative.

cerrar el grifo, y abrir la puerta de un puñetazo para así reunirme con los míos en la sala. Como si nada hubiese sucedido; a excepción de esa enorme hogaza que acabo de dejar caer. Jesús, es decir: ¿qué cuernos hacía yo comportándome como un chiquillo? ¿Las jodidas pisadas? Olvídenlo. No había nadie allí; estoy a solas con mi verga en el tercer piso de este jodido Castillo. Y además, ¿toda esa mierda de la fuente dentro de mi cabezota? No tengo ni la más puta idea de qué era todo eso. En cualquier caso, ahí se queda y ahí se los dejo. Tengo que reconocer que mi corazón estaba dando saltos de miedo como un gatito, como necesitando ser aferrado del mismo modo en que un chico necesita aferrarse a la mano de su papi. Pero, dios, ¡no era más que un jodido grifo! Soy un idiota cuando me vienen ganas de cagar. Es decir, necesito un jodido trago y no un trago de un jodido grifo. ¿Y el poema? ¿Qué mierda? ¡Alarma de imbécil! Como si un poema pudiese ayudar a alguien.

En cualquier caso. Como si existieran respuestas a las preguntas. Mi corazón, jodido como está, es la respuesta. Más vale que me levante de este cagadero y lave mis mitones. Ya no puedo sentir absolutamente nada. Quién será el jodido que sabe lo que todo esto significa. Toda esa mierda de vidas pasadas. Puf, ya se ha ido. Esas postales de mierda, el agua de mierda, el cochinillo albino: nada más basura artística y pretenciosa. Todo lo que consigue es hacerme sentir más solo.

Terminé. El resto es desperdicios.

Mis chicos esperan. Haz correr el agua de esa jodida letrina. Ya amaneció. Algunos niños corren por la calle. De eso se trata. Corre. Salta. Nada. Contempla la luna. Atardeceres. Mares.

¿Qué es lo que tenemos? Tenemos lo que perdemos.

NOTES ON THE TRANSLATIONS

I.

My German is good enough to buy a railway ticket, but probably not to the right destination. I accepted this challenge with some trepidation, and my first sight of the manuscript did nothing to allay my fears. Scanning Krasznahorkai's text, I decorated the margin with comments like "What?", "Don't get it," and "Unclear—is it me?" Happily my pal and neighbor, Howard Sharp, chats daily to German businessmen who want to invest in chains of shopping malls or finance airports or somesuch, and this turned out to be the skillset we needed. Howard produced a crib, and I wrestled with the form. Given the philosophical nature of the text (a kind of Kantian two-legged stool), I was concerned to inject some jollity: "A funny thing's the villanelle" wrote W.E. Henley. So it is, but they're rather devilish to write, I discovered. The rhyme-scheme continually pulled at the sense of the piece, now this way, now the other. The writing felt, quite literally, like keeping an ill-tempered horse in line. English is an enormous language, largely because of the successive overlays of differently sourced synonyms, but it is not particularly suited to philosophical nuance. I think I lost that dimension, so my translatee will probably (and properly) feel aggrieved. But translation is famously inexact; just to ride in the same park is an achievement. I hope these verses offer a gallop over Krasznahorkai's terrain, even if the course is different.

—Lawrence Norfolk

II.

French and I are somewhat estranged these days. In my twenties, when I worked in restaurants to make my living, I translated in my spare time, for pleasure. When I replaced restaurants with writing for my daily bread, I translated much less. As the late critic Roger Shattuck told me, it's impossible to give yourself completely to writing if you're trying to make a living as a translator: translation takes up too much writing time, and energy. So, I chose writing. Even so, I do chip away at some personal translation projects now and again, for fun or out of a feeling of virtuous duty.

Enough time has passed since I translated regularly that I don't have any particular methodology anymore. I used to. In the past, I looked up every word, especially the words I knew I knew: I was translating sixteenth-century prose and nineteenth-century poetry and some contemporary prose, and I was of a temperament that if I didn't hunt down every possible meaning of something, sleep didn't happen very readily. And one likes to sleep. Once the scholarly skullduggery was done, I'd transition what was a mind-numbingly literal draft into something closer to liberality. French syntax and English syntax differ significantly, and so the grammar needs to go. Once that's done, it licenses other changes. Even so, I'd say I tended to hew closer to the original than, now, I feel one should: literality kills, liberality thrills (or so I like to imagine the motto emblazoned on Christopher Logue's favorite coffee mug).

My approach to the text Adam sent me for this project was new for me. The French text itself was easy to read, but made little meaningful sense. Someone was hiding in a bathroom, perhaps taking a crap, in a perhaps derelict house. M'kay. It didn't make me want to leap like a jungle cat into translation action. Time passed. Deadline approached; deadline passed; guilt rose; self-hatred struck; and work happened: after dinner one night, I sat down on the couch with laptop and girlfriend, and translated the piece. Nothing was looked up; everything was felt out aurally, and typed in as I spoke it. What, in the French, felt pretentious and fussy (much of it), I rendered into pretentious, fussy English. It quickly became ridiculous. And so, after a few sentences, I started amping up the silly: reading the on-the-fly English translation in a high, unbearably pretentious British accent akin to Peter Sellers's "Chinless Wonder," from his comedy records of the early '60s.

With the amping up came amplification. Zeller's "Enterré vivant" ("Buried alive") became my "Buried alive, like a miner, in a mine, a deep, dark, dank, and—in all likelihood—Chilean mine." My girlfriend, whose French is fluent, laughed. And no, we hadn't been drinking, or not much. Dull black literality was married to hot red liberality: "As a child, this had been my recurring nightmare: I made my mother promise that, were I to expire before the first light of morning—its lemony rays gilding my soft, downy cheeks in nature's wet, hot, matutinal bizou—she'd settle me into my eternal resting place, my sorry crypt, with, why yes of course, a cell phone"—my sentence structure the same as Zeller's, but all the words in red my additions to his, to keep the voice I was going with—zany Sellersesque pedant—consistent.

Did I go too far? Of course. But, ultimately, out of this lark, I took the following semi-serious lesson: when translating, anyone can get words to cross borders. The key is to find a new voice, or what you yield isn't a text but a task. As the six-headed Krasznahorkai/Norfolk/Zeller/Mason/Fresán/Manguso translation-monster puts it, in the end: "What do we have? We have what we lose."

—Wyatt Mason

III.

1) Translating is using somebody else's hat and hoping it fits great on your head. It doesn't, of course. So you make some alterations, thinking with your head in someone

other's head. And hoping he likes what you did to his favorite/perfect/impossible-to-better hat.

2) Translating is like long-distance psychosis.

3) In translating this piece (as I usually do when I translate; I remember I did the same when I translated Denis Johnson's *Jesus' Son* and *The Name of the World* into Spanish), I didn't read the whole thing first. I read it for the first time as I translated it. Going along. Hand by hand. Into a dark forest. Then, when I'd finished a first draft, I read the original again. Took some notes. Not many. After that—without consulting the original—I polished my version.

4) Translating is like a very personal form of forgery. You respect the author, but at the same time you can't resist the temptation of "drawing"—as some kind of secret signature—a small and almost invisible figure that wasn't there before in the borders of the canvas.

5) Reading my translation again—going to press, having deleted the previous translation in this sort of babelian merry-go-round with Adam Thirlwell at the ticket stand—I discover I can't remember what I added and what I took out.

6) So, I think, it works okay for me. Hope it works for you. Here's your hat, there's the exit to the next entrance.

—*Rodrigo Fresán*

IV.

Though I can read Spanish with a dictionary and pick out its idioms clumsily, I'm not intimate enough with the language to know how *por supuesto* or *ay yi yi* sound to an informed reader. My instinct tells me they're quieter in Spanish than in English, which uses fewer articles and particles, and fewer syllables in general. When I doubted my ear, I gravitated toward cognates and strove to match, to the best of my ability, the effect of my English version to that of the Spanish version I was given.

I omitted the *por supuesto*s and the *ay yi yi*s, and I inserted several line spaces within the sections, reasoning that Spanish, closer to Latin, is more forgiving of sudden changes in verb tense. The English seemed to want to breathe between the tense changes.

I consulted my friend Alexis Romay, a bilingual writer and translator, on a few finer points, the details of which I include in footnotes.

The title, *Haciendo Tiempo*, which Alexis correctly translated as *Wasting Time*, might have been in some earlier version *Making Time*—a pun in English, at least. I have about a dozen similar suspicions.

The translation benefited from Alexis's smoothing of a few pronoun-dotted clauses and his correction of several adverbs referring to time. To preserve his professional reputation, though, I must admit I didn't take all of his corrections out of fear that being too literally correct might extinguish—something, but I couldn't say what.

—*Sarah Manguso*

XI

THE MAKING OF A MAN

a story in ENGLISH *by* RICHARD MIDDLETON

ILLUSTRATORS, IN ORDER OF APPEARANCE

Wesley Allsbrook, Ian Huebert, Mike Bertino, Erin Althea, Brianna Harden, Tim Lahan.

COMÓ SE HACE
UN HOMBRE

translated into Spanish by JAVIER MARÍAS

ERA UN EMPLEADUCHO de oficina enclenque y se había extraviado camino de la estación de Vauxhall en plena noche, y ahora caminaba temerosamente por calles sórdidas pero excepcionalmente poco frecuentadas. Temía estar perdiendo su último tren, pero, cuando se le aproximó una figura callejera, perdió los nervios y no le preguntó el camino. Pensó que podía ser un ladrón. Al mismo tiempo, sabía que la lluvia le estaba empapando y estropeando su único abrigo, y el pensamiento le hizo desgraciado. ¿Por qué no había ido a Waterloo como le había aconsejado Murray? ¿Por qué había olvidado pedir prestado un paraguas? ¿Por qué no había policías? Observó con alivio, sin embargo, que a medida que avanzaba las casas iban mejorando. Se iban haciendo más grandes y más respetables, y confió en la posibilidad de estarse aproximando a una calle principal.

Al poco vio brillar una ventana encendida en el primer piso de una de estas casas, y al acercarse a ella la puerta principal se abrió de par en par y dejó ver a una mujer, que se asomó a mirarlo con curiosidad.

Simmonds se sintió aliviado al ver su sexo, pues no temía a las mujeres. Era muy joven.

—Por favor, señorita, ¿podría usted indicarme el camino hacia la estación de Vauxhall? —preguntó, y se levantó el sombrero con satisfecha conciencia de sus buenos modales.

2

HOW TO
BECOME A MAN

translated into English by ANDREW SEAN GREER

With, hyper-translated from the Andrewseangreerish, Andres Carlstein, Laurel Fantauzzo, Justin Blackwood, Marcus Lund, Alea Adigweme, Garrin Buffo, Yaddyra Peralta, Brenda Sokolowski, and Liz McGovern.

HERE HE WAS: a runty little clerk on a hapless midnight quest for Vauxhall Station, lost in a maze of twisting, sordid little streets. He was panicked he'd miss the last train, and yet, when he finally came upon someone to ask—well, he lost his nerve. After all, they might be a thief. Meanwhile, he felt the rain beginning to soak through his only coat, ruining it, and the thought made him quite miserable. Why hadn't he gone to Waterloo as Murray suggested? Why hadn't he borrowed an umbrella? And why oh why were there no policemen about? But now came a relief—as he scurried along, he noticed the houses improving, becoming grander and more respectable, and he comforted himself with the promise that, surely, just around the next corner, he would find his way at last.

And here, ahead, he saw a window gleaming in the first floor of one of these houses. He began to approach—and the front door swung wide open! There, in the doorway, turning to him with a curious gaze, stood a woman.

What a relief for Simmonds to find a woman, because he was not afraid of women. He was, after all, very young.

"Excuse me, miss, could you tell me the way to Vauxhall Station?" he asked, and tipped his hat; he was conscious of his good breeding.

The woman stared at him fixedly, curiously, intently.

"Are you a medical student?" she asked seriously.

Simmonds was distracted, still busy noticing the details of her womanliness, her beauty, and her question left him speechless.

"Medical student?" he repeated stupidly.

"No, I can see you're not," she said to herself, and Simmonds saw her forehead wrinkle in thought.

"If I can do anything to be of assistance…" he said as grandly as a man in a novel.

She decided in the blink of an eye.

"Oh, you can be of use!" she told him. "I need help desperately." She stood to one side of the door.

Simmonds hesitated, and was on the point of fleeing, but some instinct, he did not know what, made him obey and go into the hallway, waiting below a gas lamp while the lady locked the door behind him. Simmonds assured himself she was a lady: she wore so many rings and her dress shone so brilliantly, though admittedly with a rather bad stain down the front. She had now left the door and was looking him over doubtfully, and the silence lasted almost too long for him to bear.

"It's up there," she said, and glided past him, up the stairs, leaving him to follow if he wished.

Again he hesitated, but was too badly thrown by everything to admit he was afraid. Up he went, meekly, and found her waiting on the landing with her fingers on the handle of a door. On his approach she opened it, and half pushed, half led him into the room.

"There!" she said. "There!"

Simmonds looked in and grew sick to his stomach.

It was a nicely furnished room, illuminated by a gas lamp that hissed noisily overhead. Just beneath it, on the floor, sat a metal trunk and, as if seated there: the body of a man, its throat cut ear to ear. The thing was in its shirtsleeves, and fresh blood bloomed on the crisp white cotton.

La mujer lo miró fijamente, de un modo curiosamente intenso.

—¿Es usted estudiante de medicina? —dijo con seriedad. Simmonds estaba ocupado descubriendo que se trataba de una dama, y guapa, y la pregunta lo dejó estupefacto.

—¿Estudiante de medicina? —repetió estúpidamente.

—No, ya veo que no —dijo ella para sí, y Simmonds vio cómo se le fruncía el ceño en su esfuerzo por pensar rápidamente.

—Si pudiera ser de alguna utilidad… —dijo él ampulosamente, como la gente de las novelas.

La dama tomó una decisión en un abrir y cerrar de ojos.

—Oh, si estuviera usted dispuesto —gritó. —Necesito tanta ayuda. —Y se hizo a un lado en el portal.

Simmonds vaciló y estuvo a punto de salir huyendo, pero algún instinto, no sabía qué, le hizo obedecer y pasó junto a ella al vestíbulo y esperó bajo el mechero de gas mientras ella cerraba la puerta con llave detrás de él. Simmonds estaba seguro de que debía tratarse de una dama porque llevaba muchos anillos y su vestido era brillante, aunque por su parte delantera bajaba una fea mancha. Ella se había apartado ahora de la puerta y estaba escudriñándolo como si dudara, y el silencio se hizo casi demasiado prolongado para los nervios de Simmonds.

—Es arriba —dijo ella, y pasó majestuosamente junto a él, escaleras arriba, dejando que la siguiera si lo deseaba.

Simmonds vaciló de nuevo, pero estaba muy mal echarse atrás después de todo y decir que tenía miedo. Así que subió dócilmente y la encontró esperándolo en el rellano con la mano en el picaporte de una puerta. Al acercarse él, ella la abrió, y medio lo empujó, medio lo condujo dentro de la habitación.

—¡Ahí! —dijo.

Simmonds miró y se puso mortalmente enfermo.

La habitación estaba bastante bien amueblada al modo de una sala e iluminada por un mechero de gas que crepitaba de manera abominable. Justo debajo, en el suelo, había un baúl metálico, y, como si estuviera sentado en el borde, allí estaba posado el cuerpo de un hombre con la garganta rajada de oreja a oreja. Aquella cosa no llevaba chaqueta ni chaleco, y le chorreaba sangre fresca por la camisa blanca.

Simmonds pensó en ello y dio una arcada, mientras la mujer lo miraba con curiosidad.

—¿Qué va a hacer? —le preguntó ella cuando él pareció estar mejor.

Él apenas la oyó; no podía oír nada más que el zumbido del gas encima del cadáver, y el ruido lo molestaba.

—¿Está muerto? —susurró.

—Muerto —repitió la mujer. —¡Muerto! —Se acercó a él con estas palabras, pero él la rehuyó. Había sangre en su vestido.

—Tiene que ayudarme —dijo ella con ferocidad. —¡Tiene que hacerlo! ¡Tiene que hacerlo! No puedo meterlo en el arcón. Lo he intentado una y otra vez y no he podido. Tiene que ayudarme a cortarlo en pedazos. Puede besarme. Lo que quiera, después.

Él la miró mortecinamente. Nunca había besado a nadie excepto a su madre, y eso había sido hacía mucho tiempo. No le había dado ningún placer especial, pensó. De hecho, más bien le había desagradado. Y ahora esta mujer… Por supuesto, había oído cosas en la oficina, cosas groseras. Él mismo las había dicho. Pero nunca había deseado besar a ninguna mujer. Y sin embargo… había algo… sus labios serían cálidos. A otra gente parecía gustarle…¿quizá?

—Lo que quieras, después —dijo ella automáticamente, mirándolo.

Simmonds sintió una débil agitación en sus venas, como si le apeteciera besar aquellos labios cálidos, intentarlo al menos. Se descubrió mirando el cuerpo sin horror. Pensó que casi podía ser agradable acuchillar aquellos miembros muertos. Le entraron ganas de cortar algo.

—¡Vamos! —dijo la mujer, y le mostró media docena de cuchillos. —Lo harás, ¿verdad?… por mí.

De pronto se echó hacia adelante y lo besó en los labios.

Vaya, no fue nada, después de todo…nada de nada. Y sin embargo, él supo en un instante que daría el mundo por tener aquella nada otra vez. Los labios sólo habían rozado los suyos durante un segundo: levemente, como una flor. ¿Qué habría pasado si él los hubiera apretado con fuerza contra los suyos? ¿Hasta que hubiera salido la sangre, rodeándola con los brazos? La miró con una luz nueva en sus ojos, y ella leyó bien en ellos.

—Después —dijo—. Después.

Él cogió uno de los cuchillos y se acercó al cuerpo.

—Me manchará las ropas —balbuceó.

—Pues quítatelas —dijo ella. —Dios, qué crío —porque él retrocedió sonrojándose.

Ella atravesó corriendo una puerta con cortinas que daba a la habitación de al lado y volvió con algunas ropas que arrojó a los pies de él.

—No importa que éstas se estropeen —dijo—; ya no hacen ninguna falta. —Luego, al ver que él aún dudaba—: Está bien, yo no miraré.

Y le dio la espalda mientras él se cambiaba y se ponía las ropas del hombre

---

While the woman stood by, watching, Simmonds promptly vomited.[1]

"What are you going to do?" she asked when he recovered.

He barely heard her; he could not hear anything but the lamp's ceaseless racket, a sound that nearly undid him.

"Is he dead?" he whispered.

"Dead," the woman repeated. "Dead!" She approached him with these words, but he kept his distance. There was blood on her dress.

---

[1] *Alternate translations provided by students:*

"The withdrawing room, though otherwise luxurious, had an ancient calefactor that wheezed like a consumptive, and cast dull light on the vert edges of the copper-bound chiffonier. A body had been posed atop this traveling case, in a position reminiscent of *The Thinker*. Someone's sharp blade had drawn a line between the earlobes. The corpse wore neither frock nor waistcoat, and its red essence issued freely onto a white blouse. Simmonds, moved by the sight, jettisoned a supper of beets and beaujolais in violet crescents, while the woman coolly observed." —Andres Carlstein

"The room was well appointed but lit harshly by a sputtering gas burner. A man sat on the room's metal trunk, with a wet red wound smiling across his neck. He was not a man anymore, but an object that wore objects, his white shirt brightened by blood. The woman said "Hmm," to Simmonds, who felt a wetness in his own neck, and vomited." —Laurel Fantauzzo and Justin Blackwood

"The gas burner coughed a dirty light across the clean, ornately furnished room. On the ground below was a metal trunk, and balanced atop its edge sat the body of a man, his pose frozen, his throat filleted. The body wore neither jacket nor vest, and blood, still warm, fell onto the white shirt. Simmonds gave it some thought, and then he threw up, while the woman looked at him curiously." —Marcus Lund

"The room, nice enough, was lit by a guttering gas flame. Beneath that, on the floor, sat a steamer trunk, and leaning against it there was arranged the body of a man, his throat lacerated from ear to ear. He wore neither jacket nor vest, and fresh blood flowed over his white shirt. Simmonds considered him and retched while the woman looked on curiously." —Alca Adigweme and Garrin Buffo

"You have to help me," she said fiercely. "You have to help me! You have to help me! I can't fit it into the trunk. I tried over and over and couldn't do it. You have to help me cut it into pieces. You can kiss me. And whatever else you want, after."

He looked at her solemnly. He had never kissed anyone except his mother, and not for years and years. There had been no pleasure in it, he recalled. In fact, it had been rather unpleasant. And now this woman… of course, he had heard things in the office, crude things. He himself had said them. But he had never wanted to kiss any woman. And yet… there was something… her lips looked so warm. Other people seemed to like it… well, perhaps?

"Whatever you want, after," she said automatically, staring at him.

Simmonds felt something swimming in his veins, as if he felt like kissing those lips after all, or at least trying. He found himself looking at the body now without horror. He thought it might be nice to cut up those dead parts. He felt like cutting something.

"Come on!" she said. She showed him half a dozen knives. "You'll do it, yes? For me?"

Suddenly she ran up and kissed him firmly on the lips.

Well it was nothing, after everything… nothing at all. And yet instantly he found that he would give the world to have that nothing one more time. Those lips were all that existed, brushing against his own for a moment: lightly as a flower. What would happen if he pressed his own against hers? Until the blood rushed inside him, his arms around her? He looked at her with a new light in his eyes, and she read his thoughts there.

"After," she said. "After."

He picked up one of the knives and approached the body.

"I'll stain my clothes," he jabbered.

"Then take them off," she said, and then: "For God's sake, grow up!" because he began to blush.

She disappeared through a little curtained door into the next room and returned with clothes, dumping them at his feet.

"It doesn't matter if we ruin these," she said. "There's no one to miss them." After seeing his hesitation: "Don't worry, I won't look."

As he began to change into the dead man's clothes, she averted her gaze. And would you guess it? She was more astonished than he.

muerto. Y de los dos, el de ella era el mayor asombro.

Cuando hubo acabado cogió el cuchillo y empezó, al principio mansamente y luego con ferocidad. De vez en cuando alzaba la mirada y la visión de los labios entreabiertos de ella le hacía temblar. Pero al cabo de un rato el horror de aquellos fríos pedazos de carne muerta se impuso a su pasión y trabajó mecánica pero obstinadamente sin saber por qué. Tenía que terminarlo rápidamente, rápidamente… eso era todo.

Los cuchillos estaban romos y él no sabía nada de anatomía, así que para cuando hubo terminado y la tapa estuvo cerrada, grises rayos de luz entraban por las rendijas de la persiana. Había hecho su tarea y se puso en pie. Casi se había olvidado de la mujer, y sus ropas y sus manos y su cara estaban todos moteados de sangre seca.

Con felicidad se preguntaba por qué… algo de algo… no sabía qué. Era muy viejo.

A través de una bruma vio a la mujer al otro lado de la habitación, de pie y mirándolo de forma extraña. Había algo… ¿qué era?

De pronto, ella abrió los brazos y le gritó a través del infinito espacio:

—¡Ven!

Y con aquella palabra algo pareció romperse y un feroz torrente de apasionada sangre recorrió su cuerpo.

Eso era. ¡La mujer! ¡La mujer!

Cruzó la habitación de un salto con un sollozo en los labios, la tomó en sus brazos, y con un beso sobre su rostro ardiente se despidió de su juventud.

When he was clothed again, he picked up a knife and began his job, at first gently and then fiercely. Once in a while he lifted his gaze and the sight of her parted lips made him tremble. After some time the horror of those cold pieces of dead meat beat away his passion and he worked mechanically yet stubbornly, without knowing why. He had to finish quickly, quickly… that was all.

The knives were dull and he knew nothing of anatomy, so that by the time he was done and the lid was shut, gray light glowed between the slats of the blinds. His duty done at last, he stood up. He had nearly forgotten the woman, and his clothes and hands and face were spotted with blood.

His dull mind asked what he was doing here… there was something important… he did not know what. He felt so very old.

Across the room through a haze he saw the woman, standing, watching him so strangely. There was something… what was it?

Suddenly, she opened her arms and cried across the infinite space: "Come!"

And with that word, something seemed to break inside him, and a fierce torrent of impassioned blood shot through his veins.

Here it was. The woman! The woman!

He leaped across the room with a sob on his lips, took her in his arms, and kissing her burning face he bid his youth goodbye.[2]

---

[2] *Alternate endings provided by Twitter followers:*

"In one leap he crossed the room and, with a gasp on his lips, took her in his arms, kissed her fervent face, and bid farewell to his youth." —Yaddyra Peralta

"He leapt across the room and, with a sob on his lips, took her in his arms and, passionately kissing her, said goodbye to his youth." —Brenda Sokolowski

"He leapt across the room, a sob forming on his lips, he took her in his arms and with a kiss upon the flaming petal of her cheek kissed youth goodbye." —Liz McGovern

MANN WERDEN

translated into German by JULIA FRANCK

MANHOOD

translated into English by A.S. BYATT

DAS WAR ER, ein mickriger kleiner Angestellter mitten in der Nacht auf der unglückseligen Suche nach der Haltestelle Vauxhall, verloren in einem Labyrinth elend verzweigter Gassen. In ihm wuchs die Angst, er könnte den letzten Zug verpasst haben. Doch allein der Gedanke, jemanden nach dem Weg zu fragen, legte seine Nerven blank. Jeder dahergelaufene Typ konnte schließlich ein Dieb sein. Während er so die Nerven verlor, spürte er, wie der Regen den Stoff seiner Jacke tränkte, sie durchnässte und ruinierte. Das machte ihn traurig, er arbeitete in der Textilbranche und legte stets großen Wert auf sorgfältige Kleider. Warum bloß war er nicht zur Waterloo gegangen, wie Murray es ihm geraten hatte? Warum bloß hatte er keinen Regenschirm geliehen? Und warum, ach warum bloß gab es hier keinen einzigen Polizisten? Aber während er so hastete, änderte sich etwas: immer vornehmer wurden die Häuser, größer und ansehnlicher, und der mickrige kleine Angestellte beruhigte sich in der Hoffnung, dass er ganz gewiss, gleich um die nächste Ecke, seinen Weg finden würde. Plötzlich sah er ein Lichtlein brennen. Es kam aus einem Fenster im ersten Stock eines jener Häuser. Kaum steuerte er darauf zu, öffnete sich die Haustür darunter weit. Im Türrahmen, erschien eine Frau und blickte ihn unverwandt an.

Was für ein Glück, welche Erleichterung für Simmonds ausgerechnet auf eine Frau zu stoßen, hatte er doch keine Angst vor Frauen. Obwohl er sehr jung war.

"Entschuldigen Sie bitte, meine Dame, konnten Sie mir vielleicht den Weg

THERE HE WAS, an unremarkable little clerk in the middle of the night haplessly trying to find Vauxhall station, lost in a labyrinth of mean and twisting streets. He was increasingly afraid that he had missed the last train. But even the thought of asking anyone for directions froze his nerves. Any passer-by could turn out to be a thief. And as the state of his nerves deteriorated he noticed how the rain was soaking the cloth of his coat, saturating it, ruining it. That really upset him. He worked in the drapery department, and so took great care to be smartly dressed. Why on earth had he not gone to Waterloo, as Murray had told him to? Why on earth hadn't he brought an umbrella? And why, why on earth, were there no policemen anywhere? But as he hurried on, things changed—the houses became steadily more elegant, larger and smarter, and the unremarkable little clerk calmed himself with the hope that surely—maybe at the next corner—he would now find his way. Suddenly he saw a small light burning. It was in a window on the first floor of one of those houses. No sooner had he turned toward it than the front door opened. A woman appeared, framed in the opening, and looked intently at him.

What luck, what a relief, for Simmonds to have come across a woman—he wasn't afraid of women. Although he was very young.

"Excuse me, Madam, could you perhaps tell me the way to Vauxhall station?" he asked, and raised his hat, remembering his upbringing.

The woman stared intently at him, with a searching and curious expression.

"You are a medical student?" she asked earnestly.

Simmonds didn't respond immediately, he was so taken up with her shapely form, her beauty. The question left him speechless.

"Medical student?" he repeated, in a daze.

"No, I can see you aren't," she said to herself, and Simmonds saw that she was frowning.

Proud as the hero of a romance, he said, "If there is anything I can do for you…"

She considered this for a moment. "Oh yes, indeed you can," she said. "I am dreadfully in need of help." She took a step aside. Simmonds trembled—he could still turn round and run away, but, following some obscure instinct, he went into the hallway. He waited below the gas lamp while the lady closed the door. He could see that she was a lady: she wore innumerable rings, and her dress seemed rich, although the stuff below her breast was somewhat faded. Now she had left the door and was looking doubtfully at him. The silence between them seemed unbearably long.

"It's up there," she said, and went up the stairs, leaving it to him whether to follow or not. Again he hesitated, but he was too enthralled to admit his fear. So he obeyed and followed her. She waited on the landing, her hand on the doorknob. Immediately he reached her, she opened it, and then she half beckoned, half pushed him into the room.

"There," she said. "There!"

Simmonds looked. He felt sick.

It was a nicely furnished room, bathed in the glimmering light of a gas lamp, which could be heard hissing above them. On the floor just under it there was a metal chest, and, as though it had arranged itself in there by itself, the body of a man, whose throat was cut from ear to ear. The thing was in shirtsleeves, and fresh blood welled up from the shining white cotton.

While the woman stood and looked around, Simmonds was suddenly very sick.

"What will you do?" the woman inquired, when he raised his head.

zur Vauxhall Station sagen?" fragte er und lüftete seinen Hut, er war sich seiner guten Erziehung bewusst.

Gebannt starrte ihn die Frau an, neugierig und forschend. "Sie sind Medizinstudent?" fragte sie ernst.

Simmonds reagierte nicht gleich, noch war er beschäftigt, die Einzelheiten ihrer Weiblichkeit in Augenschein zu nehmen, ihrer Schönheit, und ihre Frage machte ihn sprachlos. "Medizinstudent?" wiederholte er verdattert.

"Nein, ich seh schon, Sie sind keiner," sagte sie zu sich selbst, und Simmonds sah, dass sie die Stirn runzelte.

Großspurig wie ein Romanheld sagte er: "Wenn ich irgendetwas für Sie tun kann…"

Einen Augenblick überlegte sie. "Oh ja, das können Sie," sagte sie, "ich brauche dringend Hilfe," sie setzte einen Schritt zur Seite.

Simmonds zögerte, noch konnte er sich umdrehen und weglaufen, aber einem unbestimmten Instinkt folgend betrat er den Korridor. Unter der Gaslampe wartete er, bis die Dame die Tür geschlossen hatte. Er vergewisserte sich, dass sie eine Dame war: Sie trug unzählige Ringe und ihr Kleid erschien ihm prunkvoll, auch wenn der Stoff unterhalb ihrer Brust etwas ausgeblichen war. Jetzt hatte sie die Tür hinter sich gelassen und blickte ihn zweifelnd an, das Schweigen zwischen ihnen erschien ihm unerträglich lang.

"Es ist oben," sagte sie und stieg die Treppe hinauf, sie überließ es ihm, ob er folgen wollte.

Wieder zögerte er etwas, aber er war zu gefesselt, um seine Angst zu bekunden. Also gehorchte er und folgte ihr hinauf. Sie wartete auf dem Absatz, die Hand auf der Klinke. Kaum war er bei ihr angelangt, öffnete sie, halb lockte sie, halb stieß sie ihn in den Raum. "Da," sagte sie, "da!"

Simmonds sah hin, ihm wurde übel.

Es war ein nett eingerichtetes Zimmer, getaucht in das dämmrige Licht einer Gaslampe, die vernehmbar über ihnen zischte. Auf dem Boden gleich darunter befand sich eine metallene Kiste, und als sei er eigens platziert: die Leiche eines Mannes, dessen Kehle von einem Ohr zum anderen durchtrennt war. Das Ding steckte in Hemdsärmeln, und frisches Blut quoll aus der strahlend weißen Baumwolle.

Während die Frau herumstand und schaute, musste Simmonds unvermittelt kotzen.

"Was werden Sie tun?" erkundigte sich die Frau als er wieder den Kopf hob.

Er verstand sie kaum, nichts außer dem elenden Lärm der Gaslampe konnte er hören, ein Geräusch, das ihn fast umbrachte.

"Tot?" flüsterte er.

"Tot," sagte die Frau. "Tot!" schrie sie ihm entgegen, und wahrte doch Abstand. Da war Blut auf ihrem Kleid. "Sie müssen mir helfen," sagte sie scharf, "helfen müssen sie mir, helfen, unbedingt. Ich bekomme ihn einfach nicht in den Koffer. Ich hab es immer wieder versucht, aber es klappt einfach nicht. Sie müssen mir helfen, ihn in Stücke zu hacken. Sie dürfen mich küssen. Alles, was Sie wollen. Später."

Erschüttert blickte er sie an. Nie hatte er jemand anderen außer seiner Mutter geküsst, und das schon seit vielen, vielen Jahren nicht mehr. Es war alles andere als ein Vergnügen gewesen, soweit er sich erinnern konnte. Es war sogar eher unvergnüglich. Und nun diese Frau... sicher, im Büro hatte er Sachen gehört, echt verrückte Sachen. Manche davon hatte er selbst gesagt. Aber er hatte niemals eine Frau küssen wollen. Obwohl er sich eingestehen musste, dass es da etwas gab, an ihr, ihre Lippen sahen warm aus. Andere Menschen mochten das offenbar... vielleicht also doch?

"Alles, was Sie wollen," sagte sie automatisch und starrte ihn an.

Simmonds spürte ein Kribbeln in seinen Venen, so, als wolle er nun doch solche Lippen küssen, es zumindest versuchen, mal kosten. Er bemerkte, wie er die Leiche jetzt ganz ohne Schrecken betrachtete. Vielleicht, so dachte er jetzt, konnte es sogar ganz schön sein, ein paar tote Teile abzuschneiden. Sehr schön. Allzu gern wollte er etwas abschneiden.

"Komm schon," sagte sie und zeigte ihm ein Dutzend Messer, "du machst das für mich, ja?" Nun sprang sie auf ihn zu und küsste fest seine Lippen.

Es war nichts, überhaupt gar nichts. Und doch hätte er plötzlich am liebsten die ganze Welt für dieses Nichts getauscht. Ein letztes und erstes Mal. Diese Lippen waren alles, was existierte, wie sie die seinen kämmten, sie streiften, sanft wie eine Blüte. Was würde erst geschehen, wenn er die seinen auf die ihren presste? Das Rauschen des Blutes, die Arme um sie legen. Frohlocken, Glanz in den Augen, seine Blicke verschlangen sie, die seine Gedanken las.

"Später," sagte sie. "Später."

Er griff nach einem Messer und stach in die Leiche.

"Ich werde meine Kleidung beschmutzen," stöhnte er.

"Dann zieh sie aus," sagte sie und "mein Gott, werd erwachsen"—als er anfing zu japsen.

Sie verschwand durch einen kleinen Vorhang in den benachbarten Raum und kehrte mit einer Menge Kleidung zurück, die sie ihm vor die Füße warf.

He barely understood her, he could hear only the miserable sound of the gas lamp, a sound that almost finished him.

"Dead?" he whispered.

"Dead," said the woman. "Dead," she shrieked at him, still keeping her distance. There was blood on her dress. "You have to help me," she said harshly. "You have to help, you have simply got to help. I just can't get it into the trunk. You have got to help me cut it into pieces. You can kiss me. You can do anything you want. Afterward."

He stared at her, appalled. He had never kissed anyone except his mother, and that was now many, many years ago. It had been anything but agreeable, as far as he could remember. Indeed it had been positively disagreeable. And now this woman... it was true that he had heard things in the office, totally crazy things... A lot of them he had made up himself. But he had never wanted to kiss a woman. Although he had to admit that there was something, something about her. Her lips looked warm. Other men clearly wanted that... so, perhaps, then...

"Anything you want," she said automatically, staring at him.

Simmonds felt a prickling in his veins, as though now he did want to kiss those lips, or at least to try, to taste... He noticed that he was looking at the body altogether without qualms. Perhaps, he thought, it might even be quite interesting, chopping off a few dead chunks. Very interesting. He would quite happily chop something off.

"Well, then," she said, and showed him a bunch of knives. "You will do this for me, yes?"

Then she sprang upon him, and firmly kissed his lips. It was nothing, really nothing at all. And yet he would happily have given the whole world for this nothing. A last time, and a first. These lips were everything that was, as they brushed against his own, stroking them, soft as petals. What would come about when he pressed his own on hers? The rush of blood, clasping his arms round her... Bliss, glistening eyes, she devoured his gaze, which abandoned his thoughts.

"Later," she said. "Later."

He seized a knife and stuck it into the body.

"I am going to get my clothes dirty," he said.

"Then take them off," she said, and, "My god, grow up," as he began to pant. She disappeared behind a curtain into the neighboring room and came back with a heap of garments that she threw at his feet.

"It doesn't matter if we spoil them. There's no one now to miss them."

When she saw him hesitate, she said, "Don't worry, I won't look."

But as soon as he began to pull on the dead man's clothes she changed her expression. And can you guess how? She was horribly shocked.

As soon as he was dressed, he grabbed the knife and set to work, at first tentatively, then more and more decisively. Now and then he glanced upward—the sight of her lovely lips left him trembling. At first he was horrified by the cold lumps of dead flesh—then his misery eased, and he worked more and more mechanically, with more concentration, without knowing, nevertheless, exactly why. It had to be done fast, very fast, that was all.

The knives were blunt, and he knew nothing about anatomy. When he had finally finished, he shut his eyes; a gray light shimmered in the chink of his eyelids. He had performed his task, and stood up. He had almost forgotten the woman. His clothes, his face, and his hands were blood-spattered.

A question took shape in his mind. What was he, in fact, doing here? It didn't seem to matter, as far as he could see. He felt very old.

His gaze wandered through the room, and as if in a mist he saw the woman, who stood there, indistinct. There was something… But what? What was it?

Suddenly she flung out her arms and her cry sounded across the vast and endless space between them: "Come!"

When he heard her, something inside him seemed to shatter. A whirlwind of passion shot through his veins.

That was what it was. The woman. The woman.

He had to get his clothes off, he needed to get them off, to change the blood-soaked clothes for his own rain-soaked coat. In joyful anticipation he strode toward the woman, took her in his arms, and kissed her glowing face. And so he took leave of his youth.

"Es macht nichts, wenn wir die ruinieren, da gibt es niemanden mehr, der sie vermissen wird. Als sie sein Zögern bemerkte, sagte sie, "Keine Sorge, ich werd nicht zuschauen."

Doch sobald er begann, die Kleider des Toten anzuziehen, veränderte sich ihr Blick. Und ahnen Sie wie? Sie staunte mächtig.

Kaum war er angezogen, griff er zum Messer und verrichtete seine Arbeit, erst zaghaft, dann immer entschlossener. Hin und wieder hob er seinen Blick, die Aussicht auf ihre feinen Lippen ließ ihn beben. Nach einer Weile des Schreckens angesichts der kalten Stücke toten Fleischs, war seine Leidenschaft verflogen und er arbeitete nur mehr mechanisch, doch beflissen, ohne zu wissen, warum eigentlich. Er musste schnell fertig werden, schnell, das war alles.

Die Messer waren stumpf und er wusste nichts über Anatomie. Als er endlich fertig war, schloss er die Augen, graues Licht schimmerte zwischen den Spalt seiner Lider. Er hatte seinen Auftrag erfüllt und erhob sich. Beinahe hatte er die Frau vergessen, seine Kleider, sein Gesicht und seine Hände waren blutbefleckt.

Eine Frage dämmerte in ihm, was er eigentlich hier machte… da war nichts Wichtiges, so viel er wusste. Er fühlte sich sehr alt.

Sein Blick streifte durch den Raum, wie durch einen Nebel hindurch erkannte er die Frau, sie stand da und lauerte. Da war etwas… Aber was? Was war es?

Plötzlich breitete sie ihre Arme aus und ihr Ruf drang durch die Weite des endlosen Raum: "Komm!"

Mit diesem Wort schien etwas in ihm zu zerbrechen, ein Wirbelsturm der Leidenschaft schoss durch seine Venen.

Das war es: Die Frau! Die Frau!

Seine Kleidung würde er ausziehen müssen, sie ausziehen wollen, die blutgetränkten Kleider wieder durch seine regengetränkte Jacke eintauschen. Mit froher Erwartung auf den Lippen schritt er auf die Frau zu, nahm sie in seine Arme und küsste ihr glühendes Gesicht, so verabschiedete er seine Jugend.

5

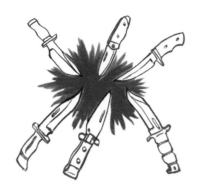

גבריות

translated into Hebrew by ORLY CASTEL-BLOOM

שׁם הוא היה, פקיד צעיר, אומלל, חסר ערך, מנסה למצוא את תחנת ווקסהול באמצע
הלילה, אבוד במבוך רחובות מרושעים ואפלים. הפחד שפספס את הרכבת האחרונה הלך
וגבר. אפילו המחשבה לבקש ממישהו הכוונה זיעזעה אותו. הלוא כל עובר אורח עלול
להתגלות כגנב. כשעצביו החלו מתערערים, הוא הבחין שהגשם מרטיב את אריג מעילו, נספג בו ו ו הורס
אותו. זה הפריע לו מאוד. הוא עבד במחלקת בדים ולכן הקפיד להתלבש בהידור.
למה לכל הרוחות הוא לא הלך לווטרלו, כפי שמורי אמר לו? למה לעזאזל הוא לא הביא מטריה?
ולמה, למה לכל השדים והרוחות, לא היו שוטרים בשומקום? אלא שככל שהוסיף ומיהר, דברים השתנו
: הבתים נעשו בהדרגה אלגנטיים יותר, גדולים והדורים יותר, והפקיד הצעיר, חסר הערך, הרגיע את
עצמו בתקווה, שבוודאי—אולי כבר בפינה הקרובה—ימצא את דרכו. פתאום ראה אור קטן מרצד.
זה היה בחלון בקומה הראשונה של אחד מאותם בניינים. בדיוק כשפנה לשם נפתחה הדלת הקדמית.
אישה הופיעה בפתח הדלת, והביטה בו בתשומת לב.

איזו הקלה! איזה מזל! היה זה עבור סימונדס להיתקל כך באישה. הוא לא פחד מנשים, למרות
שהיה מאוד צעיר.

"סליחה, גברתי, אולי תואילי לומר לי מה הדרך לתחנת ווקסהול?" שאל והסיר את הכובע, לאות
נימוס שהקפיד עליו. האישה הסתכלה עליו בעניין. הבעתה היתה סקרנית ובוחנת.

"אתה סטודנט לרפואה?" שאלה.

סימונדס לא הגיב מייד. גופה המעוצב, יופיה ושאלתה ריתקו אותו ופנייתה אליו הותירה אותו
חסר מלים.

"סטודנט לרפואה?" חזר במבוכה על דבריה.

"לא, אני רואה שלא," מלמלה לעצמה, וסימונדס ראה שקדרות התנחלה על פניה.

6

MANHOOD: STROPHES

translated into English by ADAM FOULDS

1

IT IS A QUESTION of the separation and joining of bodies, first one and then the other.

2

For example, after his fear (of being lost, of poverty and lack of law) comes his anger: the rain is soaking his coat. The wet world penetrates the fine personal fabric. This "infuriated him."

3

He turns a corner. That's better. Money engorges property. Homes enlarge and separate. They are proud. There is space between them. That's much better.

4

In the darkness a light coming on like a new thought which is *The body of a woman. The body of a woman in a doorway, is a doorway.*

5

For the achievement of Manhood, words are not essential matter. They are link work, ligature and conveyance.

Excuse me, madam. Would you kindly tell me the way to Vauxhall Station?

Are you a medical student?

A medical student?

No. I can see that you aren't.

Is there anything that I can do for you?

Yes. Yes, there is. I need help desperately.

There. That's done. In through the door.

6

"It's upstairs." *It*. It always is. Whatever the indefinite article is, it awaits you. Be a man: take a knife and cut it to define, to give it an edge.

7

Meanwhile, her coverings are interesting. Bright expensive rings. A faded expensive dress. Linger in the chambers of the social while you can. Discriminate. Be polite (while making those private financial calculations

8

that end now).

There!

A body in the room. A man. The last one.

Dead?

Dead.

9

The gaslight hiss from overhead reminds the young man of the sea at Margate sliding over pebbles in incessant dissolution, cresting and collapsing at his feet. The blankness of matter. The edge of unconsciousness. Gray water. Nothing.

This is Manhood's proper ground. He is in the right place.

10

The gray water is red and still flowing.

בגאווה שכמותה יש לגיבור מרומן, אמר לה: "אם יש משהו שאוכל לעשות עבורך..."

היא שקלה זאת לרגע. "כן, למען האמת, אתה יכול," אמרה, "אני זקוקה לעזרה נואשות."

היא זה הצידה. סימונדס רעד. עדיין אפשר היה להסתובב ולברוח, אך, בשל אינסטינקט מעורפל, הוא נכנס למסדרון. הוא המתין תחת נורת הגז בזמן שהאישה סגרה את הדלת. הוא שם לב שהיא הייתה גברת מאוד מכובדת: על אצבעותיה ענדה הרבה טבעות, וגם שמלתה נראתה יקרה, למרות שהבד מתחת לחזה היה דהוי במקצת. כעת, עזבה את הדלת, והביטה בו בפקפוק.

השתיקה ביניהם הייתה ארוכה ובלתי נסבלת.

"זה שם למעלה," אמרה וטיפסה במדרגות, משאירה לו לבחור אם לבוא אחריה. הוא שוב היסס, אך היה מוקסם מדי כדי לתת לפחד להשפיע עליו. לכן הוא ציית והלך אחריה. היא המתינה בכניסה, ידה מונחת על ידית הדלת. מייד הגיע אליה, והיא פתחה את הדלת. היא חצי הובילה אותו, חצי דחפה אותו לתוך החדה.

"שם," היא אמרה, "שם!"

סימונדס הביט סביב. הוא חש בחילה.

היה זה חדר יפה ומרוהט, שטוף אור בוהק מנורת הגז, שניתן היה לשמוע את איוושתה. על הרצפה, בדיוק מתחת לנורת הגז, הייתה שידת מתכת, וגופה של אדם שגרונו משוסף מקצה לקצה. הוא לבש חולצת שרוולים מכותנה לבנה, דם ספוג בה, וקילוח דם זרם בעדה.

בזמן שהאישה עמדה והביטה סביב, סימונדס נתקף בבחילה עוד יותר נוראית.

"מה תעשה?" שאלה האישה, כשהרים את ראשו.

הוא בקושי הבין אותה. יכול היה לשמוע רק את אוושתה המאמללת של נורת הגז, וזה כמעט חיסל אותו.

"מת?" הוא לחש.

"מת," אמרה האישה. "מת," היא צווחה לעברו, עדיין שומרת ממנו מרחק. דם נספג גם בבד שמלתה.

"אתה מוכרח לעזור לי," אמרה בנוקשות, "אתה חייב לעזור, אתה פשוט חייב לעזור. אני רק לא מצליחה להכניס את זה לתוך המזוודה. אתה מוכרח לעזור לי לחתוך את זה לחתיכות. אתה רשאי לנשק אותי. אתה רשאי לעשות בי מה שתרצה. אחר כך."

הוא נעץ בה מבט, מזועזע. מעולם לא נישק אף אחת פרט לאמו, וזה היה כבר לפני שנים כה רבות. מה גם שהוא לא זוכר שום נעימות מאותן חוויות רחוקות. שום נעימות בכלל. ועכשיו האישה הזו... זה נכון ששמע שמדברים במשרד על המון דברים משוגעים... חלק גדול מהם הוא בעצמו המציא. אך מעודו לא רצה לנשק אישה. למרות שנאלץ להודות שמשהו, משהו היה בה. השפתיים שלה נראו חמות. גברים אחרים רצו בכך באופן ברור... לכן אולי, אז...

"מה שרק תרצה," היא אמרה באופן אוטומטי, לא מסירה ממנו את מבטה.

סימונדס חש עקצוץ בווריד וו, כאילו עכשיו הוא רוצה לנשק את השפתיים האלו, או לפחות לנסות לטעום... הוא שם לב לכך שהוא מביט כעת בגופה ללא נקיפות מצפון. אולי, הרהר, זה יכול להיות דווקא די מעניין לחתוך כמה נתחים. מעניין מאוד. די בשמחה, הוא יחתוך משהו.

"ובכן," אמרה והציגה בפניו מספר סכינים, "תעשה זאת למעני, כן?"

ואז היא זינקה לעברו, ונישקה את שפתיו בחוזקה. זה היה שום כלום, באמת שום כלום, אך

בשמחה היה נותן את העולם כולו בשביל שום כלום כזה. פעם אחרונה, וראשונה. השפתיים האלו היו כל מה שקיים כרגע. כשהן התחככו בשלו, מלטפות אותן, הן היו רכות כעלי כותרת. מה יקרה כשהוא ידביק את שפתיו על שפתיה?

דמו זרם בנמרצות יתרה. הוא לפת את זרועותיו מסביב לה... אושר, עיניים נוצצות, היא טרפה את מבטו, והוא הפסיק לחשוב.

"אחר כך," אמרה. "אחר כך."

הוא אחז בסכין ונעץ אותה בגופת המת.

"אני הולך ללכלך את הבגדים שלי," הוא אמר.

"אז תוריד אותם," היא אמרה, ו—"אלוהים, תתבגר."

כשהחל מתנשף נעלמה מאחורי וילון, לתוך החדר הסמוך, וחזרה עם ערמה של בגדים וזרקה אותם לפניו.

"זה לא משנה אם נהרוס אותם, אין כאן אף אחד שיזדקק להם יותר."

הוא התמלא חשש וספק, והיא אמרה: "אל תדאג, אני לא מסתכלת."

באותו רגע שהחל ללבוש את בגדי האיש המת מבטה השתנה. ותוכלו לנחש למה? היא הייתה לגמרי בשוק.

ברגע שגמר לעטות על עצמו את הבגדים שנתנה לו, אחז בסכין והחל בעבודה, תחילה שיקשק מרוב פחד, אך אחר כך התמלא החלטיות הולכת וגוברת.

מדי פעם בפעם הציץ למעלה. מראה שפתיה החושניות הותיר אותו נרגש ומלא אמביציה. תחילה היה מזועזע מהמקור של גוש הבשר המת. אחר כך, הסבל הוקל, והוא עבד באופן יותר ויותר מכני, בריכוז גבוה יותר, מבלי לדעת, למרות הכל, בדיוק למה. זה היה צריך להיעשות מהר. מאוד מהר. זה הכל.

הסכינים היו קהים, והוא לא ידע דבר על אנטומיה. לבסוף כששסים, עצם את עיניו; אור אפרפר הבליח מבעד לסדקי עפעפיו. הוא ביצע את משימתו ונעמד. דם ניתז על בגדיו, פניו וידיו. כמעט שכח את האישה.

שאלה צצה במוחו. מה הוא בעצם עושה כאן? הוא הרגיש זקן מאוד.

מבטו נדד אל תוך החדר, וכמו מתוך ערפל ראה את האישה, עומדת שם באופן לא ברור. היה משהו... אך מה? מה זה היה?

לפתע היא הושיטה אליו את זרועותיה. מתוך החלל העצום והאין סופי שהיה ביניהם שמע את צעקתה: "בוא!"

באותו רגע נדמה היה לו שמשהו בתוכו התנפץ. מערבולת תשוקה השתלטה על כלי הדם שלו. זה היה בדיוק זה. האישה. האישה.

הוא הסיר את בגדיו. ברור שהיה חייב להיפטר מהבגדים הספוגים דם. הוא התעטף במעיל הגשם שלו. בציפייה ענוגה הוא פסע לעבר האישה, לקח אותה בזרועותיו ונישק את פניה הלוהטות. וכך בדיוק נפרד מנעוריו.

Conceived with help from Gonnem Nissim.

Still flowing, the red blood seeped through the shirt and slowly dripped into a widening puddle on the floor. While the woman stood and looked...

You have to help. You simply have to help. I can't get it into the trunk. You can kiss me. You can... you can do to me whatever you want...

11

Blankness of matter across which may surge unbounded desire. No. Not yet. First it warps inside the memory of his mother, the only woman he has ever kissed. Revolting. The tight dry pucker of her lips protruding from her face like a nipple, the surprising sharp hairs of mustache against his cheek.

12

But she! But this one! There is all the difference in the world. The shape of her body. Other men wanted exactly that in such a straightforward way. Think of them. Think of it. Staring at her. Hiss. The shape of her body.

13

Blankness of matter across which surges unbounded desire.

Perhaps, he thought, it would be interesting to cut a few pieces for her. Very interesting. He would happily cut a few pieces for her.

14

First rain, now blood. This is progress. Manhood likes progress.

To keep the wet world off him as best as she can, to keep his clothes clean, she brings him some of the dead man's. He takes his clothes off. He puts his clothes on

15

and gets to work. Manhood is work. It is a task. He dismembers her dead man, learning as he goes. Sticks in the blade and makes widening circles to increase the hole. Cutting nature at the joints. Cartilage and tendons. Feet and hands. The head. Varying weights and qualities. Piece by piece. Into the trunk. Hiss.

16

He thinks, *This is a magic trick gone wrong*. He thinks, *There is no such thing as magic*. A smile on his spattered face.

17

He works on the beach all day, forgetting everything, tiring himself out. Finally, he looks up. The woman.

Come!

18

He removes the dead man's clothes. His hands are gloved in the red of his work. He takes hold of the woman he will penetrate. Hiss.

19

The act of Manhood is blinding. A crash of surf through the brain. He does not see or remember anything. His face is a grimace of exaltation. His eyes are crushed shut. He does not think, *Who is coming up the stairs now?* He does not think, *Who will dismember me?*

With thanks to Meital Amar for her assistance.

NOTES ON THE TRANSLATIONS

I.

I translated Richard Middleton's story too many years ago, in 1989. I was preparing an anthology titled *Cuentos únicos* (Unique Tales). The main idea in it was: there are many authors who only wrote one very short masterpiece, not enough to be remembered. Their names have, therefore, fallen into oblivion in most cases. The anthology collected nineteen of those isolated masterpieces. Of course not all of the stories I chose were as good as to be called that, or by totally unknown authors (there was one by Winston Churchill, for example, another one by Lawrence Durrell). But that idea was, as it were, the alibi for the strange collection.

I decided to include one story by Middleton, whose few books I was familiar with. He died at twenty-nine, and I have always felt a great sympathy toward those talented people who died too young (the poet Keith Douglas, who died at twenty-four in Normandy, would be another case). And I considered "The Making of a Man" to be an excellent, terrible story.

Then something slightly funny happened. Most of the authors in the anthology were so unknown (at least for a Spanish readership) that I could not help including a story of my own, which I presented as by a "James Denham," for whom I invented a short biographical note. Friends knew that one of the stories was a fake, that it had been written by myself, but they did not know which one it was (I only revealed it a couple of years later, when I included the story, "Lord Rendall's Song," in *While the Women Are Sleeping*).

The funny thing is that most of my friends who guessed (including my father) could not say whether the "fake" (that is, the story I had written but had presented as a translation from the English) was the piece by "Denham" or the piece by Middleton. I was certainly flattered by their hesitations. I also thought that perhaps I should count forgotten, ill-fated Richard Middleton among my literary influences, even if he wrote so little. He died in 1911, so it has taken 101 years for him to be the object of this tribute.

—*Javier Marías*

II.

I found that after producing a literal English counterpart (the Spanish is simple enough) I was left with a lifeless, inert corpse, much like that in the story. The most difficult part, therefore, was to make the language come alive again, which meant altering literal meanings (such as that *mechero de gas que crepitaba de manera abominable*, literally a "gas burner that crepitated in an abominable manner") so the the story kept the same fun, creepy sensation of the original (itself a translation, of course). In reading Byatt's translation, however, what I found myself looking for immediately was how she handled the clerk's odd reactions: his curiosity about the kiss, his detachment after chopping up the body, and his transformation into a man. You can easily see how we both approached it—neither with the literal translation in mind. But what is most different was that odd passage when he changes into the dead man's clothes as the woman watches and, of the two, she is more surprised (*Y de los dos, el de ella era el mayor asombro*). What on earth could this mean? I decided it was his bare innocence that filled her with wonder, whereas in Byatt's it seems to be his easy transformation into a butcher that shocks her. These are very different readings, and I felt a little queasy seeing how well she'd done hers. You can also see I took these challenges and set them before my grad-school class (the tough paragraph below that crepitating lamp, in which an entire room is described, along with a body described as an "it," and a bout of vomiting—given to them in Google Translate), and put the final paragraph up on Twitter, in Spanish. The wording there seemed most important, and you can see how many possibilities there are. It all felt much riskier than I had expected—because not only did the translation feel as vulnerable as creating my own writing, it could also be dead wrong. I had not been informed of a third terror: that it could be not as good as versions by A.S. Byatt and Adam Foulds.

—*Andrew Sean Greer*

III.

I believe a translation should be as closely as possible a rendering of the original text, adding nothing and subtracting nothing. I've realized that I do believe that a piece of writing belongs in some sense to the person who wrote it—which is why I suffer a great deal from the attentions of American "line editors." I think it's important not to use anachronistic words. I also think it isn't usually a good idea to use very obtrusive or unusual words from one's own language. I read a translation from the Chinese while I was working on this, which used a lot of English provincial argot—with the result that I knew I was not in Beijing. I came to the conclusion that a translation is almost certainly—as I wrote to Adam Thirlwell—*blander* than the original.

In this case of course I was working from Julia Franck's excellent and muscular German and could only guess at the original style. I thought I could sense that Julia's German was more elegant than how I imagined the original English. Was my job to translate Julia, or to try to "feel for" the original? It was to translate Julia. My German is workmanlike (in a literary sort of way) and I had to look up several words online. I bought a new compact Oxford dictionary and in almost every problematic case there was no good translation of what I was looking for. I became so incensed with it that I wrote the only bad Amazon review I have ever written—indeed the only Amazon review I have ever written.

It is interesting how one word can set the style for a whole piece of writing. The original of our story begins: "He was a weedy clerkling." Javier Marías rendered that as "Era un empleaducho de oficina enclenque…" Andrew Sean Greer turns that into "Here he was: a runty little clerk…" Julia's version is "Das war er, ein mickriger kleiner Angestellte…" Which I translated as "There he was, an unremarkable little clerk." Of all these my version is unintentionally furthest from the original—Andrew's "runty" is closer to "weedy" than my "unremarkable"—which actually allows more space for sympathy with the character (whether or not that is a good thing).

Most of my major problems were with sex and the female body. The original simply says Simmons discovered "she was a lady and handsome." Marías translates this exactly: "una dama, y guapa." Andrew elaborates a bit—"noticing the details of her womanliness, her beauty"—and Julia elaborates more: Simmons was "beschäftigt, die Einzelheiten ihrer Weiblichkeit im Augenschein zu nehmen." I tried all sorts of things to make that long phrase work in English and ended up with "he was so taken up with her shapely form, her beauty," a phrase I was intensely dissatisfied with. I also had terrible problems with the kiss and the brushing lips soft as petals. They were too far from any sentence I myself would ever have written. There may be players of this game who would have rewritten the whole kiss—but I didn't think I had the right. My late French translator used to remark grimly that one had a duty not to make a sentence any better than it was. Since his own style was inordinately baroque and convoluted I was glad he didn't rewrite my sentences. My German translator believes one must preserve the integrity of sentences.

I was very interested to read Andrew's comments on the emotional effect of the moment when Simmonds puts on the clothes—presumably the dead man's clothes. The original reads "And of the two, hers was the greater wonder." Marias has "Y de los dos, el de ella era el mayor asombro." Andrew has "And would you guess it? She was more astonished than he." It's a dicey emotional moment—the reader has to think too much. Julia, crucially, went for simplification and cut out Simmonds's wonder altogether. "Und ahnen sie wie? Sie staunte mächtig" (*She* was greatly astounded.) I had huge trouble with this and eventually came up with "She was horribly shocked." Andrew comments that my version seems to suggest that "it was his easy transformation into a butcher that shocked her." I think what I felt also was that she was seeing the dead man alive again in his borrowed clothes. Either way it does have an emotional kick which is due to Julia's cutting.

—*A.S. Byatt*

IV.

The story I received from Orly Castel-Bloom had a rough pungency, an energetic B-movie unpleasantness that I found compelling but not quite satisfying. Trusting that more faithful translations were being made further up the chain and abetted (if not aided) by editor Adam Thirlwell, I decided to translate the text into something new, something that would stand as both a rendering and a reading of the original, something that would please me formally and intellectually. How I have gone about this should be clear enough. One note of explanation for one imported word: *Margate*. The story was reminiscent for me of the world of early T.S. Eliot poetry: the sexual unease, the gaslit and sinister city, the tightly wound unhappy clerk. Eliot mentions Margate, a seaside resort not far from London, in *The Waste Land*: "On Margate sands / I can connect / Nothing with nothing."

—*Adam Foulds*

CODA

L'INCENDIO
DI VIA KEPLERO

a story in ITALIAN *by* CARLO EMILIO GADDA

ILLUSTRATION
Wesley Allsbrook.

THE FIRE ON
CHANCE STREET

translated into English by ADAM THIRLWELL *and* FRANCESCO PACIFICO

PEOPLE CAME UP WITH 1,001 stories about the fire at number 14. Which wasn't so strange, since not even the late New York hipster Gordon Matta-Clark could have blown up that wailing tenement as comprehensively as the fire did in the course of its three-minute happening, which evicted from the building's exploding garbage and fear, in no particular order: 1) all the women in there seminaked because of the heat, and the global array of their offspring, then 2) several males, then 3) some sad old women who were in the words of one dispassionate bystander *a little unsteady on their legs*, who entered the scene all bony and disheveled, in white lace nightdresses, rather than as usual neatly and soberly arranged for the performance of their locomotions toward the Baptist Church, then 4) some gentlemen who were themselves a little—how to put this?—patched-up, then 5) Anacarsi Rotunno, an international poet, who will never be mentioned again, then 6) the careworker for the ailing anarchist on the fifth floor, then 7) Henderson with the little girl and the parrot, then 8) that kid called Flowers in his underwear and in his arms Mrs. Smith, no I mean Mrs. Maldifassi, who looked like the lord of the fucking flies was trying to personally remove her pantyhose, she was screaming so much. And then, finally—among the continuing cries, anguishes, tears, children, screams, and heartbroken shouts and random landings and bundles of stuff thrown to safety from the windows, when you could already hear the firemen arriving at top speed and two vans were already emptying themselves of some fat police beside the highspeed ambulance, the entire state security—yes finally, 9) from two windows at the right-hand side of the third floor, and then also one on the fourth, the fire managed in what was a really terrifying entrance to free its very own flames, its tongues, in staccato intervals, serpentine and red, which appeared and disappeared, along with black tortiglioni of smoke, black and greasy like some overbarbecued bo ssäm, which were libidinously morulating into spheres and multispheres or, to put it less scientifically, folks, were like the intrafolding coils of a black rat-snake, sliding out from the undergrowth and the underworld among lurid magnesium flares; and also burning farfalloni, perhaps paper or more likely fabric or burnt pegamoid, went fluttering across the smokeblackened sky, over the terror of those Mrs. and Ms. and Miss, some of them barefoot in the dust of the fucked-up street, others in their puffball slippers oblivious to the piss and dogshit, over the shricks and weepings of their infinite babies. These women who could already feel their heads and their hair, in pointless perms, erupt into a horrifying, live flame.

Take a look, panoramic reader! There were sirens already wailing on top of chimneys and nearby factories to the torrefied sky: and this cryptosymbolic electric composition harmonized with the women's desperate cries of anguish. From the flung-open doors of distant firestations escaped highspeed firetrucks, prompt and rapid impulses ready to overcome any problem the flames could pose them, while the final fireman of the fifth unit, with a leap, managed with his left hand to grab the last iron of the ladder-rest at the end of the ladder that was already turning out of the door, and viceversa with his right was still buttoning the buttons of his fireman's jacket. While, to come back to earth, the enperfumed dreaminess of what are laughably called *motorists*—who happily kneecap patient and lame geriatrics; whose interior is a languid drowsiness of MP3s and aircon while their exterior is crazed and murderous, slicing up street corners on their way out to the more metroland sidewalks of this metropolis…—was at last blockaded by these electric and premonitory tones, followed simultaneously by the transversal advent of the sirens… It was like that Saul Steinberg print where the sirens are a repeat of ovals coming from the squad car.

Do you get it, hipsters?—A Happening is an assemblage of events performed or perceived in more than one time and place. So okay, Allan Kaprow. Merci, monsieur. But it ends up looking like this.

A three-year-old girl, Berenice, the only daughter of Mr. Sol Smith (esq.), home alone with her parrot, on the high chair into which she'd been heaved and then imprisoned, was crying desperately for her mamma without being able to get down, and fat tears like harlequin pearls were dripping and descending over her cheeks in pursuit of the soaked wet bib mechanically scribbled with *Got Pizza?* until they drowned in the messy mush of her lukewarm milk where little by little she'd soaked an entire loaf of sliced white bread and a few chocolate biscuits that might have been Oreos or just those strange kind of teatime wafers but which were three years old themselves, I'm sure of that. "Mamma, Mamma!" she shouted in terror; while, at the far corner of the table, sat a multicolored bird, with a Roman nose of a beak, who kinda liked what he saw in the mirror, this bird, this arrogant bird, who'd glow and simper as soon as the kids called his name—"Snickers, Snickers!"—but if not then some sort of hopeless melancholy and lethargy would take hold of him, and so they'd incite him with "Hey, Snickers, sing!… come on… Sing 'Bad Romance'!… Hey, dumbass Snickers!" and on hearing that "Sing!"

he'd riposte with a gentle gurgle of "Szingyourfuckingself!" But now, poor creature, there was to be no Szingyourfuckingself… It's true that, without it causing him undue alarm, a certain hint of burnt matter had been already sensed by his perceptual apparatus: but when he saw those petals diagonally enter the open window and then travel through the room in their sinister magic like so many burning bats and start lapping at the shreds of the frazzled upholstery and the yellow blind, its ash slats rolled up with some threadbare cords in its box, then he too began to squawk from the hollow of his throat a range of random noises on repeat, as if he were a radio: and he skittered scared and fearful toward the girl, with abrupt motions, cut off every time, after half a meter of straining, by the inexorable malice of the little chain that was keeping him linked to his perch.

People said that he'd first belonged to a soldier, a veteran of the Falklands, then to the business maven Emmanuel Goldfarb: a restful youth spent in meditation, in Chelsea: about whose haute bourgeoisie he'd wikileak to anyone who'd listen. But now he'd completely lost it: man, he seemed about to go mad: "Roma—roma! Ma—maa!" he strangulatedly squawked, fluttering around with his little chain tied to his leg in a meteor of feathers and a shroud of burnt paper and soot, perhaps hoping that this kind of behavior would somehow propitiate Fate, while the little girl kept shouting "Mamma, mamma!" and screaming in terror as she wept, pounding on the table with the handle of her big spoon. Until eventually a man called Henderson Peters, thirty-three, who had priors in the way of larceny and was only out on parole, and therefore without current employment, and so forced, because of this lack of employment, to sleep through the day so he could be ready if need be to carry out any small jobs that needed doing at night, on the offchance, notwithstanding the curfew, just wanting to earn his bread like everyone else, the poor shnorrer, which was why to cut a long story short this man was very luckily sleeping in the room directly above, at Mrs. Kemal's, on the living-room sofa; and on sensing that he himself had only just avoided a very great danger discovered let's say a certain courage, at that precise moment, among the fear and the smoke, a smoke that was using the stairwell as a chimney, and all those women rushing down the stairs in dressing gowns and blouses, and the shouts, and the kids, and the firemen's sirens approaching in the distance. He broke down the door to the Smiths', with kicks, with shoulders, and saved the poor kid and the bird; and also a gold watch on top of the dresser, which he later forgot to give back, an absence that everyone blamed on the firehoses' water, with which, to extinguish the fire, they'd flooded the whole building.

Yes, Henderson had heard the screams: and this cat knew the girl was home alone: because around five in the afternoon was precisely when he'd disembark from the sofa onto the wharves of his reawakened conscience, so burdened as he was by his problems with the police; and he'd rub his eyes, scratch here and there, his hair in particular, and then shove his head under the tap in the sink; and he'd towel himself down—with a towel the color of a sewer rat—and then comb his hair—with his half-size pocket comb, green, plastic: and then, removing from the comb one by one with great delicacy the hairs that were stuck in it, he counted them and delivered them one after the other to the sink oozing with piles of bowls and greasy plates in the informal kitchen of Mrs. Kemal's *establishment*. Then, yawning, he'd put on some old clothes, and his sneakers, and finally he'd leave reyawning down the corridor and wander up and down the endless stairs, inventing alibis, and sometimes with the precise aid of his buccinators he'd dart a liquid arrow of saliva onto the stairs or the wall, sleepy and alert at the same time, his bones still a little tender from the sofa, hoping for a grand encounter. Encounter, you ask?—well, obviously, with one of the women in residence there, for some of them were slim, and lavish; and decisive: and then quick to slap their heels down the steps *tatìc* and *tatàc* to the ground floor, out of the building: and he'd usually find one available in front of numero 14, even though there were now many storekeepers on Chance Street, who'd recently moved there with their families. This was how, on that very day, he'd met the little girl's mother, a total fussbudget!—and so he knew that the girl was on her own with her parrot. And so he saved her. And Snickers, too. They'd see what kind of man he was, and what he was made of; and how he paid them back for their condescension; even with all the grief the police gave him, night and day. So okay: the watch: the watch, that's another story, of course: too bad if they'd left it on the dresser, just when a building evaporates in flames.

"That fire," said everyone, afterward, "was like totally one of the worst things to happen in the entire history of the world." And it's true: amid the generosity and nobility of the plastic firemen: amid cataracts of water bursting from the bathroom pipes over the pissgreen sofa, now threatened by a very savage red, and above the bedside tables and sideboards, perhaps hoarding an old nubbin of sweating cheddar, but already licked by the flame as the deer is by the python: jets, liquid needles, turbid and soaking from the hoses, and long, stabbing blows from brass hydrants, that elongate into white fringes and then cloud in the scorching August sky: and half-finished porcelain insulators falling to pieces and disintegrating against the sidewalk *kaboom!*: and wiring from burnt TVs and DVD players flying away in the twilight from their now scorching units, with black and floating islands made of cardboard and hot-air balloons of charred wallpaper, and down, between men's feet, and behind the mobile ladders, circles and curves and rearings of tubes that scatter parabolic jets from both sides of the road into the gutters, glasses in smithereens in a swamp of water and mud, buckets filled with carrots thrown down and out the window, even now! against the boots of the rescuers, of the police, of the firemen with their walkietalkies: and the arrogant and indefatigable *chic-chiàc*, and *chichìc* and *chichiàc*, of feminine slippers as they gathered up pieces of comb, or shards of mirror, and blessed images of Jesus Christ.

It was total destruction. I mean, a pregnant woman—oh, but you don't want to know! Another heartbreaking case! In her third trimester!—in the panic and anguish of the commotion and perhaps, this was also a possibility, asphyxiated by the staircase's smoke, fainted right there on the landing, as she was trying to escape from the building. And by a miracle she was saved by a certain Deepak Guha, son of the late Indira, who was thirty-eight, and worked as a porter at the Great Eastern Hotel, where he was due back on shift at six-thirty. An emissary of God!—if you consider the fact that, if you're in the business of carrying or moving Louis Vuitton trunks, you need to be practical. Humming like a kazoo, he too was leaving Mrs. Kemal's, after concluding a certain robust gallantry to which God had almost certainly kept at least one goggle-eye closed. Having said his goodbye, he was feeling buoyant and inclined more than ever to protect the weak, the forlorn: he took his beanie, adjusted it on his head, and relighting a half-finished cigarette he'd already started meditating on how he'd organize all 256 trunks and suitcases and hatcases of some conasse americanessa, the asshole and unlikeable sort, en route from Los Angeles to the Biennale.

But, instead of an americanessa, in front of him as he opened the door were just screams and frenzy and smoke from the stairs, so bad that at times he couldn't see anything. Yeah, yeah, it was a bad moment, he said later, one of the worst. He shouted at a woman who was still struggling with a tap, the toilet, some small pans and great wastes of water, who dropped everything, soap and towel and bowl and water, everything, and slipped into some sort of Chinese robe, or maybe it was Japanese, and then dissolved into screaming "Oh, my God, my God! My fur, my fur!" and wanted to take her purse out of the dresser, so he grabbed her arm and dragged her out just as she was, in that kimono from a store on Cheshire Street and without any underwear even, just some slip-on shoes one of which slipped-off on the stairs; and dragging her behind him by the hand they went in search of safety while drowning together in that terrifying suffocation. With two or three kicks, like that, pure instinct, he reduced the first window to minuscule pieces, as he passed by: from which smoke just came out as well. Then, downstairs, they almost stumbled on the fainting woman, sprawled against the door frame; and so with the help of the other woman, who was limping because of her slip-onless foot and wanted to escape on her own, no matter how, but instead he grabbed her and held her tightly and shouted in her face: "Help me, you cunt," and they both managed after an infinite effort and terror and sweat to take her all the way down, where there was already a stretcher and nurses and even, now, the firemen.

While elsewhere Mrs. Maldifassi, cousin of the famous baritone Maldifassi, Eleuterio Maldifassi—you know the name? I think he sang at Covent Garden once, back in the day, when we were happy in the twentieth century—this woman, while rushing to safety along with everyone else, slammed and dunked by the "egoism," as she reported afterward, "of the fifth-floor tenants," storming down the stairs like a bunch of hares, she didn't go and catch her stiletto between the concrete step and the badly constructed iron railing? But totally! And that, she said later, was how she broke her leg: but really she'd just sprained her ankle, slipping on the very first step because of her fear and because she didn't know how to walk in the clickclack of her heels, an ambitious attempt to expropriate another six or seven centimeters… And all because she'd wanted to save the portrait of her Eustorgio, and his precious things, all her souvenirs of Italia, and she'd rushed back to take them out of the dresser: which only that morning she'd liberated from the Cash Converter on the Bethnal Green Road, with money that Cohen woman had finally given back. Talk about luck! And imagine what she must have felt when in her fright and confusion she felt herself being slammed against the staircase's railings, and then against the wall, by the *ruthless selfishness of human nature*, and then back against the railings so hard that she was very much scared of toppling over into the void! And to the fear and faintness that were only natural to one of her sex was all at once added this rip in her foot, an improvised piercing spasm followed by a terrible pain in her entire leg, so she collapsed and then slid down on her ass a little farther, a terrible toboggan, at every bounce stair after stair bruising and rebruising her backbone, or coccyx if you prefer, so poorly guarded by the deficiency of her buttocks, with which ever since she was young she had always been so dolorously ill equipped, poor Mrs. Maldifassi! She was coughing and sneezing in the acrid soot and screaming "I'm choking! I'm choking; oh, oh my leg, save me! For the love of Christ! Oh, oh! Madonna, Madonna, my leg, my leg, I'm choking! I'm choking!" In fact, she never stopped emitting phrases like this, from the cubist mess of her mouth; from her terrified soul, her tortured body. And she had to be dragged down the stairs, among unimaginable screams of pain and in that coughing and horrible smoke, by the kind apprentice Jimmy Flowers, son of James, seventeen, from Enfield, who, basically in his underwear, was in the process of saving his own valuables too, which couldn't be converted, after all, into any cash. And here too you could see the hand of God. Because Flowers had just rushed barefoot down from the roof where he was helping repair the tiles, after the crazy hail the week before, which had fallen on all the various roofs of East London impartial and solemn, like every misfortune which is said to descend on this earth through the will of divine providence or, if you prefer, natural justice.

He was working this late because although this was London it was still August, and if you went up there in the middle of the day on those scorched tiles you'd be basically frying your brain; so his head was tightly wrapped in a red/yellow bandanna, and then further protected by the density of his hair, like a calf's fleece, if a calf's fleece were ever powdered in lime, which seems unlikely: and he'd attempted, obviously, to dress light, in a tie-dye vest, which was made of viscose and was see-through, and full of holes, so it looked like a sheet of tissue-paper drenched in sweat. His enormous feet, gnarled and fleshy, with stub toes, also fleshy, splayed and opened like a fan, offered to the biscuity porosity of the tiles a friction particularly prized by every builder in London, because to tell the truth this kid had the most agile feet in town, which meant he got sent up on the roof for fifty quid a day to move around the chimneys like a ghost, to rub, like a fearless cat, against the gutters and spouts. Absolutely, dear editor: in the words of the politicians, he had earned his *place in the world* on merit. And this uninterrupted labor was the backstory to why what remained of his basketball shorts was in the process of reaching his ankles—a banlieue Hermes, from Enfield, whose wings had frazzled to the shorts round his feet.

The builder, with lime mortar smeared over his mustache and face, all wrinkled, with a bloom of white moles, tired and overcome by the pandemonium, was calling to him lamentingly from the fearful bottom of the stairwell: "Jimmy! Oh, Jimmy!" and explained weepingly to all those women frantically fleeing in their slippers, burdened with terror and bundles and screaming children, that a boy had been left on the roof, "The kid, my kid," that up on the roof there must be "Little Jimmy, the kid": and then he went back to once more enjimmify the smoky well of the infernal staircase, from bottom to top, but was overwhelmed by everyone's screams. No one of course was going back at the thought of the kid, and most of them, at that point, couldn't even hear him. But then he appeared at the top of the stairs, exhausted, red, soaked in his own sweat, with the red/yellow bandanna tied round his head, a black mustache smeared on his cheek, with in his arms Mrs. Maldifassi screaming "Ow ow! My leg! My leg, my leg! Signor Madonna jutèmm vi alter!" but at the same time clutching a small canvas bag that she obviously wasn't going to part with no matter what: and him with his shorts in an inferior position caused by this extreme emergency, and about to fall lower, stumbling at every new stair. He'd grabbed her and was holding her from behind, under the armpits, and with one knee, then the other, on each step he'd make a sort of temporary seat under her lean bottom, her forlorn bottom, trying to keep his balance and not have the two of them fall down on top of each other to the foot of the stairs. With such success that they later honored him at the Town Hall for his bravery.

Another poor schmuck, Mr. Joyce, only just got out in time. For years he'd suffered from asthma and bronchial catarrh. The situation was so bad that even summer couldn't make it any better, which meant that by now the world was more than convinced that his state was, as they say, *incurable*. He had his own private method of painkilling, by staring at his bedroom wall until noon, and then at his kitchen table until six—on which throughout the day, while the sun performed its full ascension and declension, there was always a tablecloth (filthy) and a can of Guinness, "my secret Novocaine," he used to call it—without noticing the Guinnessstains and ketchupstains, and Nescaféstains, nor worrying about the chaos of doubled-over slices of bread and the scattered crumbs that were left long after the cheese and corned beef had vamooshed. From that can of Guinness—sitting at the table, with an elbow on the tablecloth from which dangled his left hand, inert—Mr. Joyce poured the sleepy, slackery afternoon away one glass at a time, "Just half a glass" and "Another half a glass," and with the oscillating hand, the right one, from time to time he'd place it under his mustache, I mean the glass; and so he wouldn't stop ekeing and savoring (long savorings and formidable ekeings of the palate), as though it were ambrosial nectar, that can of Guinness, which left a thin black residue on his tongue: and fat black drops, also, on his mustache. Which seemed, they shone so brightly, like drops from the Sacred Heart or tears of the Woman of Sorrows in some kitsch velvet painting, or hologram, or other form of the barocco. And his stare, also, veiled, melancholy, staring at a distant point in the lethargic sky, the twin upper halves of his eyeballs hidden by his drooping eyelids, a sort of forehead-sleep, yes his stare also had a hint of the Sacred Heart, à la Chance Street. In this way, hour after hour, with his elbow on the filth of his Guinness-and-ketchup tablecloth, with one hand dangling, and the other, when not pouring or ekeing, scratching his knee; in this way he muttered and snored for hours on end, through the entire long decline of the afternoon, sweating, in the heat and the stink of the room, full of dust, with the bed still unaired, the pillowcase the color of a hare or a whippet; with unbuttoned trousers from which emerged a bit of nightgown, with two wornout slippers on his bare greenish feet, with his short breath that seemed to run on balls of mucus, cuddling with the lovingness of a young mother his soft catacombal catarrh, like a glue that bubbled, on a slow boil, in a pot left on the hob.

This Mr. Joyce, a partner in the limited company of Chapel & Eisenberg, at 44 Ridley Road, ran a business in cheap Atlantic fish, trucked down from Rotterdam and Aberdeen; they also offered at very convenient prices some oysters, and frozen seafood from Albion's shores. And I have to admit: they weren't doing badly, handing over chunks of green sea monster that had once inhabited the marine depths to the speechless citizens of Ridley Road; citizens who, very much taken with the idea of saving money, also very much lacked anything to cook them in: these unicorns...

But no, I'm wandering: when the concept of a fire first approached the brain of Mr. Joyce, maybe occasioned by the first screams of fear from the stairs, maybe not, and however much he may have reached a consoling stupor and torpor, the old man had even attempted, in a sort of hallucinated physical pain, to try to reach the window and open it, his klutziness having reached a point of such perfection that he thought it was shut, even though it had been open the entire afternoon: a pain that was like a heat shimmer round the stump of what remained of his instincts: but he only succeeded in knocking the can of Guinness, half empty and a klutz like him; and so instead of the window what was opened wide were the cataracts of his bronchial tubes and loosened, at the same time, his otherwise tireless sphincter rings, so that among bursts of terrible coughing, in an acrid smoke, the blackest, the first to filter into the apartment through the keyhole and under the door, in his fear and sudden suffocation, gripped by the pathos of solitude, of feeling his legs like raw cookie dough precisely when he needed them most, the performance ended,

finally, with a bowel motion right there in his night shirt: at full volume: and then, for an encore, the expelling from his pulmonary chasms of more stuff than could have ever been found in the Channel, I'm sure, even with its infinite oysters.

He was rescued by the firemen, in their masks, after they'd broken the door down with hatchets. "See. Fire? You. Scram," opined the head of the squadron sagely when the rescue was over.

But the most poignant story was the one fatality—the case of the sad hidalgo Ezra Goodman, the anarchist on the fifth floor... Despite the screams of his careworker Mrs. Patrice, he'd stubbornly insisted on saving two photo albums from the era of his political youth. Now, the transport of a Cable Street veteran's photo albums, in a situation of total panic, isn't as simple as you might think. So he too ended up afflicted by asphyxiation, or something resembling asphyxiation, and the firemen had to go in to get him too. But things quickly accelerated, given his age, ninety-eight!, and his heart condition, and a painful urethral stricture he'd been suffering from for a while. And so I have to admit that the ambulance, on its fifth trip, didn't stop at the Royal London on Whitechapel Street but carried on straight to the morgue, farther out, farther out! in East Ham, exactly, along the Commercial Road, you know, after the East India Docks, and then the Prince Regent, beyond Ben Jonson, beyond the Custom House, you've got it, out there, in the middle of nowhere.

NOTES ON THE TRANSLATION

I.

I'd been told by my friend and editor, Luigi Brioschi, that Carlo Emilio Gadda was the greatest Italian novelist of the twentieth century. I relayed this opinion to another friend, the novelist Francesco Pacifico. Francesco seemed to agree; in fact, he had his own giant theories about the place of Gadda in the wider history of Italian literature. Gadda was God. But, like God, finding the works of Gadda in English was difficult—for Gadda, it turned out, was reckoned to be untranslatable. This was due to his extraordinary style—a rough description of which would include: a) a mixture of Italian dialects; b) a mixture of registers, from philosophical and academic jargon to total street obscenity; c) his dilapidated syntax, with sentences that ran down entropically, without a main verb, or with endless relative clauses, punctuated by sudden short, staccato phrases. The only piece of Gadda I could easily find was his great novel, *That Awful Mess on the Via Merulana*, translated by William Weaver, published by New York Review Books—a detective story that is really an investigation of the whole idea of causation. And, *lettore*, I was hooked.

And because I wanted to prove that maybe nothing was untranslatable, I kind of thought it would be interesting to try to translate some Gadda. Even though, or especially because, I speak no Italian.

I went back to Luigi, who told me to find a story called "L'Incendio di Via Keplero"; and I proposed to Francesco—who is not only Italian but gorgeously fluent in English too—that we make a collective translation.

Our method was that, once a week, Francesco and I would talk for hours in the stopmotion staccato of a Skype connection, as Francesco gave me a map of Gadda's story about this fire in the Via Keplero—going through the text, word by word: elaborating, fulminating, in the process outlining a whole Pacifico belief system. This process proceeded minutely. When one of Gadda's characters describes a woman he dislikes as a *dispettosa*, Francesco tried to explain this by finally saying that his ultimate image of a *dispettosa* was *Peanuts*'s Lucy van Pelt, so that eventually I happened on a Charleschulzian insult: *fussbudget*.

In this way, Francesco invented his version: a Pacifico-expanded rewrite of Gadda. Occasionally, a technical term—and Gadda loved to use the technical terms of biology or chemistry or whatever other science came to hand—would be skipped. I would then send Francesco emails with a list of these skipped terms: and this had its drama too, so that what eventually were identified as "bronchial tubes" were initially only described to me as "a part of the respiratory system," with Francesco sadly adding: "I'm on the seaside, Adriatic sea, with no dictionary, drinking caffè shakerato with

Baileys on a terrazzo in front of a roundabout, listening to bad FM radio, all the chairs are wooden movie-director-chair-like and yellow..."

Yes, this was how we entered the problem of Gadda's linguistic contamination. We worried over the degree to which the ordinary Italian reader would understand Gadda's occasional delighted descents into the total Lombard dialect, which would therefore have to condition how easily we would make it for the transatlantic reader to understand Gadda's dialects—like the moment when Mrs. Maldifassi, in pain, screams out "Signor Madonna jutèmm vi alter!", to which Francesco offered no translation, claiming that it was nonsense: a pure Gadda solipsism.

And I tried to work out what to do in English. Because one reason to love Gadda is the way he melts all the usual conventions of tone and vocabulary. I wanted to perform an equivalent operation on English as Gadda had operated on Italian—but Gadda had one extra tool at his disposal, which was the multiple dialects of his language. Whereas if suddenly the English lurched into the equivalent of an accent, into Cockney or Brooklyn or whatever, it only felt fake. So in the end my solution was to invent a kind of international dialect, a multilingual English, as a way of mimicking Gadda's antics with the varieties of Italian: but really, more precisely, trying to match the fiction to what Gadda had intricately done in this early story—the digressions, that syntax, the mock-epic raconteuring.

But when this version was ready, we started to get worried. Because, okay: one aspect of Gadda's style was this love of unmotivated shifts in register and reality. His sentences are a mess of the Latinate, of dialect, of someone's passing speech. But the unmotivated shift is also one way of identifying a bad translation—it betrays the uncertainty of tone that is elsewhere called *translationese*. So what emerged from an experiment with Gadda's "Incendio" was that the grave danger in translating Gadda was to sound like a translation, precisely because in the Italian, as it were, Gadda sounded like a translation—he destroyed all authority of tone. In Italian, however, this total refusal of authority possessed the deeper authority of Gadda himself. And while it was therefore true that if this English version of Gadda had been published as an original story then possibly this same authority would have meant that the New York or London reader could have read it as a legitimate experiment with English, with its syntax and its imagery—but reading it as a translation it was very much possible that Gadda's style could in fact just sound like translationese. And so in order to stay true to Gadda, what was in fact necessary was to come up with a substitute Gadda.

And at this time when I was starting to despair I was reading about the works of the artist Gordon Matta-Clark, whose ideas were more and more conspiring to make me think of Carlo Emilio Gadda and how to multiply him internationally. And this was partly because Matta-Clark, like Gadda, enjoyed imagining what to do with apartment blocks, I mean disintegrating them or blowing them up, but it was also because Matta-Clark like me believed that one way of investigating something was seeing what you could remove from it. He made cuttings, and splittings. And just as I'd thought about this idea of a novel as an unstable multiple, I considered the possibility that some novelists are fractal, that maybe in fact many novelists I admired were fractal—in that wherever you entered their composition the deep structure was always already present. It seemed to be true, say, of Proust, or Laurence Sterne. It was definitely true of Gadda. The reader could join anywhere in the composition, and leave whenever they liked.

And this made me wonder if the same could be true for a translator. Or at least: the novelist-translator. Because the ethics of the novelist-translator may well be different from the ethics of the translator-translator: especially if the novelist-translator is also a collective. I'd always believed in the stern ethics of translation proposed by Nabokov or Kundera. But now I was wondering if everything could belong to everyone.

There is no place, in the end, for the historical sense—or at least, not in our hazarded version of collective translation, which was collective now not only across languages but also across time. You replace the old present with the new present, so that the old present stays alive: so Milan becomes London, and the Via Keplero becomes this street in Shoreditch called Chance Street. And therefore we were free to add new linguistic dilapidations—or replace a reference to the futurist poet Marinetti with a smuggled reference to my personal avantgarde antagonist, Matta-Clark. While some characters' names were left the the same, like Mrs. Maldifassi: a small example of time travel…

It isn't the usual kind of morality, I know, but it's the one that was being forced on us by the craziness of Gadda. And I wondered if this could therefore emerge as a possible solution to the problem of multiplying Gadda in a different language—that you could give up on the idea of fidelity, this idea of fidelity to the minute flow of Gadda's structures, and do something that would be the same but different. That in fact you could remove and alter whatever you liked and still his style, this style that deforms everything it describes, would remain the same.

—*Adam Thirlwell*

II.

There's darkness in Gadda's motives and writing.

He's famous in Italy for being the guy with the best, craziest *lessico*; he uses his assortment of Italian, Lombard, Old Latin, and Generic Old Italian as if those languages were typefaces and he was an eccentric graphic designer creating his dream magazine. He isn't famous for the thing I envy him for: he crafts perfect paragraphs. The paragraph is his court.

Working on this translation I became sure of something I had only suspected, when caught and lost in the difficult task of deciphering every sentence of his—his interesting language was first and foremost a baroque choice, made to hide content from passers-by, and also, perhaps inadvertently, made to create esoteric stalwarts out of picky readers. You stumble upon Gadda's cryptic, funny, and masterful-sounding sentences, and you fall for him no matter what. But never, not even once, has an Italian writer or critic told me "I love Gadda's sentences/paragraphs." The beautiful form of his paragraphs is never the subject matter.

Here's a paragraph that you fall for, in the Italian, just because it sounds crazy, big, exciting, hardcore, real-thingy:

La sonnolenza impomatata dei guidatori d'automobili che falciano via con il parafango i ginocchi de' claudicanti vecchi alle svolte e, svaccati dentro macchina, ma saette pazze di fuori, stracciano via i cantoni ai più garibaldofrusti marciapiedi della metropoli, ecco sonerie elettriche premonitrici li bloccarono improvvisamente ai cantoni, poi, subito, l'avvento delle trasvolanti sirene. Inchiodati i tram, i cavalli trattenuti al morso dal cavallaro, disceso di serpa: i cavalli col carro contro il culo, l'occhio, all'angolo, imbiancato da un ignoto motivo di terrore.

Working on it I could finally realize that even this apparent mess is a beautifully constructed thing:

Sleepy drivers with coiffed hair cut corners and hurt limp old men on the street. They are slouched on their seats but outside they're like mad thunderbolts, and they destroy the hardest sidewalks. Then they stop when they hear ominous sirens: everyone stops to let the firemen pass. The tramways stop, the horses stop, the horseriders have dismounted, horses that carry cars have the car against their arse; in the white corner of their eyes there's panic.

Every paragraph of Gadda's gives this intense pleasure of form and hectic order.

I worked on this because there's darkness in me too: I would never make a point about Gadda in front of other people, in Italy. You cannot discuss him. We have this language that sounds so great, you see; it's impossible to state any case in favor of meaning, let alone structure. So I agreed to embark on this *impresa* in order to smuggle some Gadda outside of the usual, narrow routes that take him to the literati for enormously elitarian tasting sessions, and give him instead to this most untrustworthy British novelist, Gaddam Thirlwell. Could I trust him? I wasn't sure: he's always upbeat; he's schemey like a nine-year-old; he has these weird vibes, as if he does unorthodox things to the books he carries to the bathroom. So basically Gadda is my father's sports car, and I'm a teenager who just called this crazy friend who was desperate for it and told him to come and try the car while my parents were away.

We crashed the car. I knew I couldn't trust him, but we had to take the thing out of the garage, where it was well kept, like a secret told only to the deserving and righteous. The sports car had to be taken for a ride even though now it looks way less beautiful and polished (it looks totaled, I'd say). It was my darkness that did it, not the process itself.

It's also that, as I was working on it, I was dreading the moment a certain young Italian female critic—and Gadda expert—who hates me would find out what I'd done and punish me, write something awful against me, maybe even beat me up somehow, along with a bunch of Gaddian priests, giving me the lesson I deserve, tough love, and grounding me forever. It's this will to first escape and then be punished by that highly superior young critic that fueled my *cupio dissolvi* and made me make an ass of myself and ridicule Gadda's story through Gaddam's Gaddorable and useless linguistic inventions. What's even better—that critic hates *McSweeney's*, too. And this makes me feel even more guilty.

—*Francesco Pacifico*

NOTES ON THE ORIGINALS

SØREN KIERKEGAARD began "Writing Sampler" as a sequel to *Prefaces*, which was published in 1844. The piece remained unpublished during his lifetime. It appeared in print for the first time in 1914, in the Danish edition of *Søren Kierkegaard Papirers*. Princeton University Press first translated "Writing Sampler" into English in 2009.

"Luck," A.L. SNIJDERS's short story (or *zeer kort verhaal* ["very short story"], as the author calls it) was first published in *Brandnetels & verkeersborden*, by AFdH Publishers, March 2012.

FRANZ KAFKA's "In the Synagogue" was not published during his lifetime. It was first published by Max Brod in 1937, and appeared in *Gesammelte Schriften,* vol. 6.

The majority of KENJI MIYAZAWA's stories were published posthumously. His nine-chapter novel *Night on the Galactic Railroad* (sometimes translated as *Milky Way Railroad*, *Night Train to the Stars*, or *Fantasy Railroad In The Stars*) was written around 1927; it is within this book that "The Earthgod and the Fox" was first published, in 1934, by Bunpodō, as part of *Complete Works of Kenji Miyazawa*, vol. 3.

YOUSSEF HABCHI EL-ACHKAR, until now, has yet to be translated into a foreign language. "The Four Seasons, Without a Summer" is from the novel *Almazalla Wa Al-Malek Wa Hajees Al-Maout*.

ENRIQUE VILA-MATAS's story, "The People Below," was published in the collection *Hijos sin hijos* in 1993.

DANILO KIŠ was a Serbian novelist, short story writer, and poet. "The Shoes" has remained unpublished until now.

GIUSEPPE PONTIGGIA's "Incontrarsi" was originally published in *Vite di uomini non illustri* in 1993.

RICHARD MIDDLETON's "The Making of a Man" first appeared in *New Tales of Horror by Eminent Authors*, published by Hutchinson & Co. in 1934.

CARLO EMILIO GADDA's *Accoppiamenti giudiziosi*, the collection that included "The Fire on Chance Street," was first published in 1963. The story is dated between 1930 and 1935.

LÁSZLÓ KRASZNAHORKAI's story is part of an unpublished work in progress.

CONTRIBUTORS

ERIN ALTHEA paints and draws in Berkeley, where she lives with her family and a small black kitten.

NADEEM ASLAM was born in Pakistan and now lives in England. His novels include *Maps for Lost Lovers*, *The Wasted Vigil*, and the forthcoming *The Blind Man's Garden*.

TASH AW was born in Taipei and moved to England at the age of eighteen. He is the author of three novels, including the forthcoming *Five Star Billionaire*. His fiction has been translated into twenty-three languages.

JOHN BANVILLE is an Irish novelist, dramatist, and screenwriter. In 2005, his novel *The Sea* was awarded the Man Booker Prize. He writes crime novels under the pen name Benjamin Black.

FRÉDÉRIC BEIGBEDER has written ten books in French, one of which was translated in the U.S. as *Windows on the World* in 2003.

MIKE BERTINO lives in Berkeley, where he works as an illustrator, cartoonist, dad, and sometimes painter.

LAURENT BINET is French. He wrote *HHhH*, a novel about the 1942 assassination, in Prague, of Heydrich, head of the Gestapo and Himmler's right hand. His latest book is about the campaign of François Hollande, the new French president.

A.S. BYATT is an English writer of novels, short stories, essays, and occasional poems. Her latest books are *The Children's Book* and *Ragnarok: the End of the Gods*.

ORLY CASTEL-BLOOM has published novels, collections of short stories, and a book for children.

J.M. COETZEE is the author of thirteen works of fiction, as well as of memoirs, criticism, and translations. In 2003, he was awarded the Nobel Prize for Literature. Since 2002 he has lived in Australia, where he is Professor of Literature at the University of Adelaide.

KELSEY DAKE draws hair, letters, things, people, and gore.

LYDIA DAVIS is the author, most recently, of *The Collected Stories of Lydia Davis* and the chapbook *The Cows*.

JOE DUNTHORNE is the author of the novels *Submarine*, which was adapted for film, and *Wild Abandon*, which won the Encore Award. He was brought up in Swansea, South Wales, and now lives in London.

DAVE EGGERS's latest book is *A Hologram for the King*.

NATHAN ENGLANDER is the author of the story collections *What We Talk About When We Talk About Anne Frank* and *For the Relief of Unbearable Urges*, as well as the novel *The Ministry of Special Cases*.

ÁLVARO ENRIGUE, born in Mexico, 1969, is the author of five novels and two books of short stories. *Hypothermia* will be published in the U.S. by Dalkey Archive next spring.

PÉTER ESTERHÁZY is perhaps best known, outside of his native Hungary, for his book *Celestial Harmonies*.

JEFFREY EUGENIDES is the author of the novels *The Virgin Suicides*, *Middlesex*, and *The Marriage Plot*.

ADAM FOULDS is the author of two novels and a narrative poem. His last novel, *The Quickening Maze*, was a finalist for the Man Booker Prize. He lives in London, where he is currently finishing a novel scheduled for publication in early 2014.

JULIA FRANCK was born in Berlin in 1970. Her novel *Die Mittagsfrau* has been translated into thirty-five languages, including into English as *The Blind Side of the Heart*. Her latest novel, *Rücken an Rücken* (or *Back to Back*), will be released in the UK next year.

RODRIGO FRESÁN was born in Buenos Aires in 1963 and now lives in Barcelona. His books include *Historia Argentina*, *Esperanto*, *Kensington Gardens*, and the forthcoming *La Parte Inventada*. He has translated and edited work by Roberto Bolaño, John Cheever, Denis Johnson, and Carson McCullers, and directs the publication of criminal literature for Red & Black Mondadori.

TRISTAN GARCIA is a French writer and philosopher. He was born in Toulouse, raised in Algeria, and now lives in Chartres.

FRANCISCO GOLDMAN has published four novels and one book of non-fiction. His most recent novel is *Say Her Name*.

ANDREW SEAN GREER is the author of four works of fiction, most recently *The Story of a Marriage*. His next novel, *The Other Lives of Greta Wells*, will be out in June 2013.

ARNON GRUNBERG is a novelist and reporter. His work has been translated into twenty-five languages.

YANNICK HAENEL is the author of several novels, including *Introduction à la mort française* and *Évoluer parmi les avalanches*. *The Messenger*, published in France under the title *Jan Karski*, won the Prix Interallié and the Prix du roman FNAC in 2009.

RAWI HAGE is a writer and visual artist; his novels include *DeNiro's Game*, *Cockroach*, and *Carnival*. He was born in Lebanon and currently lives in Montreal.

BRIANNA HARDEN is an illustrator and designer living in Brooklyn.

ALEKSANDAR HEMON is the author of *The Lazarus Project*, which was a finalist for the National Book Award and the National Book Critics Circle Award, and three collections of short stories.

SHEILA HETI is the author of five books, including *How Should a Person Be?*

CHLOE HOOPER is an Australian author. Her first novel, *A Child's Book of True Crime*, was shortlisted for the Orange Prize for Literature and was a *New York Times* Notable Book.

IAN HUEBERT lives in Lincoln, Nebraska.

HEIDI JULAVITS is the author of the novels *The Mineral Palace*, *The Effect of Living Backwards*, *The Uses of Enchantment*, and *The Vanishers*.

DANIEL KEHLMANN is a German-language author of both Austrian and German nationality. His work *Die Vermessung der Welt* (translated into English as *Measuring the World*) is the best-selling novel in the German language since Patrick Süskind's *Perfume* was released in 1985.

ETGAR KERET lives in Tel Aviv. He is the author of six story collections, including, most recently, *Suddenly, a Knock on the Door*.

JONAS HASSEN KHEMIRI is the author of three novels and six plays. His work has been translated into more than fifteen languages.

LÁSZLÓ KRASZNAHORKAI worked for some years as an editor until 1984, when he became a freelance writer. He has written five novels and won numerous prizes.

TIM LAHAN lives and works in New York while eating peanut butter and banana sandwiches.

JONATHAN LETHEM is the author of the forthcoming *Dissident Gardens* and eight other novels. He lives in Los Angeles and Maine.

MARA FAYE LETHEM's recent translations include works by Patricio Pron, David Trueba, Albert Sánchez Piñol, Juan Marsé, Javier Calvo, and Pablo De Santis. Her fiction has appeared only in translation, in such anthologies as *Matar en Barcelona*. Originally from Brooklyn, she lives in Barcelona.

VALERIA LUISELLI was born in Mexico City in 1983 and now lives in New York. Her work includes ballet librettos, literary criticism, poetry translations, and personal essays; her first novel, *Faces in the Crowd*, was published in May 2012.

MA JIAN was born in Qingdao, China in 1953 and now lives in London. He is the author of *Red Dust*, *The Noodle Maker*, *Stick Out Your Tongue*, and *Beijing Coma*.

SARAH MANGUSO is the author of five books, including the memoirs *The Guardians* and *The Two Kinds of Decay* (2008) and the story collection *Hard to Admit and Harder to Escape* (2007), which was published as one volume of three in the McSweeney's collection *145 Stories in a Small Box*.

JAVIER MARÍAS has published thirteen novels, two collections of short stories, and several volumes of essays. His work has been translated into forty-two languages and won an array of international literary awards.

CLANCY MARTIN is the author of *How To Sell*.

WYATT MASON has translated Rimbaud's complete works for Modern Library, a revised and expanded version of which will appear in 2014. He serves as editor at large for the Margellos World Republic of Letters of Yale University Press, and is a contributing writer for the *New York Times Magazine*. He teaches at Bard College.

TOM MCCARTHY is a writer and artist. His latest novel, *C*, was shortlisted for the Man Booker Prize, and his first novel, *Remainder*, is currently being adapted for cinema.

DAVID MITCHELL is a British novelist. He lived in Japan for eight years, and now lives in Ireland with his family.

CEES NOOTEBOOM is the author of novels, travel books, and essays on art and poetry. His recent publications include *Letters to Poseidon* and *Self-portrait of an Other*.

LAWRENCE NORFOLK is the author of *Lemprière's Dictionary*, *The Pope's Rhinoceros*, and *In the Shape of a Boar*. His latest novel is *John Saturnall's Feast*.

JULIE ORRINGER is the author of *How to Breathe Underwater* and *The Invisible Bridge*.

FRANCESCO PACIFICO's forthcoming novel is *The Story of My Purity*.

ALAN PAULS is an Argentinian novelist, essayist, critic, and screenwriter.

JOSÉ LUÍS PEIXOTO is a Portuguese novelist. He is the author of *The Implacable Order of Things*, *Blank Gaze*, and *The Piano Cemetery*.

GARY SHTEYNGART is a book writer. He lives in New York.

SJÓN is an Icelandic author and poet. He has published numerous books of poetry and prose, as well as children's novels. In 2001 he was nominated for an Academy Award for the song "I've Seen It All," from the film *Dancer in the Dark*, alongside his co-writers Lars von Trier and Björk.

ZADIE SMITH is the author of several novels; her latest is *NW*.

PETER STAMM has written short stories, novels, and plays. His last novel was *We're Flying*.

ADAM THIRLWELL is the author of two novels, a novella, and a book about novels.

COLM TÓIBÍN is the Irene and Sidney B. Silverman Professor in the Humanities at Columbia University. His novels include *The Master* and *Brooklyn*.

CAMILLE DE TOLEDO is a filmmaker, screenwriter, and novelist.

JEAN-CHRISTOPHE VALTAT is a French writer. He is the author of *Exes*, *Aurorarama*, and *Luminous Chaos*.

VENDELA VIDA, a founding editor of the *Believer* magazine and the editor of *The Believer Book of Writers Talking to Writers*, is the author of four books. Her most recent novel is *The Lovers*.

IVAN VLADISLAVIĆ is the author of the novels *The Restless Supermarket*, *The Exploded View*, and *Double Negative*. He sometimes works with visual artists, and has edited volumes on architecture and art.

JOHN WRAY is the author, most recently, of the novel *Lowboy*.

ALEJANDRO ZAMBRA is a Chilean writer, author of *Bonsai* and *The Private Lives of Trees*. His newest novel, *Ways of Going Home*, will be released in 2013.

FLORIAN ZELLER is a French novelist and playwright. His work has been translated into a dozen languages.

Edited by
ADAM
THIRLWELL